MW01043365

Music, Liturgy, and Confraternity Devotions in Paris and Tournai, 1300–1550

Eastman Studies in Music

Ralph P. Locke, Senior Editor
Eastman School of Music

Additional Titles of Interest

A complete list of titles in the Eastman Studies in Music series
may be found on our website, www.urpress.com.

Music, Liturgy, and Confraternity Devotions in Paris and Tournai, 1300–1550

Sarah Ann Long

UNIVERSITY OF ROCHESTER PRESS

First published 2021

University of Rochester Press
668 Mt. Hope Avenue, Rochester, NY 14620, USA
www.urpress.com

and Boydell & Brewer Limited
PO Box 9, Woodbridge, Suffolk IP12 3DF, UK
www.boydellandbrewer.com

ISBN-13: 978-1-58046-996-8

ISSN: 1071-9989 ; v. 174

Cataloging-in-Publication data available from the Library of Congress.

This publication is printed on acid-free paper.

Printed in the United States of America.

For Damien

Contents

Illustrations

Figures

Examples

Tables

Acknowledgments

Since this is a project that has been fifteen years in the making, there are many individuals and organizations that have supported and encouraged me in the course of my research. I owe a great debt of gratitude to Herbert Kellman and his wife, Susan Parisi. It was while studying with Herb that I discovered my interest in chant and confraternities, which set me on a fruitful path as a researcher in France and Belgium.

From 2008 to 2013 I spent five years as a postdoctoral research fellow in Belgium at KU Leuven (formerly the Katholieke Universiteit Leuven). During that time, I was affiliated with the Alamire Foundation—International Center for the Study of Music in the Low Countries. My position was generously funded by several entities: the Flemish Minister of Culture, a Postdoctoral Bursary with the aid of the KU Leuven Musicology Research Unit, and a two-year Marie Curie Intra-European Fellowship from the European Commission. For support in all of these positions, I am particularly indebted to Bart Demuyt (director of the Alamire Foundation). Peter Bergé and Mark Delaere (KU Leuven Musicology Research Unit) were both instrumental in advocating for me at the university level. During my time in Belgium, I benefitted from the constant assistance of the research staff at the Alamire Foundation: Inga Behrendt, Stratton Bull, Veerle Francke, Nele Gabriëls, Adam Gilbert, Marianne Gillion, Ann Hasendonckx, Pieter Mannaerts, Grantley McDonald, Zoe Saunders, Karin Strinnholm Lagergren, Jo Santy, Emily Snow Thelen, Sofie Taes, Diewer van der Meijden, An Verbeeck, and Miriam Monroe Wendling. This has resulted in life-long friendships and research collaborations, for which I am truly grateful.

One person who helped me immensely as a postdoctoral fellow, and continues to be a great supporter, colleague, and friend is David Burn, professor of early music at KU Leuven. He has read numerous drafts of proposals, articles, and all the chapters of the present study. His generosity and patience are unstinting, and he is always there to provide encouragement.

There are a number of archivists and librarians who granted me access to their privately held precious collections in Belgium. First and foremost among them is Jacques Pycke, the archivist for the Bibliothèque de la

Cathédrale de Tournai. Half of this book would not have been possible to write without his kindness and generosity. He allowed me to view materials that have until now remained unknown to most scholars. His assistant, Anne Dupont, was also a great help. Other archivists in Tournai who provided ready access to sources were Monique Maillard Luypaert (Bibliothèque du Grande Seminaire), Florian Mariage (Archives de l'Etat, Tournai), and the staff of the Bibliothèque de la Ville de Tournai. In Liège, I found great assistance from Christian Dury (Archives de l'évêché de Liège), Philippe Joris (church of Ste. Croix and Musée du Grand Curtius), and Albert Lemeunier (Musée du Grand Curtius).

Throughout my time in Belgium, I benefitted from the friendship of Anne-Emmanuelle Ceulemans, who help me gain entry to several of the archives above. Additionally, she has translated a number of my articles into French, which has ensured their readership in francophone academic circles.

In Paris I am thankful for a number of archivists and librarians who helped me along the way. Yann Sordet (Bibliothèque Mazarine) allowed me to have unlimited access to manuscripts and early printed books in his collection and has continued to engage in scholarly collaborations with me. Other archivists and librarians in France who were indispensable for the project were the entire staff and director of the Bibliothèque Ste. Geneviève manuscript room, and Ghislain Brunel (Archives nationales de France).

In addition to those who aided me in official capacities in Belgium and France, there are a large number of friends and colleagues in Medieval and Renaissance studies who helped me immensely in the course of researching and writing this book to obtain materials, read drafts, and in general to provide a listening ear. In particular, I would like to thank Alison Altstatt, Jennifer Bain, Katherine Baker, Bonnie Blackburn, James Blasina, Jennifer Bloxam, James Borders, Danette Brink, Camilla Cavicchi, Raeleen Chai-Elsholz, Remi Chiu, Meredith Cohen, Marie-Alexis Colin, Julie Cumming, Daniel DiCenso, Jennifer Edwards, Liz Elmi, Justine Firnhaber-Baker, Mary Franklin-Brown, Barbara Haggh-Huglo, Kristin Hoefener, Danielle Johnson, Debra Lacoste, Jeremy Llewellyn, Chris Macklin, Rebecca Maloy, Chris Murray, Mary Natvig, Christophe Pirenne, Alejandro Planchart, Isabelle Ragnard, Anne Walters Robertson, Anna Russakoff, Molly Ryan, Catherine Saucier, Barbara Swanson, Klaas Jaap van der Meijden, and Valerie Wilhite. I also benefitted from frequent collaboration with the members and Board of the International Medieval Society, Paris. In addition, Henry Parkes, Anna Zayaruznaya, and the students of the Yale University Medieval Song Lab read a draft of one of the chapters and provided important input.

Upon returning to the United States in 2013 I found great inspiration among my colleagues at Michigan State University. I would like to thank the members of the Musicology Department: Kevin Bartig, Joanna Bosse, Nick Field, Ken Prouty, Marcie Ray, and Chris Scales. Michael Largey in particular has been a friend and mentor since my arrival in Michigan. He was always willing to read drafts of my work and talk through research ideas. This work has benefitted greatly from his attention. Dean James Forger, and Associate Dean David Rayl also provided a great deal of financial and logistical support for the project. I also received assistance with images from Leslie Van Veen McRoberts and Tad Boehmer at the Michigan State University Libraries Special Collections. Other colleagues and friends who were a constant source of encouragement are Diana Baldwin, Michael Callahan, Brandy Ellison, Lyn Goeringer, Petra Hendrickson, Juliet Hess, Cathy Illman, Nicola Imbrascio, Corey Kellicut, Steve Kunciatis, Elden Little, Stephanie Palagyi, Marisa Rinkus, Michael Rodriguez, Jennifer Shangraw, Cara Stroud, Britta Urness, and Leigh Van Handel.

In the completion of this monograph, I would like to thank Kerry McCarthy and Valerie Wilhite for reading the entire draft and helping immensely with Latin and French translations and formatting. Liza Calisesi Maidens helped with the bibliography format, and Carol Neel also provided translations of certain rubrics in appendix 6. The music examples were expertly done by Chris Kayler, and line art for appendix 3 was provided by Zachary Lloyd. I received permission to use images from the collections of the Koninklijke Bibliotheek, Nationale Bibliotheek van Nederland; Michigan State University Libraries Special Collections; and The British Library. I thank the Humanities and Arts Research Program at Michigan State University, which generously supported the editing and production of the book

Finally, I would like to thank my family. My parents, Robert and Marylee Long, have nurtured me throughout my academic pursuits, and my sister, Anna Long, has been a constant source of reassurance and optimism.

Above all, I would like to thank my husband, Damien Guillaume. This project has taken us to three different countries and many different research and teaching posts. His love and encouragement have been unwavering, even in the most difficult times. At the very end of this project our son, Mark, came into our lives and reminded me yet again that everything I do I should do with commitment and honesty.

Abbreviations

AH	*Analecta hymnica medii aevi.* Edited by Guido Maria Dreves et al. 55 vols. Leipzig: O. R. Reisland, 1886–1922
AASS	*Acta sanctorum quotquot toto orbe coluntur. Maii tomus tertius, quo dies XII, XIII, XV et XVI continentur.* Edited by Joannus Bollandus et al. 69 vols. Antwerp: Victor Palme, 1643–1940
B-Br	Bruxelles, Bibliothèque royale de Belgique
B-Gu	Gent, Universiteitsbibliotheek
BHL	*Bibliotheca hagiographica Latina antiquae et mediae aetatis.* Edited by the Society of Bollandists. Brussels: Society of Bollandists, 1898–1901, 1911
B-La	Liège, Archives de l'Etat
B-Lsc	Liège, Collégiale Sainte-Croix
BNAM	*BN Archives et manuscrits.* Accessed February 12, 2020. https://archivesetmanuscrits.bnf.fr/ark:/12148/cc793296
B-Tc	Tournai, Chapitre de la Cathédrale, Archives
B-TOb	Tongeren, Onze-Lieve-Vrouwebasiliek
B-Ts	Tournai, Bibliothèque du Grande Seminaire
B-Tv	Tournai, Bibliothèque de la Ville
Calames	*Calames: Catalogue en ligne des archives et des manuscrits de l'enseignement supérieur* Accessed February 12, 2020. http://www.calames.abes.fr/pub/#details?id=MAZA11186
CANTUS	*CANTUS: A Database for Latin Ecclesiastical Chant.* Directed by Debra Lacoste. Accessed February 12, 2020. http://cantus.uwaterloo.ca
CH-HE	Hermetschwil, Benediktinerinnenkloster St. Martin
D-Mbs	München, Bayerische Staatsbibliothek
D-TRb	Trier, Bistumsarchiv
D-TRsb	Trier, Stadtbibliothek im Palais Walderdorff

E-BUlh	Burgos, Monasterio de Santa Maria la Real de las Huelgas
E-codices	*E-codices*. Accessed February 12, 2020. https://www.e-codices.unifr.ch/en/list/one/hba/chart0151
E-Mn	Madrid, Biblioteca Nacional de España, Departamento de Musica y Audiovisuales
F-AM	Amiens, Bibliothèque Louis Aragon
F-APT	Apt, Basilique Ste. Anne
F-CA	Cambrai, Bibliothèque municipale
F-Dm	Dijon, Bibliothèque municipale
F-DOU	Douai, Bibliothèque municipale
F-Lad	Lille, Archives départementales du Nord
F-Lfc	Lille, Facultés Catholiques
F-Lm	Lille, Bibliothèque municipale
F-MOf	Montpellier, Faculté de Médecine
F-Pa	Paris, Bibliothèque de l'Arsenal
F-Pan	Paris, Archives nationales
F-Pm	Paris, Biblitothèque Mazarine
F-Pnlr	Paris, Bibliothèque nationale de France, Réserve des livres rares
F-Pnm	Paris, Bibliothèque nationale de France, Département des Manuscrits
F-Psg	Paris, Bibliothèque Sainte-Geneviève
F-RS	Reims, Bibliothèque Carnegie
F-VAL	Valenciennes, Bibliothèque municipale
GB-Lbl	London, British Library
I-AO	Aosta, Seminario Maggiore, Biblioteca
I-BAas	Bari, Archivio di Stato Bari
I-Bc	Bologna, Museo internazionale e biblioteca della musica di Bologna
I-CFm	Cividale del Friuli, Museo Archeologico Nazionale
I-IV	Ivrea, Biblioteca capitolare

I-Rsm	Roma, Archivio capitolare della Basilica papale di Santa Maria Maggiore
LU	*The Liber Usualis: With Introduction and Rubrics in English.* Edited by the Benedictines of Solesmes. Tournai: Desclée, 1961
NL-DHk	Den Haag, Koninklijke Bibliotheek, Nationale Bibliotheek van Nederland
P-Cug	Coimbra, Biblioteca Geral de Universidade
PL-WRu	Wroclaw (Breslau), Biblioteka Uniwersytecka
US-BAw	Baltimore, Walters Art Gallery
US-Bp	Boston, Boston Public Library, Music Department
US-Cn	Chicago, Newberry Library
US-ELmsu	East Lansing, Michigan State University Libraries

Editorial Procedures for Foreign Languages and Music Examples

All transcriptions from the original Latin, French, and Dutch sources are semi-diplomatic. The original spellings and capitalization have been retained directly from the primary sources, but abbreviations are resolved without brackets. This means that in most cases, representation of i/j do not follow classical Latin conventions, thus a word like *Jesu* will usually appear as *Iesu*, and *ae* is often truncated to *e*, so a word like *caeli* will appear as *celi*, and so forth. In cases where there are multiple spellings for one word in different sources, the most common spelling among all the sources will be used. All French institution proper names are translated, though when dedicated to a saint, holy figure, or relic the original French name for the dedicatee is retained. For instance, L'Eglise Sainte-Croix in Liège is referred to as the Church of Ste. Croix, L'Hôpital Ste. Catherine in Paris is referred to as the Hospital of Ste. Catherine, L'Eglise St. Jacques is referred to as the Church of St. Jacques, etc. Dutch names follow the same rules, except in instances where a church or basilica is dedicated to the Virgin Mary, in which case the full institution name will be given in Dutch. For instance, the Church of Our Lady in Maastricht is called the Onze-Lieve-Vrouwekerk. Confraternity names follow the same general principal being translated into English, but also with the patron saint's name in English (Confraternity of the Spice Dealers and Apothecaries, Confraternity of St. Catherine, etc.) unless there is no proper English equivalent (the Confraternity of Notre Dame de la Gésine, for example). Institutions with original Greek names are also given in English. When needed, English translations of song texts and other prose are given in the main body of the text, with transcriptions of the original in the endnotes. There are several instances where the meaning of short Latin, French, or Dutch phrases are evident in the original, and thus will not be translated into English. While I retain the original orthography for transcriptions, in translations I take liberties with punctuation and capital-ization. Parts of the Mass use standardized texts and modern capitalization conventions when discussed in the text of the book itself (Agnus Dei, Ite Missa Est, Benedicamus Domino), whereas in the musical examples, original spellings and capitalizations are retained. English translations are mine unless otherwise indicated, and any exceptions to the rules above are indicated in the notes.

Regular slurs are used in the music examples to indicate neumes in unme-tered chant, whereas square brackets are used to indicate ligatures in the cantus fractus and polyphonic repertory. Flats, naturals, any other acciden-tals, and rests are only given when they appear in the original manuscript or printed source.

Note on Online Material

The following material can be found on the book's companion website, located at https://boydellandbrewer.com/music-liturgy-and-confraternity-devotions-in-paris-and-tournai-1300-1550.html:

Appendix 4: Inventories of Sources from Parisian Confraternities
Appendix 5: Comparison Tables

Appendix 6: The Kyriale in the *Misse familiares*

Introduction

> Sickness ceases, pestilence ceases when the altar has been built. Holy
> martyr, witness of Christ, beseech God for us, that the epidemic which
> is scourging our native land might cease, and that the will of God
> might hasten with mercy, and that when the misery of this perishing
> world is finished, we might be with you in glory: let every one of us say
> Amen.[1]

This sequence text, which first appeared at the end of a fifteenth-century notated missal used in Paris, is a plea to St. Sebastian. Although the saint is not mentioned by name, it is one of several similar texts set to music that appear in manuscripts containing votive masses for him. It is a personal, direct appeal for the saint to intervene and protect his supplicants from one of the most devastating illnesses to affect Western Europe in the Middle Ages: the bubonic plague. The medieval laity believed that such settings served as vehicles to carry their words directly to these protective figures, and through them to God.

Plague epidemics affected everyone, forcing men and women of all walks of life to come face to face with their mortality. The disease first appeared in Western Europe in 1347, recurring every ten to fifteen years until well into the eighteenth century, and had a profound effect on the populace. For instance, before 1433, the city of Paris had a population of approximately two hundred fifty thousand people, but between 1433 and 1444, a mere decade, the plague took the lives of over forty-eight thousand Parisians.[2] This is a rather large figure for a late-medieval urban population. One can imagine a certain helplessness that people felt when confronted with this disease, causing them to routinely seek divine intervention from patron saints thought to have special protective powers.[3]

St. Sebastian was viewed as one of the most powerful protectors from the plague in northern France from the fourteenth through the sixteenth centuries, but he was not alone. He was one of a group of saints called the fourteen holy helpers, who were commonly invoked for protection against sickness and death in the region.[4] St. Barbara, St. Nicholas of Myra, and St. Catherine of Alexandria were all thought to protect one against an untimely death, as was the Virgin Mary. Starting in the fourteenth century and developing throughout the fifteenth and early sixteenth centuries, new Mass propers, sequences, hymns, and offices composed in their honor appear in multiple liturgical books and are a testament to their popularity. Intercession and healing were the focus of these chant texts, which were commonly used in combination with well-known chant melodies to create contrafacta (chants using preexisting melodies set with new texts). These musical and textual relationships served to bolster a saint's power by sonically associating him or her with the Virgin Mary and with Christ.

Devotions to the fourteen holy helpers were promoted by the laity through the formation of confraternities. From the fourteenth through the sixteenth centuries these communities were a driving force in popular piety, and they had an effect on the development of new devotional practices.[5] Many of these organizations consisted of men and women practicing specific trades, and within them there were members of different social standing (masters, journeymen, apprentices) who came together regularly to celebrate masses and offices for their patron saint.[6] Confraternities played an important part in supporting the creation of new music and texts for their services.

Music, Liturgy, and Confraternity Devotions in Paris and Tournai, 1300–1550 is the first study to explore the role of confraternities as patrons of new plainchant and polyphony for masses and offices in honor of saints thought to have healing powers. It assesses the important place these works occupied in the devotional landscape of northern France from the fourteenth through early sixteenth centuries.[7] The members of these communities believed that they were procuring divine protection from untimely sickness and death by promoting the construction of specialized liturgical practices celebrating popular patron saints, the Virgin Mary, and divine cults (such as the Transfiguration of Christ).[8] Newly uncovered liturgical books and archival sources, investigated for the first time here, show that these compositions circulated throughout the region in lay devotional contexts and were eventually incorporated into liturgical books used in the main sanctuaries of cathedrals and parishes. While these practices emerged in the fourteenth century, by the first decades of the sixteenth century printed chant books marketed more broadly to different devotional communities included similar services.

At the heart of this study are fourteen books containing masses, offices, and extra-liturgical music that formed a central part of confraternity devotions in two important economic and artistic centers in northern France: Paris and Tournai.[9] I have chosen to focus on these two cities because they are associated with the largest number of surviving books that preserve music of this sort.[10] These books are only a fraction of what once existed and represent a much larger medieval phenomenon. Liturgical books containing music and texts for confraternity services serve as a window into late medieval devotional preferences and religiosity. In some cases, confraternity books are the only surviving record of the liturgical practices taking place within a given establishment, making them important to our knowledge of the history of religious devotions.[11] The contents of these sources also reveal that Paris and Tournai were artistically connected through shared musical repertoires. Ultimately, they show a possible confraternal network that existed within the diocesan purview. Such networks were facilitated by contact between individuals associated with different trades and ecclesiastical institutions.

My focus on liturgical books provides new information about how confraternity devotions were structured. The contents of the books reflect these organizations' religious values over several centuries, illuminating for the first time the prominent role of plainchant in these communities. Most of the liturgical books discussed here have remained either unknown or unstudied by scholars of late medieval and early modern music and history. Most studies have explored the liturgical practices of larger ecclesiastical and political institutions, for which we have a more substantial body of archival sources.[12] As a result, our understanding of the liturgy is often directed primarily by the practices of major monastic institutions and cathedrals. Plainchant and polyphony were of course fundamental to the performance of the Mass and Office at these locations. This is evident, for instance, in the development of Notre Dame organum and the motet and conductus repertory emanating from Paris starting in the twelfth century. I show here how musical and liturgical innovation was also cultivated in smaller institutions having lay membership. Evidence of this is found in the books that are the foundation for this study, which are rich in newly composed plainchant and polyphony. In some cases, these works appear exclusively in confraternity sources.

This monograph illustrates how the contents of liturgical books produced for confraternities coincide with popular devotional trends in northern France starting in the fourteenth century and developing throughout the fifteenth. For most confraternities in Paris and Tournai, liturgical books are the only surviving witnesses to the daily practices of these organizations. The existing account registers, rule books, membership registers, and other archival documents do not outline these communities' liturgical practices, those responsible for compiling and carrying them out, or the extent to which they were subject to episcopal oversight. While documents of these types have survived with more regularity than liturgical books for confraternities, there are still not many of them. Furthermore, these sources are often vague regarding the musical details of the religious rituals that were at the very heart of these organizations' founding and which marked the daily life of those taking part in them. The only surviving documents of this sort that are connected to the confraternities in the present study come from one organization—the Confraternity of the Spice Dealers and Apothecaries discussed in chapter 2. Craig Wright has uncovered some information on the practices of the Confraternity of St. John the Evangelist that worshipped at Notre Dame in Paris. His overall conclusion regarding confraternities at the cathedral was that they exercised some degree of autonomy in their services but "were held in check by the conservative thinking of the canons of Paris as to what constituted appropriate liturgical music."[13] Without sources giving specific indications of diocesan regulation of confraternities at other institutions in Paris and Tournai, it is not possible to give details regarding the clerics, musicians, and others who were presumably paid by the confraternities to compile their services, and perform the Mass and Office. Consequently, this study takes a broader approach to the contents of their surviving liturgical books and investigates the connections they have to different devotional trends.

Because of the lack of information on the everyday aspects of confraternity devotions, most musicological scholarship on confraternity devotions in northern France and the Low Countries has focused more on communities with royal Burgundian patronage. There are more surviving archival resources and manuscripts for these organizations, making it possible to explore the patronage of polyphony in the late fifteenth and early sixteenth centuries.[14] Recent work on these confraternities indicates that urban *puys* (poetic societies, also called chambers of rhetoric) organized around the amateur creation of poetry and music were responsible for creating new liturgies. This is the case for the repertory appearing in manuscripts produced by the scribe Petrus Alamire, who was employed by the Burgundian court.[15] While there are a few surviving confraternity books from further north in the Low Countries that contain both chant and polyphony, there are not many liturgical books preserving these communities' order of service.[16] Thus, out of necessity, most scholarship on confraternities and music in the southern Low Countries and northern France relies heavily on the few surviving archival resources that contain scant references to music and liturgy.[17] These are the same types of documents that many historians have used in their investigations of confraternities in France and the Low Countries, but music and liturgy has not been an integral part of that discussion.[18]

The liturgical books discussed in the subsequent chapters were all produced between ca. 1300–1540. The early part of this timeframe is when trade guilds were first widely established in Northern French towns; it ends at a time when the reforms of the bishop of Paris sought to standardize the music and text of the liturgy in the diocese of Paris.[19] It was within this two-hundred-fifty-year time period that the formation of confraternities, and the increase in popular devotions to certain saints, grew with particular fervor. In this book, I explore how newly composed plainchant mirrors this trend. The chant repertory in the sources central to this study undergoes some change from the early to the later period of this time frame, but the rate of this change does not differ greatly based on the medium (manuscript or print). Therefore, the contents of printed books produced in the sixteenth century (commonly thought of as the beginning of the early modern period) represent the continuation of a process with its roots in the Middle Ages. For this reason, I refer to the entire era, as it relates to the liturgy, as late medieval.

Confraternities, Institutions, and Popular Piety

Trade and devotional confraternities, which were first formed with regularity in the fourteenth century and continued to develop throughout the fifteenth and sixteenth, played both social and spiritual roles in late medieval life. Their members paid yearly dues in order that the community could effectively fulfill its responsibilities. The social role of these communities was to serve the temporal needs of their members: trade confraternities (or guilds), for instance, regulated trade but also provided charity, such as food and burial costs, for destitute members. Purely devotional confraternities served the same functions, but they were not connected to specific trades. While both types of organizations were devotional in nature, I use the term "trade confraternity" to describe organizations regulated by profession and the term "devotional confraternity" to distinguish those organizations that were purely devotional in nature with no connection to trades.[20] The spiritual role of all confraternities—both trade and devotional—was to ensure the salvation of the souls of the members through their participation in public annual processions and their frequent (usually weekly) attendance at a privately held Mass and/or Office. The performances of these services were held at the altar established by the organization in local ecclesiastical and monastic institutions, which I call "sheltering houses."[21]

While processions served to publicly reinforce the place of confraternities as prominent civic institutions, I discuss how private devotions during the Mass and Office bonded the community together in communal worship. These services were meant to exalt the patron saint of the confraternity, who was seen as the spiritual protector of the community, through the liturgical use of specialized chants and texts in the saint's honor. Carol Symes describes how such private devotions reinforced public displays in confraternal contexts by promoting the idea that "the celebration of Mass is a celebration of community."[22]

In this book, I explore a range of different networks of tradespeople living in Paris and Tournai during the fourteenth through sixteenth centuries. More specifically, I interrogate the possible effects these connections had on the creation of new liturgical practices associated with confraternities.[23] At a very basic level, members of trade confraternities in both cities had contact with practitioners of other trades through proximity (living in the same neighborhoods) and professional necessity. The same is true for members of purely devotional confraternities who belonged to different trades. These men and women would also become members of devotional communities at their own parish churches, which put them into contact with other tradespeople. This becomes most evident in the fifteenth century, for in 1467, King Louis XI organized the city of Paris into sixty-one trade banner districts, which placed people of different trades into particular quarters of the city.[24] In order to practice a trade in Paris in the fifteenth and sixteenth centuries, artisans were required to be members of the local guild, a requirement that was enforced by their peers.[25] These guilds also had foreigners as members, for people occasionally travelled to different towns to learn their trades. Due to this, there is some evidence that artisans were familiar with trade confraternity practices outside of their own city.[26]

As shown above, individuals had the capacity to move through different social spaces, and this may have had an impact on the dissemination of liturgical practices. The situation is further complicated by the fact that multiple trade organizations would worship at the same institutions, thus occupying the same physical space. The worship of multiple confraternities at the same chapels (although at different times) was an important part of how new liturgical practices migrated into a variety of liturgical books. Confraternities were also known to move from one institution to another for different reasons, which provided further avenues for the dissemination of devotional practices within an urban center (see chapters 2 and 4). While the chant repertory and most of the polyphonic settings in the books investigated here are anonymous, these works were likely composed by clerics who would have had the skills to write both chant and polyphony (see chapter 1).[27] The chaplains of the sheltering houses were charged with ensuring that the Mass and Office were properly done for all confraternities who rented chapels there. This may explain the similarities between some of the masses and offices in the present study (see chapter 2). In this way, confraternity patronage was an important driving force in the development of new liturgies.

My exploration of the liturgical books used by confraternities reveals that these organizations did not stand in a simple center versus periphery relationship to the diocesan authorities of Tournai and Paris. Instead, they deferred to and acted independently of those authorities in various ways over time. The diocesan usages (rituals and orders of service) observed in secular institutions (cathedrals and parishes) in the two cities differed in many ways from the usages of the various confraternities that existed in these locations. Diocesan manuscripts produced in the thirteenth and fourteenth centuries contained votive masses for different saints at the end, which were done in the side chapels of the city's institutions. Sometimes these services were endowed by individuals, but often they were performed for confraternities. Such masses normally drew directly from the chants and texts used on the main feast day, or from the Common of Saints.[28] By the fifteenth century, votive masses often differed in their content from the high masses celebrated in the main sanctuaries of cathedrals and parishes in that they used newly composed texts and music. This shift in the fifteenth century is especially notable in Paris, while the surviving sources from Tournai show change over an even longer period, starting ca. 1300.

The development of specialized liturgies in the middle of the fifteenth century coincides in large part with growing concerns for salvation in the face of sickness and death. These liturgical texts bear marked similarities to those found in Books of Hours and other devotional literature.[29] In this respect, they are intimately connected to private devotions, which are often explored by scholars separately from the liturgical practices of the diocese.[30] Erika Honisch points out that there was much more overlap in elite and popular traditions than is often recognized, as many see the two as binaries.[31] I argue that, consequently, the terms "liturgy" and "devotions" have come to carry different connotations in modern scholarship that go against medieval practice. The term liturgy often implies an air of official authority, while devotion has come to mean something informal and popular in nature—in other words, it is "unofficial."[32] Here, I use the words devotion and liturgy synonymously to describe the worship practices of confraternities, as their liturgical texts are imbued with ideas circulating in popular devotional literature to an extent that is not often present in the liturgy of the diocese as a whole. In this way, they served a different, more specialized religious function.

The new music and texts used in confraternity devotions reflect the medieval laity's obsession with the lives and deeds of the saints, brought on in large part by fear of plague and the belief that focusing on specific figures would save one from an untimely death. This fascination with mortality resulted in the production of new literature that circulated widely, first in manuscripts and later in print. What any layperson in the fifteenth century knew about the lives of the saints would have likely come from the *Legenda aurea* (*Golden Legend*), written in Latin by the Dominican Jacobus de Voragine in 1275 and produced in hundreds of editions well into the sixteenth century (see chapter 1). Intriguing connections between this type of popular hagiographical literature and the composition of new music emerge in the liturgical practices developed under confraternity patronage. New Mass propers and pieces based on rhymed poetry (hymns, sequences, and *historiae*) were composed with increasing frequency in honor of the Virgin Mary and certain saints who had local importance; for example, in Paris and Tournai the most prominent figures were St. Barbara, St. Nicholas, St. Catherine, and St. Sebastian (see chapters 1 through 3). A detailed study of the contents of liturgical books produced for confraternities reveals why specific chant melodies were chosen and how contrafacta were carefully crafted with an awareness of the theology they expressed. These two components (music and text) work together to become spiritual mechanisms for entire communities.[33]

Tournai, Paris, and Their Sources

The connections between Paris and Tournai, which are reflected in the confraternity manuscripts from these two centers, were reinforced through uniquely overlapping political and ecclesiastical boundaries. This permitted the movement of tradespeople and members of the church to different cities throughout northern France (under the jurisdiction of the French throne) and the Low Countries (under Burgundian control). In the examples given in the previous section, I noted how the movement of individuals to different locations and institutions was important in the circulation of popular devotions among confraternities, and that this movement sometimes involved their travel across dynastic boundaries. Politically, Tournai held a precarious position between the French and Burgundian territories, which allowed for influences from both France and the Low Countries. Throughout the Middle Ages, Tournai was part of France, but by 1521, it had officially become territory of the Burgundian Low Countries under the control of Charles V. Tournai's place on the Scheldt (Escaut) River, which runs through the center of town, made it an important post for communications with other major city centers along the river in the north, such as the Burgundian cities of Ghent, Bruges, and Antwerp. In fact, Tournai rivaled the city of Bruges in population in the late fourteenth century and was among the most prominent trade centers in the area.[34] The city served as the seat of the Tournai diocese, but the Scheldt functioned as a natural ecclesiastical boundary between the diocese of Tournai and the diocese of Cambrai, splitting the city into two different bishoprics. Institutions on the eastern side of the river were subject to the diocese of Cambrai (under Burgundian control), and those to the west (including the cathedral) were subject to the diocese of Tournai (under French control).[35] This led to strong French and Burgundian presences in the city, and most importantly for the present study, composers moved around to different institutions in both kingdoms (see chapter 4). Its situation on the river between French and Burgundian lands made it vital for the French kings to hold on to the territory, giving it a privileged place.[36] While Paris was the heart of France, Tournai, as a border city, was important in maintaining and solidifying the power of the French monarchy.

Many intellectual and artistic activities took place in Paris, which were fostered by the constant influx of students coming from abroad to study at the university. The city's role as a major center for book production also had a direct impact on the construction of popular devotional practices and their dissemination in both manuscript and print (see chapter 5). While the liturgical practices of confraternities in Tournai were shaped by the city's position between French and Burgundian lands (see chapter 4), those in Paris were influenced by its position as an international center of learning. Paris was the largest student center in Europe, with scholars who came from all over Western Europe and beyond. The inclusion of texts and music in Parisian confraternity books that have no connection to the diocese of Paris could be attributed to foreigners at the university.[37] These students were divided into four different *nationes* (nations), which were groups that congregated for special activities.[38] Each of the four nations had its own confraternities and devotional practices; thus the potential for the influx of different liturgical practices, texts, and music to Paris through these individuals was very great.[39] More importantly, the nations encouraged a sense of group identity through common heritage, which was reinforced through religious worship (see chapter 5).

In addition to common origin, I explore how group identity formation manifested itself in confraternity devotions to specific patron saints tied to the land through the presence of relics (see chapter 3).[40] Related to the notion of student *nationes* is the idea of patron saints that were thought to protect large geographical areas, or even entire kingdoms. Naturally, the associations of modern scholars with the words "nationalism" and "nation" are ahistorical to the time period, and thus not the same as those perceived in the Middle Ages. Nevertheless, it is clear that the term "nation" did have cultural connotations. One of the most prevalent forms of "national" awareness in France in the late fifteenth century was based on the idea of France as the Most Christian Kingdom with the Most Christian King, and the French church as the ultimate authority. These ideas had given rise to the emergence of French national saints throughout the Middle Ages—St. Louis, St. Denis, St. Clovis, and St. Michael.[41] This awareness also affected liturgical practices at the cathedral of Notre Dame, at collegiate and parish churches, and in confraternities (see chapters 2, 3, and 5). The development of civic communities such as trade guilds and devotional confraternities, for instance, gives some evidence of group identity that was legitimized through worship of a patron saint.

In order to illustrate personal connections between different confraternity members, I turn to existing notarial documents, particularly in relation to the members of the book trade, who all belonged to the Confraternity of St. John the Evangelist.[42] This group of artisans and merchants was very different from nearly all others both because of the nature of the trade and of its centralization in Paris. Members of the community had documented contact with other artisans and merchants in the city, revealing an intricate web of connections between printers of chant books and other city inhabitants. They are also unique in the influence they exercised over the production of liturgical books sold all over France and the Low Countries (see chapter 5).

The only evidence we have for music and confraternities in Tournai has to do with priests and other literate men who were involved in the day-to-day workings of the diocese and who also happened to be members of confraternities. The Confraternity of the Notaries is an example of a mixed organization that contained laymen and clerics together, all of whom had close access to the bishop. On the other hand, the Confraternity of the Transfiguration consisted only of priests who held positions at the cathedral (see chapters 1 and 4).

The extant liturgical books draw our attention to trade confraternities in Paris, and to ecclesiastical and mixed ecclesiastical and lay confraternities in Tournai—a dichotomy that could be misleading unless one takes into account the number of sources that survive in relation to the number of confraternities that once existed (see chapters 1 and 2). Most archives pertaining to the city of Tournai and its institutions were destroyed during World War II, leaving us with only a handful of documents currently held at the Bibliothèque de la Cathédrale de Tournai, a private institution providing limited access. Paris has fared better with documents held in national and regional archives (such as the Archives nationales and the Archives départementales du Nord).

Chapter Summaries

Each of the following chapters explores a different aspect of confraternity devotions and shows how these organizations were involved in the promotion of new liturgical practices devoted to divine cults and saints thought to have healing properties. In addition to five chapters, the book contains six appendices with detailed descriptions of the confraternity manuscripts; analyses of scribal hands and gathering structures for the Tournai manuscripts (which have not to this point been considered together); comparison tables of chant texts and melodies; Mass ordinary comparison tables; and a transcription of the kyriale rubrics for the printed *Misse familiares*.

The first three chapters explore devotions to specific patron saints by confraternities in Tournai and Paris, discussing the composition of new Mass propers and offices that reflect local beliefs about these figures. Chapter 1 shows how the Confraternity of the Notaries' devotions to St. Barbara were constructed in the fourteenth century and eventually found their way into books used in the main sanctuary of the Tournai cathedral over the fifteenth century. It explores the circulation of mainstream hagiographical literature and shows how a saint known initially almost exclusively in the popular realm in this geographical area came to achieve official diocesan recognition.

Chapter 2 shows how two widely venerated saints who were officially recognized within the dioceses of Paris and Tournai took on specific properties as healers in confraternity devotions in the course of the fifteenth century and into the early sixteenth. The chapter investigates in detail two confraternity manuscripts that were used by different communities that worshiped at the Hospital of Ste. Catherine in Paris—the Confraternity of the Doublet

Makers and the Confraternity of the Spice Dealers and Apothecaries. The chant texts in these books portray the translation of the relics of St. Nicholas and the finding of the relics of St. Catherine. Relic translation from one place to another came to serve as a focal point commemorating a saint's healing power, and new chants for the Mass and Office were composed for confraternities with this in mind.

Chapter 3 investigates a third dimension of confraternity practice, showing how organizations in the city of Paris promoted devotions to St. Sebastian as a response to fear of the plague in the second half of the fifteenth century and into the early sixteenth. The manuscript F-Pa 204, which was produced for the Confraternity of the Bourgeois Archers, contains unique music and texts in honor of St. Sebastian and others thought to protect against an untimely death. These sources draw on historical and royal imagery in addition to popular folklore in order to place St. Sebastian as a local saint and protector of the French realm, much in the same way that the archers were meant to protect the city of Paris.

While the first three chapters explore the Mass proper and offices, chapter 4 investigates how compositional practice and personal networks affected the dissemination of monophonic and polyphonic Mass ordinaries used on feast days celebrated by confraternities. Some Mass ordinary chants were more popular with confraternities than others, and the chapter traces those conventions in usage at different points in time from the fourteenth through the sixteenth centuries. One way of praising the patron saint of a community was through more elaborately composed music, such as chants written in mensural notation (a technique known as cantus fractus) and polyphony, which was seen as a high expression of devotion. The chants in cantus fractus show links between old and new in confraternity practices at the Tournai cathedral, as well as links to confraternities in Paris and practices in Cambrai. These are connected to a political network established earlier on in the fourteenth century and are illustrated through different compositional procedures in certain movements of the first polyphonic Mass ordinary compilation known to exist from the early fourteenth century, commonly called the "Tournai Mass."

The fifth, and final, chapter of this monograph discusses the role of the Parisian book production community in the dissemination of the different settings for the Mass proper and Mass ordinary in the early sixteenth century discussed in chapters 1 through 4. It takes as its point of departure a series of printed liturgical books produced in the first decades of the sixteenth century that appear to have been marketed to a broad audience that would have included confraternities—the *Misse familiares*, *Misse solenniores*, and *Communes prosa*. Ultimately, confraternity devotions to St. Barbara, the Virgin Mary, and St. Sebastian find their way into diocesan missals as votive masses for the usages of Paris, Tournai, and Cambrai due to the recognition on the part of Parisian printers that these devotions were prominent enough to merit their inclusion as appendices. This chapter explores both how the printers may have come into contact with devotional practices cultivated by confraternities and their role in spreading these practices to other cities and dioceses. In order to understand the many votive masses newly appearing in printed diocesan missals, one must understand the history of confraternity devotions and the roles played in them by interactions between different communities.

Music, Liturgy, and Confraternity Devotions explores different popular devotional networks that existed as a result of the decentralized nature of religious and spiritual authority from the fourteenth through sixteenth centuries. The primary catalyst for this was the desire of the laity to procure divine protection from sickness and untimely death. As a result of these findings, it is evident that liturgical practices were in part facilitated by networks of individuals associated with different trades and ecclesiastical institutions, rather than by diocesan officials. Consequently, confraternities exercised the power to cultivate devotional practices that reflected their sense of group identity, which came to be recognized by dioceses throughout northern France.

Chapter One

Confraternities and Popular Devotions to St. Barbara in Tournai

O beautiful violet, seedling of paradise, he has crowned you, holy Barbara, with the eminent double halo of virgin and martyr: make us to be rendered worthy of the laurel of heaven.[1]

This antiphon text is one of many examples of intercessory prayers found in popular devotions meant to establish a direct connection between saint and supplicant. It appears as part of the Office for St. Barbara in Tournai, Archives et Bibliothèque de la Cathédrale MS A 12 (B-Tc A 12), a chant manuscript with additions from the thirteenth through sixteenth centuries used by the Confraternity of the Notaries at the Cathedral of Notre Dame in Tournai. Many of the chants for the Mass and Office in liturgical books used by confraternities are in first person narrative and end with the formula "Ora pro nobis," or "pray for us," and indeed, this text asks the saint to "make us to be rendered worthy of the laurel of heaven." In addition to laudatory texts like the one above, devotional literature (Books of Hours, Miracles of the Virgin, the *Golden Legend*) and the liturgies that developed from it encouraged the laity to identify with the suffering of the saints by focusing on the details of their martyrdom. Music, text, and image all worked together to engage the "emotional imagination," creating a personal experience of the saint's pain and salvation.[2] New liturgical texts and music created for confraternities in the fourteenth through sixteenth centuries were integral to this process.

In this chapter, I explore the material culture of the Confraternity of the Notaries at the Tournai cathedral—in particular, three manuscripts they owned—and what it can tell us about the development of liturgical practices in private devotional communities at this institution. In the absence of any archival documents recording the everyday acts of the confraternity (how they interacted with the diocese, payment of musicians, and all other sundry activities), these manuscripts are the only existing sources reflecting their rituals and place within the cathedral. Since the discovery of these books in the nineteenth century, scholars have investigated isolated parts of their contents but have not sought to view each one as a whole. By conducting a detailed study of how the books were constructed in relationship to their contents, it is possible to gain an understanding of how they were all used together and what they can tell us about this organization's belief system. As a case study, I focus on a unique Office and Mass for St. Barbara that appears in B-Tc A 12 as an addition from the late fourteenth century. In this context, material culture reflects the confraternity's identity, and the inclusion of new services for St. Barbara shows how that identity underwent change over a period of several centuries. This transformation is mirrored more broadly in how St. Barbara is represented in different northern French hagiographical traditions, and in the construction of new masses and offices for her in neighboring dioceses. After first appearing in the confraternity's liturgical books, devotions to St. Barbara played an increasingly important role in the diocese of Tournai as a whole during the course of the fifteenth century and into the early sixteenth, as represented in different liturgical sources used in the main sanctuary of the cathedral. New music and texts from this era produced for services in her honor highlight the place of confraternities in Tournai as patrons of new music composition based on popular devotional practices.

The intercessory prayer to St. Barbara given above would have been a fitting choice for the people of Tournai during the turbulent times of the fourteenth century. The city was besieged by the English in 1340 at the beginning of the Hundred Years War, leaving the citizenry destitute and without supplies. At the end of the decade, in 1349, a plague epidemic took hundreds of lives.[3] The inhabitants of Tournai were certainly faced with their own mortality during this era, and as one of the fourteen holy helpers thought to protect against an untimely death, it is no surprise that St. Barbara's popularity increased.[4] This belief has its roots in the story of her life and martyrdom, wherein it is said that after she was beheaded by her father, he himself was unexpectedly struck down by lightning as a divine punishment for taking her life. St. Barbara was the patron saint of artillery makers, a reference to both the instrument of her martyrdom (a sword) and the unexpected death of her father by lightning. She was also the patron saint of coal miners, a dangerous line of work in which one could be buried alive underground at any time.[5] In the face of all this uncertainty, people turned to St. Barbara for aid.

St. Barbara was not the only figure that people sought in times of need— it was the Virgin Mary who served as the patron and protector of the city of Tournai as a whole.[6] The people of Tournai would often collectively pray to her for aid. One example is during the siege of 1340, when the inhabitants of the city gathered at the cathedral to keep vigil before the statue of the Virgin. Jacques Pycke, in his research on devotions to the Virgin Mary at the Tournai cathedral, has gathered information pertaining to endowments for masses to be sung in her honor. One in particular is a 1349 foundation for a Mass "cum nota," which he has speculated could be the famous polyphonic "Tournai Mass" found in one of the Confraternity of the Notaries' existing manuscripts (B-Tc A 27), although there is nothing that firmly ties the existing setting to that context (see chapter 4).[7] Nevertheless, it is clear that processions, special masses, and other devotions to the Virgin were widespread at the cathedral, and that most of these events took place in the main sanctuary before her statue.

Both St. Barbara and the Virgin Mary were subjects of devotion for the Confraternity of the Notaries in service to the bishop at the Tournai cathedral, even though some of the liturgical celebrations in their honor were not initially observed in the cathedral at large. In particular, the Office and Mass for St. Barbara in the confraternity's existing manuscripts offer rare examples of new chant composition in the diocese, with roots in confraternal settings. The central portions of this chapter examine how the liturgical practices of the Confraternity of the Notaries at the Tournai cathedral were constructed, and the possible role of this community in introducing local popular devotions into the diocesan usage of the cathedral. The notaries would have moved frequently with the bishop, as they were an important part of his close entourage.[8] Due to this, they were always present at major political functions and would have been exposed to a variety of different musical practices on official occasions. The notaries were thus in a unique position to come into contact with music and texts used outside of the diocese of Tournai, and as the contents of their liturgical books show, they were free to incorporate them as part of the rituals of their own confraternity. An analysis of the contents, compilation, and scribal hands found in the confraternity's manuscripts provides a timeline for the introduction of the Mass and Office for St. Barbara into the organization's devotional cursus, and more broadly, the changing nature of their liturgy over time.

The Confraternity of the Notaries and their Liturgical Books

The Confraternity of the Notaries was one of around thirty confraternities in the city prior to the seventeenth century, and one of only two for which there are surviving liturgical books containing music.[9] Overall, we have few details about the role of music in the activities of confraternities that met at the parishes of Tournai. What does exist comes from private contexts, such as endowments for offices and masses that the confraternity members were required to attend, rather than processions that would have been observed publicly (for which there is no surviving information). Agatha Nys has studied what little documentation survives for confraternities in Tournai and has found references to both music for masses founded for dead members (called obits) and masses celebrated for their main feasts throughout the year. A certain number of clerics and choristers were needed to sing during the services, but no details are provided concerning how many took part in these performances or what was sung. Aside from references to paying organists to play during confraternity services, there is no mention of any instrumentalists.[10]

Devotions to the Virgin Mary are well documented for confraternities in the city, but again, without surviving music. By the fourteenth and fifteenth centuries, the Confraternity of Notre Dame de la Gésine at the church of St. Jacques, and the Confraternity of Notre Dame at the church of Ste. Marie Madeleine celebrated five main Marian masses throughout the year (Purification on February 2, Annunciation on March 25, Assumption on August 15, Nativity on September 8, and Conception on December 8).[11] There is also a foundation from around 1350 by Jaquèmes Cauwe for a Marian Mass to be performed every Saturday at the church of St. Piat, which indicates that there was a regular group of singers who specialized in performing a polyphonic Mass in her honor, a "compagnie de le messe Nostre-Dame."[12] Despite these references, there is not one surviving liturgical book with music from any of the communities that worshipped at these institutions.

Although most existing documentation provides references to private contexts where music would have been performed for the Mass and Office, there is also plenty of evidence that there was once a vibrant and very public musical culture in Tournai itself in the fourteenth and fifteenth centuries. The unique monophonic and polyphonic compositions found in the notaries' liturgical books may be viewed as part of that artistic legacy. Instrumentalists from Tournai were among the most prominent musicians in France during the fourteenth and fifteenth centuries, and references to their employment

appear in documents from Paris, northern centers like Lille and surrounding towns, and as far south as Toulouse and Montpellier. These musicians
were in the employ of both cities and confraternities and were known to play
during annual processions as well as for private masses.[13] At the same time,
there was a confraternity focused on the composition of music and poetry in
Tournai (called a *puy,* or chamber of rhetoric) in the early fourteenth century,
based on the famous Confraternity of the Jongleurs in Arras.[14] Moreover,
the city of Tournai is the setting for "The Boy and the Blind Man," a vernacular religious play that was well known throughout northern France.[15]
The references to Tournai and music above are compelling, but what little
documentation there is about artistic practices emanating from the city, and
any mention of its instrumentalists, comes from other urban centers. These
sources do not give information about the private masses and offices that
were celebrated regularly by confraternities in Tournai.

Among the vestiges of Tournai's prominent musical heritage are the three
liturgical books used by the Confraternity of the Notaries, which are some
of the few sources containing music from the city during the thirteenth
through sixteenth centuries. These books, which are currently held at the
Bibliothèque de la Cathédrale de Tournai, not only preserve unique musical
settings for the Mass and Office composed during that time but also provide
most of the information we have about the confraternity, its members, and
how they interacted with the diocesan infrastructure. All that can be established about the confraternity's membership is that it was comprised of clerics
and married laymen, who were episcopal notaries in service to the bishop.[16]
The many different layers in the community's three existing manuscripts
allow for a sense of how they were used over a period of several centuries;
in addition, they represent the changing liturgical practices of this organization. B-Tc A 12 and B-Tc A 27, both mentioned previously, were used along
with another book, B-Tc A 13. The detailed inventories of the three manuscripts in appendix 1 show that the Confraternity of the Notaries celebrated
a significant number of masses and offices together, indicating that they met
regularly and were able to financially support frequent performances of these
services. It is not clear in which chapel the organization met, but the Mass
and Office for St. Vincent in B-Tc A 12 implies that the confraternity was
housed in the episcopal chapel of St. Vincent, erected on the southwest side
of the cathedral.[17] This is the largest of the three books, with its earliest layers
dating from the thirteenth century (ca. 1280), and contains additions from
well into the sixteenth century.[18] B-Tc A 13 yields some clues about the
members of the community, as it includes a list of eight names—likely those

of the confraternity provosts—copied on the recto of the opening flyleaf in a sixteenth-century hand with the caption "notarii anno 47."[19] This distinction is probably a reference to the year 1547, since two of the names on the list are also found in other cathedral documents dating from 1526–70. One of these men, Joannes Corvillain, held an administrative post directly delegated by the bishop of Tournai, which gives an idea of the rank and prestige enjoyed by certain members of the organization.[20] Although the manuscript contains handwritten addenda from the sixteenth century, like B-Tc A 12, the bulk of its chants and texts date from the late thirteenth century.

The liturgical practices of the Confraternity of the Notaries may have exercised a gradual influence on those taking place in the main sanctuary of the cathedral, and the set of devotions to St. Barbara offers a good case study for this, as I will show later in the chapter.[21] Despite her inconsistent appearance in well-known sources such as Jacobus de Voragine's *Golden Legend*, existing hagiographical material for her from northern France and the Low Countries shows that she was very much a local saint in the area, and one with a large popular following. At the same time, devotions to St. Barbara were relatively new to this confraternity in the late fourteenth century, showing that the confraternity's liturgical practices underwent some change in response to the increasing popularity of different saints in the region. A detailed examination of the structure of this community's only surviving books helps to establish a timeline for the introduction of new feasts in the confraternity, especially when the Mass and Office for St. Barbara were introduced. In this way, the material culture of the confraternity gives us an idea of the organization's devotional ethos.

Gathering Structures and Scribal Hands

Much can be learned about the history and place of popular devotions in Tournai by studying how all three of the confraternity's liturgical books were put together and looking at their contents side by side—a task that has only recently been possible. In the absence of archival documents recording the practices of the notaries and their interaction with the bishop and diocesan infrastructures, it is the material evidence in the books themselves that illustrates a rich process of accretions to the liturgy. While there have been individual unpublished codicological studies of two of the manuscripts (B-Tc A 12 and B-Tc A 13), this is the first attempt to show exactly how all three of them correspond to each other, which aids in contextualizing their contents.[22] In the end, these are the only sources available to reconstruct the practices of the notaries. As we shall see at the end of the following discussion, of all of the services transmitted in these sources, the Mass and Office for St. Barbara stand out as significant later additions.

An overview of the manuscripts' contents, and writings about them, shows that how they have been viewed since their discovery in the nineteenth century has in some cases limited our ability to see these sources in their cultural context. The descriptions in appendix 2 indicate that all of the manuscripts have scribal hands dating from the thirteenth through sixteenth centuries, and appendix 3 illustrates how the scribal hands match up with the gathering structures of the three books.[23] The only one of the three manuscripts that has been discussed at length is B-Tc A 27, as it contains the polyphonic Tournai Mass. This work is heralded as one of the first polyphonic Mass ordinary compilations and has been the subject of a number of studies (see chapter 4).[24] In 1862, Edmund de Coussemaker was the first to mention the manuscript, but he focused exclusively on the polyphonic setting. Subsequent authors were also solely interested in this work among the manuscript's contents, as it fed nineteenth-century scholars' captivation with composers and works that served as models for what they perceived to be significant developments in Western art music. In this discourse, the Tournai Mass was viewed as an important precursor to the works of Du Fay, Binchois, Josquin, and others, with Coussemaker an often-cited authority on the matter.[25] As a consequence, the context of the Mass and the contents of the manuscript as a whole were of secondary importance.

Coussemaker implied that B-Tc A 27 was associated with the Confraternity of the Notaries, but without the examination of any proof; thus, the entirety of its contents and their role in confraternity devotions has never been the subject of scholarly attention. My study of the sources reveals that the manuscript bears striking similarities to B-Tc A 12 and B-Tc A 13, both of which we know were used by the Confraternity of the Notaries. Appendix 2 shows that B-Tc A 27 contains several monophonic masses in honor of the Virgin Mary; masses from the Temporale; chants for St. Catherine and St. Nicholas; a series of Marian sequences almost identical to the one appearing in B-Tc A 12; a commemoration Mass for the Virgin; and numerous Mass ordinary chants.[26] Also, like B-Tc A 12 and B-Tc A 13, B-Tc A 27 includes many handwritten addenda from the fourteenth, fifteenth, and sixteenth centuries. There is, however, one scribe who is found in all three books. As shown in appendix 3, Scribe O in B-Tc A 12, Scribe C in B-Tc A 13, and Scribe K in B-Tc A 27 are the same hand. This indicates that the Confraternity of the

Notaries used the three manuscripts together. This newly demonstrated association of B-Tc A 27 with the other two books now places it and its chant contents within the larger discussion of confraternity practice at Tournai, a point to which I will return in chapter 4.

B-Tc A 12 and 13 give insight into other aspects of the confraternity's religious practices. The smallest of the three books, B-Tc A 13, has only recently become a subject of study.[27] Its contents exclusively focus on the Virgin Mary, St. Catherine, and St. Nicholas. Unlike the other manuscripts, which contain only chant and polyphony, this source includes numerous readings to be done during the confraternity's services, within which there are rubrics pertaining directly to the notaries. One of the many examples is on folio 26r, which indicates that a reading from the book of Maccabees (2 Maccabees 12: 43–46) is to be done during an annual commemorative Mass for dead brothers, which would have taken place on the feast day of one of the confraternity's patron saints.[28]

Of all three sources, the material composition of B-Tc A 12 tells us the most about when certain feasts were incorporated into the confraternity's devotional cursus, something that is more difficult to establish in the other two books. It is the only one of the confraternity's manuscripts to contain both masses and offices for the feasts they celebrated. This is also the only known surviving source from an institution in Tournai to contain music for the Office, which makes it important for liturgical studies in the city as a whole. Two items included in this book, when viewed closely together, shed light on the development of the confraternity's liturgical practices. The first is the index of its contents in an early fourteenth-century hand, with the rubric "Order of incipits for the offices in this existing book";[29] and the second is an early fourteenth-century inventory of the confraternity's belongings (commonly known as a "fabric") appearing directly after the index.

Starting in the nineteenth century, the fabric in B-Tc A 12 became the most studied part of this manuscript. Similar to scholars' preoccupation with the Tournai Mass in B-Tc A 27, interest in this portion of B-Tc A 12 has prevented historians and musicologists from seeing the contents of the tome in its entirety. B-Tc A 12 is first mentioned in an article from 1860, written by the vicar general of Tournai, Charles-Joseph Voisin.[30] Voisin was interested in liturgical drama at the cathedral, and in this work he explores some of the more dramatic aspects of the Christmas services and how they relate to the usage of the diocese. Since the manuscript had never been discussed in print before, Voisin took it upon himself to transcribe the fabric and include a translation of it into French. From the very beginning, he indicates that the manuscript belonged to the Confraternity of the Notaries and that much of its contents can be dated to the thirteenth century.[31] The role of the book as it was used by the confraternity, transmitting the quotidian devotional practices of the notaries, was not his focus. Interest in the manuscript for its fabric arose again in the early twenty-first century, as it appears in Albert Derolez's work on medieval booklists in the southern Low Countries.[32] In this case it is viewed as an example of medieval material culture, but its significance for exploring the services celebrated by the confraternity fell outside the scope of Derolez's work. Hence the chant contents of B-Tc A 12 remained unstudied until 2011.[33]

Upon closer inspection, this fabric is much more than just a list of the confraternity's material objects—it also allows for an idea of the genesis of B-Tc A 12 and the confraternity's original devotional focus in the thirteenth and early fourteenth centuries. A timeline for this can be established by viewing the fabric alongside the index and accounting for how these two inclusions match up with the book's gathering structure and different scribal hands. The index and the fabric are in two different early-fourteenth century hands (the index was written by Scribe A and the fabric by Scribe B, see appendix 3). Appendix 2 shows the index appearing as the first item in the book, on the verso of the opening flyleaf; it contains the services present in whatever form the manuscript existed at the beginning of the fourteenth century. Most of the contents of the book are recorded in this index, but not all, a point to which I will return below. The fabric is the second item in the manuscript, appearing directly after the index, and shows that the confraternity owned numerous devotional images and statues, as well as other liturgical books and ornaments.[34]

The variation in scribal hands in B-Tc A 12 in many respects matches the manuscript's gathering structure, indicating that this book could consist of portions of several different sources from the thirteenth and early fourteenth centuries that were bound together. Appendix 3 shows that there are twenty different scribal hands in B-Tc A 12. One in particular appears in noncontinuous parts of the manuscript, and the various scribes use different notation styles—both Messine and square notation. For instance, Scribe K, a late thirteenth-century hand using Messine notation, copied all of the music in gatherings 5–18 and 22–24, which is over half of the book (150 folios). Scribe K's contribution consists of all the offices, the masses of the Temporale, and the thirteen Marian sequences. Gatherings 19–21 (fols. 132r–155v) were all copied by Scribe M—an early fourteenth-century hand using square notation for the Marian masses of the Assumption, the Nativity, the Purification, and the Annunciation; the masses for St. Catherine and St. Nicholas; and several troped Kyries.

When the gathering structure and scribal hands are viewed together with the contents of the fabric, it becomes evident that the portions of the manuscript described above match up in some ways to the *quaterni*, or "quires" owned by the confraternity that are mentioned in the fabric, which are listed in figure 1.1 below. The confraternity's quires, and perhaps sections of a larger liturgical book that was dismantled, could have been assembled into one tome at some point in the early fourteenth century to facilitate the performance of the confraternity's services. Figure 1.1 shows that among these quires was one containing the offices of St. Nicholas, St. Catherine, and the Purification; there were two others containing offices for the Virgin Mary. In addition to the small quires, this inventory reveals that there was a book containing masses for the entire year. An examination of the isolated gatherings in B-Tc A 12 shows that Gathering 10 (fols. 59r–66v) solely comprises the Office for the Nativity of the Virgin; Gatherings 11–12 (fols. 67r–80v) are exclusively devoted to the Office for St. Catherine; and Gatherings 13–16 (fols. 81r–114v) include the offices for St. Nicholas and the Nativity. Scribe K copied all of these gatherings, and it is likely that they could be some of the *quaterni* mentioned in the inventory of the confraternity's holdings, which were then later bound together in this volume. The contents of these gatherings represent the earliest round of offices celebrated by the Confraternity of the Notaries since the thirteenth century. The manuscript's inclusion of high masses of the Temporale (three Nativity masses, and one for Epiphany), also copied by Scribe K, may likewise be inclusions from the book containing masses for the entire year, mentioned in the fabric.[35]

The discussion above shows just how much information about the confraternity's religious practices can be gained by looking in-depth at the material composition of the books. On a larger scale, the fabric also gives us some idea about the material wealth of the confraternity from the thirteenth century through the middle of the fourteenth. It is evident that they owned a number of books to carry out their services, and that the devotional focus of the organization at that time was the Virgin Mary, St. Catherine, and St. Nicholas. This is clear also in the number of statues and devotional images they had, which portrayed the likeness of these three figures. For instance, one of the entries in the fabric lists (along with other decorations and vestments they owned) a statue of the Virgin, a statue of St. Nicholas, and a statue of St. Catherine that the confraternity "bought with their money."[36]

Figure 1.1. Books listed in the confraternity's fabric in B-Tc A 12.

> First, four psalters
>
> Then two red books and a plate for communion masses
>
> Then one quire with a fur cover, containing the offices of St. Nicholas, St. Catherine, and the Purification
>
> Then another quire for the choir in which, at the end, is found the entire office of the Nativity of Our Lord
>
> Then, two quires of offices of the Conception of the Holy Virgin Mary
>
> Then one quire containing the Office of the Dedication, Vespers, Matins, and Mass
>
> Then three quires containing the notated Office of the Conception
>
> Then one quire containing the readings for the Conception and for the Nativity of Our Lord
>
> Then four pairs of books containing vigils
>
> Then one book containing only the masses for the entire year

Individuals associated with the Confraternity of the Notaries are not often mentioned in the books, but here there are two proper names appearing in the fabric, one of which could give some indication of the status of the organization within the cathedral. The confraternity owned a gold covering cloth that was donated by a certain "Master Walter Liebart," whose name does not appear in other documents from the cathedral, but he was likely a member. More significantly, the fabric mentions among the confraternity's holdings a piece of white wool cloth ornamented with "armed beasts," given to the organization by Jean des Prés, bishop of Tournai. This is a later addition to the fabric, which would have been added sometime either during his reign as bishop (1342–49) or after. As mentioned previously in relationship to B-Tc A 13, in the sixteenth century some of the confraternity members held high administrative positions at the cathedral, which required close contact with the bishop, and this gift is evidence of that relationship as early as the fourteenth century.

Devotions to St. Barbara at Tournai

To this point, I have explored the *inclusion* of services and objects in the index and fabric of B-Tc A 12, but equally as much can be learned from the *exclusion* of certain items in these two sections. One glaring omission from the index is the Mass and Office for St. Barbara that appears on gatherings two and three as the first round of services in B-Tc A 12. These were added to the book in the late fourteenth or early fifteenth century, after the index and fabric were created, and they reflect the growing importance of popular devotions in the diocese. This marks a distinctly new layer to the confraternity's practices at the close of the fourteenth century.

There is some evidence that St. Barbara was not a central part of the official cycle of liturgy at the Tournai cathedral, even as music in her honor was starting to appear in cathedral books during the course of the fifteenth century. Among the manuscripts used by the confraternity, and also those used in the main sanctuary of the cathedral, a Mass and Office for St. Barbara appear first in B-Tc A 12. During the fifteenth century, however, masses for her were ultimately incorporated into the liturgical usage of the diocese as a whole. That process of inclusion is best traced through additions to other service books, and especially those used in the main sanctuary of the cathedral. The incorporation of the feast of St. Barbara at the cathedral is first evident in accretions to the calendars of liturgical books used there, and new chants added to these sources by later hands. For instance, the cathedral manuscript B-Tc A 10 (see appendix 2), a notated missal produced in the middle of the thirteenth century, contains several addenda at the beginning and the end from the fifteenth and sixteenth centuries. There is a full fifteenth-century calendar included at the beginning of the book, but on fol. 7r there is a remnant of the original thirteenth-century calendar for December, allowing for comparison. The two December calendars both show that December fourth was the feast of St. Barbara, but there is no feast rank indicated, and there is no mention of her among the other saints in the Sanctorale.[37] St. Barbara is a later addition to the original calendar, but she appears in the main fifteenth-century hand for the newly added calendar. The information in this and other sources shows that she was a saint of growing importance in the diocese at some point in the late fourteenth or early fifteenth century. St. Barbara's feast rank was elevated to duplex at some point during the fifteenth century before 1498, as reflected in the calendar of a printed missal for Tournai produced in that year.[38]

It was after this point that a new Mass for St. Barbara appears among several other masses with music added at the end of B-Tc A 10, all in the same hand as the fifteenth-century calendar, showing them to be representative of a larger devotional trend in the diocese.[39] Additions of this type could have been entered into the calendar for practical reasons, as the cathedral canons needed to be aware that a group within its walls would be observing a saint's feast day.[40] It was also the clergy who would have been obligated to carry out the Mass and Office for the confraternity, and they may have copied the texts and music into their own books for convenience.

These votive masses are tied in some ways to religious settings that were already established within the cathedral, as they used newly composed texts set to preexisting music, or contrafacta. The technique of contrafactum is employed in intriguing ways in confraternity devotions, which will be discussed more fully in chapters 2 and 3, but in the masses for St. Barbara at Tournai, the method is employed in its simplest form. Here, well-known chant melodies sung on the feast days of other saints are reused in their entirety and set with new texts for St. Barbara. In order to discuss these musical and textual pairings and their implications, the words and the melodies must be approached separately.[41]

It is apparent in appendix 5 ✌ that the chant texts of the Mass proper for St. Barbara differ in all the cathedral and confraternity books, indicating that their inspiration came from multiple sources rather than being passed along directly. Unique texts for St. Barbara first appear in B-Tc A 12, implying that the confraternity was the catalyst for this. The specialized nature of devotions for St. Barbara, however, is not reflected as prominently in the Mass chants in the confraternity manuscript as it is in the later additions to the cathedral manuscripts. The only proper element of the Mass in B-Tc A 12 is the alleluia verse *Inclita virgo barbara colens*, whereas those chants added at the end of the cathedral manuscript B-Tc A 10 contain the most specialized texts in her honor (see appendix 5 ✌).

Melody adds a different component, as the contrafacta musically make reference to the Virgin Mary. For instance, in B-Tc A 10, the offertory and the alleluia verse present similarities to certain melodies used during the feast of the Nativity; to chants for diverse Marian feasts appearing in the cathedral sources; and those used for other services in B-Tc A 12. The offertory *Ave barbara celorum virgo regis*, for example, is a contrafactum created with the melody of *Ave maria gratia plena*, used on Thursdays in Advent and for most of the Marian feasts in B-Tc A 10, 11, and 12. In this setting, melody and text work together, with the text praising St. Barbara as "second only to Mary."

Hail, Barbara, virgin of the heavens
of the king of angels,
the flower of virgins second only to Mary,
like a rose or a lily,

pour out prayers to the Lord
for the salvation of the faithful.[42]

The communion chant, *Barbara virginis oratio*, and the alleluia verse from B-Tc A 12, *Inclita virgo barbara colens*, are not modeled directly on the usage of the cathedral but could equally be contrafacta created with melodies from outside this context.

So far, there are a number of sources containing music for the Mass for St. Barbara that allow for comparison in the city of Tournai, and they establish that the method of new chant composition for that service was primarily textual, through the creation of contrafacta. The most complex example of new liturgical composition in the books owned by the Confraternity of the Notaries is the Office for St. Barbara in B-Tc A 12. The appearance of music and text for St. Barbara first in the confraternity sources and later in those for the cathedral suggests that religious observances in her honor were promoted first and foremost in a confraternity setting, at a time when devotional fervor for her was growing in the region.

The Life of St. Barbara

St. Barbara's life and martyrdom is included inconsistently in northern French hagiographical sources from the fourteenth and fifteenth centuries and in this respect reflects the irregular appearance of her feast in liturgical books from Tournai. This new focus on St. Barbara goes hand in hand with the development of hagiographical literature meant for consumption by the laity, which was a result of the increase in late medieval devotional consciousness. Consequently, there are many different versions of St. Barbara's vita that circulated in northern France from the thirteenth through the sixteenth centuries. Approaching the transmission of popular devotional practices more broadly allows for a nuanced understanding of how new music and texts for St. Barbara took hold in Tournai. Since most lay people of the time were not literate, this transmission was largely indirect.

All confraternity members would have been familiar with the folklore surrounding the lives of their patron saints through a combination of visual, textual, and aural representations readily available to them, and we can view St. Barbara against this mediascape. It can be assumed that all those taking part in confraternity devotions knew the basic articles of the Christian faith, the prayers and the symbolism related through the Church, and the legends associated with the saints. These connections were achieved in large part through the use of images and iconography.[43] The most likely sources would have been through visual representations in stained glass windows, sculpture, and illuminations and woodcuts in devotional books; as well as in public theatrical and musical displays.[44] The importance that people placed on the display of pious images in their homes is evidence of the central place of iconography in identifying with the lives of the saints.[45] Such associations are further strengthened by the production of thousands of devotional books by Parisian printers in the late fifteenth and early sixteenth centuries. These editions were exported to cities throughout France, the Low Countries, and beyond, and many of them contained woodcuts portraying the lives of the saints and stories from the Bible. From what is known about the ownership of these printed prayer books, it is evident that the audience was not strictly elite, but that men and women of varying socioeconomic formations owned and used them, whether they were able to read and understand the text—in either Latin, French, or a mixture of the two—or not. Praying aloud was common, and whether or not the supplicant understood the words they were saying did not detract from the power these texts were thought to carry, which some scholars have characterized as a sort of "charisma."[46] Most merchants and artisans of the time, including those who were members of the confraternities discussed throughout this book, were usually literate in their vernacular language because their work required it, and the majority had a practical education in Latin through attending celebrations of the Mass and Office.[47] The episcopal notaries in service to the bishop of Tournai were obviously literate, as their profession was based on producing written text. All of these individuals, both literate and non-literate, were part of the market for the various printed editions of the *Golden Legend* (discussed below), collections of miracles of the Virgin Mary, and prayers in Books of Hours, all of which circulated widely in manuscript and later in print.[48]

So far, I have shown how physical objects (books, icons, stained glass windows, etc.) had a hand in reinforcing literacy, but there are also accounts that show how public displays of music and theater were used to the same end. Plays depicting the Annunciation and other stories from the Bible were well known and performed in churches throughout northern France, but in the course of the thirteenth and fourteenth centuries such dramatic representations were also done outside of the church in the vernacular.[49] Carol Symes shows how vernacular plays, particularly the French *Jeu de Saint Nicolas* by Jehan Bodel, are related to vernacular preaching in the city of Arras when she writes, "It is not surprising that Picardy marched in the vanguard of a movement that produced biblical translations, exempla, and other texts that facilitated communication with the laity."[50] Arras provides a good comparison to Tournai, as both were important northern trade centers, and as mentioned previously, they were both places known to have musical cultures perpetuated by the urban *puys* that encouraged writing new poetry and song. These new compositions were performed publicly for anyone in the city of Arras to hear. Evidence from cities all over France, and those further south in Italy, make similar references to urban minstrels performing vernacular plays and songs portraying the lives of the saints. In this respect, Tournai would not have been an exception.[51]

The artistic creations discussed above are in many cases tied to the acquisition of relics by ecclesiastical and monastic institutions in different geographical areas, and this is the case for St. Barbara. Her local popularity in Tournai grew out of the movement of her relics to different institutions in the diocese, which gave way to a rich hagiographical tradition there. The earliest recorded account of St. Barbara's life comes from Egypt, written in the seventh century, but there was a history of devotions to her before that time in Edessa (fourth century) and Cairo (seventh century).[52] The history of her relics in the West is obscured, as there are several different accounts. One source of her vita posits that they went to Constantinople in the sixth century, and after that to Torcello, by way of Venice. Another source from the late fourteenth century indicates that they went directly to Rome in the sixth century and were placed in the Cemetery of Calixtus. In 985, a portion of St. Barbara's relics were moved from Rome to Ghent (which was in the diocese of Tournai), and in 1150, part of her left hand and arm were moved to the church of St. Basile in Bruges (also in the same diocese).[53]

The presence of St. Barbara's relics in the north provided her with a new role as local protector, for saints' relics were thought to have special divine powers. The need for such protection intensified in the fourteenth and fifteenth centuries due to the plague, which led to an outgrowth of local devotional literature and new music compositions during this time, and even shortly before. For instance, there are several notable thirteenth- and fourteenth-century versions of St. Barbara's vita originating in northern France and the Low Countries. Among these is a Latin version from Douai, F-DOU MS 838, dating from the thirteenth century (this is *BHL* Suppl. 913a). Another (*BHL* 918, 920, and 926), was produced in 1380 by Jean de Wackerzeele, also known as Jean de Louvain.[54] There is also a French poetic text that was copied in the 1420s by Jehan Vagus in Hainault.[55] All of these retellings of St. Barbara's life differ in small details, but they show that the legend was widely disseminated in France and further north.[56]

Perhaps the most famous Latin hagiographical work of the late Middle Ages is Jacobus de Voragine's *Golden Legend*, which was originally written in 1275. Despite St. Barbara's popularity in northern France and the Low Countries, which started to increase as early as the thirteenth century, the first version of this work did not include her vita. The *Golden Legend* was paramount in the transmission of local legends surrounding the lives of the saints, and St. Barbara stands out as an example of its variability. Jacobus truncates the vitae into easily digestible abridged versions put together in one tome, which was meant to be used by individuals who did not regularly have access to extensive hagiographical sources (rural parish priests, monks, other religious individuals, and the laity). Favorite episodes from this work were publicly portrayed in devotional images in churches, and in Books of Hours. Its impact on the devotional landscape of Western Europe in general is evident through the number of editions and copies produced. According to Brenda Dunn-Lardeau, the *Golden Legend* was the most transcribed work of the Middle Ages, and by the fifteenth century, copies of it outnumbered those of the Bible. Over 900 manuscripts and 150 printed editions of the *Golden Legend* currently survive and that is only a fraction of what there once was (this number includes translations into English, French, and other vernaculars dating from the fifteenth century and before).[57] Since each geographical region had saints that were important only locally but were perhaps not venerated in other dioceses—or distinctly local stories about widespread saints who were celebrated in a number of places—editors and scribes who copied this work would add new details to the saints' lives. In some cases, they would add completely new vitae in honor of saints not originally included by Jacobus. Thus, local editors and printers had the power to disseminate texts celebrating regional figures and the legends associated with them on a broad scale.

These changes reveal something of the variability of recorded saints' lives, as well as the values of different audiences. Such omissions and inclusions in the *Golden Legend* are further evidence that St. Barbara was of primarily local importance in northern France and the Low Countries. In places where she was revered there was a considerable amount of artistic production (vitae, images, and music) in celebration of her.[58] St. Barbara's prevalence in specific regions led to a variety of marked differences among the later versions of her vita, particularly in printed editions from the late fifteenth century. Multiple editions of the *Golden Legend* provide some of the most variations, as printers and editors took the liberty of adding local saints and their legends to these works. This is evident when the original French version translated by Jean de Vignay (1333–48) is compared with Jean Batallier's well-known revised translation done in 1476. Neither of these editions included the vita of St. Barbara, but when Batallier's 1476 text was printed in Paris by Antoine Vérard twenty years later in 1496, Vérard added a legend of St. Barbara to the Batallier edition.[59] This was not the first time that a printer had included her vita in the *Golden Legend*, for Caxton's 1483 edition in English (volume 6) also has the legend of St. Barbara. The Caxton and Vérard prints are quite different in tone. While Caxton strays from previous vernacular versions in smaller details, the Vérard rendition is a complete departure.[60] Whether Vérard himself was the creator of this vita is unknown, but the story is heavily truncated, and instead of giving information about the events of her life, this legend lingers almost entirely on the act of her martyrdom.[61] The freedom of printers and editors to introduce new vitae is a testament to the fact that there was not a standardized group of saints recognized by all dioceses.

I have drawn primarily from two sources to give the following account of St. Barbara's life: the thirteenth-century vita from Douai (*BHL* Suppl. 913a), and Caxton's printed edition of 1483. The events given here formed the basis of her liturgy, but the texts of the Office chants (there are no readings for Matins in the confraternity books), which I will discuss below, paraphrase the vita rather than quoting directly from it. According to the hagiographical sources, St. Barbara was the daughter of Dioscorus, a rich pagan who lived in the third century under the rule of Maximian. She was said to be incredibly beautiful, so her father, wishing to keep her safe, enclosed her in a tower so that none would see her. Many princes asked for Barbara's hand in marriage, but she begged her father not to force her to marry. Before going on a long trip to survey his lands, Dioscorus had a bathhouse erected for Barbara near her tower and had asked the builders to put two windows in it. Barbara, however, asked them to add a third window as a symbol of the Trinity. The men resisted, fearing her father's anger, but Barbara insisted, telling them that she herself would deal with her father's displeasure when he came home.[62] In the bathhouse, Barbara blessed the water making the sign of the cross with her finger, and it became a healing pool where she was then baptized.[63] While her father was away, she prayed in her tower and condemned idol worshippers. When Dioscorus came back, he was furious about the windows and confronted Barbara. She explained that the three windows let in the light of God, as they symbolized the Holy Trinity. Her father became enraged and tried to kill her with his sword, but Barbara was saved by the grace of God, and taken away to the top of a mountain where two shepherds kept their sheep.

Barbara's father followed her to the mountain, and along the way he asked the shepherds where his daughter was. One ignored him, but the other revealed her whereabouts. In retaliation, she cursed the shepherd who pointed her out by turning his sheep into locusts. After catching her, Dioscorus dragged Barbara down the mountain by her hair and threw her into prison. Barbara then went before Marcian the judge who, charmed by her beauty, gave her a choice: sacrifice to the pagan idols to give penance, or be tortured. Barbara proclaimed that she loved Jesus and denounced all who believed in false idols. In response to this, Marcian ordered Barbara to be stripped naked and beaten, and salt was rubbed into her wounds. She was taken to her cell, and the next morning her wounds were completely healed. The judge proclaimed that it was the pagan gods who healed her, but Barbara said that it was the divine power of Jesus. The judge then ordered her to be hung between two trees, where her sides were burnt with heat lamps; she was whipped; her head was bludgeoned; and her breasts were cut off. After her torture, she was dragged naked through the streets and humiliated. Her final act was to ask God to cover her nakedness, and he did so by adorning her in a white robe. Dioscorus then led Barbara up a mountain to decapitate her, and after brutally murdering his daughter, he himself was struck by lightning and died.

Although this rather grisly story is the basis for the texts of offices and masses for St. Barbara, these works vary in their presentation of the events of her life and martyrdom. There were at least seventeen different offices in her honor circulating in the Low Countries alone from the thirteenth through sixteenth centuries that are found in modern indices and chant databases, but the one on the added gathering in B-Tc A 12 does not appear among them.[64] This particular Office for St. Barbara had an unconventional transmission history and was only celebrated in a handful of areas in neighboring dioceses to the east—Liège and Trier. Through each pass to a new location, the Office was modified both musically and textually, showing that it was subject to as much local variation as the stories about her life and martyrdom. The Office in B-Tc A 12 shows that the Confraternity of the Notaries played an equal part to major cathedrals and parishes in this process, as I demonstrate in the following section.

Sources for the Office of St. Barbara

What does it mean to "compose" a new Office? What methods were used? These are central questions surrounding the Office for St. Barbara in B-Tc A 12. This work is an *historia*, which gives a detailed account of a saint's vita in chronological order through the chants and lesson readings of Vespers, Matins, and Lauds.[65] The chant texts are found in several different sources from Cambrai, Trier, and Liège, but the music in the Tournai version is unique, having no relationship at all to what was used in other locations.[66] Composing new music and setting it to a text already found in other sources, although similar in concept to the technique of contrafactum in its use of preexisting material, is a different process. The term "contrafactum" was already in use in the fifteenth century and essentially means "to imitate," which results in the creation of something new.[67] I use the word contrafactum here to describe a compositional technique meant to establish dual meanings through modeling. In the Mass for St. Barbara discussed earlier in the chapter, I described one type of contrafactum, which involved adding new text to a preexisting melody. In other cases, melodies are manipulated to accommodate new texts or are used as inspiration for an entirely new melody. The chant melodies used to create contrafacta have meaning associated with them through their original texts, therefore adding a new text to a melody that was known in other contexts establishes a symbolic connection to the source (this will be discussed more fully in chapters 2 and 3). Composing completely new melodies and setting them to preexisting texts does not carry such dual meanings. Both are significant undertakings, and they are acts made with the intent to create something new, but in the end, they achieve different results. In composing new melodies not based on pre-circulating models, the focus becomes artistic musical expression, whereas setting new texts to preexisting melodies establishes dual meanings associated with the original text and liturgical function of the source melody.[68] The text of the St. Barbara Office and all of its musical settings in different geographical areas discussed here are anonymous, and no evidence has yet come to light that could indicate who composed them. More broadly, however, these offices yield a good deal of information about local chant composition during the fourteenth century.[69]

A close look at the chant texts and melodies for the St. Barbara Office in B-Tc A 12 and other sources provides details about the types of changes it underwent locally as it was transmitted from one place to another. The late fourteenth-century gathering in B-Tc A 12 that contains the Office and Mass for St. Barbara was added within a 150-year time period during which an Office for St. Barbara appears in a number of other manuscripts and printed books from the dioceses of Cambrai, Liège, and Trier. Figure 1.2 lists all the sources that contain an Office for St. Barbara having some relationship to the one in B-Tc A 12 and indicates which portions of the Office appear in these books (Vespers, Matins, Lauds, or all three together), whether or not the source contains music notation, and the diocese from which it came (the numbers below correspond to appendix 1). The information in figure 1.2 will be referred to in the following discussion of the Office for St. Barbara, and the source numbers are used in the comparison tables in appendix 5⌀.[70]

Three of the earliest manuscripts in figure 1.2, dating from the middle of the fourteenth century, contain chant texts almost identical to those appearing in B-Tc A 12 (see sources 6, 25, and 112). The same Vespers antiphons appear in an additional five books, the latest of which was produced in the early sixteenth century (see sources 3, 15, 42, 101, and 120). Of the three mid-fourteenth-century manuscripts listed above, I will only discuss in detail those with musical notation (a total of two sources) and refer to the other books in figure 1.2 only in cases where they help to establish dating and geographical provenance.[71] The earliest of the two notated manuscripts is an uncatalogued antiphoner held at the church of Ste. Croix in Liège, which was produced between 1333 and 1334 (source 6 in figure 1.2); it contains Vespers, Matins, and Lauds.[72] The later of the two manuscripts is a mid-fourteenth-century notated breviary from the Cathedral of Trier (D-TRb 480), which only contains Matins and Lauds for St. Barbara (source 25 in figure 1.2).[73] Of the three manuscripts containing music, B-Tc A 12 is the most recent, having been copied at some point in the late fourteenth or even early fifteenth century, and represents a later stage in an already established tradition of Office modification.

The St. Barbara Office in the sources above was part of a living tradition, being re-created at different times and places to fit the needs of local communities. Several of these manuscripts and printed books have been discussed in other contexts, and while the Office for St. Barbara has in some cases been a part of those studies, this is the first comparison of its local variations. In order to study how the office changed over time, it is important to establish a timeline for its introduction into three of the earliest manuscripts in figure 1.2. Two of the books were produced between 1333–1373 in the diocese of Liège: the Ste. Croix antiphoner (source 6) and the Maastricht ordinal (source 112). The third source is the mid fourteenth-century manuscript from the

Figure 1.2. Sources for the Office of St. Barbara in the dioceses of Tournai, Cambrai, Liège, and Trier.

3. B-Br 6434	Late fifteenth-century antiphoner from an unidentified institution. Only Vespers and Lauds are included for St. Barbara, and both contain music. Diocese of Liège.
6. B-Lsc 1	Antiphoner produced between 1333 and 1334, used at the church of Sainte-Croix in Liège. Contains Vespers, Matins, and Lauds for the Office for St. Barbara. Diocese of Liège.[i]
10. B-Tc A 12	See appendix 2 for a full description. Contains Vespers, Matins, and Lauds. Diocese of Tournai.
15. B-TOb 63	Antiphoner produced c.1375–1400 used at the Onze-Lieve-Vrouwekerk in Tongeren. It is nearly identical to MS 64, listed below, showing that it was likely produced for one side of the choir, but there are handwritten addenda indicating that the transmission history of the two sources is separate. While the manuscript contains Vespers, Matins, and Lauds for St. Barbara, only Vespers is similar to the Office in B-Tc A 12. Diocese of Liège.[ii]
16. B-TOb 64	Antiphoner produced c. 1375–1400 used at the Onze-Lieve-Vrouwekerk in Tongeren. It is nearly identical to MS 63, listed above, showing that it was likely produced for one side of the choir, but there are handwritten addenda indicating that the transmission history of the two sources is separate. Due to lacunae, Vespers is missing, and the Office for St. Barbara begins in the middle of Matins and continues through Lauds. Diocese of Liège.[iii]
25. D-TRb 480	Notated breviary from the Cathedral of St. Peter in Trier, produced in the middle of the fourteenth century. This source does not contain Vespers, but rather begins with the Magnificat antiphon, *Dulci voce resonet*, and then goes on to Matins and Lauds.[iv] Diocese of Trier.
26. D-TRb 486	Antiphoner produced at the end of the fourteenth century and used at Koblenz. Diocese of Trier.
27. D-TRb 488a	Antiphoner produced in the fifteenth century and used at Dietkirchen. Diocese of Trier.
28. D-TRb 498a	Antiphoner produced in the fifteenth century and used at the Cathedral of Trier. Diocese of Trier.

—(continued)

Figure 1.2—*continued*

29. D-TRsb 427/1250	Breviary from the church of St. Simeon in Trier dating from the fourteenth century. A rubric before first Vespers indicates that this Office was done at the Cathedral as well. Diocese of Trier.
42. F-CA Impr. XVI C 4	Printed antiphoner from Cambrai, produced in Paris by Simon Vostre between 1508 and 1518. Contains only Vespers for St. Barbara.[v] Diocese of Cambrai.
101. F-Psg OEXV 828 (3) Rés	*Breviarium Tornacense* (Pars hyemalis). Printed breviary for the diocese of Cambrai, produced in Paris in 1497 by Jean Higman. Contains no music, but the antiphons for Vespers are the same as in B-Tc A 12, and it is identical to the Vespers Office appearing in Source 42 above.[vi]
112. NL-DHk 71 A 13	Ordinal produced between 1354–73 for the Onze-Lieve-Vrouwekerk in Maastricht. Short chant text incipits for Vespers, Matins, and Lauds for St. Barbara. No responsory verses are provided. No music. Diocese of Liège.[vii]
120. US-Cn Inc. 9344.5	Breviary for the diocese of Liège (usage of the Cathedral of St. Lambert) printed in 1484 in Brussels by the Frères de la vie commune in 1484. The source contains the chant texts for Vespers, Matins, and Lauds for St. Barbara but no music. Diocese of Liège.[viii]

Notes:

[i] See Frisque, "Les manuscrits liturgiques notés," 77–78.

[ii] See Long and Behrendt, *Antiphonaria*, 110–12. The full manuscript is indexed in *CANTUS*.

[iii] See Long and Behrendt, *Antiphonaria*, 113–15. The full manuscript is indexed in *CANTUS*.

[iv] See Brink, "Historiae Trevirenses" (419–42) for a detailed discussion of the St. Barbara Office in the Trier sources (sources 25–29 above).

[v] This Office was discussed by Haggh in *Two Cambrai Antiphoners*, xxix.

[vi] A scanned version of the copy at Ste. Geneviève is available online via *The Internet Archive* https://archive.org/details/OEXV828_3a (Accessed April 1, 2019).

[vii] Discussed by Saucier, "Sacred Music and Musicians," 176–200; and Tagage, *De Ordinarius van de Collegiale*, 129–30.

[viii] See Saucier, "Sacred Music and Musicians," 157, 192–204; Frisque, "Les manuscrits liturgiques notés," 176–200; and Saucier, *A Paradise of Priests*, 157.

cathedral of Trier (source 25). This book was recently discovered by Danette Brink, who conducted a detailed study of the St. Barbara Office, translating the texts of Matins and Lauds into English and providing a detailed musical analysis of the reciting tones and cadences.[74] Both Xavier Frisque and Catherine Saucier have discussed the music of the St. Barbara Office found in the Ste. Croix manuscript. Frisque did a detailed modal analysis of the chants, while Saucier showed its connection to the Office in the Maastrict ordinal and discussed the use of a contrafactum for the magnificat antiphon *Dulci voce resonet* (which is set to the *Salve regina* melody).[75]

None of these authors were aware of the St. Barbara Office in B-Tc A 12; nor were they aware of each other's work, but viewing the Ste. Croix antiphoner and the Maastricht ordinal (sources 6 and 112 respectively, both from the diocese of Liège) in context with all of the manuscripts in Trier helps to clarify its origin. In source 29, from the collegiate church of St. Simeon in Trier, the Office of Vespers carries a rubric indicating that it was sung at the cathedral.[76] Brink argues that the Office was written in Trier and relates it to a testament from 1238 by Tymar, principal of the cathedral school. This document attests that Tymar endowed an Office for St. Barbara, indicating that it was newly composed.[77] The testament does not identify exactly which Office this is, and although the distinctive local Office for St. Barbara does appear in two cathedral sources (source 25 and source 27), the earliest one (source 25) was produced ca. 1350, over one hundred years after Tymar's foundation. This Office may have been composed in the thirteenth century in Trier and only survived in later sources, but there is no concrete way to determine that. In light of this, the earliest datable manuscript with music for the Office of St. Barbara is the Ste. Croix antiphoner from the 1330s.

As I established previously in the discussion of contrafacta for the Mass, music and text circulated independently, and this is the case for the Office as well. While all of the St. Barbara offices in the sources shown in figure 1.2 share much of the same chant texts, the musical settings are different. Looking at the components separately yields information about how local traditions are related to those in other regions and contexts. The result of my comparisons of the music and text in appendix 5 ❧ are condensed in tables 1.1 and 1.2 to show the textual and musical relationships in the St. Barbara Office among those sources that have musical notation. Textually, the Office in B-Tc A 12 (figure 1.2, source 10) and the one in D-TRb 480 (figure 1.2, source 25) are nearly identical and will be hereafter referred to as

Table 1.1. Textual concordances among the three sources containing music for the Office of St. Barbara.

Sources compared to B-Tc A 12 (figure 1.2, Source 10)	Texts the same when compared to B-Tc A 12 (figure 1.2, Source 10)
D-TRb 480 (figure 1.2, Source 25)	Yes
B-Lsc 1 (figure 1.2, Source 6)	No
Textual Traditions	Tournai/Trier and Liège Ste. Croix

the Tournai/Trier Office, while the one from B-Lsc 1 (figure 1.2, source 6) differs, and will be referred to as the Ste. Croix Office.

Although there are two different traditions for the Office chant texts, the music does not fall so neatly into these categories. Melodically, there are separate lines of development for the liturgical books containing Vespers and those that contain Matins and Lauds. Vespers was the most widespread of the offices, and music for it appears in a total of five sources (figure 1.2, sources 3, 6, 10, 15, and 42).[78] Music for Matins and Lauds appears in only three sources: B-Tc A 12 (source 10), the Ste. Croix antiphoner (source 6), and Trier (source 25). The comparisons in appendix 5 ☝ show that when the chant texts in Ste. Croix and Trier are the same, which they are for all portions except the Matins responsories and verses, so is the music. While the chant texts in B-Tc A 12 are also almost exactly the same in Trier, the music in the Tournai manuscript has no relationship to any of the other settings. Thus, table 1.2 shows that there are two broad melodic traditions for the offices of Matins and Lauds, which I refer to as Tournai and Ste. Croix/Trier. My discussions of melody and musical style will specifically focus on Tournai and Ste. Croix in Liège.[79] How these offices differ, and the distinctive characteristics of each, will be the basis of the following discussion.

Local variants in the Office for St. Barbara show how different communities cultivated new music and text in her honor focusing on particular events in her vita; thus, the most logical place to start this investigation is with the text. All the chant texts for the *historia* paraphrase her life and recount well-known and widely circulating legends from it. These are manipulated in different ways due to variations in their narrative structure as a result of using divergent responsories and verses during Matins, which changes the way these events unfold.[80]

The antiphons are the most stably transmitted part of the Tournai/Trier Office and the Ste. Croix Office and establish the overall narrative structure

Table 1.2. Melodic concordances among the three sources containing music for the Office of St. Barbara.

Sources containing chant melodies	Music the same when compared to Source 10	Music the same when compared to Source 6	Music the same when compared to Source 25
D-TRb 480 (figure 1.2, Source 25)	No	Yes	(This is Source 25)
B-Lsc 1 (figure 1.2, Source 6)	No	(This is Source 6)	Yes
B-Tc A 12 (figure 1.2, Source 10)	(This is Source 10)	No	No
Melodic Traditions	Tournai	Ste. Croix/Trier	Ste. Croix/Trier

and devotional focus to St. Barbara. Vespers, Matins, and Lauds portray scenes from St. Barbara's life in various ways, but there are some similarities among them. For instance, the Vespers antiphons give general praise to St. Barbara, referencing her pagan ancestry and conquering of idols, the act of her torture with lamps, her pain, and her beheading. The responsory and verse refer again to the lamps of fire, but also her bravery, emphasizing her martyrdom. Table 1.3 gives the full texts of the antiphons for Vespers with English translations and shows their appearance in all the sources.[81]

The comparisons above show that the rhymed antiphons are more or less the same in all books, with only one textual outlier (antiphon 5). Table 1.3 shows that the text is similar across the manuscripts—and indeed it is the same in Tournai, the cathedral of Liège, and Maastricht (sources 10, 120, and 112)—but the Ste. Croix and Cambrai sources each have their own variations on it (similarities are highlighted with italics). The Ste. Croix text is a mangled reading of the Cambrai version, leaving out the words "celica" and "dona," which breaks the meter and obscures the text. It also contains elements of the chant in the Tournai source, as it starts with "Virgo" rather than "Barbara." Because the Ste. Croix manuscript from the 1330s predates the Cambrai print (produced between 1508 and 1518), it shows that some version of the text in the Cambrai book was in circulation in other sources in

Table 1.3. Vespers. Close comparison of antiphons in Tournai, Liège (Ste. Croix), and Cambrai (see figure 1.2 for corresponding source numbers). Similarities in the different versions of antiphon 5 are highlighted in italics.

Antiphons	Latin text	English text	3	6	10	15	42	112	120
Antiphon 1	Barbara virgo dei virtute probata trophei igne flagrans fidei sacrat huius festa diei.	Barbara, virgin of God, proven in the strength of victory, ablaze with the fire of faith, consecrates the festivities of this day.	X	X	X	X	X	X	X
Antiphon 2	Virgo fide sana de stirpe creata prophana gaudia mundana posponit et ydola vana.	The virgin, sound in faith, born of profane lineage, sets aside worldly joys and vain idols.	X	X	X	X	X	X	X
Antiphon 3	Carceris horrore roseo perfusa cruore lampadis ardore patitur cruciata dolore.	In the horror of prison, covered with red blood, she suffers by the burning of a torch, tormented by pain.	X	X	X	X	X	X	X
Antiphon 4	Ubere truncata vestimentis spoliata hinc decollata conscendit regna beata.	With her breast cut off, stripped of her garments, then beheaded, she rises to the blessed kingdom.	X	X	X	X	X	X	X

—(continued)

Table 1.3—*concluded*

Antiphons	Latin text	English text	3	6	10	15	42	112	120
Antiphon 5	*Virgo morte bona vite redimita corona* iusticie zona precingi nos prece dona.	Virgin wreathed with the garland of life by a good death, grant us by your prayer to be girded with the belt of righteousness.	X		X	X		X	X
	Virgo morte bona vite redimita corona dans nos salves sancta patrona.	(Mangled version of the text below)		X					
	Barbara morte bona vitae redimita corona celica *dans* dona *nos salves sancta patrona.*	Barbara, wreathed with the garland of life by a good death, giving heavenly gifts, save us, holy protector.					X		

the early fourteenth century, almost two hundred years before it was printed by Simon Vostre in Paris.

While Vespers gives a general overview of her life and torture, the Matins antiphons proceed to give a detailed account of St. Barbara's vita in chronological order, which is common in *historiae*. During the first nocturn, the antiphon texts discuss her lineage, her life in the tower, and the marriage proposals she received. The second nocturn antiphons narrate her baptism in the holy water of the pool, her judgment of pagans, and her description of the Trinity symbolism in the bathhouse windows. The third nocturn antiphons describe her imprisonment, the miraculous healing of her wounds, and her denunciation of pagan gods. Lauds continues the dramatic action with antiphons portraying Barbara's pain and martyrdom, starting with Marcian's final order for her to be tortured and her father's promise to execute her. There are also several texts of general praise in honor of St. Barbara in the

Figure 1.3. Antiphons 1 and 2 in the Ste. Croix antiphoner (B-Lsc 1).

> Antiphon 1. The governor, enraged at the answers of the glorious martyr Barbara, orders her sides to be savagely torn and burning torches to be applied to her.
>
> Antiphon 2. The governor orders the virgin's head to be beaten with a hammer and her breasts to be cut off with a sword.

Lauds antiphons, as well as allusions to her father's death after her martyrdom. Appendix 5 ⁀ shows that the Lauds antiphons are arranged differently in the Ste. Croix Office when compared to the Tournai/Trier Office, and that in some cases there are altogether different antiphon texts. These variations do not change the story, but some of the unique antiphons in the Ste. Croix antiphoner, such as *Iratus preses* (antiphon 1) and *Iubet preses* (antiphon 2), make direct and detailed references to her torture with the burning lamps, her head wounds, and the amputation of her breasts. (See figure 1.3).[82] In the Tournai/Trier Office, the antiphons are arranged so that there are allusions to her torture coupled with general texts of praise, so there is a balance in the texts between references to the act of her martydom, and to her holiness.

The responsories and verses done after the antiphons for each nocturn of Matins are the main place where the Ste. Croix Office and the Tournai/Trier Office differ. Responsories are often moved around in offices as they are adapted locally, but in these two there are in some cases different texts.[83] In the Ste. Croix Office, most of the responsories and verses are unica both musically and textually, and they contain either general praise for St. Barbara or a reflection on the content of the antiphons (usually focusing on the heinous events of her martyrdom), rather than continuous dramatic action. In this way, the Ste. Croix Office is versatile, as it is possible to move the responsories and verses around without ruining the narrative structure. Table 1.4 gives the texts and translations of the unique responsories in the Ste. Croix manuscript.[84]

In the Tournai/Trier Office, the responsories and verses for Matins continue the narrative action and play an equal part to the antiphons in the continuation of the story's dramatic plot (see the Latin incipits of the chant texts in appendix 5 ⁀).[85] In nocturn 1 they discuss her demand for a third window in the bathhouse and its symbolism, her blessing of the water with the sign of the cross, and the healing virtues of the pool. In nocturn 2, the responsories and verses recount St. Barbara's flight to the mountain and the shepherd's betrayal, her revenge by turning his sheep into locusts, her trial by jury, her whipping, and the miraculous healing of her wounds (the content of the last responsory and verse overlap with the first antiphon of the third nocturn). And finally, in nocturn 3 these chants detail her condemnation to be tortured and burnt with heat lamps, and have her breasts cut off and her head bludgeoned. This again provides overlap with the first Lauds antiphon that describes how the judge ordered her to be tortured.

The discussion above shows that in the later fourteenth century, the text of the St. Barbara Office took on a more cohesive form in Tournai and Trier in comparison to the one in the Ste. Croix manuscript, because the antiphons and responsories are reliant on each other. The primary use of antiphon texts to carry dramatic action in the Ste. Croix Office perhaps made it more versatile, so the responsories could easily be rearranged if need be. Since this is the earliest source for the Office, with the Trier manuscript being the next in chronology, we see how it changed textually over time and in different places.

Local changes are even more apparent when melody is taken into consideration, and the most compelling examples come from Ste. Croix and Tournai. Table 1.2 shows that the categories above are realigned when both music and text are considered together, and in this respect there are two broadly established melodic traditions for these offices: Tournai and Ste. Croix/Trier. Although local compositional features can be established by analyzing the music, it is not as easy to determine chronology based on musical analysis. Musical markers of chant composition from the fourteenth through sixteenth centuries have only recently become the subject of scholarly attention and cannot yet easily be compared with the older repertory, making it difficult to identify a timeframe for the composition of the music for the St. Barbara Office in B-Tc A 12 or in the other manuscripts. Characteristics that have been put forth as representative of repertories created after the tenth century also hold true for a number of chants in the earlier repertory, such as their wide ambitus (up to an eleventh), and use of melodic formulae.[86] The newer repertory appears to display these traits more regularly, as well as using chant models as the basis for new composition, long scalar passages and melismas, contrafacta, and classical poetic meters.[87] All of these are present in the offices under consideration here, but to different degrees. Looking at the music does not add to our understanding of chronology, but it does add to our understanding of local compositional characteristics.

What stands out structurally about the Tournai Office in comparison with the Ste. Croix/Trier Office is the use of modal order for the antiphons and responsories, which is a hallmark of later chant composition.[88] The chants in the Tournai and Ste. Croix/Trier offices all proceed in some sort of modal

Table 1.4. Matins. Unique responsories and verses in B-Lsc 1.

Chant	Latin text (words in italics are highlighted by long melismas)	English text (words in italics are highlighted by long melismas)
NOCTURN 1		
Nocturn 1 responsory 1	Die ista preclara virgo et martyr barbara exuta carnis sarcina venit ad solamina Christo iuncta qui hanc rexit in quem credidit quem dilexit.	On this day the illustrious virgin and martyr Barbara, having laid aside the burden of the flesh, arrives at consolations: joined to Christ who guided her, in whom she believed, whom she loved.
Verse	Coronatur fidelis Christicola inter sacras virgines aureola.	The faithful Christian is crowned with a halo among the holy virgins.
Nocturn 1 responsory 2	In eterno speculo previsa barbara virgo pia ex prophana stirpe progenita amirabili pulcritudine nituit sed fide moribus pulchrior Altissimo domino *complacuit.*	Foreseen in an eternal mirror, the holy virgin Barbara, born of profane lineage, shone in admirable beauty, but even more beautifully in faith and behavior: she was *pleasing* to the most high Lord.
Verse	Pulcra facie virgo beata sed pulcrior fide.	The blessed virgin was beautiful in appearance but more beautiful in faith.
NOCTURN 2		
Nocturn 2 responsory 1	*Virgo* flagellatur acerrime nervis taurinis et texturis defricatur atrociter cilicinis Ex plagis illatis defluebant gutte *sanguinis.*	*The virgin* is flogged severely with cords of ox-hide and is scoured violently with woven haircloths: drops of *blood* flowed from the wounds inflicted.
Verse	Incarceratur virgo prophani iudicis precepto.	The virgin is imprisoned at the order of the impious judge.

—(*continued*)

Table 1.4—*continued*

Chant	Latin text (words in italics are highlighted by long melismas)	English text (words in italics are highlighted by long melismas)
Nocturn 2 responsory 2	Barbara virgo sanctissima succensa igne interius divini *amoris constanter* In *suo* corpore tormentorum sustinuit *cruciatus*.	Barbara, the most holy virgin, internally ablaze with the fire of divine *love*, *resolutely* endures the anguish of *tortures* in *her* body.
Verse	Cuius intercessio veniam nobis optineat et perhennis vite gloriam.	By her intercession may she obtain pardon for us and the glory of eternal life.
Nocturn 2 responsory 3	In carcere nocte media lux de celis refulsit in qua salvator apparuit beate barbare consolans eam et dicens ei Confortare filia quia ego tecum sum.	In the prison at midnight a light shone from heaven, in which the Savior appeared to blessed Barbara, consoling her and saying: Be courageous, daughter, because I am with you.
Verse	Gaudet virgo super visitatione domini et statim omnia vulnera ei illata non comparent.	The virgin rejoices at the Lord's visitation and immediately all the wounds inflicted on her are no longer present.
NOCTURN 3		
Nocturn 3 responsory 1	Conturbatur preses in verbis virginis qui latera eius iubet discerpi et lampades ardentes applicari ei Et malleo caput eius crudeliter *iubet* tondi.	The governor was dismayed at the words of the virgin; he gave orders for her sides to be torn and for burning torches to be applied to her: and he *ordered* her head to be cruelly beaten with a hammer.
Verse	Et mamillas eius ipse crudelis gladio iubet amputari.	And he himself, the cruel one, ordered her breasts to be cut off with a sword.

—(*continued*)

Table 1.4—*concluded*

Chant	Latin text (words in italics are highlighted by long melismas)	English text (words in italics are highlighted by long melismas)
Nocturn 3 responsory 2	Suscipitur *sanctissima* Christi martyr barbara a crudeli patre suo et ducitur supra montem Que perseverans in confessione nominis *domini decollatur* ibi.	Barbara, the *most holy* martyr of Christ, is taken by her cruel father and led to the top of a mountain: persevering in the acknowledgment of the *Lord's* name, she is *beheaded* there.
Verse	Festinabat virgo gaudens ut bravium victorie mereretur accipere.	The virgin hastened, rejoicing that she was worthy of receiving the prize of victory.
Nocturn 3 responsory 3	Christum patris filium laudet chorus fidelium cuius imitari barbara vestigia virgo pia studuit Preclara fide et castitate.	Let the chorus of the faithful praise Christ, Son of the Father, in whose footsteps the holy virgin Barbara was eager to follow, illustrious in faith and chastity.
Verse	Ora pro nobis virgo pia ut mereamur in patria eterna frui gloria.	Pray for us, holy virgin, that we may be worthy to enjoy eternal glory in our heavenly home.

sequence. Table 1.5 shows that the antiphons in the Ste. Croix antiphoner proceed in modal order, 123: 456: 781, but the responsories do not.[89] The Tournai Office has a different type of modal order for the antiphons, 111: 222: 333, and the responsories, as in the Ste. Croix manuscript, are not in modal order at all. This reveals that the responsories in all three offices are the most variable element not only textually, as I showed above, but also musically.[90]

Modal ordering is a larger organizing principal, but there are also internal structural markers indicating local compositional practices, primarily having to do with the use of long melismas on important words, which was not noted by previous scholars. Although there are two different chant melodies for the responsory *Virgo christi barbara* (one in Tournai, and one in Ste. Croix/Trier), the composers of both melodies used long melismas to put special emphasis on certain words in order to enhance the meaning of the text. In this case, it draws attention to the healing power of the pool in St.

Table 1.5. Modal ordering for the Tournai and Liège Ste. Croix/Trier offices.

Chants	B-Tc A 12	B-Lsc 1	D-TRb 480
Nocturn 1			
Antiphon 1	Mode 1	Mode 1	Mode 1
Antiphon 2	Mode 1	Mode 2	Mode 2
Antiphon 3	Mode 1	Mode 3	Mode 3
Responsory 1	Mode 1	Mode 5	Mode 3
Responsory 2	Mode 8	Mode 5	Mode 3
Responsory 3	Mode 7	Mode 5	Mode 6
Nocturn 2			
Antiphon 4	Mode 2	Mode 4	Mode 4
Antiphon 5	Mode 2	Mode 5	Mode 5
Antiphon 6	Mode 2	Mode 6	Mode 6
Responsory 4	Mode 5	Mode 7	Mode 6 (transposed)
Responsory 5	Mode 8	Mode 7	Mode 7
Responsory 6	Mode 5	Mode 2	Mode 7
Nocturn 3			
Antiphon 7	Mode 3	Mode 7	Mode 7
Antiphon 8	Mode 3	Mode 8	Mode 8
Antiphon 9	Mode 3	Mode 1	Mode 1
Responsory 7	Mode 7	Mode 8	Mode 5
Responsory 8	Mode 3	Mode 2	Mode 6 (transposed)
Responsory 9	Mode 1	Mode 8	Mode 6 (transposed)

Barbara's bathhouse, and the word "remedia" (cure) contains long melismas in both versions (see example 1.1 and example 1.2).

Examples of this occur throughout the Office in all sources, but it is worth pointing out that the melismas portray stylistic differences, and I use the responsory melodies in Tournai and Ste. Croix to illustrate this. Melismas in the Tournai Office rarely surpass ten notes, whereas those in the Ste. Croix Office are normally more than twice as long; they often appear at the end of a responsory, indicating that at least part of their function was musical. Those instances where there are words with exceptionally long melismas in the Ste.

Example 1.1. Nocturn 1 responsory 3, *Virgo christi barbara* in B-Tc A 12 (Tournai)

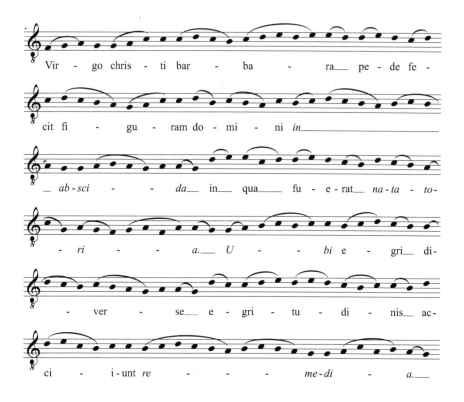

Croix antiphoner are highlighted in italics in table 1.4; in some cases they appear singularly on words like "pleasing" (complacuit) in nocturn 1 responsory 2 (see example 1.3), and "ordered" (iubet) in nocturn 3 responsory 1 (see example 1.4). In three responsories, more than one word is highlighted, always having associations with blood, torture, and martyrdom: "The Virgin … blood" (Virgo … sanguinis) in nocturn 2 responsory 1 (example 1.5); "love resolutely … her … tortures" (amoris constanter … suo … cruciatus) in nocturn 2 responsory 2 (see example 1.6); and "most holy … Lord … beheaded" (sanctissima … domini decollatur) in nocturn 3 responsory 2 (see

Example 1.2. Nocturn 1 responsory 3, *Virgo christi barbara* in B-Lsc 1 (Liège).

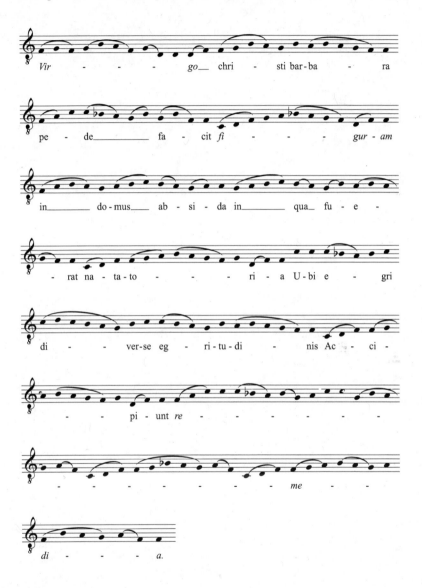

Example 1.3. Nocturn 1 responsory 2, *In eterno speculo* in B-Lsc 1 (Liège).

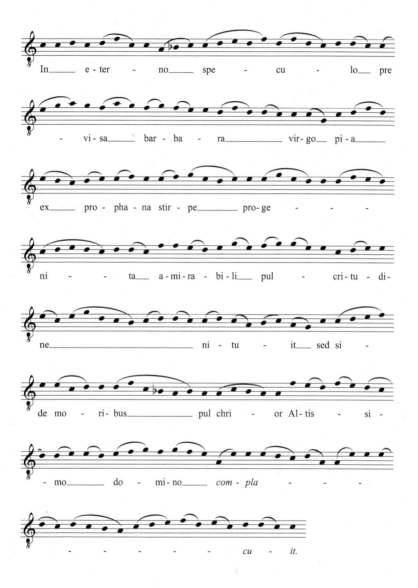

Example 1.4. Nocturn 3 responsory 1, *Conturbatur preses* in B-Lsc 1 (Liège).

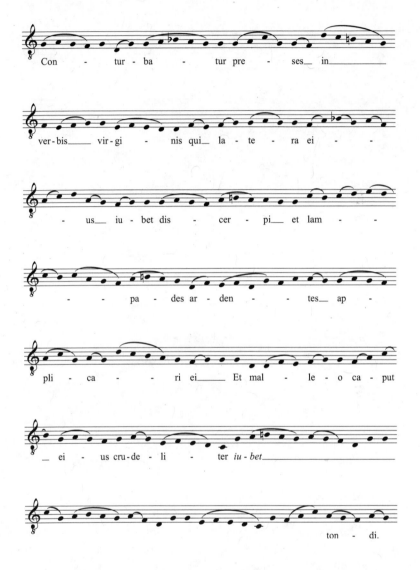

Example 1.5. Nocturn 2 responsory 1, *Virgo flagelletur* in B-Lsc 1 (Liège).

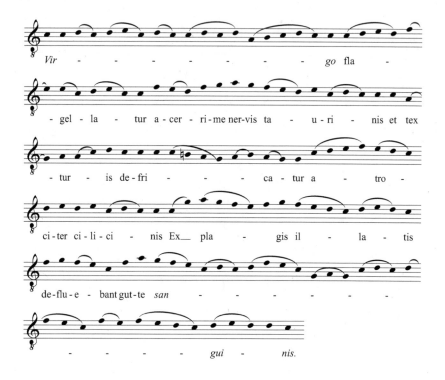

example 1.7). In these cases, the composer of the Ste. Croix Office draws the listener's attention to important parts of St. Barbara's martyrdom.

The analysis above shows that the composer of the Ste. Croix responsories was concerned with music and textual meaning. In contrast, the Tournai version is more subtle in its use of melismas, and it is in some cases more formulaic. To illustrate this, I turn again to the responsory *Virgo christi barbara*. I showed previously how the longest melisma is on the last word (remedia), but there are also shorter melismas on "in abscida," "natatoria," and "ubi." The first, on "in abscida," bears marked similarities to the scalar passages in the long melisma at the end, as they use the same melodic motives in the upward rise from B to D and then fall back down to A (see example 1.1). Similar uses of melodic motives occur in the third responsory of nocturn 3,

Example 1.6. Nocturn 2 responsory 2, *Barbara virgo* in B-Lsc 1 (Liège).

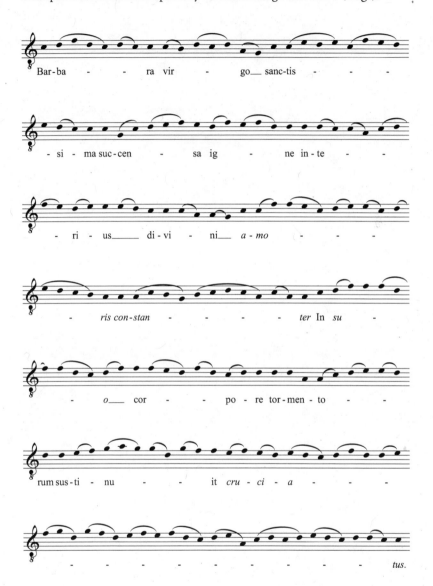

Example 1.7. Nocturn 3 responsory 2, *Suscipitur sanctissima* in B-Lsc 1 (Liège).

Example 1.8. Nocturn 3 responsory 3, *Honor deo pro tropheo* in B-Tc A 12 (Tournai).

Honor deo pro tropheo. In this chant, there are distinguished internal leaps of a fifth on words like "deo" (God) that are followed by a short melisma; "thronum" (throne) and "virtutum" (mighty works) again have opening leaps followed by short melismas. The words "et virtutum" at the end have a repeated falling scalar passage emphasizing the fifth from A to D (see example 1.8).[91]

What does this tell us about chant composition in Tournai and Liège? Without knowing who wrote these offices, it is difficult to say with any degree of certainty that they came from specific locations, but the variants above show that composers had a number of techniques to draw from. The composer of the Ste. Croix Matins responsories took care to emphasize important words with melismas, doing so mostly at the ends of phrases. The composer of the Tournai Office also artfully composed melodies that reinforced certain pitch centers through the use of melodic motives. Both these approaches reflect what we know of chant composition in the fourteenth century and provide more examples of these procedures in the repertory.

Perhaps the most important discovery here is that these offices are all part of a tradition marked by local modifications, and that confraternities, such as the Confraternity of the Notaries, are an integral part of this process along with important collegiate churches (like Ste. Croix in Liège) and cathedrals in neighboring dioceses (like the cathedral of St. Peter in Trier). The text of the St. Barbara Office was familiar to people in the dioceses of Liège and Trier by the middle decades of the fourteenth century, and it could have arrived in Tournai in any number of ways. Among the possible avenues are traveling clerics and even correspondence by post, as such liturgical items were known to have traveled in this manner in the dioceses of Liège and Cambrai in the fourteenth and fifteenth centuries.[92] Since the notaries were clerics who would have traveled with the bishop, it is tempting to think that they themselves could have been responsible for bringing the text to Tournai. The melodies of the Tournai Office were created after the chant texts had already been in circulation and undergone a number of different local artistic modifications in neighboring dioceses to the east. All that can be established for certain is that B-Tc A 12 is the only source from Tournai to contain music for the Office of St. Barbara, and there is no evidence that her feast was celebrated outside of confraternal settings until at least the late fifteenth century, which is when Mass chants for votive masses in her honor were added at the end of cathedral books like B-Tc A 10, discussed previously. The distinctive chant melodies of the Tournai Office speak to a value placed on new music composition in the confraternity, which is related to celebrations for St. Barbara in similar communities outside of Tournai.

St. Barbara's Place in Confraternity Devotions and Beyond

The Office for St. Barbara in B-Tc A 12 illustrates the opposite of the type of new chant composition most commonly found in confraternity books, which are usually contrafacta. In this case, the composer took previously circulating texts and set new music to them. I addressed the possible avenues for how the Office text may have ended up in Tournai, but we are now left with two more questions. How do confraternity practices honoring St. Barbara in other locations parallel those of the notaries in Tournai, and who could have composed the music for the Office in B-Tc A 12?

To answer the first question, it is necessary to look at neighboring cities in which St. Barbara had a large following, and the one closest in proximity to Tournai is the city of Liège, where the Ste. Croix antiphoner comes from. St. Barbara was venerated among the laity and in prominent ecclesiastical institutions in the city, which is significant considering the appearance of the same Office text for her in both B-Tc A 12 and the Ste. Croix antiphoner. This could imply that the text of the St. Barbara Office came to Tournai from

this location. Devotions to St. Barbara in Liège resulted in numerous foundations for votive services in her honor, as well as modifications to her liturgy. For instance, the cathedral chapter of Liège elevated St. Barbara's feast
to duplex rank in 1365 and commissioned proper chants to be composed
for the occasion.[93] This seems to have started a trend within the diocese, and
other institutions followed suit, which is evident in two Liègeois sources held
at the Bibliothèque royale de Belgique in Brussels, where her feast rank is
also listed as duplex.[94]

Evidence of her popularity among the laity in the late fifteenth and early
sixteenth centuries is demonstrated through the records of one of the most
prestigious freestanding confraternities in Liège, the Confraternity of St.
Barbara, which met at the chapel of St. Barbara on the Pont des Arches. The
rules of the confraternity, recorded in a register from 1514 currently held
at the Archives de l'État in Liège, are a prime example of the types of information pertaining to confraternity devotions that are commonly recorded
in archival sources. Such rulebooks and account registers rarely give musical
details, but they are rich in logistics.[95]

What is apparent in this document is that although the confraternity rules
are very specific regarding when and where services were to be celebrated,
they do not indicate exactly which Office or Mass was sung. Since there
were many different offices for St. Barbara circulating in the Low Countries,
the confraternity could have used the same Office as the Cathedral of St.
Lambert, or the one in use at the church of Ste. Croix, or something completely different. It is clear through the seven articles in the register that this
confraternity celebrated St. Barbara's feast day with high ceremony. The organization met regularly, sometimes in the chapel of St. Barbara at St. Lambert,
but the location differed depending on the occasion. According to article 1,
the confraternity members were to meet in the afternoon on the vigil of St.
Barbara at the chapel on the Pont des Arches to sing first Vespers for the said
feast. On the next day, after Matins was finished, they were to process to St.
Lambert where the confraternity members would congregate in the chapel of
St. Barbara to sing high Mass, and in the afternoon, to sing second Vespers.
Articles 4, 5, 6, and 7 also give similar information.

The closest anyone has ever come to identifying a composer for the music
of the St. Barbara Office is in relation to the Office of Vespers at Cambrai,
which is the same as that found in the Tournai books. In her 1995 edition of
the two Cambrai antiphoners, Barbara Haggh speculated on the likelihood
that the Office was composed by Jean de Wackerzeele, also known as Jean de
Louvain.[96] Wackerzeele was born in the middle of the fourteenth century,

joining the Augustinian order in 1370 and later residing in Cologne where he is known to have written a version of the life and miracles of St. Barbara around 1380. This work circulated widely in the Low Countries starting in the late fourteenth century.[97] Given the sources that were available during the indexing of the two Cambrai antiphoners, Jean de Wackerzeele as the composer of the St. Barbara Office was a very reasonable conclusion. In fact, the sources for the Office in the *AH*, cited by Haggh, are two breviaries printed in 1497 without music, one from Cambrai and one from Tournai (the Tournai breviary is appendix 1, source 101).[98] This easily led to the assumption that the Office in the printed Cambrai antiphoner was a much later composition.

While Jean de Wackerzeele was certainly capable of writing a St. Barbara *historia*, it is not possible for him to have composed the one under consideration here because the dates do not line up with the sources. Vespers, which is the same in all of them, was copied into the Maastricht Ordinal between 1354 and 1373, well before Wackerzeele wrote his life of St. Barbara. Furthermore, it appears in both existing Liègeoise sources, with the one from Ste. Croix dating from the 1330s. As I showed earlier, the events of St. Barbara's life and martyrdom had circulated widely in northern France since the thirteenth century, for the details in the Douai vita closely match those reflected in all the offices discussed here.

The types of relationships that the Tournai notaries may have established in other places remain largely undocumented for this period, so how the Office text came to Tournai continues to be unexplained. What is particularly compelling here is the fact that the music for the Office of St. Barbara in B-Tc A 12 is not the only unique work in the Tournai confraternity books (see chapter 4). While there are no cathedral records relaying information about the composition of the Office, or the composition of any of the works in the liturgical books that are explored in this study, there is some circumstantial evidence that casts light on the creative circle from which they emerged, showing that Tournai was a place known for the creation of music. For instance, Gilles Li Muisis, abbot of St. Martin at Tournai and a famous chronicler, discusses the vibrant artistic life of the city in the fourteenth century; he mentions several composers whose works were known there, such as Guillaume de Machaut and Philippe de Vitry.[99] Neither composer was from Tournai, and there is no evidence that either of them ever spent time there, but they were part of the same creative milieu as the poet Jehan de le Mote and the local composer Jehan Campion (see chapter 4).[100]

CONFRATERNITIES AND POPULAR DEVOTIONS TO ST. BARBARA   59

In addition to the importance of the city as a musical center, the cathedral of Notre Dame in Tournai was the seat of an important bishopric, and it was an institution with a strong musical heritage about which much information has been lost. We can, however, bring together some details about the possible role of music in the daily celebration of services there around the time the new music for this Office was written. Anne Dupont estimates that the total number of those in service to the choir (choirboys, canons, chaplains, etc., not just those who took part in singing but the complete clergy more broadly) was around 130 men and boys in the fifteenth century, and Craig Wright gives a similar estimate for the choir of Notre Dame in Paris.[101] Performing votive masses, like those found in B-Tc A 12, 13, and 27 was a regular duty for the clergy of the institution. For instance, at the altar of St. Jacques there were fifteen daily masses that the clergy were obligated to carry out. There was also an altar for St. Sebastian with seven daily masses with a chaplaincy attached to it for these occasions that paid for a chaplain priest. Furthermore, there was a parish altar on the interior of the cathedral dedicated to St. Nicholas, with five chaplains designated to officiate services there, but we have no idea of the place of music in these ceremonies.[102] All of this shows that the Cathedral of Tournai played an important part in the devotional life of the city, much in the same way that the Parisian institutions of Notre Dame and the Ste. Chapelle provided this function in that urban setting (see chapter 2).

As for the notaries' familiarity with the liturgy, it is likely that at least some of the those who were clergy could have come up through the ranks into that position after starting as young choirboys in the cathedral school, or *maîtrise*, giving them the musical skills needed to compose an Office. Most of the existing detailed information about such organizations comes from the dioceses of Cambrai and Paris. Many of the boys who entered the *maîtrise* would be sent on to study at the University of Paris or other prominent northern institutions when they came of age, and would eventually obtain high positions at ecclesiastical institutions.[103] At Notre Dame in Paris, choirboys learned plainsong, counterpoint, and discant, and we can assume that similar studies were pursued by choirboys at Tournai cathedral.[104] Although choirboys would have not had the freedom to work as freelance musicians or take part in secular activities, Carol Symes provides evidence from Arras that cathedral canons as well as monks were members of the local confraternity of jongleurs, and ranked among the city's trouvères.[105] It appears, therefore, that both sacred and secular musical knowledge was a common part of clerical life in the north.

Through their education and chosen career paths, notaries were well placed to have contact with artistic circles in the fourteenth century. They were certainly present at official functions where music was performed, and some of them (including Vitry and Machaut) were also composers.[106] There was a long list of composers who were notaries in service to various French royal houses as well as the papal chapel in Rome. Evidence of their output exists in the form of music notation in documents they drafted, and it was notaries who were responsible for the creation of the famous Roman de Fauvel.[107] These facts, combined with the material evidence of the musical setting for St. Barbara in B-Tc A 12, indicate that the Confraternity of the Notaries in Tournai may have included several men who were capable of composing chant and polyphony for their own services. It is known that in other northern cities, like Arras, rhetoric guilds that promoted the composition of music and poetry comprised a combination of artisans, clerics, and priests, so this would not be out of the realm of possibility.[108] This would show them to be important actors in the construction of their own devotions.

Conclusion

In conclusion, we may look back to where this investigation started: three unique liturgical books used by the Confraternity of the Notaries at the Tournai cathedral. By investigating their contents in detail, we unlock a rich devotional matrix that facilitated the creation of new music and liturgical practices in a city known for its cutting-edge artistry. The Confraternity of the Notaries' devotions to St. Barbara serve as a witness to the organization's individuality as it was formed musically, through the composition of new Office chants. The Office of St. Barbara illustrates different possible processes by which popular devotional practices came to be incorporated into confraternity and cathedral books at Tournai. When viewed in comparison with sources from nearby cities, we have a rare opportunity to see how this Office changed as it travelled to different institutions, and the different compositional processes employed by local composers. All of this shows not only that popular piety was a driving force in the construction of new liturgies but also that confraternities stood alongside cathedrals and parishes as important patrons of new chant composition.

Chapter Two

Relic Translation and Healing in Liturgies for St. Catherine and St. Nicholas in Paris

> Alleluya. O Nicholas, your tomb drips oil, of which a small stream pre-
> serves the care of the sick; protect the present from fevers that cause a
> death that is everlasting.[1]

St. Nicholas, a bishop of Myra in the fourth century, captured the imagina-
tions of many writers and composers from the high Middle Ages through the
Renaissance. This alleluia verse appears as part of the Mass for St. Nicholas
in two confraternity manuscripts from northern France: Paris, Bibliothèque
Mazarine MS 464 (F-Pm 464), for the Confraternity of the Spice Dealers and
Apothecaries in Paris; and B-Tc A 13, for the Confraternity of the Notaries
at the Tournai cathedral (see chapter 1).[2] The text calls upon him for protection from "fevers that cause a death that is everlasting," a reference to the
plague, which was seen as God's wrath on earth. It also alludes to one of his
most celebrated virtues, as St. Nicholas was, according to legend, a myroblyte, whose relics were believed to secrete a holy oil, or myrrh, with healing
attributes. For this reason, his popularity grew in Western Europe after the
theft of his relics from Myra and their relocation to Bari in 1087. From this
point on, St. Nicholas became one of the most widely venerated saints of the
Catholic Church, and his feast was normally celebrated at the high rank of
duplex in cathedrals and parishes in northern France. He also assumed an
important role in devotions among the laity, becoming the subject of miracle
plays and the patron saint of countless groups of people, including students
and scholars, children, those seeking to become pregnant, merchants, and
sailors. This resulted in the hundreds of devotional and trade confraternities

adopting St. Nicholas as their patron, making these communities a driving force in the creation of new music and text in his honor.

In this chapter, I explore new masses and offices focused on healing narratives for the Translation of the Relics of St. Nicholas and the Finding of the Relics of St. Catherine of Alexandria, which appear exclusively in Parisian confraternity manuscripts.[3] These two saints were commonly associated with each other and often appear together, for like St. Nicholas, St. Catherine was also a myroblyte and had the same healing power. Furthermore, portions of both saints' relics were "translated" (meaning moved) to northern France around the same time, at the end of the eleventh century. Although by the fifteenth century the feasts of St. Catherine (November 25) and St. Nicholas (December 6) were highly ranked in most northern French diocesan calendars, the translation and finding of their relics were of lesser importance in the main sanctuaries of cathedrals and parishes. The Translation of St. Nicholas on May 9 is found in the majority most diocesan calendars, but the Finding of the Relics of St. Catherine on May 13 was not celebrated at all in northern French institutions.[4]

Both St. Catherine and St. Nicholas were revered as patron saints of northern French confraternities, and movement, both physical (through relic translation) and spiritual (through healing narratives constructed as a result of relic translation), accounts for their popularity in the city of Paris and beyond. Although masses and offices in confraternity devotions in general were performed privately only for the members of the confraternity, such services gave the community a sense of corporate identity by focusing on a patron saint.[5] This identity was ultimately displayed publicly in contexts where the confraternity took part in processions, such as those on the patron saint's feast day, which highlighted their roles as prominent Parisian civic communities.[6] Celebrating the confraternity's civic power became part of how these organizations constructed their shared identity. Moreover, a confraternity would occasionally have need to move their devotions to a different location by renting a chapel at another institution, which served to disseminate their liturgical practices throughout the city.

The ecclesiastical and monastic institutions of Paris provided an important infrastructure for confraternities, and they would financially benefit from the money gained through renting their chapels to these organizations. Privately held confraternity services would come to the attention of the musicians (such as cantors and other members of the clergy) at those places, many of which already housed other confraternities. Members of the large number of Parisian trade organizations who worshipped in the chapels of the city's different churches and monastic houses would have therefore paid some of the same musicians to compile and perform their services, which led to the spread of different devotional ideas and music.[7]

In this chapter, I show how these musicians, who remain anonymous in this context, were acutely aware of how music and text could come together to create meaning not only in enhancing and solidifying the healing powers of the two saints relics but also in connecting them to local Parisian institutions. The role of Parisian confraternities as patrons of new liturgical practices is evident in unique masses and offices I have identified for the Translation of St. Nicholas and the Finding of the Relics of St. Catherine. These appear in two liturgical books produced for confraternities that met in the chapel of St. Nicholas at the Hospital of Ste. Catherine on the rue St. Denis in Paris: F-Pm 464 (mentioned above) for the Confraternity of the Spice Dealers and Apothecaries in honor of St. Nicholas; and Den Haag, Koninklijke Bibliotheek MS 76 E 18 (hereafter referred to as NL-DHk 76 E 18) for the Confraternity of the Doublet Makers in honor of St. Catherine.[8] The contents of the manuscripts have so far escaped scholarly attention by musicologists, but they are significant to our understanding of the spiritual identities of these organizations. Because the original meeting place for both confraternities, the Hospital of Ste. Catherine in Paris, was a place of healing, this could account for their devotion to restorative oils and healing narratives.

Relic Translation and the Roles of St. Catherine and St. Nicholas

Both St. Catherine and St. Nicholas increasingly became prominent objects for adoration among the laity throughout the late Middle Ages, a phenomenon that has to do with the dissemination of their relics. While Bari was the new home of most of St. Nicholas's relics starting in the eleventh century, pieces of them were taken to France and other geographical areas in subsequent centuries. Stories about St. Nicholas and his healing properties start to appear in northern France following his translation to Bari, which was at that time under Norman rule. Because of the pivotal role that merchants played in the translation story (to be discussed later in the chapter), Norman sailors residing in this area adopted St. Nicholas as their patron saint.[9] At the same time, several institutions in the region acquired portions of his relics, which led to a number of musical displays in his honor.[10] For instance, he became a saint of some importance in Paris, as his finger was one of the relics held at Notre Dame, which resulted in a long history of extra-liturgical worship of him at this institution. The three-voiced motet *Psallat chorus*, which was based on a responsory for St. Nicholas, was produced for one of these occasions; and there are numerous St. Nicholas plays and other compositions for him.[11] Two of the most famous dramas featuring St. Nicholas were written in French by poets from further north, such as Jehan Bodel (a jongleur from Arras at the beginning of the thirteenth century) and the twelfth-century Anglo-Norman poet Robert Wace.[12] Musical and dramatic pieces for St. Nicholas are not as well documented in the city of Tournai, but the cathedral did have an ampoule of his holy oil.[13]

St. Catherine's popularity started with the translation of a portion of her relics to Rouen in the eleventh century. According to the acquisition accounts, her body was laid to rest at the monastery of the Virgin Mary on Mount Sinai. At some point between 1031 and 1054 her finger bones were transported by the monk Simeon of Trier to the monastery of the Holy Trinity in Rouen, which was founded around 1030 on a hill east of the city. After this translation of her relics, several collections of miracles were recorded in Normandy featuring St. Catherine along with other already widely revered local saints in an effort to elevate her healing power.[14] A series of miracles from Rouen has to do with her healing various ailments through the aid of her "holy oil"; others have her providing pregnancies in the face of sterility, curing blindness, and providing protection from a host of other hardships. St. Catherine's association with the monastery in Rouen was so great that by 1250 the institution became known as Ste. Catherine-du-Mont.[15] Starting in the thirteenth century, there were foundations in her honor for other parishes and monastic communities in the area, particularly in Paris: the Augustinian house of Ste. Catherine Val des Ecoliers, the Hospital of Ste. Catherine on the rue St. Denis (mentioned previously), and the chapel of St. Catherine founded in 1373 at the College of Navarre.[16] Her importance in Tournai is evident through the foundation of a chapel for St. Catherine at the cathedral, and there is a 1475 testament referring to a confraternity in her honor at the parish of Ste. Catherine in the city.[17]

While the broad-reaching popularity of St. Catherine and St. Nicholas in this geographical enclave is clear, the middle of the fifteenth century saw a distinctly new concentration in Paris on their roles as healers.[18] The focal point of this devotion was the Translation (*Translatio*) and Finding, or Discovery (*Inventio*), of their relics. Translation and Finding narratives in fifteenth-century confraternity devotions commemorated relic movements as a way of coming into contact with the physical object, and most importantly, the holy oil. The alleluia verse for St. Nicholas at the beginning of the chapter heavily emphasizes objects: his relics, his tomb, and his healing oil. Medieval writers believed that while the spirits of all saints resided in heaven, their presence was closely tied to the body they inhabited in life, which is why relics and tombs were so often the preoccupation of popular piety.[19] The oil of St. Nicholas was also very powerful, for it was considered to be a type of secondary relic known as a contact relic. Contact relics were objects or substances that had contact with a saint's body—oil, blood, shrouds, etc.—and therefore embodied the saint's presence. Unlike the actual bones, which were specially guarded objects held at ecclesiastical and monastic institutions, contact relics like oils and holy waters were accessible to most worshippers, as they were sometimes sold as souvenirs at pilgrimage sites.[20] *Ampullae* (pilgrim flasks) were often used at pilgrimage sites to harvest water or oil that had come into contact with a saint's tomb and were worn around the neck as souvenirs.[21] Because of its accessibility to the laity, the healing oil of St. Nicholas became the focus of popular piety. The origin of his popularity in general, and the strong belief in his healing oil, is directly connected to the translation of his relics from Myra to Bari.

Relic translation works on two levels: it is an act involving physical movement, and through this movement it becomes a symbol of a saint's healing and prestige. As a result, the theme of translation narratives was not the saint's vita but rather the posthumous capabilities of his or her relics and miracles.[22] Complicating matters, relics were often used as political tools by the institutions that housed them, and as Caroline Goodson points out, "the translation of relics was a movement between social spaces as much as physical spaces," thereby adding symbolic value to both social and physical place.[23] Translations were official celebrations in cathedrals, parishes, and monastic communities, and were used in those settings to exercise a community's power through the public display of relics, a dynamic that also applied to the finding of relics.[24] Finding, Translation, and Elevation (*Elevatio*) are all symbolic references that bring the saint into the public eye and renew and reaffirm his or her power.[25] The celebration of these acts gave increased visibility to religious institutions, and in some cases made them centers of pilgrimage.

Even in the absence of the objects themselves, liturgical texts in Parisian confraternities praise St. Nicholas and St. Catherine through reference to relics and contact relics by concentrating on their movement. Being present for musical displays that meditated on these objects parallels practices of praying before pictorial representations of the relic, an act that in some cases carried an indulgence for the supplicant.[26] All of this indicates a belief on the part of confraternity members that they would procure divine aid and healing through corporate displays of devotion to relic translation and finding.

Confraternities at the Hospital of Ste. Catherine in Paris

The Confraternity of the Spice Dealers and Apothecaries and the Confraternity of the Doublet Makers were central in the construction of new worship practices in Paris related to the translation and finding of relics. This is evident through the contents of their existing liturgical books and confraternity registers, as well as the notarial documents mentioning their practices. To understand how these communities worshipped, it is first necessary to recognize the important place that the Hospital of Ste. Catherine occupied in Parisian city life throughout the Middle Ages, for this institution was their common meeting point. There was originally an Augustinian abbey founded on this site in 770 under the name Ste. Opportune, and by 1188 a hospital was also constructed there. In 1222, both a new chapel and the old hospital were consecrated in the name of St. Catherine. Over the course of the twelfth and thirteenth centuries the male community waned, and by 1328, there was an independent female convent on site with a secular clergy named by the bishop. The Parisian population called this female community "Catherines" or "Catherinettes." According to their statutes, they were to do three main things: provide hospitality; care for the sick; and prepare the cadavers from the Châtelet prison, those washed up from the river, and those found on the city street in the parish of St. Jacques-de-la-Boucherie.[27] By 1480 there is also mention of a chapel for St. Nicholas founded at the institution.[28]

There are no existing liturgical books from the hospital that record the daily round of masses and offices that would have been performed for the Catherinettes; nor is there a fabric inventorying the objects in the hospital chapels. Outside of the two confraternity manuscripts discussed here, the only information that we can gather regarding services said at the institution is in relation to the burying of the dead, which was a major role that the Catherinettes played in the city.[29] The clergy appointed by the bishop are not named, so it is not possible to have a firm grasp of who may have performed services for the sisters, let alone who may have been paid to perform services at the chapel for the two confraternities.

Different types of documentation exist for the Confraternity of St. Nicholas and the Confraternity of St. Catherine, and they illustrate these communities' devotional practices in distinct ways. They appear to be the only two Parisian confraternities that worshipped at the hospital.[30] Overall, there is more information concerning the Confraternity of St. Nicholas than the Confraternity of St. Catherine, for in addition to the liturgical book owned by the organization (F-Pm 464) there is also a confraternity register preserved at the Bibliothèque royale de Belgique, MS 17939 (B-Br 17939), which dates from 1311–1534. This source provides information about how the apothecary trade functioned, royal decrees, punishments for infractions, the organization's place in the Parisian merchant community, and their religious practices.[31]

Apothecaries and spice dealers sold materials that were used to heal certain ailments—an attribute that St. Nicholas had through his holy oil. Throughout the course of the thirteenth and fourteenth centuries, the terms spice dealer and apothecary were used synonymously, since both sold condiments, jams, wax, and medicines in their shops. The spice dealers and apothecaries were united under the same banner in 1467, but in 1484, there was an attempt to make a clear distinction between the two trades: spice dealers were merchants who merely sold raw materials that could be used as medicines in their shops, but they only had the right to make condiments; apothecaries could sell the same raw materials as spice dealers, but they also had the right to make medicines. As a general rule, all apothecaries could continue to function as spice dealers, but spice dealers could not function as apothecaries. Despite the separation of the two trades, the spice dealers and apothecaries were still united under the same banner in the early sixteenth century, which is affirmed by the renewal of their statutes in 1514.[32] St. Nicholas was a likely choice to be the patron saint of their confraternity, for he was seen as the protector of sailors, and by association merchants who benefitted from the transportation of goods by sea.

I have uncovered pertinent information about this community's devotions and affluence through my analysis of the confraternity register B-Br 17939 in comparison with the liturgical book F-Pm 464. I provide a brief inventory of F-Pm 464 below (see figure 2.1), but a fuller description of its contents is given in appendix 4 ✁. The following text from the register, which dates from around 1502, tells us much about how often the confraternity worshipped together and which feast days they celebrated, showing that the organization had enough money to be able to pay musicians and priests to perform their services:

This is the service that is done during the year for the brothers and sisters of the Confraternity of St. Nicholas for the master spice dealers and apothecaries of the city of Paris in the church of the Hospital of Ste. Catherine on the great rue St. Denis in Paris.

And first, every Sunday of the year, holy water, a high mass with deacon and subdeacon, holy bread, and after a *de profundis* for trespasses in the accustomed manner.

Also, the two feast days of St. Nicholas, the same service and double vespers.

Also, three other masses of the week; that is to say Monday, Tuesday, and Thursday. And the increase made in the year 1502.

Also, the two feast days of St. Nicholas, Matins, with 9 psalms and 9 lessons.

Also, the day after the two feast days of St. Nicholas, vigils and remembrances, with 9 psalms and 9 lessons, with a high requiem mass and *libera* for trespasses.

Also, on the day of trespasses the same service, and all this in return for the sum of 32 *livres tournoys* to be paid for each year.[33]

The text above from the confraternity register directly reflects the contents of F-Pm 464 (see figure 2.1 and appendix 4 ᔒ), which contains a Mass for St. Nicholas and a Mass for his Translation; three full offices (two for the Translation and one for the feast of St. Nicholas); and an Office and Mass for the dead. The opening inscription also indicates that the confraternity consisted of master spice dealers and apothecaries ("maistres espiciers et apothicaires"), showing that while the two trades were connected at that time, the confraternity did not include everyone in the trade, but only those at the very top. This is significant, for during the sixteenth century many trade confraternities became separated, with masters forming a separate community from journeymen and apprentices, resulting in several confraternities associated with one trade.[34]

The ability to celebrate several masses and offices, and commission works of art, lecterns, and other such items are a testament to this organization's financial position. For instance, in addition to the confraternity register, there is also a document from 1529 that makes mention of a lectern commissioned by the masters of the confraternity: Claude Rubentel, Hélie Saulmon, and Valleran de Bais. According to the commission, this lectern was constructed for the chapel of St. Nicholas in the hospital church of Ste. Catherine.[35]

The Confraternity of St. Nicholas moved to several different institutions in Paris throughout the course of the sixteenth century, and the documents outlining this make important reference to the organization's payment of

Figure 2.1. Brief inventory of F-Pm 464 (see appendix 4 ✄ for detailed inventory).

Fol. [i]r	Alleluia verse *O nicholae* with music (later scribal hand)
Fols. 1r–34v	antiphons and invitatories for the entire year
Fols. 35r–47r	first Office for the Translation of St. Nicholas (only one Matins nocturn. After the third Matins antiphon, there is the following rubric, "Lessons for the Translation of St. Nicholas below")[i]
Fols. 47r–66v	(reading) the Translation of St. Nicholas by Nicephorus of Bari (divided into three sections with the rubrics "Lectio prima," "Lectio secunda," and "Lectio tercia." The third reading is further subdivided into four sections. The full text is concordant with *BHL* 6179)
Fols. 66v–68v	(prosa) *Previst le createur du ciel* (later scribal hand)
Fols. 69r–114v	Office for the Feast of St. Nicholas (contains full Matins and all readings)
Fols. 115r–45v	(reading) the Life and Miracles of St. Nicholas by John the Deacon (various popular miracles found in many sources that have been published in *BHL* 6140, 6140b, 6142, 6145b, 6149, 6161, 6167, 6108. Each new miracle is introduced with the rubric "aliud miraculum.")
Fols. 145v–46v	(prosa) *Sancte nicholae beate pontifex* (later scribal hand)
Fols. 147r–59v	Mass for the Feast of St. Nicholas
Fols. 159v–60v	(prosa) *Letabundus laudet Nicholao* (later scribal hand)
Fols. 161r–203r	Office for the Dead
Fols. 203r–v	(prosa) *Clemens fotor pauperum* (later scribal hand)
Fols. 204r–11v	Requiem Mass
Fols. 212r–25r	second Office for the Translation of St. Nicholas (only one Matins nocturn. No readings indicated.)
Fols. 225v–27v	(prosa) *Dies irae* (later scribal hand)

Note:

[i] Lectiones de translatione sanctissimi nicholay quere infra.

priests and others to carry out their services. The earliest mention of the confraternity at the hospital comes from a will dated 1412, where Jean Angelin, an apothecary, left "cent solz parisis" to the confraternity. The community continued to worship there until the middle of the sixteenth century, when they made the first of several moves to different institutions.[36] While there may have been a variety of factors that influenced the move, some scholars have speculated that above all the smell of the morgue proved to be overpowering for the community.[37] At some point before 1546, the confraternity moved to the Benedictine abbey of St. Magloire and was housed there until 1572, at which time the convent was closed to make way for the construction of Catherine de Médici's Hôtel de la Reine. The masters of the confraternity voted and chose to move to the church of Ste. Opportune, a process that is well documented in detail regarding the payment of musicians, choirboys, and priests.[38] Shortly after moving to their new place of worship, the confraternity entered into a conflict with the church canons, who raised their prices and refused to honor the original agreement of 1572.[39] The confraternity found its final resting place in 1589 at the Augustinian house of St. Victor, where it remained until 1777.[40]

The confraternity register mentions the names of many men and women throughout who were masters of the trade from the fourteenth through the sixteenth centuries, showing that this was a rather powerful community. In 1498 alone there are 145 names of male and female merchants in Paris, with the women being listed as widows.[41] Georges Huisman notes that some of the spice dealers and apothecaries belonged to families which were devoted to the protection of the interests of the Parisian population as a whole, and were thus very prominent in the city: Bartillon, Malingre, and Potier.[42]

While there is documentation of the worship and trade practices of the Confraternity of the Spice Dealers and Apothecaries, we have limited information about this for the Confraternity of the Doublet Makers. Doublets were jackets that had padding, which were originally designed to be worn underneath armor in the fourteenth and fifteenth centuries; in later eras they became fashionable as a type of outerwear for men. These clothing items were commonly made by tailors, but in the early fourteenth century in Paris, it appears that certain tailors specialized in producing these vestments and were thus associated more closely with armorers and bronze casters who manufactured military equipment than with members of the broader tailor trade.[43] There was also an increased demand for armor and accessories in fourteenth-century France, as the country entered the Hundred Years' War in 1337. The choice of St. Catherine as patron saint for the doublet makers was likely due to her promotion in France in the fourteenth century, along with St. Michael the Archangel, as the patron saint of soldiers. This involved an embellishment in her vita that indicates St. Michael took her to heaven after her death.[44] The doublet makers made the decision to establish their own trade statutes separate from the tailors in 1323, fifteen years before this major military conflict. Their statutes were confirmed in that year, outlining the dues that each member of the trade was to pay, the length of apprenticeships, and other aspects related to regulation of the trade.[45] In 1406, the new patent letters for the organization indicated that the members of the trade were to pay money that would be used to aid their colleagues who were less fortunate, and secure beds for them at the Hospital of Ste. Catherine. By 1655, the doublet makers were reunited with the tailors, and there is no evidence that they continued as a separate confraternity.[46]

Aside from their statutes, most of what we know about this confraternity comes from its only surviving liturgical book, NL-DHk 76 E 18. The inscription at the end of the manuscript on fol. 119r (see appendix 4 ❧ and figure 2.2 below) gives some detail about the confraternity and its members, informing us that the organization was founded at the Hospital of Ste. Catherine on the rue St. Denis. It contains the date 1450 and lists the names of the governors of the confraternity at that time: Robin de la Baie, Jehan Maillet, Jehan Denis, and Jehan Grenet.[47] The inscription also gives an accounting of the contents of the manuscript, which reflects the book's present structure (see figure 2.2 below). This source contains a full Requiem, Vespers for the Office of St. Catherine and a Mass in her honor, Vespers for the Office of the Finding of St. Catherine's Relics; interspersed with this material are Mass ordinary chants.[48] In contrast to F-Pm 464, there are no readings in the book, such as the Miracles of St. Catherine or other well-known hagiographical texts, nor are there readings for the Mass and Office. The appearance of several alleluia verses used at different times of the year, and a few Kyries, indicates that the confraternity hired priests to celebrate a Mass and Office for their patron saint perhaps more than once a year.[49]

Several chant genres in the liturgical books for the Confraternity of St. Catherine and the Confraternity of St. Nicholas served as vehicles for the illustration of different aspects of confraternity worship that will be discussed in the following sections. These devotional components consist of celebrating the virtues of the patron saint, connecting the saint to specifically Parisian devotional contexts, and celebrating the civic power of the confraternity. This is done primarily through antiphons, prosas, hymns, and alleluia verses. Popular circulating stories about the lives of St. Catherine and St. Nicholas

Figure 2.2. Brief inventory of NL-DHk 76 E 18 (see appendix 4 ᵗ for detailed inventory).

Fols. 1r–14v	Psalms for Offices throughout the week
Fols. 15r–18v	Compline
Fols. 19r–64v	Office of the Dead (with illumination at the beginning, contains readings.)
Fols. 64v–71v	Vespers for St. Catherine (with illumination at the beginning)
Fols. 72r–79v	Mass Ordinary chants
Fols. 80r–92v	Mass for St. Catherine
Fols. 92v–94v	Second Vespers
Fol. 94v	Mass Ordinary chants (later scribal hand)
Fols. 95r–102v	Vespers for the Finding of St. Catherine (with illumination at the beginning)
Fols. 103r–9v	Requiem Mass
Fols. 111r–14r	(prosa) *Dies irae* (later scribal hand)
Fols. 114r–17r	(prosa) *Lux gentibus* (later scribal hand)
Fol. 119r	Inscription of ownership by the confraternity

were a direct outgrowth of the translation of their relics and provided the basis for the liturgical texts found in these manuscripts. Some chant texts in Parisian confraternity manuscripts also appear in the Tournai notary manuscripts, but in both cases, they have no connection to practices at the cathedrals or parishes in the two cities.[50] These types of variations show just how much confraternity practices differed from those of the diocese at large; they also indicate that certain chants circulated more widely in confraternal contexts than they did in others.

The St. Catherine Mass and certain portions of the Office found in NL-DHk 76 E 18 are based on the Mass and Office for St. Nicholas used in Parisian institutions. Despite these similarities, the services for St. Catherine and St. Nicholas that appear in confraternity manuscripts used by communities at the Hospital of Ste. Catherine illustrate two distinctly different processes of composition that are not wholly dependent on each other. The St. Catherine Office is an example of an almost completely new liturgical composition both in text and music, whereas the St. Nicholas Office and Mass rely on modeling and contrafacta using melodies borrowed from other liturgical occasions. I will start the discussion that follows with the St. Catherine Office, as it provides a succinct case study of an office that is mostly free of

Figure 2.3. The Finding of St. Catherine of Alexandria in NL-DHk 76 E 18, fol. 95r. Image reproduced courtesy of the Koninklijke Bibliotheek, Nationale Bibliotheek van Nederland.

previous melodic models. I will then move on to explore the multifaceted sources for the unique St. Nicholas liturgy observed by the Confraternity of the Spice Dealers and Apothecaries.

Figure 2.3 is an illumination from NL-DHk 76 E 18. It appears before the first Vespers antiphon for an Office that formed a central part of the Confraternity of the Doublet Makers' devotional practices. The image depicts an important act in the story of the Finding of the Relics of St. Catherine of Alexandria, featuring six Greek Orthodox monks with long beards holding shovels and other digging instruments. Several of the men are putting their hands up signaling the others to stop, for they have uncovered the body of a beautiful woman, perfectly intact; the halo surrounding her head indicates that she is a holy figure. Directly underneath the illumination, there is a small inscription: "In inventione beate katherine virginis" (For the Finding of the Virgin St. Catherine). The first Vespers antiphon reaffirms this with the following text: "You who grant to us to honor the discovery of the body of Catherine today, give devotion to those who honor her, we beg you, bountiful king of glory, alleluia" (see table 2.1 for original Latin text).

The Finding of St. Catherine by the monks at the Orthodox monastery of the Virgin Mary on Mount Sinai is the event responsible for launching her popularity in Western Europe.[51] The circumstances surrounding this occasion are unclear, but it appears that the fixation on pilgrimage and its potential financial and social profits for institutions in the holy land had something to do with it. The economic advantages of pilgrimage encouraged a desire for churches and monasteries to acquire relics and likely led to St. Catherine's "discovery" in the tenth century at this location, without any documentation. According to her vita, her body was carried to Mount Sinai by angels and laid to rest after her martyrdom in Alexandria.[52] This is one of several stories from St. Catherine's passio that served as the basis for distinctive liturgical texts in celebration of her.

Over one hundred copies of the Latin vita of St. Catherine have survived as evidence of her popularity after the miraculous finding of her relics, with many more vernacular translations in addition to these sources. Like St. Barbara, St. Catherine was not an actual historical figure. Instead, she stands for a mixture of different female saints from Alexandria in the fourth century.[53] Jacobus de Voragine used the Latin vulgate *passio* as the basis for her life in his original edition of the *Golden Legend*, and it appears in many subsequent vernacular versions of the work.[54] According to these texts, Catherine was the daughter of King Costi, a local ruler in Alexandria. She was a Christian who was beautiful and highly educated, having studied languages, literature, and medicine. The events leading to her martyrdom were set into motion when the Emperor Maxentius was in Alexandria, ordering animal sacrifices to the pagan gods. Catherine, being a devout woman, refused, and instead tried to convert him to Christianity. During this process, Catherine demonstrated her exceptional intellectual abilities, and as a result the emperor could not win an argument with her. In hopes of subduing her, he finally gathered fifty philosophers to debate with Catherine, but she ended up converting them all to Christianity. Maxentius, furious with this turn of events, ordered the philosophers to be executed and had Catherine imprisoned. In the meantime, Maxentius's wife, the queen, took pity on Catherine and she herself, along with the leader of the imperial guard, Porphyry, converted to Christianity at Catherine's behest. Throughout all of this, Maxentius became taken with Catherine's beauty and offered her the opportunity to join him as a ruler in his realm. She denied him, which once again filled Maxentius with rage, leading him to give her an ultimatum: make a sacrifice to the pagan gods or be tortured. Caxton's 1483 edition gives Catherine's response, "I desire to offer to God my blood and my flesh like as he offered for me; he is my God, my father, my friend, and mine only spouse."[55] Maxentius upheld his ruling, ordering her to be tortured on the wheel of torment as an example to all Christians. Once again,

Catherine prevailed, for during her punishment, an angel of the lord broke the wheel and its pieces struck her torturers. The queen, having witnessed this, approached Maxentius and chastised him for his cruelty, begging for Catherine's life. In response to her plea, he had his wife executed. After the death of the queen, Maxentius appealed to Catherine one last time, now asking her to be his new queen. Catherine then gave her final refusal, and he had her beheaded. After her death, angels took her body and laid it at the top of Mount Sinai, which was more than twenty days' journey, and there a healing oil flowed from her bones. According to legend, Catherine was eighteen years old when she was martyred in the year 310.

As mentioned at the beginning of the chapter, St. Catherine was widely revered throughout the Middle Ages and Early Modern periods for her healing power as a myroblyte. This is directly related to her vita, as it was said that after her bones were found on Mount Sinai in the tenth century, an oil continued to flow from them. From that point on the Orthodox monastery of the Virgin Mary became a major pilgrimage site where people would go to collect this holy oil. Due to this, the institution eventually came to be known as the monastery of St. Catherine. After the translation of her finger bones to Rouen in the eleventh century, and the resulting healing miracles that circulated in that area, St. Catherine's vita became well known throughout Western Europe.[56]

Miracles concentrating on the healing oil of St. Catherine gave rise to a number of new liturgical texts, as did the events of her martyrdom, but the finding of her relics on Mount Sinai is not described in any of the St. Catherine offices uncovered so far, making this the only source known to do so. This unique Office was likely commissioned by the confraternity in the fifteenth century. The texts of the antiphons in table 2.1 make no mention of the events of her life recorded in her vita, but instead make general references to her purity and the discovery of her relics.[57] This is depicted visually in the illumination at the beginning of the Office (see figure 2.3), and the second antiphon explains that her body was uncorrupted by worms and remained perfectly intact. The fourth antiphon addresses the movement of her body to Mount Sinai directly after her martyrdom, and the fifth antiphon calls upon St. Catherine to intercede for her supplicants and protect them from the dangers of the world. The rhyme scheme for the Office is consistent, which implies that it was written with continuity in mind.[58] The presence of three Magnificat antiphons is a testament to the frequency of its performance, for these could be used on different occasions to add variety—much in the same way different Mass propers for frequently said votive masses are often written in confraternity books—a point to which I shall return later.[59]

Table 2.1. Vespers for the Finding of St. Catherine in NL-DHk 76 E 18.

Chant	Latin text	English translation
Antiphon 1	Qui colere das inventionem katherine corporis hodie colentibus da devotionem te precamur rex alme glorie alleluya.	You who grant to us to honor the discovery of the body of Catherine today, give devotion to those who honor her, we beg you, bountiful king of glory, alleluia.
Antiphon 2	Annis centum trigintaque tribus et amplius hoc corpus in syna non corruptum nec vermium cibus requievit virtute divina alleluya.	For one hundred thirty-three years and more, this body rested in Sinai by divine power, not decayed nor food for worms, alleluia.
Antiphon 3	Serpentinum pre multitudine deserentes loca corde tristi consolantur hoc ergo famine. hiis obvians virgo mater xpisti alleluya.	Leaving the regions with a sad heart because of the multitude of serpents, they are then consoled by this word. Meeting them, the virgin mother of Christ [says], alleluia:
Antiphon 4	Cur heremum fugitis merentes redite nunc modice fidei katherine martyris querentes sanctum corpus synay vertice alleluya.	Why do you flee the desert, mourning? Return now, you of little faith, seeking the holy body of the martyr Catherine at the summit of Sinai, alleluia.
Antiphon 5	Nam ipsius cito suffragia liberabunt vos a periculis vite dabunt et necessaria sic ab horum recessit oculis alleluya.	For her intercessions will set you free quickly from the dangers of life, and will give you the things that are necessary: thus she withdrew from their eyes, alleluia.
Responsory	Ex eius membris virgineis sacrum resudat oleum quo hinti sanantur ceci surdis auditus redditur et debilis quisquem sospes regreditur	From her virginal limbs there exudes a holy oil: anointed with it the blind are cured, hearing is restored to the deaf, and every lame one will return safe and sound.
Verse	Catervatim ruunt populi cernere cupientes que per eam fiunt mirabilia.	In throngs the people run, eager to see the wonders that were done through her

Table 2.1—*continued*

Chant	Latin text	English translation
Prosa	Sospitati dedit egros olei perfusio. Katherina disputantum affuit presidio. Candor mentis fusi lactis monstratur indicio. Sepelitur ministrante celesti solatio. Baptizatur uxor regis simul cum porphirio. O quam probat sanctam dei rotarum confractio. Ergo laudes katherine concinat hec concio. Nam qui corde poscit illam propulsato vitio. Sospes regreditur.	The pouring of oil returned the sick to health. Catherine was present as a help to those who debated. The pure radiance of the mind is shown by the evidence of the poured-out milk. She is buried by the attendant with heavenly solace. The wife of the king is baptized at once with Porphyrius. O how the shattering of the wheels proves the holy woman of God. Therefore let this assembly sing together the praises of Catherine: for whoever asks her in his heart, having driven out vice, will return safe and sound.
Magnificat antiphon 1	O quam tui felix inventio corporis est virgo katherina quam de celis descendans solio revelavit virginum regina propter quod prebuit concio angelorum iter montem synay ut translatum cum cordis gaudio coletetur in valle vacua alleluya.	O how blessed is the finding of your body, virgin Catherine, whom the queen of virgins revealed, descending from the heavenly throne: because of this, an assembly of angels showed the road to Mount Sinai, so that, transferred with joy of heart, they might rejoice together in the desert valley, alleluia.
Magnificat antiphon 2	Katherine reperto corpore translatoque de qua celum gaudet non nunc solum sed omni tempore omnis deum spiritus collaudet alleluya.	The body of Catherine having been discovered and transferred, in whom heaven rejoices, not only now but at all times, let every spirit praise God together, alleluia.

—(*continued*)

Table 2.1—*concluded*

Chant	Latin text	English translation
Magnificat antiphon 3	Magnificet omnis creatura creatorem mundi mente pura refertaque bine dulcedine per quem sina repertum beatum ac in vallem moysi translatum est hodie corpus Katherine celebremus omnes diem istum ut precibus eius apud xpistum invenire cordis et corporis hic queamus salutis gratiam et ad celi transferri gloriam nostri cursu finito temporis alleluya.	With pure mind and overflowing with twofold sweetness, let every creature magnify the creator of the world, through whom the blessed body of Catherine was discovered on Sinai and transferred into the valley of Moses today: let us all celebrate this day, that by her prayers we might be able to find the grace of health of heart and body here, and to be transferred to the glory of heaven when the course of our time is done, alleluia.

Because the texts above do not adhere to any known version of St. Catherine's vita or miracles, it is not possible to identify a source for them, leaving us to speculate on their origin and meaning. These antiphons revere her as a healer, for the very act of finding her relics brought stories of her healing power to the populace. By the time this Office text was written in the fifteenth century, legends of her restorative abilities were well known, but antiphons three and four have curious references to serpents in the desert and an exodus of people mourning. This could allude to the fall of Constantinople, which passed into the hands of the Turks in 1453 and had a profound impact on the West. In this case, the serpents would refer to Muslims, and those fleeing the desert mourning would be Christians. In antiphons four and five the Virgin Mary appears to validate St. Catherine's role as a healer and protector in the face of adversity and urges the saint's supplicants to go on pilgrimage to Mount Sinai, where her relics resided.

When the chant melodies are observed in relation to the texts, connections between her healing powers and those of St. Nicholas are highlighted. Chants focusing on his healing oil, *Ex eius tumba, Catervatim ruunt populi,* and *Sospitati dedit egros,* are also found in F-Pm 464 and other Parisian sources for the Office of St. Nicholas.[60] The texts for the responsory and versicle are identical for both saints, but the word "tumba" from the St. Nicholas version has been changed to "membris" for St. Catherine to refer to her relics rather than to her tomb. These chants appear in other sources for St. Catherine, but much less often than for St. Nicholas.[61]

The prosa, *Sospitati dedit egros*, goes beyond changing a few words in the text in order to tailor it to St. Catherine, reworking the poem to make specific references to St. Catherine's life. While both the St. Nicholas and St. Catherine versions begin with the mention of healing oil, they then diverge, with the text for St. Catherine outlining her help to those who debate, her intellectual abilities, and her baptism of the king's wife and the leader of the guard, Porphyry. The St. Catherine and St. Nicholas versions then become nearly identical at the end, with the words "Therefore let this assembly sing together the praises of Catherine (or Nicholas): for whoever asks her (or him) in his heart, having driven out vice, will return safe and sound."

Characteristics of new chant composition in the fifteenth century are difficult to identify with regularity. Several scholars have indicated range, scalar passages over single words or phrases, subtonal cadences with repetitions of the end tone (so-called "Gallican" cadences), recurring melismas, technical artifice, formulaic use of mode, modal order, etc. as being markers of style after the eleventh century (see chapter 1).[62] Although the prosa in the St. Catherine Office is a contrafactum, and the responsory and versicle are nearly identical to those from the St. Nicholas Office, the antiphons for this Vespers were newly composed and have no melodic or textual concordances in Paris or elsewhere. As was the case for the St. Barbara Office in chapter 1, the composer of this Office uses extended scalar melismas on important words, with one of the largest appearing on the word "rex" (king) in antiphon 1. The composer also broke free of previous melodic models, yet reliably adhered to modal formulae. This is especially evident in antiphon 1 (mode 1) and antiphon 2 (mode 2), both of which clearly establish modal formulae in their opening (see examples 2.1 and 2.2).

The Office for the Finding of St. Catherine illustrates several of the types of compositional methods used for constructing new confraternity services. The antiphons were all newly composed, but the composer also used contrafacta. This special Office for a devotional practice known only within the Confraternity of the Doublet Makers shows us the kinds of connections that were made musically and textually between St. Catherine and St. Nicholas. Much of St. Catherine's liturgy was borrowed from that of St. Nicholas, which is apparent in the use of contrafacta for the prosa, responsory, and versicle melodies; and it extends to the Mass by using the same technique for the alleluia verses. These compositional procedures, and others, are also featured in the offices and masses for St. Nicholas.

Example 2.1. Vespers. Antiphon 1, *Qui colere das* in NL-DHk 76 E 18.

Qui__ co - le - re das____ in - ven - ti - o - nem_ ka-the-ri-ne_
_ cor - po - ris ho - di - e co-len-ti-bus____ da de-vo-ti - o-
nem te__ pre - ca-mur *rex*____ al-me glo - ri-e al - le -
lu - ia. Seculorum__ amen.____

Example 2.2. Vespers. Antiphon 2, *Annis centum trigintaque* in NL-DHk 76 E 18.

An - nis____ cen - tum____ tri - gin - ta-que_ tri - bus et am - pli
- us hoc____ cor - pus_ in____ sy-na non cor - rup - tum
nec ver - mi-um ci-bus re-qui-e - vit vir-tu - te di - vi-na al-le -
lu - ya. Seculorum__ a-men.

Confraternity Masses for St. Nicholas

Many of the contrafacta in confraternity services draw from popular folklore about the lives of the saints. They were created by using widely circulating chant melodies from the Temporale and Sanctorale, thus establishing symbolic references to the life of Christ and to other devotional figures.[63] The chant texts for the St. Nicholas and St. Catherine masses in all of the confraternity books appear in appendix 5 ᷍, but an examination of chants for St. Nicholas in particular in these sources shows how text and melody were manipulated to establish new meanings based on the saint's attributes.

The alleluia verses for St. Nicholas provide a good case study illustrating how text and melody circulated independently in confraternity devotions for two reasons. First, it is the primary chant genre of the Mass proper to vary significantly when confraternity usages are compared to diocesan usages; and second, there are many of them in the confraternity manuscripts from Paris and Tournai, allowing for fruitful comparison. In these sources, melody adds to the meaning of the text, which is accomplished through the assignment of chants drawn from different sections of the diocesan usage. Most of the chants for St. Nicholas (both his Nativity and his Translation) in the diocesan usages of Paris and Tournai came from the Common of Saints for One Confessor—in other words, they were general texts that were used in services for many different saints. The overall popularity of St. Nicholas could easily have led to this type of uniformity, for the masses in both dioceses are almost identical, as they are in many other locations.[64]

The most widespread alleluia verses for St. Nicholas in confraternity manuscripts from these two cities focus on his healing attributes, and particularly in Paris, the Translation of his relics. This is shown in a total of four alleluia verses for St. Nicholas distributed among the confraternity manuscripts, which appear either rarely or not at all in diocesan sources: *Tumba sancti nicholai*, *Summe dei confessor nycholae*, *O nicholae tumulus tuus distillat* (given at the beginning of the chapter), and *Egregie christi confessor nicholae*. As I have shown elsewhere, F-Pm 464 contains three of the four verses here, and so do the Tournai confraternity manuscripts B-Tc A 12, 13, and 27.[65] This means that several of these alleluia verses started to appear in confraternity manuscripts as early as the thirteenth century in Tournai, and by the fifteenth century, they are included in Parisian confraternity manuscripts. Although it is not possible to establish a dissemination trajectory, we can say that their occurrence primarily in confraternity sources, and over several centuries, shows that they were preferred chants to be used in that context.

The subject matter of the chant texts—the healing oil of St. Nicholas—is based on the focal point of the Translation narrative, which was recorded in 1087 by a priest called Nicephorus of Bari.[66] This story is also included in F-Pm 464 (see figure 2.1), showing that it had a central place in the worship practices of the Confraternity of the Spice Dealers and Apothecaries.[67] According to Nicephorus, St. Nicholas was thought to have divine protection at his tomb in Myra, as his shrine supposedly resisted many different assaults in previous decades. In 1081 the Turks had destroyed many churches and holy objects in the area, which led the merchants of Bari to construct a scheme to steal his relics and bring them to safety. This plan was put into action in 1087, when the men of Bari set sail for Myra on their mission. Upon arrival at the tomb, they were met by the guardians of the relics, who argued with them about whether they had a right to take the saint's bones from their original resting place. After a lengthy discussion, the guardians of the tomb confessed that St. Nicholas had appeared a year previously in a vision and told them that he wished to move to another location, as his relics were not well guarded in Myra due to the Turkish threat. After this, one of the men of Bari broke into the tomb, and within it he found the body of St. Nicholas floating in a sweet-smelling holy oil. Because the man remained unscathed during this action, the guardians of the tomb took this as a sign that St. Nicholas favored the men of Bari, and that he indeed had chosen a new resting place, so they reluctantly allowed the relics to be removed. The men of Bari left an ampoule of the saint's oil behind for the people of Myra before quickly carrying the relics to their ship and sailing back to Bari.

The oil becomes a major theme in this story, for according to lore, removing a saint's relics from his or her resting place could cause disaster, even resulting in death, if it is not the saint's wish for their bones to be displaced.[68] The corollary to this was the belief that saints chose their resting places, and in this case, St. Nicholas chose to go to Bari. The intent of St. Nicholas is reinforced through both the appearance of the healing oil and the fact that the man of Bari who broke the tomb did not succumb to an immediate death.

While the alleluia verses *Tumba sancti nicholai* and *O nicholae* make both direct and symbolic references to healing through the oil, the actual act of relic translation described above is topically referenced in another alleluia verse for St. Nicholas, *Egregie christi*. This chant appears only in F-Pm 464 and focuses on the removal of his body from the tomb in Myra. The use of first person in the text serves as an affirmation of the spice dealers' and apothecaries' veneration of the Translation of St. Nicholas in the form of an intercessory prayer.

> Alleluia. Nicholas, illustrious confessor of Christ, for us who venerate the miraculous removal of your body, intercede.[69]

The last alleluia verse to contain a specific text for St. Nicholas is *Summe dei confessor nicholae*, which is a general call to him for protection. The text of this verse is found in the Tournai confraternity manuscripts B-Tc A 12 and B-Tc A 13 as well as in the sources used in the main sanctuary of the Tournai cathedral dating from the thirteenth century:[70]

> Alleluya. Greatest confessor of God, Nicholas, protect those who venerate you, for indeed we believe we can be saved by your prayers.[71]

Several themes emerge in the assignment of melodies and texts, allowing us to establish possible patterns in the different compilers' choices for the St. Nicholas masses observed by the Confraternity of the Spice Dealers and Apothecaries and the Confraternity of the Notaries. Table 2.2 below shows text usage in the first three columns, and melodic usage in the last three columns. The first column gives the opening text incipits of the four alleluia verses discussed above. Column 2 lists the other confraternity sources containing the text specific to St. Nicholas, and column 3 gives the diocesan manuscripts and printed books that also include it. Column 4 provides the name of the source melody for each chant, while column 5 lists the texts for other saints and devotional figures that are also set to these melodies. Column 6 gives a list of all sources from Paris and Tournai that contain the source melodies (regardless of the text). For instance, column 2 shows that the *Tumba sancti nicholai* text is found in the confraternity manuscripts F-Pm 464, F-Pnm lat. 10506, B-Tc A 27, F-Pnm lat. 862, and F-Pnm lat. 17311; and column 3 gives a number of Parisian diocesan sources that contain the text. Column 4 indicates that the original source melody for the chant was *Tumba sancti nicholai*, with column 5 showing that the melody is also assigned text for St. Catherine. The last column shows that this melody appeared frequently in both confraternity and diocesan sources from Paris, as well as one from Tournai (B-Tc A 27).

Table 2.2 shows two important things: first, two of the four chants discussed above (in column 1) are contrafacta created with melodies for the Virgin Mary and other saints, which is a testament to their popularity. Second, the original source texts of these melodies (in honor of Mary and

Table 2.2. Contrafacta for St. Nicholas, source melodies (the first three columns refer to text, and the last three refer to melody).

Chant text	Confraternity sources containing the text (set to music)	Diocesan sources from Paris and Tournai containing the original chant text (with or without music)	Melody	Associations with other devotional figures (with chant texts from Tournai and Paris in parentheses)	Sources from Paris and Tournai containing the melody (both confraternity and diocesan, regardless of the text)
Tumba sancti nicholai	F-Pm 464; F-Pnm lat. 10506; B-Tc A 27; F-Pnm lat. 862; F-Pnm lat. 17311	F-Pnm lat. 830; GB-Lbl Add. 38723; F-Pa 110; F-Pnm lat. 12065; F-Pnm lat. 14282; F-Psg lat. 15616; F-Psg OEXV 54²; F-Psg Fol. BB 97 INV 102 Rés	Tumba sancti nicholai	St. Catherine of Alexandria (Tumba sancte katherine)	F-Pm 464; F-Pa 110; F-Pnm lat. 10506; F-Pnm lat. 830; F-Pnm lat. 15616; GB-Lbl Add. 38723; F-Pnm lat. 17311; B-Tc A 27
O nicholae	F-Pm 464; B-Tc A 12; B-Tc A 13	None	O consolatrix pauperum	St. Catherine of Alexandria (O beata katherina; Dulcis martir dulcis virgo diversa); Virgin Mary (Dulcis mater dulcis virgo dulcia); St. Barbara; St. Mellonie; Christ	F-Pm 464; B-Tc A 12; B-Tc A 13; F-Pnlr Rés. B 27762
Egregie christi confessor nicholae	F-Pm 464	None	Iustus germinabit	Common of Saints for One Confessor in Parisian missals and graduals	Parisian missals and graduals for the usage of Paris, thirteenth through sixteenth centuries.
Summe dei confessor nicholae	B-Tc A 12; B-Tc A 13	B-Tc A 10; B-Tc A 11; B-Ts Inc. 27	Summe dei confessor nicholae	St. Nicholas	B-Tc A 12; B-Tc A 13; B-Tc A 10; B-Tc A 11

other saints) worked together with the chant texts for St. Nicholas to associate him with important religious figures. In some cases, these melodies appear multiple times, each with a different text, in one source.

The role of St. Nicholas as a confessor is likely the reason for using the alleluia verse melody for *Iustus germinabit*, which comes from the Parisian Common of Saints for One Confessor. The original text alludes to righteousness, so the pairing of this melody with the *Egregie christi* text serves both as a confession of devotion to the translation of relics and as melodic praise of the saint's virtue:

> Alleluya. The righteous man will sprout like the lily and he will blossom in eternity before God.[72]

The alleluia verse *O consolatrix pauperum* illustrates the different types of connections that were possible both melodically and textually in alleluia verses. It is one of the most frequently used alleluia verse melodies in the confraternity sources from Paris and Tournai, appearing a total of six times.[73] Although it was regularly used in confraternity services, the chant does not appear in liturgical books from the cathedral or parishes of Paris or Tournai, again showing a certain amount of freedom that confraternities exercised within the two dioceses. This alleluia verse was favored in several other northern French usages, such as those of Autun, Troyes, and Reims, with many melodic variants.[74] In these dioceses, the melody was assigned texts in lauding the Virgin Mary, St. Barbara, St. Catherine, St. Nicholas, St. Mellonie, and Christ. The melody in F-Pm 464 closely matches a version of the chant from Reims (F-RS 264).[75] Example 2.3 shows the relationship of the melodies in F-Pm 464, B-Tc A 13, and F-RS 264. While I provide incipits only of the opening Alleluia statement, the same types of melodic similarities and variations also appear in the verses. Example 2.3 shows these differences to be small.

A closer look at some of the texts in honor of other saints that were set to the *O consolatrix pauperum* melody shows us how it enhances the text for St. Nicholas. The F-RS 264 version of the chant (see example 2.3) is for St. Barbara, and it is also similar in theme to the *O nicholae* text transcribed at the outset of the chapter, giving hope for salvation after death.

> Alleluya. O comforter of the poor, renowned Virgin Barbara, fragrant with the odor of virtue, protect your servants, see to it that when life runs its course, we will come into enduring joys with you.[76]

Example 2.3. *Alleluia O consolatrix pauperum* (F-RS 264)/*O nicholae* (F-Pm 464 and B-Tc A 13).

O consolatrix pauperum appears several times in B-Tc A 12, first with a text for St. Catherine, and then later in the manuscript with a text for the Virgin Mary, but they both break away from a concentration on sickness.

> Alleluya. Sweet martyr, sweet virgin, bearing various blows, merciful Catherine, pray for us to the King and Lord of the heavens.[77]

> Alleluya. Sweet mother, sweet virgin, bearing sweet breasts, who alone was worthy to give milk to the King and Lord of the heavens.[78]

These two texts are almost identical, the only differences being that the one for St. Catherine makes reference to her martyrdom in the form of an intercessory prayer, where the supplicants ask her to "pray for us"; and that the one for the Virgin Mary mentions her role as Christ's mother. There is another Christological allusion here, as both are based on the alleluia verse for the Exultation of the Cross, *Dulce lignum, dulces clavos*, which was widespread throughout northern France and the Low Countries, and melodically similar to the various versions of *O consolatrix pauperum*.[79]

The musical and textual associations here are compelling, and whether the confraternity members themselves were aware of them or not, the performance of these chants during the service would have held significance, calling upon the saint for intercession. The number of alleluia verses in F-Pm 464 for St. Nicholas directly reflects the regular meetings of the confraternity to celebrate the Mass in honor of their patron saint, which I established previously through the confraternity register. The fact that the *O nicholae* text also appears in the notary confraternity manuscripts from Tournai shows the broader importance of this textual and melodic pairing in confraternity devotions. All people were meant to model their behavior on the life of Christ and the Virgin Mary, and the source melodies reinforce these values. This is but one manifestation of the innovative nature of contrafacta and its use to establish multiple meanings through music and text. These types of manipulations take place in other chant genres in different ways, which I explore below.[80]

The Office for the Translation of St. Nicholas

The greatest testament to the importance of the Translation of St. Nicholas for the Confraternity of the Spice Dealers and Apothecaries in the fifteenth century are the offices that appear in F-Pm 464. As shown in figure 2.1, the manuscript contains three offices for St. Nicholas with music: one for the Feast of St. Nicholas on December 6; and two for the Translation of St. Nicholas on May 9, which I will hereafter call Translation Office 1 and Translation Office 2.[81] There are no instructions in the manuscript that indicate when the two Translation offices are to be performed, but we can infer that they are two possible options for the confraternity's celebration of the Translation of St. Nicholas on May 9.[82] Translation Office 1 is not special to this confraternity as it is copied from the diocesan usage of Paris, which reuses chants from the Feast of St. Nicholas. In contrast, Translation Office 2 contains very specific and direct references to the Translation of St. Nicholas.

The chants of Translation Office 2 emphasize different parts of the translation narrative, moving beyond the holy oil as a focal point and instead lingering on the act of translation as recorded by Nicephorus, discussed earlier. The Office is unique, as it contains newly composed antiphon and responsory texts that are not found in any other sources from the fifteenth century, or in modern chant indices.[83] Only Vespers, the first nocturn of Matins, and Lauds were copied into the manuscript, but the narrative between Matins and Lauds is continuous, so the Office was likely conceived in its present form with one Matins nocturn instead of three.[84] While at times the chants dwell on specific events of the Translation story, they largely paraphrase Nicephorus's text rather than directly quoting it.

Like Vespers offices for other saints, such as the one for St. Barbara discussed in chapter 1, the antiphons in table 2.3 give general praise for St. Nicholas's miracles and call for intercession. The responsory and verse make specific reference to the head of the saint, which is not in the Translation story written by Nicephorus. This is related to other Translation offices for St. Nicholas in circulation in the fifteenth and sixteenth centuries, and likely before. For example, it is found almost word for word in *De probatis sanctorum historiis* by Laurentius Surius, which appeared in 1581. Although published well into the sixteenth century, this work was based on preexisting *Translatio* narratives, so this aspect of the story was certainly in circulation in the fifteenth century.[85]

Although one portion of the Vespers studied here has concordances elsewhere, Matins is not related to any other Office that has been identified so far. Matins is usually where the saint's vita is articulated complete with details of martyrdom, but since St. Nicholas was a confessor, the chants primarily outline the difficulties faced by the citizens of Bari on the way back from Myra. The lessons would normally give more detail, but they are not included in F-Pm 464, or at least they are not marked clearly, as I will show below.

The Matins antiphons in table 2.4 portray the arduous voyage of the merchants of Bari with the body of St. Nicholas in tow after leaving Myra. The texts provide a climactic sense of suspense, so in some ways they, too, capture the more sensational aspects of a martyr's Office (see Matins for St. Barbara in chapter 1, for example). The heightened emotional appeal is present in the first responsory and verse, which is from the point of view of the people of Myra. It describes how they chased the merchants to their ship, dramatically lamenting the "pillage" and pleading with the men of Bari to leave the relics behind.[86] This is the only chant text from the point of view of the citizens of Myra, while all the others describe the actions of the citizens of Bari and their feelings upon leaving the city with the relics. Did they make a mistake? Did St. Nicholas really choose Bari as his new resting place, or are they all doomed? There is a pervasive sense of doubt in the texts that adds to the suspense, and in particular, the third antiphon and second responsory draw upon beliefs concerning the dangers of relic displacement, discussed earlier.

Although Translation Office 2 does not have readings, nor any rubrics indicating where they might be found, Translation Office 1 includes the following rubric after the third Matins antiphon of nocturn 1, "Lectiones de translatione sanctissimi nicholay quere infra" (see figure 2.1). This indicates that the readings came from the Translation story by Nicephorus, which

Table 2.3. Translation Office 2. Vespers (portions based on *De probatis sanctorum historiis* are highlighted with italics).

Chant	Latin text	English text
Antiphon 1	Sanctus confessor Nicholaus ut apostolicus pro maximo thesauro iesum cristum sacrato ferebat in pectore alleluya.	The holy confessor Nicholas, as an apostolic man, carried Jesus Christ in his heart as the greatest sacred treasure, alleluia.
Antiphon 2	Replebantur populi stupore miraculorum et in pectoribus omnium fides catholica firmabitur alleluya.	The nations were filled with stupefaction at the miracles, and the Catholic faith was strengthened in the hearts of all, alleluia.
Antiphon 3	O sancte Nicholae confessor christi preciose in tua translacione quesumus ora pro nobis alleluya.	O holy Nicholas, confessor of Christ, precious in your Translation, we beg you, pray for us, alleluia.
Antiphon 4	Sancte Nicholae confessor domini gloriose adesto nostris precibus pius et propicius alleluya.	Holy Nicholas, glorious confessor of the Lord, devoted and favorable, attend to our prayers, alleluia.
Antiphon 5	Tu in celo choruscas inter choros sanctorum simplex ut columba cuius fint dignitatis vox de celo nuncia beate nicholae ora pro nobis mundi salvatorem alleluya.	You shine in heaven among the choirs of saints, simple as a dove, of whose worthiness a voice from heaven was the herald: blessed Nicholas, pray to the Savior of the world for us, alleluia.
Responsory	*Expositis* quidem *membris ceteris* beati nicholai *confuse ac temere caput adhuc deerat. Quo nondum reperto tristes aliquantulum sunt effecti.* Alleluya.	When the other members of blessed Nicholas were set out in a confused and rash way, the head was still missing. As it had not yet been found, they became somewhat sad. Alleluia.
Verse	Cum autem collocassent corpus beati nicholai adhuc caput deerat.	When they had set the body of blessed Nicholas in its place, the head was still missing.

—(*continued*)

Table 2.3—*concluded*

Chant	Latin text	English text
Magnificat antiphon	Concurrebant itaque ex universis provinciis hysperie cristicolarum multitudines diverse pro divinis virtutibus miraculisque stupendis et innumeris qui quotidie ibi fiebant alleluya.	Therefore various multitudes of Christians came running from all the provinces of Hisperia[i] for the divine powers and the astounding and innumerable miracles which were taking place there every day, alleluia.

Note:
[i] This refers to Italy.

Table 2.4. Translation Office 2. Matins.

Chant	Latin text	English text
Antiphon 1	Redeuntibus nautis tempestas valida exoritur que nec ultra nec retro nautas ire desinebat alleluya.	As the sailors were returning, a powerful storm arose which did not cease to advance on the sailors beyond or behind, alleluia.
Antiphon 2	Unde quidem mutuo colloquentes turbatis animis aiebant alleluya.	Because of this, speaking to one another with troubled minds, they said, alleluia.
Antiphon 3	Quare nobis hec adversitas opponitur forcitan aliud nobiscum gerimus aut si veraciter gerimus sibi non placet alleluya.	Why is this adversity set against us? Perhaps we are carrying some other thing with us, or, if we are carrying truly, it is not pleasing to him, alleluia.
Responsory 1	Tempore quid miseris heu nobis accidit isto quo patrie nostre dedecus aspicimus.	What has fallen upon us wretches, alas, in this time, in which we behold the disgrace of our native land?
Verse	Munera namque dei servata diu rapiuntur orbe dolente sua gens lacrimat misera.	For indeed the long-preserved gifts of God are pillaged; as the world grieves, his miserable nation weeps.

—(*continued*)

Table 2.4—*concluded*

Chant	Latin text	English text
Responsory 2	Naute quidem tribus noctibus et geminis diebus boream flantem in unum contrarium habuerunt. Unde quidem mutuo colloquentes dubitantibus animis et turbatis aiebant forsitan aliud nobiscum gerimus non autem illud quod amamus alleluya.	For three nights and two days together the sailors had the north wind blowing against them. Because of this, speaking to one another with doubting and troubled minds, they said: Perhaps we are carrying some other thing with us, but not what we love, alleluia.
Verse	Quare nobis flaminis huius adversitas opposita est nec quiescit.	Why is the adversity of this wind opposed to us, nor does it rest?
Responsory 3	Inter cives barrenses orta est disencio. Et sedicio exoriens in geminas partes est divisa. Alleluya.	A disagreement arose among the citizens of Bari. And the insurrection which rose up was divided into two parts. Alleluia.
Verse	Una pars in una parte civitatis altera vero pars in altera sanctum nicholaum collocare nitebantur.	One part struggled to place Saint Nicholas in one part of the city, the other part in another.
Prosa	Laus tibi sit domine regum rex eterne. Qui regnas in ethere cum patre et matre. Tecum sancti gaudent nicholausque. Quem barrenses receperunt hodie. Gaudentes de tam sancto pontifice. Quem disposueras eis donare. Certantes in qua locaretur parte. Et eorum lis cum discensione. In duas est partes divisa. Alleluya.	Praise be to you, Lord, eternal king of kings, who reigns in heaven with the Father and Mother. The saints rejoice with you, and Nicholas, whom the people of Bari recovered today, rejoicing in such a holy bishop, whom you ordained to give to them, disputing in which part he should be placed, and their quarrel and disagreement was divided into two parts. Alleluia.

happens to appear directly after Translation Office 1 on fols. 47r–66v of the manuscript. Figure 2.1 shows that this reading is divided into three substantial sections with the rubrics "Lectio prima," "Lectio secunda," and "Lectio tercia." This division, however, does not fit well with the narrative structure of the Matins responsories in Translation Office 2, making it unlikely that they were distributed this way in the performance of this Office. The first reading starts with the preparation of the merchants of Bari to go to Myra, the second begins with the men of Bari arguing with the guardians of St. Nicholas's tomb in Myra, and the third commences with the breaking of the tomb. The third antiphon and all the responsories in Translation Office 2 are about the journey back to Bari, which is another chapter in the story altogether.

The reading marked "Lectio tercia" is further subdivided into four sections, with each rubric simply indicating "de eodem," showing that they could also be used as individual readings as well. They are divided in the following way: 1—the moment when the body of St. Nicholas is placed on the ship for the journey back to Bari; 2—the arrival of the ship at the port of St. Gregory in Bari; and 3 and 4—the miracles performed in Bari. The divisions of this reading fit better with the structure of the antiphon and responsory texts, so it is possible that they were read during Translation Office 2. Either way, these texts were options for those in charge of performing the confraternity's services.

The Lauds antiphons in table 2.5 dwell on the high point of the Translation story—the arrival of St. Nicholas at the port of St. Gregory near Bari, where he performed miracles curing the sick. The chant texts are specific, making reference to the movement of the relics from the port of St. Gregory to the city of Bari, the dispatch of messengers to signal their arrival, and the "intense gazes" of the citizens.[87] The entire Office ends with the final Magnificat antiphon from second Vespers as a prayer to St. Nicholas to look after the laity in both death and in life.

As was the case with the alleluia verses, melody is also used in Translation Office 2 to provide dual meanings. The chant texts give insight into the specific parts of the translation narrative that carry important ideas concerning the movement of St. Nicholas's relics and their healing power. Table 2.6 gives all of the antiphon texts from F-Pm 464 in column 2 and establishes their melodic connections to chants from Parisian liturgical usage in column 3. It then provides the text of the original source melody in the diocesan usage (column 4) and the connection of the source melody to feast days in Parisian

Table 2.5. Translation Office 2. Lauds and Vespers 2 Magnificat antiphon.

Chant	Latin text	English text
Antiphon 1	Navigantes leti paucis diebus portum sancti gregorii advenerunt qui locus a barrinis menibus adest quasi quinque miliariis alleluya.	The joyful seafarers arrived in a few days at the port of Saint Gregory, a place which is about five miles from the city walls of Bari, alleluia.
Antiphon 2	Hic autem illo de vasculo quod prenotavimus sanctas extrahentes reliquias in lignea capsellula honorifice concluserunt alleluya.	There, removing the holy relics from that small container which we have described before, they enclosed them honorably in a small wooden box, alleluia.
Antiphon 3	Dum concluserunt corpus beati nicholai premiserunt quosdem barrenses ad clerum et populum nuncios alleluya.	When they had enclosed the body of blessed Nicholas, they sent ahead some citizens of Bari as messengers to the clergy and the people, alleluia.
Antiphon 4	Quibus nunciantibus confestim tota civitas mirabili gaudio repleta concurrit ad lictora alleluya.	As they made their announcement, the whole city, filled with marvelous joy, immediately came running to the seashore, alleluia.
Antiphon 5	Homines et mulieres senes et iuvenes anus et iuvencule pueri et adolescentule infantuli et infantule naves se predictas tantam leticiam afferentes in tantis obtutibus expectabant alleluya.	Men and women, old men and young men, old women and young women, boys and girls, male and female infants, awaited with such intense gazes the predicted ships bringing them such joy, alleluia.
Benedictus Antiphon	Cum deposuissent beatum nicholaum ad ecclesiam sancti benedicti primo in die infirmi numero triginta utriusque sexus omnis etatis a multitudinis infirmitatibus liberati sunt alleluya.	When they had laid blessed Nicholas in the church of Saint Benedict, on the first day, thirty sick people, of both sexes, of all ages, were set free of great numbers of sicknesses, alleluia.

—(continued)

Table 2.5—*concluded*

Chant	Latin text	English text
Magnificat Antiphon	Magne pater sancte nicholae mortis hora nos tecum suscipe et hic semper nos pie respice alleluya.	Great father Saint Nicholas, receive us with you at the hour of death, and always look graciously on us here, alleluia.

Table 2.6. Antiphons in F-Pm 464 for Translation Office 2.

Service	Chant text (F-Pm 464)	Melodic concordance in Parisian usage	Source melody in Parisian usage	Feast day for source melody in Parisian usage
Vespers	*Sanctus confessor Nicholaus*	Yes	*Tecum principium*	Nativity
			Ave maria gratia plena	Suffrage for the Annunciation
	Replebantur populi	Yes	*Dum steteritis*	Common of Apostles
	O sancte Nicholae confessor	No	–	–
	Sancte Nicholae confessor	No	–	-
	Tu in caelo chorus	No	–	–
Matins	*Redeuntibus nautis*	Yes	*Nobilissimus siquidem*	Feast of St. Nicholas
	Unde quidem	Yes (tenuous)	*Postquam domi puerilem*	Feast of St. Nicholas
			Reges intellegite	Crown of Thorns
	Quare nobis	No	–	–

—(continued)

Table 2.6—*concluded*

Service	Chant text (F-Pm 464)	Melodic concordance in Parisian usage	Source melody in Parisian usage	Feast day for source melody in Parisian usage
Lauds	*Navigantes laeti paucis*	Yes (tenuous)	*Quid hic statis tota die*	Hebd. Septuagesima
	Hic autem illo	Yes (tenuous)	*Ecclesie sancte frequentans*	Feast of St. Nicholas
	Dum concluserunt	No	–	–
	Quibus nunciantibus	Yes	*Sacerdotes sacerdoti*	Crown of Thorns
	Homines et mulieres	No	–	–

liturgical usage (column 5). Column 3 shows that four of the antiphons are contrafacta created from chants in the diocesan usage.[88]

The composer of Translation Office 2 takes a slightly different approach to contrafacta compared to the widely employed method discussed previously for the alleluia verses.[89] First and foremost, the meaning of the source melody text was a factor in the composer's choice of antiphon melodies in F-Pm 464, which was also the case for the alleluia verses. What is different is that the composer of this Office has altered the melodies of the chants to accommodate the new chant texts, which was not common in the alleluia verses, as they required little to no melodic alteration. For instance, example 2.4, *Sanctus confessor Nicholaus*, has thirty-nine syllables, whereas the source melody *Ave maria gratia plena* has only twenty-six. The same is true in example 2.7, *Sacerdotes sacerdoti*, which has thirty syllables, whereas the new text for St. Nicholas, *Quibus nunciantibus*, has thirty-six syllables. Similar differences in syllable count appear in the other musical examples as well (examples 2.5–2.6). The musical similarities could, at first sight, be attributed to the use of the same chant formulae, but they go beyond just the first few notes and continue throughout.[90] Example 2.4 gives a good illustration of the common Mode 1 formula, with incipits from two examples from the diocesan usage compared to the first Vespers antiphon of Translation Office 2. The first seven notes establish the modal formula, but the similarities with

Example 2.4. Vespers. Antiphon 1, *Sanctus confessor Nicholaus* in F-Pm 464.

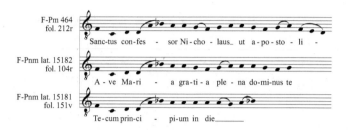

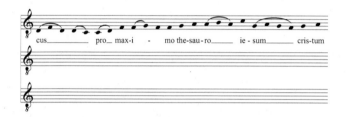

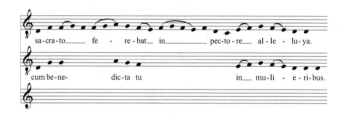

the antiphon in F-Pm 464 move beyond this. The chants end the same in example 2.4 as well. There is a similar process at work for examples 2.5–2.7, for all show the Translation Office 2 chants to have connections with melodies from the diocesan usage that eventually diverge.[91]

There are several possible reasons for this selection of chant melodies, and among them are two that are of interest here: first, the composer would have chosen chants that he knew well or that were readily available to him as models; and second, the composer chose source melodies that added depth to the meaning of the text for St. Nicholas. Those melodies from the common of saints, like *Dum steteritis*, would have been among the chants known to the composer, as would *Ave maria gratia plena*. There are also logical connections

Example 2.5. Vespers. Antiphon 2, *Replebantur populi* in F-Pm 464.

Example 2.6. Matins. Antiphon 1, *Redeuntibus nautis* in F-Pm 464.

Example 2.7. Lauds. Antiphon 4, *Quibus nunciantibus* in F-Pm 464.

in choosing a chant from the Feast of St. Nicholas, such as *Nobilissimus siqui-dem*, as a source melody for the Translation.

Some links between the new texts and the source melodies above are symbolic and were likely meant to establish spiritual or thematic connections. For instance, table 2.6 shows that the first Vespers antiphon, *Sanctus confessor Nicholaus*, is based on the well-known melody *Ave maria gratia plena*. The contrafactum text is, "Nicholas, as an apostolic man, carried Jesus Christ in his heart." This might guide an adaptor to choose the melody *Ave maria gratia plena*, "Hail Mary, full of grace the Lord is with thee: blessed art thou among women," the connection being Mary carrying Jesus in her womb. St. Nicholas was the patron saint of sterile women, so associations with Mary carrying Christ would have added to this symbolism.

Connections to relics, processions, and Parisian institutions as sources of civic pride are evoked through the composer's use of an antiphon from the Crown of Thorns Office in the diocese of Paris, *Sacerdotes sacerdoti*, discussed above (example 2.7). King Louis IX (who was later canonized as St. Louis, see chapter 3) obtained the Crown of Thorns and a portion of the True Cross from Constantinople in 1239 and built the Ste. Chapelle (completed in 1248) to house it. A very detailed account describes how upon its arrival in Paris on August 18, 1239, Louis IX and his brother Robert of Artois carried the relic in a procession to different locations in the city, among them Notre Dame (where a Mass was said). They ultimately found their temporary resting place at the chapel of St. Nicholas in the king's palace. The event was celebrated yearly on August 11 throughout the diocese for centuries after, and it appears in the calendar of all Parisian manuscript and printed liturgical books.[92] This public display was important in solidifying Louis IX's sacral kingship, for he would subsequently publicly carry the Crown of Thorns in processions around the city on feast days. According to William of St. Pathus, who wrote the Life of St. Louis in the early fourteenth century, "both the clergy and the people of Paris joined him."[93] Table 2.6 shows that the Parisian Office for the main feast day of St. Nicholas and the Parisian Crown of Thorns Office both use the same Matins antiphon melody with different texts (*Postquam domi puerilem* for St. Nicholas, and *Reges intellegite* for the Crown of Thorns). While these two offices were connected in the diocesan usage, the composer of Translation Office 2 drew different chant melodies from the Crown of Thorns. Table 2.5 gives the antiphon text for *Quibus nunciantibus*, which describes how the people of Bari, upon hearing of the arrival of the relics of St. Nicholas, came to the seashore to witness the event. The original text from the Crown of Thorns antiphon, *Sacerdotes sacerdoti*, is "All priests, bless the highest priest, and subject us as heirs to the sacred crown." Just as the Parisians became heirs to the Crown of Thorns relic, so did the people of Bari become heirs to the relics of St. Nicholas—both happened through Translation.

The choice of a chant from the Crown of Thorns Office also draws references more generally to the Ste. Chapelle as a place of pilgrimage, where Parisians and those from afar would come and take part in difference services. Meredith Cohen has demonstrated that all inhabitants of the city—the poor, merchants, and those of all social ranks—were given incentive to celebrate public services in the lower chapel through an indulgence granted by Pope Innocent IV in 1244. From that point on, the Ste. Chapelle served as a place of pilgrimage for centuries, and the laity would have been able to observe a Mass in honor of the relics from the feast of the Purification through Quinquagesima, and the full liturgy of the Crown of Thorns on all days of its octave, with the exception of days with feasts of nine lessons or more.[94] In light of this, the composer's choice of the chant melody *Sacerdotes sacerdoti*, which praises the blessing of the Crown of Thorns in Paris, could have also been because it came from an Office that was celebrated with a high level of public ceremony at the Ste. Chapelle, with which he was familiar.

Translation Office 2 demonstrates the act of translation and focuses specifically on the relic itself, rather than healing, which was the narrative concentration of the alleluia verses. Along with these spiritual connections are ideas about civic pride, which makes Translation Office 2 truly Parisian in its composition. We see these worldly references as well as other healing narratives take shape in hymns and prosas.

The Power of Hymns and Prosas for the Translation of St. Nicholas

The Translation of St. Nicholas is also a theme in the hymns and prosas found in F-Pm 464, and due to their lengthy texts, they add another dimension to the confraternity's devotions—reinforcing miracles that were important to the community. Tables 2.7 and 2.8 below show that there are five prosas and six hymns in the manuscript that carry new and specific texts for St. Nicholas.[95] These chants are interesting both for their musical and textual associations and for what their placement in the manuscript may indicate about overall performance practice and the role of confraternity members in participation in the musical portion of their services.

Most of the hymns for Translation Office 2 in table 2.7, with the exception of *Exultet aula regia letetur* and *Pange lingua nicholai*, appear only in F-Pm 464.[96] The majority of the hymns and prosas are contrafacta, and in the case of the hymns, most are set to melodies from the Parisian Temporale and Sanctorale, showing again the same compositional approach as in the alleluia verses. The prosas, on the other hand, have very little in common with the usage of Paris, but their source melodies are among some of the most popular and widespread chants in northern France.[97]

The musical and textual structure of hymns and prosas allow for more detailed references to a saint's protective powers. These genres feature lengthy rhymed poetic texts composed in verses set to melodies in strophic and double cursus form, making them ideal for popular consumption.[98] The composers of the meditative texts in F-Pm 464 referred to the miracles of St. Nicholas, his relics, and his Translation. For instance, the short prosa, *Laus tibi*, makes direct mention of the Translation of St. Nicholas to Bari, and his role in settling disputes. These actions are wrapped up in general praise for him, as shown below. The hymn texts *Adest nunc dies* and *Nicolay preconia* similarly follow suit.[99]

> Praise be to you, Lord, eternal king of kings, who reigns in heaven with the Father and Mother. The saints rejoice with you, and Nicholas, whom the people of Bari recovered today, rejoicing in such a holy bishop, whom you ordained to

Table 2.7. Hymns for St. Nicholas in F-Pm 464.

Hymns in F-Pm 464	Source melody	Source melody in diocesan usage
Pange lingua nicholai – *AH* vol. 52, 207	*Pange lingua gloriosi proelium*	yes – Passion Sunday
Exultet aula regia letetur	*Eterna rex*	yes – Ascension
Presulis sancti gesta nicholai – AH vol. 12, 377	*O quam glorifica*	yes – Conception of the Virgin
Adest nunc dies – AH vol. 12, 379	*Eterna rex*	yes – Ascension
Nicholay preconia – AH vol. 12, 380	*Eterna rex*	yes – Ascension
Fecundavit hic steriles – *AH* vol. 19, 402	*Iesu nostra redemptio*	yes – Ascension, Pentecost, Trinity

Table 2.8. Prosas for St. Nicholas in F-Pm 464.

Prosas in F-Pm 464	Source melody	Source melody in diocesan usage
Previst le createur du ciel	*Mittit ad virginem*	no
Sancte nicholae beate pontifex - AH vol. 9, 313	*Mittit ad virginem*	no
Letabundus laudet nicholao - AH vol. 9, 312	*Letabundus exultet*	yes – Nativity
Laus tibi sit domine	unidentified	no
Clemens fotor pauperum – AH vol. 40, 297	*Veni sancte spiritus*	no

give to them, disputing in which part he should be placed, and their quarrel and disagreement was divided into two parts. Alleluia.[100]

The prosa melody that appears with the greatest frequency in F-Pm 464 is *Mittit ad virginem*, which was one of the most widely disseminated Marian sequences in northern France and the Low Countries and was used as the basis for several polyphonic works in the fifteenth and sixteenth centuries.[101] The chant was normally notated rhythmically in cantus fractus, and in both of its occurrences in F-Pm 464 it is written in this way.[102] In this manuscript, the melody appears with a full text in French, *Previst le createur du ciel*, followed by a short Latin incipit, *Previdit conditor celi*; and at another point in the book with the text *Sancte nicholae beate pontifex* (see example 2.8).[103]

The incorporation of *Mittit ad virginem* into confraternity manuscripts is one possible example of music used to aurally reference doctrine that was taught through liturgical drama, vernacular devotional literature, and prayer books with images (see chapter 1). As a Marian sequence, its popularity is due to its connection with the Annunciation, which is a central moment in the retelling of the life of Christ (as the beginning of human salvation) and the life of Mary (referencing her place as the Mother of God).[104] The feast was celebrated at the time of year when there were numerous liturgical plays, and it was a popular theme for these events, which catered to the laity.[105] For instance, at the Tournai cathedral *Mittit ad virginem* was part of the Annunciation drama performed in the main sanctuary on Ember Wednesday during Advent, where at the end of the ceremony, the prosa was sung with organ and discant.[106] These types of associations would have been fresh in the minds of the medieval laity, who would likely have known this melody due to its dramatic context. In addition, doctrinal associations between Christ and Mary circulated widely in vernacular literature, such as the Miracles of the Virgin and Meditations on the Life of Christ, which included many devotional images along with the texts.[107] The use of contrafacta praising St. Nicholas set to well-known prosa and hymn melodies was meant to invoke identification with these events and elevate and exalt the saint as Christlike.[108]

The use of the vernacular in *Previst le createur du ciel* signals that a value was placed on aural comprehension of the text for St. Nicholas, and that confraternity members played an active role in participation.[109] The text of the prosa, which appears uniquely in F-Pm 464, is translated into English in appendix 5 ♫.[110] Its subject matter is similar to other prosa texts in its praise of St. Nicholas, his life and miracles, and the healing oil of his relics.

Example 2.8. Prosa. *Previst le createur* in F-Pm 464.

The opening verse features a direct and personal confession of faith: "The creator foresaw the heavens from the firmament: The true keeper of faith, as well should be, its defender. I, who am wanting, firmly rejecting the devil, as a disciple I worship with awe the true religion."[111] Members of confraternities in other locations were known to have engaged in communal singing, and this prosa shows that was likely the case for this confraternity as well.[112]

A clue to the possible inspiration for the French setting appears on fol. 97r of the confraternity register discussed earlier in the chapter, B-Br 17939, which indicates that the spice dealers and apothecaries were granted the privilege of carrying "le ciel," or canopy, for kings, queens, and all high-ranking persons during processions from the church of St. Leu-St. Gilles until the fountain of the Holy Innocents. This was part of a standard Parisian processional route, with different groups given the honor of carrying the canopy for short stretches. It was a sign of prestige for Parisian trade guilds to have this right, and those communities upon which it was bestowed were very proud to have the role.[113] There is no evidence that confraternities provided the music during these processions, but this prosa could have been sung by the confraternity members during one of their own private services, and served to reinforce their public identity. Only male members of confraternities in Italy during this era engaged in public communal singing, but there is no evidence that this was the case in private settings in Parisian communities, so it is possible that both male and female members of the confraternity participated in this activity.[114] If we assume that the text in the vernacular was meant to exalt the confraternity, "du ciel" mentioned at the beginning could have triple meaning: praising the creator of the heavens, praising their patron saint, and praising the Confraternity of the Spice Dealers and Apothecaries who were charged with carrying the canopy. In this case, the prosa text could have both spiritual and corporate implications.

The Role of Physical Movement in Devotions to
St. Nicholas and St. Catherine

If we return to the idea put forth at the beginning of this chapter, that the movement of confraternities and the individuals taking part in them is both a social and spiritual practice, we can begin to see how such organizations navigated physical space together. The previous sections highlighted the role of clerics at institutions who housed multiple confraternities in the construction of their services. Socially, the contact that practitioners of different trades had with each other is another avenue for the transmission of devotional practices among confraternities in the city. As established in the introduction to this book, tradespeople in Paris, Tournai, and other urban centers in the French kingdom lived and worked in banner districts, but there is evidence that they also inhabited other quarters throughout the city.[115] Members of different trades interacted with each other within their local parish, within the parish or monastic community where their confraternities worshipped, and in general through public displays of confraternity devotions at different times of the year, according to their statutes.

Specific examples of such individual movement and its possible relationship to devotional practices exist in notarial registers for the city of Paris.[116] In many cases bakers, coopers, spice dealers, candle makers, members of the book production community, apothecaries, etc. lived in the same neighborhoods and attended services for Christmas, Easter, and other major feasts in the same parishes. There were also many links of marriage between practitioners of different trades. One example of members of various trade communities having contact in different religious institutions comes from the parish of St. Benoît-le-bien-tourné. François Regnault and Claude Chevallon, both of whom were printers and booksellers, are known to have been churchwardens at this institution, as well as Thielmann Kerver and Jean Petit, who were also major figures in the trade.[117] In a 1522 notarial document, Kerver, Chevallon, and Petit, along with eleven other men, are mentioned as parishioners.[118] This document concerns the acceptance on the part of the parish, represented by these (altogether) fourteen men, of an endowment for a church service by a certain Antoinette de Gannay, widow of Pierre Barthomier.[119] While six of the men other than the ones mentioned above are not easily identified, five of them are known: Josse Bade—printer, Gervais Dodier—bailiff for the French chancery, Conrad Resch—bookseller, Jean Périer—candle maker, and Jean Eschart—spice dealer.[120] Although this particular parish had a community of members from various trades, there is no evidence at this point of a trade confraternity at St. Benoît.[121] In fact, Kerver, Chevallon, Petit, Bade, and Resch would have been members of the Confraternity of St. John the Evangelist for the Book Production Community at the parish of St. André des Arts; Périer would have been a member of the Confraternity of St. John the Evangelist for the Oilers and Candle Makers at Notre Dame; and Eschart would have been a member of the Confraternity of St. Nicholas for the Spice Dealers and Apothecaries at the Hospital of Ste. Catherine. The information gathered from this document is a good example of the financial role of laypeople in the workings of a medieval parish, and the contact they had with each other. To what extent this influenced content of confraternity devotions is unknown.

Conclusion

Each of the chant genres discussed in this chapter show how different aspects of *Inventio* and *Translatio* narratives for St. Catherine and St. Nicholas are reflected in newly constructed liturgical practices throughout the fifteenth century. Although one of the prosas in F-Pm 464 makes possible reference to the role of the Confraternity of the Spice Dealers and Apothecaries in processions as canopy bearers, the music I have explored here was performed in private contexts, meant specifically for the confraternity members.[122] These communities had the resources to commission new compositions, and while I have not been able to identify composers for the masses and offices, it is possible to make some broad comments on the compositional methods they employed.

The Office was an important genre for both new musical and textual composition—a point that should already be clear from discussions in chapter 1. The antiphons for the Finding of St. Catherine were entirely newly composed, and because of the regularity in text and melody, we can assume it was written by one composer. The method of contrafactum was employed in Translation Office 2 in such a way as to also imply that it was the product of a single composer. The text is suspenseful and draws out the act of translation, and this individual's artful choice of source melodies as models served to ground the Office as a Parisian work, referring to institutions in the city known for other famous relic translations, such as that of the Crown of Thorns.

For the Mass, the mode of composition was primarily textual, using contrafacta in the strictest sense, and it was concentrated on the alleluia verse and prosa. Both chant genres exalt the finding and translation of relics by referencing healing and miracles rather than martyrdom and life events. These chants served a slightly different function from those of the Office, which worked to establish the legitimacy and narrative stories surrounding these acts. Alleluia verses and prosas became genres suitable for transmitting popular ideas about the patron saints of confraternities, and contrafacta created from widespread melodies aided in the transmission of these practices. On a broader level, liturgical texts in the vernacular hint at audience participation and the use of the liturgy to bond a community together by privately celebrating and reinforcing its affluence and place in the larger social fabric of the city. In the end, for the doublet makers and the spice dealers and apothecaries, finding and translation reference the same basic act: the exaltation of relics as healing objects, meant to bring protective power closer to the people. The liturgical books of confraternities invite us into rich devotional contexts, perpetuated by individuals who were deeply entrenched in the everyday workings of urban merchant life. The contents of these sources highlight the pivotal role of lay communities in promoting popular religious practices focused on relics and healing. I have shown here how music and text were used in different ways to accomplish this.

Chapter Three

Historical Narratives and the Importance of Place in Masses for St. Sebastian

Illustrious martyr, glory of the soldiery, champion of Christ, born in the sight of God in order that he might avert for us God's anger. Martyr who piously poured out judgments so that the epidemic may not be harmful. In this fatherland and in others which request your help. Hear [your] praises. And with pious prayer may rewards be given. Quick, soldier, help us. Alleluya.[1]

This is a Mass offertory for St. Sebastian found in Paris, Bibliothèque de l'Arsenal MS 204 (F-Pa 204), a fifteenth-century Parisian liturgical book for the Confraternity of the Bourgeois Archers. This organization comprised men of different trades, who resided in neighborhoods throughout the city but came together to function as the citizen's guard of Paris.[2] It is personal and urgent in nature, calling upon the saint directly with the plea, "Quick, soldier, help us." This prayer to St. Sebastian alludes to his power as a plague saint and healer, which is based on his ability to deflect the anger of God. It is not unlike the other laudatory texts discussed in chapters 1 and 2 that made references to a saint's healing ability, martyrdom, and miracles. St. Sebastian was one of the most revered plague saints in northern France, along with others counted among the fourteen holy helpers in this geographical area.[3] The contents of this confraternity manuscript reveal St. Sebastian to be the most important figure of veneration for the archers, for the saint himself was shot with arrows in an attempted execution at the hands of the Roman emperor Diocletian. This is the only source in the present study that is devoted exclusively to plague saints, as it also contains masses for St. Roche, St. Anthony the Abbot, and St. Genevieve.[4] In this chapter I explore how

Parisian confraternities in the fifteenth century refashioned St. Sebastian into a local protector through textual and melodic references to historical persons and places—and in particular, places that held relics.

In addition to the text's allusion to healing, it has a notable reference to place through the line "In this fatherland and in others which request your help." The composers of liturgical texts gave great attention to their construction, and in light of this, the presence of geographical markers here is significant. This is one of many such references within the masses for St. Sebastian that appear in this manuscript and in other Parisian sources. The texts discuss the Italian region of Lombardy and the city of Milan, which is where St. Sebastian was born and raised, but along with these allusions to St. Sebastian's Italian heritage are mentions of Francia, the kingdom of the Franks that included most of modern-day France. More specifically, one of the prosas for the Mass mentions the northern French city of Soissons. Its prominence at the beginning of a liturgical text for St. Sebastian at first seems out of place—what would an Italian saint like Sebastian have to do with the kingdom of Francia, or the city of Soissons?

The answer to this has to do with St. Sebastian's relics, for in the early ninth century, a portion of them were translated from Rome to the abbey of St. Médard in Soissons, making it an important pilgrimage site in northern France during times of sickness and plague.[5] Pilgrimage was a central component of medieval religious devotions, and references to it appear throughout popular literary genres of the time. Individuals residing in northern France who were able and willing would be likely to embark on a pilgrimage to a local site, such as Soissons.

St. Sebastian's relics originally came to France in the ninth century as a political maneuver on the part of Charlemagne's grandson, Lothair. The choice of Soissons for their resting place was strategically calculated to send the message that St. Sebastian was a protector of the French realm.[6] Subsequently, St. Sebastian's popularity spread throughout the region starting in the fourteenth century, for during a 1348 plague outbreak, Foulques de Chanac, bishop of Paris, granted an indulgence of forty days to all who paid homage to the newly erected altar for St. Sebastian at the abbey of St. Victor on the outskirts of the city, which housed some of the relics that had previously resided in Soissons.[7] The increase in his popularity in confraternity devotions in the fifteenth century is directly related to the Parisian plague epidemics of the 1430s, which claimed over forty-eight thousand lives.

In the masses in F-Pa 204, healing narratives and geography are intertwined, giving rise to a new emphasis on St. Sebastian as a local protector in

France. The construction of local and national identities through representation of historical places and events in hagiography and liturgy has been well studied in France, particularly with regard to St. Louis (King Louis IX of France).[8] Historical references in the lives of saints are often used in an effort to tie these figures to specific geographical locations in order to heighten their protective power over local communities.[9] The composer (or composers) of the new liturgical texts and chants found in this manuscript and in other Parisian sources containing masses for St. Sebastian drew upon historical narratives. Through contrafacta mentioning geographical areas in France, those who composed these new chants provided dual textual and melodic cues to exalt St. Sebastian as a protector of the realm. This construction of the saint's identity became central in private lay devotions to him in northern France and could be seen as an effort to unify the citizenry. Popular devotions to St. Sebastian became so powerful that they were promoted publicly by the time of Francis I's reign in 1515, to the point where he held a privileged place in French royal processions. Well before this, however, masses for St. Sebastian formed part of the original devotional fabric of confraternities in the city; they start to appear in diocesan manuscripts produced in the late fifteenth and early sixteenth centuries, along with the weekly round of votive masses to be said in other institutions in the diocese of Paris. This could be due to the intensity of adoration that surrounded him in confraternal contexts and the residence of individuals from the citizen's guard in different areas of the city.

The Confraternity of the Bourgeois Archers in Paris

F-Pa 204 serves as a window into the devotional practices of the bourgeois archers in Paris, while at the same time providing some contextual information concerning the place of this organization in the Parisian trade network. Both of these aspects are important to the larger context and longevity of devotions to plague saints in northern France.[10] The first clue concerning the book's origins is found on its front binding, where it is embossed with the text "For the Confraternity of Mr. St. Sebastien for the Bourgeois Archers of Paris, 1658," followed by the device of the organization (an image of an archer).[11] The contents of the manuscript were produced in the middle of the fifteenth century, but there is a significant amount of handwritten addenda that dates from well into the seventeenth century. Like the other confraternity manuscripts discussed in chapters 1 and 2, the handwritten addenda in this book show that it was used over a span of several centuries.

The second clue concerning the membership of this confraternity is the distinction of the archers as "bourgeois," a term that had a slightly different meaning in the fifteenth and sixteenth centuries when compared to later periods. In the documents of the Notaries of Paris at this time, only masters of trades are listed as "Bourgeois de Paris," meaning they were among those persons financially responsible enough to take part in urban administration—in other words, they were citizens.[12] Indeed, some scholars have argued that guilds, with their political influence in urban centers during this time period, provided financial security to their members, thus offering a type of citizenship. This civic structure remained intact throughout the seventeenth century but collapsed at the end of the ancien régime in the eighteenth century.[13]

The term "bourgeois" in relation to the archers designates not only financial responsibility and citizenship, but in this context, it refers to a very specific group of people—the citizens' watch, or "guet Bourgeois." The citizens' watch of Paris consisted of artisans practicing different trades and residing in different areas throughout the city. The watch was not their main occupation, for they were involved in many different guilds and professions. Beginning in the thirteenth century and continuing until 1559, the citizen's guard was regulated by the Provost of Merchants, and their mission was to serve as archers protecting the different trade quarters of the city. The group was disbanded in 1559 and then reestablished in 1561 during the wars of religion. At that time they officially became part of the royal Paris guard, which was their affiliation in 1658 when this book was embossed with the organization's name.[14] Nevertheless, the inscription indicates that there were still citizen members of the guard at that time, and that they worshipped together in their own confraternity.[15]

Where this confraternity worshipped is a subject that is open to question. There is evidence of a St. Sebastian confraternity in the chapel of St. Sebastian at Notre Dame since the middle of the fifteenth century, starting in 1434, one year after the 1433 Parisian plague epidemic. The documents from Notre Dame do not mention anything specifically about the archers, but it is possible that the St. Sebastian confraternity mentioned in the documents is the Confraternity of the Bourgeois Archers, to whom this manuscript belonged.[16]

The contents of F-Pa 204 show a heavy focus on St. Sebastian, including two masses dedicated to him. As was the case with masses for St. Catherine

Figure 3.1. Masses in F-Pa 204.

Fols. 1r–4r	*Missa pro mortalitate subitanea evitanda*
Fols. 4r–12r	St. Sebastian
Fols. 12r–15v	St. Anthony the Abbot
Fols. 16r–19v	St. Genevieve
Fols. 25v–27v	St. Sebastian
Fols. 29r–34r	St. Roche

and St. Nicholas in chapter 2, the appearance of several services may speak to the frequency with which the confraternity met, as they would be performed at different times of the year. The manuscript also contains masses for other saints thought to protect against a variety of different ailments (see figure 3.1).

St. Sebastian, St. Anthony, and St. Roche were venerated with particular fervor in Italy and southern France for their abilities to heal various skin diseases; thus it is not surprising to find them grouped together here. Due to this popularity, they were commonly invoked along with the fourteen holy helpers, whose intercession was thought to be effective against a variety of ailments. This confraternity's preoccupation with plague is reinforced through the inclusion of a rare musical setting of the Mass to avoid an untimely death, the text of which was written under the direction of Pope Clement VI at Avignon in 1348.[17] While the focus of this chapter is St. Sebastian, it is important to have an understanding of these figures in relation to him, as the illnesses for which they provided protection were clear concerns for all members of the population at the time. Furthermore, allusions to the different diseases and the connections between them are present in the liturgy, as I will show later in the chapter.

St. Anthony the Abbot, whose feast is celebrated on January 17 in the Catholic Church, was widely called upon for protection against all epidemics in the fourteenth and fifteenth centuries. Heralded as the father of Christian monasticism, by the eleventh century his relics ended up at the abbey of St. Antoine-en-Viennois in the Rhone Alps region of France, near Grenoble. It is at this final resting place that numerous miracles were reported, all of which were related to miraculous cures of several skin ailments that came to be known as "St. Anthony's Fire."[18]

There are two main diseases associated with St. Anthony's Fire, the first being gangrenous ergotism, known as "Holy Fire," which was marked by rashes and a burning sensation in the extremities brought on by a fungus that contaminated rye and wheat. In its most serious form, the disease caused hallucinations and psychosis. The second was erysipelas, which was a bacterial staph infection of the skin, and, similar to ergotism, caused bright red rashes and burning. Most medieval texts and prayers for St. Anthony focus on bringing respite from the physical burning sensations of these afflictions. By the late Middle Ages, the "burning" of St. Anthony's Fire came to be synonymously associated with the flames of hell and purgatory.[19]

St. Roche, whose feast day was August 16, was a relatively recent saint, born in Montpellier in 1295. He was believed to have travelled throughout Italy dressed as a mendicant pilgrim, curing the bubonic plague along the way, before he was imprisoned in Montpellier, where he died in 1327. His far-reaching popularity as a plague saint took hold in 1414 during the Council of Constance, when plague broke out. The fathers of the council ordered prayers and processions in his honor, thus supposedly causing the plague to cease. Although many prayers and masses to St. Roche appear in manuscripts throughout France, Italy, and the Low Countries, an official Office for him was not approved until the time of Pope Urban VIII in the seventeenth century.[20]

Neither St. Anthony nor St. Roche were formally recognized by diocesan authorities in Paris during the fifteenth century when F-Pa 204 was produced, as their names do not appear in the calendars of diocesan graduals and missals. This shows that devotions to them existed exclusively in private contexts at that time. As a result, there is no music or text for masses in their honor in the Parisian liturgical books of this era. Despite this, both saints appear in countless Books of Hours, with images showing that they were part of popular devotional consciousness, which also holds true for St. Sebastian. The only one of the four saints in this manuscript who was officially recognized in Paris was St. Genevieve.

The feast of St. Genevieve was celebrated in all Parisian institutions on January 3, and she was known as the protector of the city. Born in 420 at Nanterre, she spent her life as a nun and was known as a seer and a mind reader. Her status as patroness of Paris has to do with several events during her lifetime, as well as reported miracles she performed after her death. The first of these is the belief that through her fervent prayers, she saved Paris from invasion by Huns in 451. This event is what led Parisians to invoke her as a patroness of the city in times of crisis, such as the Norman attack of 885, and the rampant floods of the thirteenth century. St. Genevieve also held great importance for the French aristocracy, as she was instrumental in the conversion of Clovis, the first king of the Franks, to Christianity.[21]

By the fifteenth century, St. Genevieve was widely called upon for protection from the plague, which explains her appearance in F-Pa 204. Belief in her healing attributes goes back to at least 1129, when the citizens of Paris asked for her protection against the Mal des Ardents, or "burning sickness," which is another one of the many names for ergotism. It is reported that when all cures for this disease did not work, Stephen of Senlis, bishop of Paris, organized and headed a supplicatory procession with St. Genevieve's relics, which departed from her shrine in the city and ended at the cathedral. After this public display, the sickness subsided.[22]

It is evident that St. Anthony, St. Roche, and St. Genevieve were all known for their protection against both "Holy Fire" and the plague; the presence of offices to all of them in the manuscript of interest here shows that this confraternity had a clear focus on healing and preservation. The members of the confraternity were, after all, the archers of the citizen's guard, and St. Sebastian, due to his martyrdom by arrows, was their patron saint. St. Anthony and St. Roche very commonly go along with St. Sebastian as a protector from the plague throughout France and Italy. St. Genevieve was a local saint and defender of the city of Paris, and her presence in F-Pa 204 is one of the hallmarks of this manuscript's Parisian origins. The theme of protection for the archers is important not only in the context of their devotion to plague saints and fear of sickness but may also allude to their role as guardians of the city. In this way, it is possible that the contents of the manuscript go beyond the purely devotional, and reflect the worldly function of this organization within the fabric of city life.

In addition to St. Genevieve, St. Anthony and St. Roche also have some ties to the kingdom of France, indicating that these martyrs could have been chosen for their importance to the geographical area in addition to their healing attributes. Nevertheless, of all the saints represented in F-Pa 204, the masses for St. Sebastian present the most direct references to place. The following section explores the healing narratives in the St. Sebastian liturgy, for this provides the foundation for the geographical and royal connections discussed later in the chapter.

The Life of St. Sebastian and Arrow Imagery

Symbolic references to St. Sebastian's martyrdom and healing power are found throughout the chants for the Mass and are related directly to the events of his martyrdom, which were disseminated in popular literature in the late fifteenth and early sixteenth centuries. The life of St. Sebastian was included both in Jacobus de Voragine's original Latin version of the *Golden Legend* in 1260, and in later French and English translations; this text was itself a truncated version of the saint's vita written in the fourth century by St. Ambrose.[23] According to these sources, St. Sebastian was a native of Narbonne in southern France, but became a citizen of Milan and spent most of his life there. He was a soldier assigned to the personal guard of the Roman emperors Maximian and Diocletian, and it is said that he took this post only in order to use his high-ranking military position to be able to help and console those Christians who were persecuted under the emperors. The most detailed example of this has to do with two young men, the twins Marcellinus and Marcus, who were to be beheaded because they had refused to renounce Christianity. Their parents and wives tried to convince them to yield and renounce their faith, so that they would be saved from death. After much pleading from their loved ones, the twins' courage started to weaken. Sebastian, who was present during these events, encouraged the twins to be brave and die for "the eternal crown."[24]

After saying these words, Sebastian was illuminated with light from the heavens and performed many miracles in the following days. Upon hearing this, the emperor Diocletian denounced him and claimed that, as his personal guard, Sebastian had betrayed him and the Roman gods. As punishment, Diocletian ordered Sebastian to be shot with arrows in a field, after which he was left for dead. His body was found by the Christian widow Irene, who discovered that he was, in fact, alive, and she helped to nurse him back to full health. Several days later, he went to confront the emperor, which led to much confusion, since he believed Sebastian had been executed. In response to this, Sebastian proclaimed, "The Lord has resurrected me to reproach you for the ill you do to the servants of Christ!"[25] Sebastian was then beaten to death by the emperor's guards and thrown into a gutter. The following night he appeared to St. Lucina, revealing where his corpse was located and instructing her to bury him.[26]

St. Sebastian was viewed by some late-medieval theologians as a double martyr. According to the French version of the *Golden Legend* (cited above), he was "resurrected" (ressucité) by God after being shot with arrows, implying that he had suffered a physical death but was then revived before Irene found him. This belief is also reflected in the *Summa theologica moralis*, written in the middle of the fifteenth century by Archbishop Antoninus of Florence. Louise Marshall shows how, in this work, Antoninus says "through two deaths, [Sebastian] possesses two crowns of martyrdom."[27]

Until the late thirteenth century, earlier legends had mentioned only Italy as the site of St. Sebastian's healing power, and it was in fact Jacobus who was responsible for the dissemination of one of these legends throughout western Europe. St. Sebastian's role as a healer has its roots in a story from Paul the Deacon's History of the Lombards, written in 680, in which he explains that God commanded an altar to be built in honor of St. Sebastian in Pavia, whereupon the plague vanished.[28] Jacobus included this miracle in the *Golden Legend*, and from there it travelled throughout France and northern Europe. In the course of the fourteenth century, after the plague epidemics had devastated western Europe, the legend took on great importance, and by the middle of the fifteenth century, there were many prayers and iconographical depictions of St. Sebastian in the French Books of Hours, all of which show the influence of Jacobus's work.

St. Sebastian's attempted execution by arrows is the emotional high point of his vita, and it was depicted visually and aurally in a number of ways. The popularity of the *Golden Legend* coincided with the production of other types of devotional literature and images, all of which include representations of his healing power and ability to protect against the plague. Art historians have demonstrated at length that St. Sebastian's iconography throughout the fifteenth century in woodcuts and Books of Hours shows him being pierced with arrows. This is a reference not only to his torture but also to his protective power against sickness.[29] By meditating on these images, the medieval laity called upon St. Sebastian as a divine protector to intervene on their behalf.[30] Visual representations and prayers in devotional books drew on biblical imagery, in which arrows in general symbolize illness and God's punishment. This is deeply rooted in Old Testament scripture, and several examples may be found in the Psalms and the book of Job. For instance, Psalm 64:7 states, "But God shall shoot at them with an arrow; suddenly shall they be wounded"; and Job 6:4 says, "For the arrows of the almighty are in me; my spirit drinks their poison; the terrors of God are arrayed against me."[31] These passages are representative of many that associate arrows with sickness.

The story of St. Sebastian's martyrdom and the role of the arrow in scripture were interconnected in the minds of medieval theologians and the laity, and this is reflected in both image and text. One example is an Italian panel painting by Pietro Perugino, showing St. Sebastian pierced with arrows along with an inscription of a text from Psalm 38:1–3, which Marshall translates as follows: "O Lord, rebuke me not in thy anger … for thy arrows have struck fast in me … there is no health in my flesh because of thy indignation."[32] The outcome of this synthesis was that St. Sebastian's resurrection after being shot by arrows was taken to mean that he had special powers to protect against God's wrath on earth—which was manifested in the plague—and that he would attract God's plague arrows into his own body, thus drawing them away from the living, as a way of protecting humanity.[33]

The Masses for St. Sebastian

St. Sebastian's martyrdom is represented in a variety of different ways in the chant texts and music in F-Pa 204. The two masses for St. Sebastian appearing in this manuscript both illustrate different devotional trends for him and for other plague saints. This is also reflected in other Parisian manuscripts, and an investigation of these sources together establishes a timeline for the introduction of services in St. Sebastian's honor in the diocese as a whole. Votive masses for St. Sebastian appear in five Parisian manuscript sources, and two of them, F-Pa 204 and F-Pnm lat. 10506, were used by confraternities (see figure 3.2 for a list of these manuscripts and appendix 4 ✒ for inventories and descriptions of the two confraternity manuscripts).[34] All of the specialized texts of these masses paraphrase the events of his martyrdom and miracles outlined in his vita. The other three liturgical books were used by unidentified Parisian institutions. None of these sources can be firmly dated—all that can be said of them is that most were produced in the second half of the fifteenth century. What is significant here is that sources 53 and 95 in figure 3.2 (two diocesan missals) both have votive masses for St. Sebastian added in a late fifteenth- or early sixteenth-century hand, indicating that he was not part of the original devotional corpus of these volumes. In the two confraternity sources, masses for St. Sebastian appear in the original hand within the body of the manuscript, showing that within some confraternities, he held a prominent place. This is a testament to St. Sebastian's growing popularity in the late fifteenth century, and by 1504, all printed missals for the usage of Paris included a votive Mass for him (figure 3.2 source 100 is an example of one of these printed liturgical books). Brief descriptions of the sources containing masses for St. Sebastian are given here. In appendix 5 ✒, I have identified four different St. Sebastian votive masses in the Parisian

Figure 3.2. Sources and inventories (source numbers conform to appendix 1).

51. F-Pa 204	missal with music notation throughout, produced in the late fifteenth century, with additions from the sixteenth and seventeenth centuries. Used by the Confraternity of the Bourgeois Archers in Paris. See Appendix 4 ⏗ for full inventory.
53. F-Pa 620	diocesan missal for the usage of Paris with music notation throughout, produced in the second half of the fifteenth century for an unidentified Parisian institution. Contains music and texts for the feasts of the Temporale, Sanctorale, and Common of Saints, as well as the kyriale—all according to the usage of Paris. Music and texts for St. Sebastian Mass 2 and the prosas *Pange dulcis francia*, *Militis inuicti laudes*, and *Cessat morbus cessat pestis* are added by a different hand (late fifteenth- or early sixteenth-century) at the end of the book.
71. F-Pnm lat. 859	diocesan missal for the usage of Paris without music notation (with the exception of Prefaces) produced in the second half of the fifteenth century for an unidentified Parisian institution. Contains all texts for the Temporale, Sanctorale, and Common of Saints according to the usage of Paris. Brief text incipits (without music) for the two masses for St. Sebastian appear at the end of the book with the votive masses. Mass 2 appears first, then the rubric "Alia missa sancti Sebastiani" followed by Mass 3.
82. F-Pnm lat. 10506	missal with music notation throughout, produced in the second half of the fifteenth century. Used by the Confraternity of the Barrel Makers in Paris. See Appendix 4 ⏗ for a full inventory.
95. F-Psg 97	diocesan missal for the usage of Paris without music notation (with the exception of Prefaces) produced in the fourteenth century for an unidentified Parisian institution. Contains all texts for the Temporale, Sanctorale, and Common of Saints according to the usage of Paris. There is a partial Mass for St. Sebastian (without offertory and communion, and without music) added at the end of the book in a late fifteenth-century hand.
100. F-Psg OEXV 54²	diocesan printed missal for the usage of Paris without music notation (with the exception of Prefaces, Genealogies, Holy Week, and Purification chants). Contains all texts for the Temporale, Sanctorale, and Common of Saints according to the usage of Paris. Full chant texts for several St. Sebastian masses appear at the end of the book with the votive masses.

books (labeled Masses 1–4), traced the origins of the chant texts and melodies, and compared them all to each other.[35]

St. Sebastian never appeared on his own in the Parisian liturgical calendar, although there was a feast of nine lessons for St. Sebastian and St. Fabian going back well into the thirteenth century.[36] The Mass for this feast day has no connection to the votive masses discussed here, for it draws primarily from the Common of Saints and is unremarkable in terms of its use of specialized music and text.[37] Because of this, masses specifically for St. Sebastian existed only within the popular realm, as he was part of a growing devotional phenomenon focused on saints with healing powers who are represented in diocesan service books from the late fifteenth and early sixteenth centuries. The masses for St. Sebastian in figure 3.2 sources 53, 71, and 95 (all three are diocesan manuscripts from unidentified institutions) appear at the end of these books with the normal round of six votive masses to be said throughout the week, which are given in figure 3.3.

By the sixteenth century, the list of votive masses had expanded in diocesan sources, and this is best illustrated through the table of contents in a missal for the usage of Paris, printed in 1504 by Simon Vostre (figure 3.2, source 100). The list in figure 3.4 shows that all of the martyrs present in F-Pa 204, and the *Missa pro mortalitate subitanea evitanda*, are also included in the printed missal. Additionally, there are several other votive masses that appear, such as a Mass for St. Barbara (see chapter 1). In comparison to these later sources, the overall contents of F-Pa 204 represent a larger phenomenon focused on the increasing attention to plague saints in Parisian confraternity devotions.

It is only in the second half of the fifteenth century that these masses appear in Parisian liturgical books, as evident in the sources listed in figure 3.2, thus indicating that their inclusion may have its roots in the plague epidemics of the 1430s. Within this trend of highlighting plague saints, a close look at the St. Sebastian masses reveals the types of variety found in Parisian popular devotions. The tables in appendix 5 ♰ show numerous textual variations in the St. Sebastian masses among all of the sources, along with the musical and textual relationships these masses have with the diocesan usage of Paris. These relationships are manipulated in various ways to evoke special meanings in the masses for St. Sebastian.

Only one Mass among all of those in appendix 5 ♰ was composed specifically for St. Sebastian with texts referring to his martyrdom, namely Mass 2 in F-Pa 204 (see table 3.1). While the chant texts for Mass 2 appear in four books, only two of those have musical notation: source 51—F-Pa 204;

Figure 3.3. Common votive masses in fifteenth-century Parisian missals.

Mass for the Trinity
Mass for the Angels
Mass for the Holy Cross
Mass for the Holy Spirit
Mass for the Virgin Mary
Mass for the Sick

Figure 3.4. Votive masses listed in the missal for the usage of Paris printed in 1504 (F-Psg OEXV 54²). Table of contents.

St. Genevieve	xxiii.
St. Sebastian	xxiii.
All Saints	xxiiii.
Missa pro mortalitate subitanea evitanda	xxxv.
In the Name of Christ	xxxv.
For Peace	xxvi.
For the Sick	xxvii.
For the Suffering	xxviii.
The Commendation of the Dead	xxxii.
For the Dead	xxxii.
The Compassion of the Virgin	xxxvii.
St. Roche	xxxviii.
St. Claude	xxxviii.
St. Anthony	xxxix.
St. Barbara	xl.
The Five Wounds of the Crucifixion	xlvi.
Raphael the Archangel	xlvii.
Masses for Every Day of the Week	
Sunday. For the Trinity	xvi.
Monday. For the Angels	xvii.

—(continued)

Figure 3.4—*continued*

Tuesday. For the Holy Spirit	xviii.
Wednesday. For the Dead	xxxii.
Thursday. For the Holy Sacrament	xviii.
Friday. For the Holy Cross	xix.
Saturday. For the Commemoration of the Virgin.	xix.

and source 53—the diocesan missal F-Pa 620 (see figure 3.2). The far-right column in table 3.1 compares the text and music in sources 51 and 53. All of the other missals in figure 3.2 draw from the Common of Saints for their material, but those masses prove to be less prevalent when they are compared to each other. Table 3.2 is a comparison of all of the chant texts in the sources in figure 3.2 together and shows that the chants for Mass 2, which are each highlighted with an asterisk, became the most widespread in the diocese of Paris.[38]

References to St. Sebastian's suffering, and the imagery of the arrow, are all found in Mass 2 more so than in any of the other masses in appendix 5 ⌁. The anonymous composer of this Mass drew on a varied set of textual and musical devices to associate St. Sebastian with other important religious figures and contexts. These create an intricate web of meaning drawn from hagiography and historical events meant to establish and validate St. Sebastian locally. In the following sections, I explore these implications in detail before going on to describe their importance to the Confraternity of the Bourgeois Archers.

Textual and Melodic Imagery

Every single one of the Mass proper chants calls upon St. Sebastian directly for protection in some way, and sometimes with urgency. Such specialized texts were a new development in Parisian votive masses of the fifteenth century (see introduction). The offertory discussed at the outset of this chapter provides a good example of such personal invocations. It also refers to the belief in St. Sebastian's power to deflect God's anger, through the words "born in the sight of God in order that he might avert for us God's anger." Most of the chant texts linger on St. Sebastian in the field, a symbol of his

Table 3.1. St. Sebastian votive Mass 2 in F-Pa 204, fol. 25v-27v (also found in F-Pa 620, F-Pnm lat. 859, and F-Psg 97). Numbers in the top row refer to the source numbers in figure 3.2.

Chant	Text	51	53	71	95	Connection to diocesan usage of Paris (Temporale, Sanctorale, Common of Saints); and music compared in F-Pa 204 and F-Pa 620
Introit	*Egregie martir sebastiane*	X	X	X	X	Text – none Music – none Comparison of F-Pa 204 and F-Pa 620 text – same Comparison of F-Pa 204 and F-Pa 620 music – same, but with melodic variation
Gradual	*O sebastiane christi athleta*	X	X	X	X	Text – none Music – none Comparison of F-Pa 204 and F-Pa 620 text – same Comparison of F-Pa 204 and F-Pa 620 music – not the same
Gradual Verse	*O sebastiane christi martir*	X	X	X	X	Text – none Music – none Comparison of F-Pa 204 and F-Pa 620 text – same Comparison of F-Pa 204 and F-Pa 620 music – not the same
Alleluia Verse	*O sancte sebastiane imploramus*	X			X	Text – none Music – *Felix corona francie* (Feast of St. Louis IX)
	O sancte sebastiane militie		X			Text – none Music – *Pater sancte ludovice* (Feast of St. Louis IX)

—*(continued)*

Table 3.1—*continued*

Chant	Text	51	53	71	95	Connection to diocesan usage of Paris (Temporale, Sanctorale, Common of Saints); and music compared in F-Pa 204 and F-Pa 620
	O sancte sebastiane			X		Text – none No music in source
Prosa	*Pange dulcis francia*	X	X			Text – none Music – *Mane prima sabbati* (Feria 2 after Easter)
	Adest dies			X	X	Only text in these two sources.
	Militis inuicti laudes	X	X			Text – none Music – *Victime paschali laudes* (Easter Sunday in F-Pnm lat. 1112)
	Cessat morbus cessat pestis		X			This prosa is tacked on to the end of *Adest dies* in F-Pa 204 Mass 1 (see appendix 5 ⏏ table 7), with no indication of it being a separate piece. The musical structure is indeed completely different from that of *Adest dies*. In F-Pa 620 it appears directly after *Militis inuicti laudes*, and it is clear it is a separate piece. The text, *Cessat morbus cessat pestis*, is identical to a tract in F-Pa 204 for St. Roche, with the words "Sancte Roche," substituted "Sancte martyr."

—(*continued*)

Table 3.1—*concluded*

Chant	Text	51	53	71	95	Connection to diocesan usage of Paris (Temporale, Sanctorale, Common of Saints); and music compared in F-Pa 204 and F-Pa 620
Tract	*Beatus es tu egregie*				X	No music in source
	Beatus es tu egregie		X			Text – none Music – *Qui seminant* (Feast of St. Agatha; Feast of Sts. Fabian and Sebastian)
Offertory	*Martir egregie decus*	X	X	X		Text – none Music – none Comparison of F-Pa 204 and F-Pa 620 text – same Comparison of F-Pa 204 and F-Pa 620 music – same, but with melodic variation
Communion	*Beatus es et bene*	X	X	X		Text – none Music – none Comparison of F-Pa 204 and F-Pa 620 text – same Comparison of F-Pa 204 and F-Pa 620 music – same
	Beatus es et bene	X				Text – none Music – none Comparison of F-Pa 204 and F-Pa 620 text – same Comparison of F-Pa 204 and F-Pa 620 music – not the same

Table 3.2. Comparison of all the Parisian sources together along with those from Amiens and Soissons (which are source numbers 34 and 99 in appendix 1). Sources 51 and 82 are liturgical books used by confraternities (see figure 3.2).

Chant	Text	34	51	53	71	82	95	99	100
Introit	*Letabitur iustus in domino*		X			X	X		
	Egregie martir sebastiane*	X	X	X	X		X		X
	Protexisti		X			X			X
Psalm	*Exaudi deus orationem*		X		X	X	X		X
	Ora pro nobis	X		X	X				X
Gradual	*Posuisti domine*		X			X	X		
	O sebastiane christi athleta*	X	X	X	X		X		X
	Alleluia				X				
Gradual Verse	*Desiderium*		X			X	X		
	O sebastiane christi martir*	X	X	X	X		X		
	O sancte sebastiane christi martir				X				X
Alleluia Verse	*Letabitur*		X			X			
	O sancte sebastiane*				X				
	O sancte sebastiane imploramus*	X	X				X		
	O sancte sebastiane militie*			X					X
	Sancte sebastiane tu dulcedo	X							

—(continued)

Table 3.2—*continued*

Chant	Text	34	51	53	71	82	95	99	100
	Surrexit dominus				X				
	Christus resurgens		X						
	In die resurrectionis		X						X
	Non vos relinquam		X						X
	Veni sancte spiritus		X						X
	Beatus vir							X	
Prosa	*Mirabilis deus*					X		X	
	*Pange dulcis francia**	X	X	X					
	*Militis inuicti laudes**		X	X	X				
	*Adest dies**		X		X	X			
	*Cessat morbus cessat pestis**		X	X					X
	Athleta sebastianus					X			
Tract	*Beatus vir qui timet*		X						
	Desiderium					X		X	X
	*Beatus es tu egregie**			X	X				
	Nobilis prosapia	X							
Offertory	*Gloria et honore*		X			X		X	X
	*Martir egregie**	X	X	X	X				
	Posuisti				X				

—(*continued*)

Table 3.2—*concluded*

Chant	Text	34	51	53	71	82	95	99	100
	Confitebuntur		X						X
Communion	*Posuisti domine*					X			
	Beatus es*	X	X	X	X				X
	Ego sum		X		X				
	Qui vult venire		X						
	Multitudo							X	X
	Letabitur								X

Table 3.3. Text of St. Sebastian Mass 2 (according to F-Pa 204).

Chant	Latin	English
Introit	Egregie martir sebastiane princeps ac propagator sanctissimorum preceptorum ecce nomen tuum in libro vite celestis ascriptum est et memoria letuum non derelinquetur in secula	Illustrious martyr Sebastian, prince and propagator of the order of the Blessed Sacrament, this your name has been written in the book of celestial life and your memory will not be neglected in the future.
Psalm	Ora pro nobis beate martir sebastiane: ut digni.	Pray for us, blessed martyr Sebastian.
Gradual	O sebastiane christi athleta gloriose qui pro christo reliquisti terrene milicie principatum et suscepisti magnum supplicium intercedas pro nobis ad dominum.	O Sebastian, Christ's glorious champion, who for Christ relinquished your earthly military command and received great suffering, intercede for us unto the Lord.
Verse	O sebastiane christi martir egregie cuius meritis tota lumbardia fuit liberate a mortifera peste libera no sab ipsa et a maligno hoste.	O Sebastian, Christ's illustrious martyr, by whose merits all of Lombardy was freed from the deadly plague, free us from that very thing and from the malicious enemy.

—*(continued)*

Table 3.3—*concluded*

Chant	Latin	English
Alleluia verse	O sancte sebastiane imploramus tibi mane tuum clemens auxilium ut possimus obtinere per te pestis mortifere apud ihesum remedium	O holy Sebastian, we beg you early in the morning for your merciful help, that through you we might be able to obtain a remedy for the deadly pestilence in the presence of Jesus.
Prosa	Pange dulcis francia martiris preconia mediolanensium. Gaudeat suessio in regali gremio tantum claudens precium........	Sing, sweet Francia, the praises of the Milanese martyr. Let Soissons rejoice, enclosing so great a reward in its royal bosom.....
Offertory	Martir egregie decus milicie athleta fidei ora natum dei ut avertat a nobis indignationem suam. Martir suffragia effunde pia. Ut epydeimia non sit noxia. In hac patria aut in alia. Que subsidia poscit tua. Audi talia tu preconia. Hic precepia dantur premia miles eya nobis. Alleluya.	Illustrious martyr, glory of the soldiery, athlete of faith, born in the sight of God in order that he might avert for us God's anger. Martyr who piously poured out judgments so that the epidemic may not be harmful. In this fatherland and in others which request your help. Hear [your] praises. And with pious prayer may rewards be given. Quick, soldier, help us. Alleluya.
Communion	Beatus es et bene tibi erit egregie martir sebastiane quia cum sanctis gaudebis et cum angelis exultabis in eternum. Alleluya. Alleluya.	Blessed and good are you illustrious martyr Sebastian. For you will rejoice with the Saints and exult with the angels for eternity. Alleluya alleluya.

Figure 3.5. St. Sebastian at the Column in US-ELmsu MS 2 fol. [178]v. Image reproduced courtesy of Michigan State University Libraries, Special Collections, East Lansing, Michigan.

torture and ability to protect against the plague. Others, such as the gradual verse, refer to St. Sebastian's protection of the Lombards of Pavia. The texts and translations of the full Mass are given in table 3.3.[39]

St. Sebastian's suffering for others made him Christlike in the eyes of the medieval laity, which was an important association that added to his healing power and legitimacy. This is promoted visually in Books of Hours, panel paintings, and other works of art throughout western Europe. Louise Marshall demonstrates that St. Sebastian is often depicted against a column in a pose that was well known at the time, modeled on the crucifixion (Christ at the Column). It became so popular that Albrecht Dürer uses it as the subject of his 1500 print entitled "St. Sebastian at the Column."[40] This crucifixion image circulated widely in the fifteenth and sixteenth centuries, and St. Sebastian is shown in this pose pierced with arrows in French Books of Hours and more broadly in other manuscripts of the time period. Figure 3.5 shows an historiated initial from a fifteenth-century Book of Hours from northern France (likely Paris), with St. Sebastian at the Column.[41] All saints were meant to be viewed by believers as Christlike, but this was not always portrayed in their iconography. Here, it is visually implied that St. Sebastian suffered similarly to Christ.

The association of St. Sebastian with Christ is also referenced aurally in the Mass through contrafacta constructed with prosa melodies from Christological feasts of the church year. Table 3.4 shows that many of the prosas for St. Sebastian found in confraternity manuscripts (F-Pa 204 and F-Pnm lat. 10506) and in diocesan sources containing music and text for Mass 2 (such as F-Pa 620) were constructed with melodies from the Easter season.[42]

The most prevalent of these is the tune *Mane prima sabbati*, or "Early in the morning on the Sabbath," sung on the Tuesday after Easter, with a text referring to Mary Magdalene and Christ's Resurrection. Table 3.4 shows that this is the source melody for the prosas *Pange dulcis francia* and *Adest dies*. The melody was used with contrafacta as early as the thirteenth century in Paris, and Margot Fassler demonstrates how new texts set to it drew connections between Christ and other saints.[43]

As was the case with the prosas for St. Nicholas and St. Catherine in chapter 2, the texts for St. Sebastian draw upon many of his miracles and the events of his martyrdom. There is, for example, a very detailed account of his martyrdom that recounts the same events as those found in the *Golden Legend* discussed previously, in verses 15a–20b of the prosa *Adest dies*, presented in table 3.5.[44]

It is apparent that at least some of the references to St. Sebastian's suffering in the chant texts are further established through melodic associations with Christ's suffering in the votive masses. The textual and melodic pairings in the prosas discussed above, combined with the iconographic tradition relating his attempted martyrdom to the crucifixion of Christ, sets St. Sebastian apart from the other patron saints in this study. Here, he is portrayed as a double martyr who suffered similarly to the Son of God.

Geographical References in the Liturgy

Lineage and place both play an important part in devotions to St. Sebastian, and this mirrors a trend in other types of religiously driven popular practices, all of which manifest themselves in different ways for different audiences. For noble audiences in particular, Christ's lineage from David is important, for

Table 3.4. Prosa texts and source melodies in F-Pa 204, F-Pa 620, and F-Pnm lat. 10506.

Prosa text	F-Pa 204	F-Pa 620	F-Pnm lat. 10506	Connection to diocesan usage of Paris
Adest dies	X			Text – None Music – *Mane prima sabbati* (prosa for Feria 2 after Easter)
Cessat morbus cessat pestis	X	X		Text – None Music – None
Pange dulcis francia	X	X		Text – None Music – *Mane prima sabbati* (Feria 2 after Easter)
Militis inuicti laudes	X	X		Text – None Music – *Victime paschali laudes* (Easter Sunday in F-Pnm lat. 1112)
Mirabilis deus			X	Feast of Sts. Sebastian and Fabian (January 20)
Athleta sebastianus			X	None

rulers traditionally ascended to the throne based on hereditary line. David is portrayed in medieval courtly literature as a loyal personality, the original great knight who followed his descendant, Christ. Inherent in this body of literature is the idea that one followed Christ as a knight would follow his lord, which sent the message that Christianity was a "noble service."[45] The emphasis on Christ's lineage is portrayed in the liturgy through the singing of the genealogies at Christmas and Epiphany, which traces his ancestral line from Abraham. Although the audience is different for trade confraternity liturgies, noble lineage as it relates to a geographical area and a sense of belonging to a specific place was still important, as it forged a sense of French identity. Saints were integral in this construction.[46]

In northern French confraternity liturgies for St. Sebastian, geographical references were used to transform him into a local protector. Like David, he too is referred to as a "chevalier" in French vernacular texts of the fourteenth

Table 3.5. *Adest dies* (verses 15a–20b).

Verse	Latin	English
15a	Carnifices ad stipitem Palam sacratum militem Ligaverunt atrociter	The executioners bound the consecrated soldier cruelly and publicly to the stake
15b	Nequissima sentential; Nam pro salute regia Deum rogabat iugiter.	By the most wicked sentence; he was asking God continually for the well-being of the emperor.
16a	Tunc nequitiae ministri Iussu impii magistri Arcus aptant velocius	Then the ministers of wickedness, at the command of their impious master, prepare their bows swiftly,
16b	Et sanctam reddunt consutum Sagittis atque hirsutum Ut est spinis ericius.	And make the saint into a patchwork of arrows, bristling with them as a hedgehog is bristling with spines.
17a	Tunc recedunt, quia credunt Fatue Ipsum morti traditum.	Then they withdraw, because they believe foolishly that he has been delivered over to death.
17b	Venientis et videntis Viduae Palpitantem spiritum	He is taken down, a trembling spirit, by the kindness of the widow who comes and sees,
18a	Deponitur officio, Et eidem corde pio Exhibuit opera Misericordiae Et pietatis;	And, with a tender heart, she shows works of mercy and pity
18b	Qui in membris et corpore Sanatus brevi tempore Exsecratur scelera Imperatoriae Crudelitatis.	To him who, healed in his limbs and body within a short time, curses the crimes of the imperial cruelty.
19a	Tunc super hippodromium Ibi iuxta palatium Laceratur crudeliter.	Then, at the hippodrome next to the palace, he is cruelly mangled.
19b	Sanctum emisit spiritum, Ad cuius cantant exitum Angeli sancti dulciter.	He gave up his spirit, at whose departure the holy angels sing sweetly.

—*(continued)*

Table 3.5—*concluded*

Verse	Latin	English
20a	In cloaca aduncatur Corpus sacrati militis, Ne ut martyr habeatur Venerandus pro meritis.	The body of the consecrated soldier is hung on a hook in the sewer, lest he be considered a martyr to be venerated for his merits.
20b	Tunc per sanctum admonitae Lucinae, matri inclitae, Diligenter fuit curae Illud dare sepulturae.	Then it was the concern of Lucina, the illustrious matron advised by the saint, to carefully give him burial.

century. His title as "Champion of Christ" (*Christi Athleta*), a designation that was commonly used to describe early Christian military martyrs, is referenced in liturgical texts playing up his noble service.[47] The transformation of St. Sebastian into a local protector manifests itself in references to the resting place of his relics (his place in death) and their perceived healing power. The texts of Mass 2 draw simultaneously on St. Sebastian's healing ability, his Milanese heritage, his role as a soldier, and ties to specific places (see table 3.3). The prosas also exalt St. Sebastian as a healer and dwell on his miracles. These texts are most important for their extensive references to his military role, as well as his ties to France. *Cessat morbus cessat pestis* (table 3.6) is a short prosa that is appended to the end of *Adest dies* in F-Pa 204, where it also appears later in the manuscript as a tract for St. Roche, set to different music. The text gained widespread circulation in printed missals for the usage of Paris in the early sixteenth century and likely was composed somewhere in northern France. *Cessat morbus cessat pestis* is a communal appeal to St. Sebastian for protection, and the text is very direct in nature, with, for example, verse 2a referring to the pestilence "scourging our native land."[48]

While this is a subtle allusion to France, there are several overt references in two of the other prosa texts found in F-Pa 204 and other sources. For instance, the opening verses of *Adest dies* in table 3.7 describe St. Sebastian's lineage, mention his nobility, and outline his ties to France.[49]

Verse 2a specifically notes his nobility, which is a common theme in hagiographical traditions for other saints. Important here are the geographical references. Narbonne became part of the Carolingian Empire in the eighth century, so in that respect Narbonne was part of France, and St. Sebastian's origins there tie him to the realm.[50]

The clearest references to France with regard to St. Sebastian are through the prosa text *Pange dulcis francia*. The full text of the prosa is given in

Table 3.6. *Cessat morbus cessat pestis.*

Verse	Latin	English
1a	Cessat morbus, cessat pestis Altari aedificato.	Sickness ceases, pestilence ceases when the altar has been built.
1b	Sancte martyr, Christi testis, Pro nobis Deum orato,	Holy martyr, witness of Christ, beseech God for us,
2a	Ut cesset epidemia, Qua flagellatur patria,	That the epidemic which is scourging our native land might cease,
2b	Et cum misericordia Currat Dei sententia,	And that the will of God might hasten with mercy,
3a	Finitaque miseria Huius labentis saeculi	And that when the misery of this perishing world is finished,
3b	Tecum simus in gloria; Dicamus Amen singuli.	We might be with you in glory: let every one of us say Amen.

appendix 5 ❧, but the verses that refer to Francia and Gaul, noble lineage, and double martyrdom are given here in table 3.8.[51]

The opening lines of this prosa refer to the city of Soissons, located north of Paris in Picardy, the great reward it holds, and its royal connections. Geographical ties like this are more common in prosa texts for local saints, therefore one in honor of St. Sebastian appears to reflect an effort to bind him to this location.[52] *Pange dulcis francia* celebrates the translation of a portion of St. Sebastian's relics from Rome to the Benedictine abbey of St. Médard at Soissons in the ninth century, which had deep political meaning at the time, but also in later centuries. This was done in 826 under the direction of Charlemagne's grandson, Lothair, whose acquisition of holy relics figured in his claim to the legacy of imperial Rome as Holy Roman Emperor. All of this took place during a time when the Frankish dynasty became increasingly fragmented and Lothair and his brothers disputed over the throne.[53] St. Sebastian was politically significant, for already in the sixth century he had been declared by Pope Gregory the Great to be Rome's third patron saint, after Peter and Paul. Since they were gifts of the pontificate, the translation of St. Sebastian's relics functioned as a political alliance between Rome and the Frankish empire. When relics were freely given, they remained the property of the donor, but the saint's healing power travelled with the objects, thereby providing protection for both the donor and the recipient.

Table 3.7. *Adest dies* (verses 1a–4a).

Verse	Latin	English
1a	Adest dies celebris Sebastiani, crebris Intendamus laudibus,	The famous day of Sebastian is here; let us exert ourselves in abundant praises.
1b	Qui contemptis idolis Bonae puer indolis Claruit virtutibus.	Despising idols, child of good character, he was illuminated with virtues.
2a	Nobilis prosapiae Narbonensis patriae Sanctum Sebastianum	Of noble lineage, of the native land of Narbonne,
2b	Transtulit emerita Militia et vita Clara Mediolanum.	His military service and illustrious life conveyed holy Sebastian to Milan.
3a	Christianum militem, Christi sequens tramitem, Militari	He concealed a Christian soldier, following the path of Christ,
3b	Tegebat sub chlamyde, Pugnae vacans fervide Saeculari.	Under a military cloak, free from the fiery battle of the world.
4a	Hic in regis curia Praefuit industria Ceteris proceribus,	At the royal court, he led the other nobles in diligence,

In this respect, the translation of St. Sebastian's relics to Gaul established loyalty between the two domains.[54]

The placement of St. Sebastian's relics at Soissons was the first step in a process of refashioning him as a Frankish martyr. In addition to the alliance with Rome that St. Sebastian's relics established, the city of Soissons held a special place in France for a number of other reasons, again having to do with lineage and nobility. In the sixth century it was the residence of Chlothair I, who was the son of the first king of the Franks, Clovis I. Clovis was the first to unite the Frankish kingdom and also the first of the Frankish kings to convert to Christianity, under the urging of St. Genevieve.[55] As a royal coronation site of great importance to the Franks, Soissons was strategically chosen for deposit of the relics, for it was there that Clovis had defeated the last Roman ruler in Gaul in 486, thus marking the beginning of the Frankish

Table 3.8. *Pange dulcis francia* (select verses).

Verse	Latin	English
1a	Pange, dulcis Francia, Martyris praeconia Mediolanensium;	Celebrate, sweet Francia, the praises of the martyr of the Milanese;
1b	Gaudeat Suessio In regali gremio Tantum claudens pretium.	Let Soissons rejoice, enclosing such a treasure in its royal bosom.
7a	Ut triumphi duplet sortem, Pilis hirtus differt mortem, Donec resumptis viribus Christo mactatur fustibus.	So that he might double the fortune of his triumph, bristling with spears, he postpones death, until, with his strength recovered, he is sacrificed with clubs for Christ.
7b	Unco pendens in cloaca Scrobe sursum ab opaca Fertur herilis victima, Quo sancta iussit anima.	Hanging by a hook in the sewer, the noble victim is brought up from the dark ditch to the place where the holy soul commanded.
8a	Sic accinctus in agone Militavit spe coronae, Iam in pacis regione Discinctus post proelia.	Thus girded in his struggle, he waged war in the hope of a crown, now ungirded in the country of peace after the battle.
8b	Sancti ducis interventu, Cuius risit in adventu, Victrix vivat cum obtentu Regni Dei Gallia,	By the intervention of the holy commander, at whose arrival she smiled, may Gaul live victorious with the possession of the kingdom of God,
9	Iugi fruens Gloria.	Enjoying continual glory.

Merovingian dynasty. Later, in 752 at the same location, Pepin the Short (the father of Charlemagne) was crowned first ruler of the Carolingians. In light of this, acquiring the relics of a Roman martyr like St. Sebastian, and placing them within one of the Franks' most sacred institutions, had significant political implications for Lothair's claims to the throne.[56] Soissons continued to be important for devotions to St. Sebastian in later centuries, for in the twelfth century, and perhaps before, the feast of the Arrival of St. Sebastian was celebrated in the city on December 9.[57] The commemoration of this event continued into the sixteenth century, as a printed missal for the usage of the diocese produced in 1509 includes it in the calendar at the rank of three lessons.[58]

The text of *Pange dulcis francia* draws on the history of the Frankish kingdom and the translation of St. Sebastian's relics, but it only starts to appear in liturgical books in the late fifteenth and early sixteenth centuries, showing that it was likely a newer composition. The earliest datable sources containing the prosa are all books printed in Paris for other northern French dioceses. For instance, there is a printed missal for the usage of Reims, produced in 1491, followed by another printed liturgical book for the same diocese produced in 1513.[59] The prosa also appears in a missal for the usage of Amiens, printed in Paris in 1529 by Jean Petit (see appendix 1, source 34). While it is included in several printed sources, the only Parisian books to contain the prosa are manuscripts. It appears copied at the end of the fifteenth century diocesan manuscript F-Pa 620 (see figure 3.2, source 53) and was certainly added by a later hand in the confraternity manuscript F-Pa 204 with the following rubric: "De Sancto Sebastiano. Prosa. 1535." Its origins are unclear, and although it praises Soissons, none of the surviving liturgical books from that city contain it. Nevertheless, its appearance in other northern French liturgical books indicates that the praise for Soissons could be related directly to the city's popularity as a pilgrimage site.

As a result of the translation of St. Sebastian's relics, Soissons became a major place of pilgrimage in times of sickness, as it was believed that his relics had special healing powers. The importance of Soissons is discussed by Abbot Gilles Li Muisis of Tournai, who says the following in his chronicle of 1350: "While the pestilence raged in France, pilgrims of both sexes and every social class also poured from all parts of France into the monastery of St. Médard at Soissons, where the body of that martyr St. Sebastian was said to lie. But when the disaster came to an end, the pilgrimage and devotion ended too."[60] As the plague took hold every several decades throughout the fourteenth and fifteenth centuries, with each recurrence pilgrims voyaged to St. Médard to pray for aid.

Soissons was not the only place in northern France to house St. Sebastian's relics, for at some point in the fourteenth century, a portion of them were translated from St. Médard to the abbey of St. Victor in Paris.[61] The bishop, Foulques de Chanac, issued a decree on November 18, 1348, granting an indulgence of forty days to all who came to St. Victor to pray at the altar erected in St. Sebastian's honor. This indulgence was also honored at other institutions in possession of his relics.[62] There are no special instructions for a Mass, Office, or procession for St. Sebastian in liturgical books from St.

Victor, but in January, the feast of Fabian and Sebastian was celebrated at the highest rank of duplex at this institution, as opposed to all other Parisian churches where this was a lower ranking feast of nine lessons.[63]

Royal Imagery

It is clear that St. Sebastian's popularity grew in northern France during the fourteenth century, and that by the late fifteenth century there were a number of specialized chant texts composed in his honor that refer to France. The focus of these texts is not on Paris, where he was particularly popular in confraternities and other lay contexts, but Soissons, where his relics were held. St. Sebastian's ties to France are also presented musically, through the use of contrafacta. Most of the chants for Votive Mass 2 have no musical or textual concordances and were likely composed specifically for it, although there are a few notable exceptions. Example 3.1 shows that in F-Pa 204, the alleluia verse text *O sancte sebastiane imploramus* is a contrafactum created with the tune of *Felix corona francie*, which has the following text: "O blessed French crown, Louis, in your mighty works, whose crown of glory shines in the heavens."[64] This was one of four different alleluia verses in the diocesan usage of Paris performed on the feast of St. Louis.

Here, there is an effort to associate St. Sebastian with King Louis IX of France, who was canonized in the late thirteenth century. As established in chapter 2, the technique of contrafactum was widely employed by composers who wrote new masses for confraternities in order to establish ties to other saints and feasts in the church calendar. The example above shows numerous variants, but the version in F-Pa 204 is indeed based on the alleluia verse for St. Louis in diocesan manuscripts from Paris. The only other source to transmit full music and text for Mass 2 is the Parisian diocesan missal F-Pa 620 (see figure 3.2, source 53). The Mass is almost identical but contains a different alleluia verse text, *O sancte sebastiane militie*. Example 3.2 shows this to be a contrafactum of another alleluia verse for St. Louis, *Pater sancte ludovice*, "Holy father Louis, pour out your prayers to God in turn: release the guilty from the net of sins and from punishment."[65] *O sancte sebastiane militie* is the textual variation of these two contrafacta that became the most widespread, as it was disseminated in printed books for the usage of Paris and other dioceses. Like the other contrafactum, this chant also varies a bit from its model in the diocesan usage.

Example 3.1. Alleluia *O sancte sebastiane imploramus* (F-Pa 204)/*Felix corona francie* (US-BAw 302).

Example 3.2. Alleluia *O sancte sebastiane militie* (F-Pa 620)/*Pater sancte ludovice* (US-BAw 302).

Here are two examples of different alleluia verses for St. Sebastian that are both based on chants for St. Louis. As was the case with the alleluia verses in chapter 2, the similarities and differences in the opening alleluia statement carry on through the whole chant, into the verse section.[66] This indicates a trend that may have had its roots in confraternity devotions, through its appearance in F-Pa 204, and was then later copied into the end of diocesan manuscripts like F-Pa 620 with other votive masses. The connection between the two saints likely has to do with the role of St. Louis as a French saint, as well as his perceived healing ability. Cecilia Gaposchkin describes how descent from Louis IX was commonly emphasized by the Valois kings as legitimizing their dynasty and royal authority. His canonization reaffirmed Capetian dynastic notions of holy lineage in relation to Christ, and most importantly, it laid the ground for St. Louis to become a symbol of French identity.[67] Louis IX was seen as the defender of the Catholic faith and the most Christian king—a model to all those after him. Within Mass 2, the sonic invocation of St. Louis in the alleluia verses with textual references to Soissons as a royal outpost in the prosa (which is set to a melody from the Resurrection) work together to send the message that St. Sebastian, as a Champion of Christ, is a protector of the French realm through his resting place on sacred Frankish ground.[68]

St. Sebastian's perceived healing attributes are evident in the chant texts, but St. Louis was also thought to have restorative powers. King Louis IX of France was heralded in life for his good works, and many images in French prayer books show him with the sick, or burying the dead. In the late thirteenth century, as a result of his canonization, both Geoffroy de Beaulieu and Guillaume de Chartres composed vitae outlining his life and miracles.[69] There were other collections of miracles produced in the early fourteenth century, in particular, the Life and Miracles of St. Louis written in 1303 by Guillaume de St. Pathus. This was based on an inquest between 1282–83, in which 330 witnesses were interviewed who described sixty-three of the miracles he performed after his death. Those who were questioned were mostly Parisians of all walks of life. Sharon Farmer has shown that St. Louis was, from that point on, a saint who lived in popular consciousness in France as a healer and protector of the poor.[70]

More generally, starting in the fifth century with Clovis, all French kings were thought to have curative abilities, especially against scrofula, which was cited among the miracles performed by St. Louis. Scrofula bore similar physical characteristics to the plague, such as the swelling of glands in the neck causing bulbous growths. Figure 3.6 depicts St. Louis touching a man afflicted with the disease. The perceived power of French kings to heal this ailment led it to be called the "King's Evil," which was healed by what was known as the "King's Touch."[71]

The importance of St. Louis to France continued throughout the fifteenth and sixteenth centuries, as he became the patron saint of several Parisian trade confraternities.[72] Furthermore, the Ste. Chapelle stood as a constant reminder of Louis IX and his legacy. As shown in chapter 2, this institution held services that were open to the public, so it also played an important role in the devotional fabric of the city. If one approaches the alleluia verses in Mass 2, as well as the prosas, from the perspective of a composer, those for the Easter season, such as *Mane prima sabbati*, would have been well known to him. The two alleluia verses for St. Louis are found in Parisian diocesan sources with the proper chants for his feast day, so it would not have been difficult for the composer to find them. Their use in masses for St. Sebastian

Figure 3.6. Louis IX curing scrofula in GB-Lbl MS Royal 16 G VI, fol. 424v. Image reproduced courtesy of The British Library. © The British Library Board.

indicate a deliberate attempt to associate the two healers—St. Sebastian and St. Louis—with each other.

Movement, Place, and the Larger Context of F-Pa 204

Healing, protection, and connection to place are all themes in Mass 2, and this imagery was meant to bolster a sense of community among members of the Confraternity of the Bourgeois Archers as protectors of the city. The confraternity's devotions to St. Sebastian can be placed within their larger context in two main ways: by viewing them in relation to the masses in F-Pa 204 for other locally venerated saints; and putting them in dialogue with local uses of movement and place. When the masses and extra sequences in F-Pa 204 for St. Anthony, St. Roche, and St. Genevieve are taken into account along with those for St. Sebastian, similar patterns emerge in the use of melody and text—particularly in the reuse of sequence melodies from Easter—again showing conventions in the construction of confraternity liturgies. For instance, the prosa *Mane prima sabbati* is set with a different text, *Virtutes paschales*, for St. Genevieve. Likewise, *Victime paschali laudes* is set with a text for St. Anthony, *Anthonius humilis*.

Some of the chant texts for other saints in F-Pa 204 function as prayers addressed directly to St. Anthony, St. Genevieve, and St. Roche, just as they did for St. Sebastian. This is most evident in the alleluia verses. For example, *Anthoni pastor* is a prayer to St. Anthony to extinguish the heat of the fire (a reference to St. Anthony's Fire).

> Anthony, illustrious shepherd, who restores those who are tormented,
> heals and destroys sicknesses, quenches the heat of fire:
> loyal father, pray to the Lord for us miserable ones.[73]

The alleluia *Ora pro nobis* for St. Genevieve makes a more general plea to her but does refer to her ability to produce numerous miracles:

> Pray for us miserable ones, holy virgin Genevieve, now rejoicing in the heavens,
> resplendent with countless miracles by divine power.[74]

And finally, *O beate confessor sancte roche* is a prayer for deliverance from the plague:

> O blessed confessor St. Roche, how great are your merits in the sight of God, by

which we believe we are able to be set free from the sickness of the epidemic and to be granted temperate weather.[75]

These texts are reminiscent of prayers to saints in Books of Hours, showing their close ties to popular devotional literature.

The influence of confraternities on the creation of new liturgies and the movement of popular devotions into diocesan contexts is shown here, as it was in chapters 1 and 2. Like the masses for St. Sebastian, those for St. Anthony and St. Roche appear only as votive masses in Parisian sources, either at the end of printed liturgical books or written as later additions by hand at the end of missals. Their regular incorporation into printed missals indicates their acceptance as votive masses in the diocese as a whole. As was the case for St. Catherine and St. Nicholas discussed in chapter 2, a Mass for St. Genevieve does appear in the diocesan usage on her feast day (January 3). I showed in that chapter how devotions to these two widely revered saints in the diocese of Paris were modified and carefully crafted for confraternities. In similar fashion here, the votive Mass for St. Genevieve in F-Pa 204 contains very specialized texts that have no connection to the one performed on her feast day. By the early sixteenth century, she becomes a common inclusion with other votive masses appearing in printed Parisian missals.[76] The creation of specialized texts is typical of new votive masses in the fifteenth century. Moreover, the methods of composition employed here are also very similar to those used for composing votive masses in other confraternity settings. Rather than composing completely new melodies and texts, contrafacta are created using chants from the Easter season, and chant melodies used on other feast days are embellished melodically.

Movement and place are inherent in the composition of votive masses for St. Sebastian. The translation of a portion of his relics first from Rome to St. Médard in Soissons, and then later to St. Victor on the outskirts of Paris, provides a road map for the dissemination of devotions to him, as well as perceived protection from the plague in these areas. It shows an effort on behalf of the laity to protect themselves in the face of uncertainty.[77] References to St. Sebastian's healing properties abound in the prosa texts, but his role as a healer takes a more prominent place in the Mass proper texts, where they make direct reference to his restorative powers in Lombardy. Among the many references and pleas for protection, the gradual verse in table 3.3 refers to the popular legend of his protection of the Lombards of Pavia from plague: "O Sebastian, Christ's illustrious martyr, by whose merits all of Lombardia was freed from the deadly plague, free us from that very thing and from the malicious enemy." The physical movement of his relics is intertwined with the spiritual movement of the saint's healing power related to the presence of these objects in specific places.

Through devotions to St. Sebastian, whether privately at home or publicly in the presence of his relics, the laity would procure divine protection against the plague. Although the Confraternity of the Bourgeois Archers worshipped together, public gatherings during plague outbreaks were rightly viewed as health risks. For this reason, in the late sixteenth century, people under quarantine in Milan were advised to engage in private devotions in their homes and thus take part in what Remi Chiu describes as "imaginative attendance" in religious services.[78] While it is easier to assess public records of devotions, especially processions, private devotions in the home were also an important part of religious practices.

There is an extensive body of literature produced in the fifteenth century that was meant to take people on spiritual, or virtual, pilgrimage journeys, which differed from the pilgrim guides that provided practical information for those embarking on a physical journey. These served as spiritual guidebooks with stories that drew on the senses of the reader, meant to help them emotionally and actively participate in such a spiritual journey, drawing on the supplicant's emotional imagination.[79] The creation of this type of devotional literature implies that religious devotions could take place anywhere, either publicly and physically through processions and travel, or in private settings.

Movement and relic translation are at the root of devotions to St. Sebastian, and as a consequence, there is an effort in liturgical texts to call upon him as a regional protector. While the Translatio narratives discussed in chapter 2 were devoted to the power of the saint's relics, and in particular, contact relics like healing oils, the St. Sebastian liturgy in northern France focuses on his relics being tied to specific locations. Texts pointing to certain cities and institutions in France and historical Gallo Roman provinces, and the use of melody to associate him with St. Louis, show efforts to refashion St. Sebastian as a French saint.

Constructions of St. Sebastian as a local saint and healer first gained widespread popularity through Jacobus de Voragine's *Golden Legend*, but the use of this text by both lay audiences and ecclesiastical figures sheds important light on the circulation of popular beliefs and miracles. Although it was by no means the only source of stories concerning the lives of the saints, the impact of the *Golden Legend* on popular devotional practices and its importance for the liturgy has been a theme throughout the first few chapters of the present study.[80] Its influence in ecclesiastical circles is evident in the 1348 indulgence granted by Foulques de Chanac. The bishop specifically referred to the *Golden Legend* and the power of St. Sebastian's relics in Pavia as the reason for granting this indulgence for prayers at the altar at St. Victor.[81] This is an example of how local legends, through repetition and inclusion in written sources, gain a type of authority, thus making it possible for votive masses having their roots in popular devotional practices among the laity to eventually gain acceptance by the diocese.

In addition to the symbolic movement of St. Sebastian's healing ability and efforts to fashion him as a protector of the French realm, liturgical practices in his honor took hold in northern France through actual physical movement and proximity of individuals. There are no names of the members of the Confraternity of the Bourgeois Archers in F-Pa 204, and there are no existing statutes outlining their regular meetings. Furthermore, there are no indications of who composed the music in this book, or who carried out the confraternity's services. Nevertheless, its contents show a clear affinity both for plague saints and for those who were thought to be local Parisian protectors, which may reflect the status of the confraternity members as protectors of the city. On a very basic level, contact between members from different trades who served in the citizen's guard happened within this confraternity, as they were all artisans associated with different businesses throughout the city. In addition to being members of this confraternity, these men also belonged to their respective trade guilds, which would have been at least partly responsible for the spread of different devotional practices.

St. Sebastian took on an official and public role in Paris starting in April of 1515, when King Francis I ordered general processions around the city, the first of which was in celebration of peace with Henry VIII and Charles V. These were led by a statue of the Virgin Mary and an image of St. Sebastian, implying special protective power.[82] The monarchy and its religious protectors were put on public display in these processions for all inhabitants of the city.[83] This is the ultimate solidification of St. Sebastian as a local protector. Music likely played an important part in such processions. It is tempting to think that the inclusion of the prosa *Pange dulcis francia*, with its text lauding Soissons and Gaul copied into F-Pa 204 in 1535, was a result of its popularity in these contexts.

Ultimately, devotions to St. Sebastian, which emerged and grew in the course of the fifteenth century, became recognized by all inhabitants of Paris by the sixteenth. The distinct royal imagery in the newly constructed St. Sebastian liturgy was meant for popular consumption by the laity. As shown in previous chapters, the role of the confraternity in general was to give a sense of belonging through membership, and provide a feeling of corporate unity and power. Liturgical practices reinforced the prominence of the community.[84] While there are political overtones here, the unique liturgical practices emerging within these contexts reinvented historical narratives to unite communities at a time when such constructions gained traction in France, leading to a growing sense of national pride. The theme throughout is protection, and that was the primary function of the Confraternity of the Bourgeois Archers—to protect the trade quarters of the city of Paris. The liturgy for St. Sebastian shows how this was used privately to bond the community and celebrate their civic role.

Chapter Four

Compositional Practice, Networks, and the Dissemination of the Mass Ordinary in Confraternity Sources

Holy, Holy, Holy, Lord God of Sabaoth, *you who were present on Mount Thabor and shone more brightly than the sun*, Heaven and earth are full of your glory, *Because on that day you mercifully appeared to your disciples, whom you have nourished.* Hosanna in the highest. Blessed is he that comes in the name of the Lord *to redeem the sins of the world, to whom we pray in supplication.* Hosanna in the highest.[1]

The opening of the text above is easily recognizable as that of the Sanctus, which is sung year-round as part of the Mass ordinary. The added words in italics are a trope text that was included with the chant in B-Tc A 58, a manuscript used by the Confraternity of the Transfiguration in Tournai. This troped Sanctus is known as the Sanctus "Vineux;" it alludes to the metamorphosis of Christ, commonly known as his Transfiguration, on Mount Thabor before the disciples Peter, James, and John. Although the Transfiguration was long celebrated as a feast in the Eastern Church, it only became officially recognized in the Western Church in 1457 (celebrated on August 6). It was not a common theme in popular devotions among the laity before the early decades of the fifteenth century but was celebrated in clerical circles like the Confraternity of the Transfiguration before 1457. This organization consisted exclusively of priests and chaplains who held benefices at the Tournai cathedral.[2]

The Sanctus "Vineux" is a good example of a work appearing in a number of sources that could illustrate personal connections between confraternities, ecclesiastical communities, and composers. The original melody is written in cantus fractus and also appears as the tenor of two polyphonic settings—one by Guillaume Du Fay and one by his presumed teacher, Richard de Locqueville—in the manuscript I-Bc Q 15. In this source, the word "Vineux" appears after an inscription just before the polyphonic setting by Locqueville: "Sanctus vineux secundum Locqueville." It is also indicated with the name "Vineux" in several manuscripts where it appears in cantus fractus, implying that "Vineux" applies specifically to the monophonic tenor.[3] This chant is included not only in B-Tc A 58 but also in F-Pa 204 for the Confraternity of the Bourgeois Archers (see chapter 3) showing its place in confraternity worship at both Tournai and Paris.

In this chapter I explore the role of confraternities as patrons of new Mass ordinary compositions. I show how looking at these compositions in relationship to networks of confraternities and composers provides fresh insight into the transmission of new polyphonic and monophonic works. Investigating the extent to which these organizations promoted the creation of liturgical settings in cantus fractus and polyphony is central to this study. The liturgical books from Tournai for the Confraternity of the Transfiguration and the Confraternity of the Notaries contain cantus fractus and polyphonic settings of the Mass ordinary that appear in a much larger international network of manuscript sources than those discussed in previous chapters. Portions of these works eventually found their way into a variety of books in northern France and further south in Avignon and Italy. Among these settings are the cantus fractus versions of the Sanctus and Agnus Dei "Vineux" and certain movements of the polyphonic Tournai Mass appearing in the manuscript B-Tc A 27 for the Confraternity of the Notaries. The creation and dissemination of these pieces is intertwined with the movement of confraternity members and musicians between the dioceses of Tournai and Cambrai, as well as further south to the city of Paris.

In the first three chapters of this book, I have shown how confraternity liturgies, and in particular Mass propers and offices, were constructed based on texts drawn from popular devotional literature and hagiography. The trope above shows that Mass ordinary chants were also embellished textually to reflect the specific spiritual focus of these communities, a practice that was already well established in diocesan and monastic liturgical usages by the late Middle Ages.[4] The primary mode of composition for the Mass ordinary, however, was musical rather than textual. In the course of the fourteenth through sixteenth centuries, confraternities and other communities devised new and innovative methods of composition as a way of embellishing the music of the Mass ordinary in honor of their patron saints, the Virgin Mary, or other devotions to which they adhered. Adorning the church service with polyphony and chants in cantus fractus was an important way that confraternities would praise their patron saints or gain the favor of the Virgin Mary, Christ, or God himself. It was also a marker of the affluence of the community, for money was necessary to procure musicians with the skills to perform this type of music, and commission composers to write it.

The Organization of Mass Ordinary Cycles in Confraternity Sources

The way that Mass ordinaries were organized in confraternity worship differed from their use in the diocese. My investigation reveals that certain melodies were employed more widely in confraternities than they were in the cathedrals and parishes of Paris and Tournai. Untangling the similarities and differences in how Mass ordinary chants were used in confraternal and diocesan contexts is important for our understanding of how these liturgical items would come to serve as the basis for new compositions. At the most basic level, Mass ordinaries were organized into cycles in books known as kyriales, with extensive rubrics describing the feast days on which they should be performed. This method of arrangement developed in the thirteenth century and was initiated by scribes.[5] In the course of the fourteenth and fifteenth centuries, the way these chants were grouped in kyriales differed by diocese, thereby making them important liturgical markers that can serve to distinguish liturgical usage in specific geographical areas. The manipulation of Mass ordinary cycles in confraternity sources shows how these chants were used in praise of the community's object of adoration (saints, the Virgin Mary, or a divine cult). Confraternity books show a process of drawing from the kyriales of their home dioceses while at the same time including chant melodies from other places, showing again that these organizations had some freedom in the construction of their own devotions. More importantly, it shows the contact these communities may have had with others outside of the diocese.

Mass ordinary chants in confraternity sources differ in two main ways from those found in diocesan liturgical books: through their organization and placement in cycles and through their use of non-diocesan chants. The Mass ordinaries in confraternity books from Paris and Tournai are not strictly organized into cycles. It is evident that more often than not, these chants are integrated with the Mass propers in the position where they would be sung during the service, as can be seen in appendices 2 and 4 ❧.[6] In others, like B-Tc A 12 and B-Tc A 27 for the Confraternity of the Notaries, there are Mass ordinaries that appear integrated with the Mass propers as well as those organized into cycles.

In some ways, the cycles used in the confraternity books are associated with the same masses that they would be according to the diocesan kyriale, but a closer comparison shows that some chants appear to have circulated only in private devotional contexts. Appendix 5 ❧ records all of the Mass Ordinary chants in the confraternity books from Paris and Tournai, their relationships to each other, and to other published sources for the kyriale in northern France.[7] Parisian confraternities provide a good case study for the connections between the diocesan kyriale and those used in private devotional communities, since there are so many existing sources that preserve the kyriale from the diocese of Paris. On the other hand, there are no manuscripts or printed sources that contain the diocesan kyriale of Tournai for comparison with confraternity sources in that city. All that exists as vestiges of diocesan practice for the Mass ordinary from Tournai are those chants found in the confraternity manuscripts B-Tc A 12, B-Tc A 13, B-Tc A 27, and B-Tc A 58.

Since the confraternity sources contain some of the main masses of the church year in addition to masses for their patron saints, one would expect to find only the cycles of Mass ordinary material associated with high-ranking feast days.[8] Appendix 5 ❧ shows this to be the case in some of the sources, with most of the available information coming from Paris. The most common Mass ordinary chants used in the Parisian confraternity manuscripts are the Kyrie, Gloria, Sanctus, and Agnus Dei that correspond to Parisian Cycle 2, which in the diocesan usage is the one to be used on Easter, Pentecost, and all feast days carrying the rank of "annual" and duplex in the manuscripts.[9] Other Mass ordinaries in the Parisian sources also show that they have the same function as they did in the diocesan usage. F-Pm 464, for example, includes a Requiem Mass with a Kyrie melody that corresponds to Cycle 15 for the same Mass in the diocesan usage.[10]

F-Pnm lat. 10506 for the Confraternity of the Barrel Makers (see appendix 4 ⁀) contains the most Mass ordinary chants of all the Parisian confraternity sources and illustrates well the types of similarities and differences in these books when they are compared to diocesan kyriales. The distribution of the chants in this manuscript is related to the diocesan usage in some ways. One of many examples is the Gloria from Parisian Cycle 5, which appears in F-Pnm lat. 10506 just after the feast of St. John at the Latin Gate.[11] This makes sense given the rubric for the melody in the diocesan sources indicating that Cycle 5 was used for feasts of the Evangelists.

The rest of the Mass ordinary chants in F-Pnm lat. 10506 are assigned in a rather unconventional way when one considers the instructional rubrics in the diocesan manuscripts. For example, in the midst of the votive Mass for the Commemoration of the Virgin, there is a Kyrie and a Gloria that correspond to Parisian Cycle 9, to be used on Saturdays when the Office of the Virgin is sung.[12] The Sanctus and Agnus Dei for this Mass are drawn from different cycles in the diocesan kyriale. The Sanctus corresponds to Cycle 2 and the Agnus Dei corresponds to Cycle 5.[13] While the connection of Cycle 5 with feasts of the Evangelists was discussed above, this cycle was used in the diocese on a host of other feast days, although there is nothing in the diocesan rubric to indicate that it was in any way associated with the votive Mass for the Commemoration of the Virgin.[14] This cycle is one of several examples of such reassignments in F-Pnm lat. 10506.[15]

The Parisian manuscript that contains the most Mass ordinary chants having no connection to the diocesan usage of Paris is F-Pa 204, for the Confraternity of the Bourgeois Archers (see chapter 3 and appendix 4 ⁀). This source contains two Mass ordinary cycles on fols. 19v–23r.[16] Of the two Kyrie melodies, only the first has any similarity to one used in a Parisian diocesan source. The opening formula of this particular melody is similar to that of Cycle 9 in the diocesan kyriale discussed above, but they are clearly two different chants, with the one in F-Pa 204 being notated a third higher (see example 4.1).[17] This Kyrie melody appears in the *Liber Usualis* and is called the Kyrie "De Angelis." It is also found in two other Parisian confraternity manuscripts: F-Pnm lat. 10506, and NL-DHk 76 E 18 for the Confraternity of the Doublet Makers (see chapter 2), showing that the chant was known in other private devotional settings in the city, even if it was not part of the diocesan usage.

The second Kyrie melody in F-Pa 204 has no counterpart in the diocesan usage of Paris, or in any of the other confraternity books from the city (see

Example 4.1. Kyrie (diocesan Cycle 9)

Example 4.2. Second Kyrie in F-Pa 204.

example 4.2). It is, however, found in Tournai in B-Tc A 13 and B-Tc A 27 (both used by the Confraternity of the Notaries).[18]

Although the Kyries in F-Pa 204 only appear in other confraternity sources from Paris and Tournai, the two Gloria melodies on fols. 20r and 21r match Parisian Cycles 4 and 5 respectively, showing some connection to the diocesan usage.[19] The first Sanctus and Agnus Dei chants do not show such ties to diocesan usages, but they are found in Benedictine and Dominican sources from Paris, Douai, and Rheims.[20]

Overall, Parisian confraternities drew from the usage of Paris, but the use of Mass ordinary chants in confraternity manuscripts for certain feasts was sometimes disconnected from the days indicated in the rubrics of the diocesan cycles. There were also some chants from outside the diocese, showing the movement of this repertory. Such occurrences of foreign chants appearing in isolated sources may parallel contact between individuals in different ecclesiastical and compositional circles. I will return to this point later in the chapter.

What do these different Mass ordinary functions mean in the context of confraternity devotions? Reassigning a Mass ordinary chant from the diocese to a different feast day appears to have been acceptable in these communities, but it is worth noting that such a reorganization does not carry the same type of spiritual weight as the use of contrafacta for the Mass proper discussed in the previous three chapters. This is because the Mass ordinary texts remained the same throughout the year, and the assignment of a musical setting to a feast merely implied a certain level of ceremony. This also made the Mass ordinary chants more likely to be those embellished with rhythmic notation and improvised polyphony, which then gave way to entirely new polyphonic compositions. Chants in cantus fractus, such as the Sanctus and Agnus Dei "Vineux" in F-Pa 204 and B-Tc A 58, are examples of this type of embellishment. Their isolated appearance in sources used in different locations shows the types of connections that existed between artistic circles in those places. Tournai is a particularly fruitful city for studying such interactions.

The Confraternity of the Transfiguration at Tournai and Movement between Dioceses

The contents of two manuscripts produced for the Confraternity of the Transfiguration illustrate how practices from outside the diocese of Tournai mixed with those within due to the confraternity's movement between institutions. This is most evident in their use of chants in cantus fractus.[21] B-Tc A 58 is a liturgical book containing chant and polyphony used by the confraternity; B-Tc B 29 is a confraternity register outlining the rules of the organization before 1540, together with its amendments until the end of the seventeenth century (1688).[22] The confraternity was made up of a fixed number of eight priests and chaplains who held benefices at the Tournai cathedral, but they celebrated their private services together at several different institutions in the city.[23] The musical devotions of the Confraternity of the Transfiguration in particular are representative of a process of exchange between the dioceses of Cambrai and Tournai, and quite possibly beyond. Given the musical legacy and proximity of these cities, it is not altogether surprising that certain practices might be shared between Tournai and Cambrai, but to date, few sources have come to light illustrating them.

Viewing B-Tc A 58 in relation to the sources used by the Confraternity of the Notaries discussed in chapter 1 yields information on how confraternity practices traveled within the city of Tournai and in neighboring dioceses. Only recently has it been possible to investigate the music and liturgy of the Confraternity of the Transfiguration in detail, as B-Tc A 58 was thought by some scholars to have perished in the late 1940s.[24] In 2006 the manuscript was returned to the Tournai cathedral archive after sitting for years in a private collection. Since its rediscovery, both Anne-Emmanuelle Ceulemans and Jacques Pycke have done work on the confraternity, its history, and musical devotions.[25] Its recent reappearance makes it possible for the first time to reexamine the manuscript in the present study alongside the notary confraternity manuscripts and those from Paris.

The Confraternity of the Transfiguration sat at the boundary of the dioceses of Cambrai and Tournai, which accounts for some of the liturgical practices present in their surviving liturgical book and confraternity register. This organization was founded in the fifteenth century, before 1445, at the parish church of Mont-Saint-Aubert (also called Mont de la Trinité) in Tournai. The parish was on the east side of the Escaut River, under the jurisdiction of the diocese of Cambrai. At some point between 1530 and 1540, for reasons unknown, the confraternity had moved its services across the river to the Tournai cathedral.[26]

Private devotions to the Transfiguration at Tournai arose some time after the appearance of celebrations of the feast at the cathedral in the thirteenth century, long before it was officially recognized by the Western Church in 1457. These practices were first supported by trade confraternities in the early decades of the fifteenth century.[27] Both Anne-Emmanuelle Ceulemans and Jacques Pycke have pointed out that the contents of B-Tc A 58—especially the text of the sequence, *Thabor superficie*, and the trope text for the Sanctus discussed at the outset of this chapter—indicate connections to the Taborites, a reformist movement promoted in the early fifteenth century by the disciples of Jean Hus, a native of Prague. The Taborites believed that both bread and wine should be administered to the laity during communion, which was seen as heretical doctrine by Catholic authorities. They had their own settlement outside of Prague called Tabor, named after the place of Christ's Transfiguration on Mount Thabor. Adoration of the Transfiguration became important to the followers of this movement, which quickly spread beyond Bohemia and further west to France and the Low Countries. Pierre d'Ailly, bishop of Cambrai, expressed concern about these developments in 1411, as there was a group in Brussels who were followers of Hus, and his ideas were taking root in the area. There are accounts of several individuals from the region of Tournai and Lille who were in Prague around 1418–20. Among them was Gilles Merseult, a native of Tournai, who returned to his hometown to circulate the doctrine there and was ultimately put to death.[28] Nevertheless, the trend spread, and by 1423 Tournai's booming tapestry trade was playing an important role in promoting devotions to the Transfiguration. In that year the tapestry makers established a confraternity under their own banner in honor of the Transfiguration, marking the earliest mention of this practice in private devotions in the city, around twenty years before the clerical confraternity which owned B-Tc A 58 was formed.[29]

Devotions to the Transfiguration then spread beyond the city of Tournai to Cambrai, which is reflected in similarities between the liturgies for that day in the two dioceses.[30]

The Confraternity of the Transfiguration was formed at a time in the middle of the fifteenth century when private devotional fervor for the Transfiguration was at its height in Tournai. The manuscript B-Tc A 58 reflects this through its inclusion of specialized music for the celebration of the eponymous feast (August 6). In addition, the manuscript contains vestiges of the community's celebration of the feasts of St. Aubert Bishop of Cambrai (December 13), and the Holy Trinity. As shown in the inventory in appendix 2, B-Tc A 58 contains several polyphonic settings, all in connection with the feasts of the Transfiguration and the Trinity: an anonymous *Missa Sancta Trinitas* (early sixteenth century), a *Sancta Trinitas* motet by Févin, and an anonymous polyphonic setting of the sequence *Thabor superficie* (late sixteenth century). It also contains four chants in cantus fractus: the sequence *Thabor superficie* (fols. 15r–17v); the offertory *Deus enim omnium* (fol. 18v); the Sanctus "Vineux," with trope *Qui vertice thabor affuisti* (fols. 19v–20v); and the Agnus Dei "Vineux" (fols. 20v–21v).[31]

As I have shown in the previous chapters, the manuscripts that have survived from confraternities are not necessarily representative of these organizations' complete worship practices, and B-Tc A 58 is no exception. These communities often owned many liturgical books, but only a handful have survived. For instance, there are references to music in the confraternity register B-Tc B 29 that do not appear in the liturgical book B-Tc A 58. This is most apparent in the rules for the confraternity from 1540, where there are four items that mention music. Items 2 and 4 refer to a Requiem Mass to be done on the day after the feast of the Transfiguration, for which there is no music or text in B-Tc A 58. In the same items, there is also mention of Vespers and Matins, again, with no music in B-Tc A 58.[32]

The most direct references to the musical practices of this confraternity in the register are Items 5 and 19, both of which refer to communal singing. Item 5 indicates that the members should "dire ung hymne *O nata lux*, versus *Benedictus dominus Deus Israel*, repons *Qui fait mirabilia solus*, avecq la collecte *Deus qui hodierna* [sic]."[33] The texts for the hymn, verse, response, and collect all appear on folios 1r–3r, but there is no music. The word used here is "dire" rather than "chanter," but the hymn *O nata lux* was surely sung. While the previous three items pre-date 1540, Item 19 appears with the new rules of August 7th, 1540 (fol. 9–9v). This rule is in a later hand and indicates that the confraternity members must sing (chanter) an antiphon for the Holy Trinity with a collect after grace is said before dinner, and the *De Profundis* after dinner for the dead confraternity members.[34] There is an antiphon on fol. 24r of B-Tc A 58 with music, *Benedicta sit creatrix et gubernatrix*, followed by a rubric for a collect. It is possible that this was the antiphon sung by the confraternity members, as it is the only antiphon for the Trinity in the two books.[35]

There is a considerable amount of crossover between the confraternity's surviving register and liturgical book, but details that could allow us to construct the complete practices of the confraternity are missing. Since the members of the confraternity were clerics, it is likely that they performed the Mass themselves. No records survive recording their payment of musicians, but polyphony and other forms of musical elaboration clearly played an important role in this confraternity's devotions. It is possible that at least several of the members would have had the music education needed to be able to perform these works (see chapter 1). Overall, B-Tc A 58 shows distinct influences from both Cambrai and Tournai, which is reflective of the connections between the two dioceses. This manifests itself musically in the creation of chants in cantus fractus.

The Role of Confraternities in the Development of a Cantus Fractus Repertory at Tournai: Credo I and the Sanctus and Agnus Dei "Vineux"

While scholars have long recognized that there was a cantus fractus repertory cultivated at the Cambrai cathedral in the early fifteenth century, I show here that this type of composition was also produced at the Tournai cathedral even earlier, starting in the fourteenth century, as a part of confraternity services. This was shaped by links between the two dioceses. At first sight, the musical traditions of the Confraternity of the Notaries and the Confraternity of the Transfiguration appear to have no relationship to each other when the contents of their liturgical books are compared. It is actually a fragment from Cambrai, currently included in a bundle of other fragments, held in Lille at the Archives départementales du Nord (F-Lad 134 no. 12) that establishes a connection between the practices of the two organizations. F-Lad 134 no. 12 contains the monophonic Sanctus "Vineux" in cantus fractus—the same one that is found in both B-Tc A 58 and in F-Pa 204 (see table 4.1 for the sources containing the Sanctus "Vineux").[36] This piece of parchment was used to bind a will at the chapter of Ste. Croix in Cambrai in the seventeenth

Table 4.1. Appearances of the Sanctus "Vineux" in manuscripts.

Source	Monophonic (cantus fractus)	Polyphonic	Trope text *Qui ianuas mortis confregisti*	Trope text *Qui vertice Thabor affuisti*	Composer
B-Tc A 58	X			X	unknown
F-Lad 134 no.12	X		X		unknown
I-Bc Q 15		X	X		2 settings: 1 by Du Fay and 1 by Loqueville
I-AO 15	X		X		unknown
F-Dm 2837		X	X		unknown
F-Pa 204	X		X		unknown

century, implying its origin there. The fragment also contains the Credo I in cantus fractus, for which nearly identical versions are found in two of the notary manuscripts, B-Tc A 12 and B-Tc A 27, as well as a fourteenth-century missal and ritual used in a chapel at the Tournai cathedral that is currently held at the Bibliothèque de la Ville in Tournai (B-Tv 13) (see figure 4.1).[37] This fragment illustrates how the Transfiguration and Notary confraternity sources represent two overlapping traditions, a link between the old and the new, in the performance of the Mass ordinary at the Tournai cathedral. The Sanctus "Vineux" and Credo I reveal different dissemination patterns between the dioceses of Cambrai and Tournai, showing connections to other practices as far south as Paris, Dijon, and Avignon.

Several important themes intersect in F-Lad 134 no. 12. First and foremost, this fragment has played a role in studies of Du Fay's biography and compositional practice, as he wrote a polyphonic setting of the Sanctus

Figure 4.1. Appearances of the Credo I in cantus fractus in manuscript sources from Cambrai and Tournai.

> F-Lad 134, no. 12 (Unidentified institution in Cambrai)
>
> B-Tc A 12 (Confraternity of the Notaries at Tournai Cathedral)
>
> B-Tc A 27 (Confraternity of the Notaries at Tournai Cathedral)
>
> B-Tv 13 (Unidentified institution in Tournai)

"Vineux."[38] To date, the fragment has primarily been discussed in this context, although it also establishes a variety of connections to other subjects. For instance, its inclusion of rhythmic chant notation is equally pertinent to the study of hymn settings in cantus fractus and improvised polyphony in manuscripts from Cambrai and Avignon.[39]

Research on the rhythmic Credo I in Italy has revealed that cantus fractus settings like the ones in F-Lad 134 no. 12, B-Tc A 12, B-Tc A 27, and B-Tv 13 are directly tied to local improvised polyphonic traditions in the fourteenth century.[40] These practices are thought to have first appeared in Avignon with northern composers working there in the late thirteenth and early fourteenth centuries, and made their way north to the Low Countries, and south to Italy.[41] This practice was encouraged by Pope John XXII in a papal bull of 1324/5 and continued into the fifteenth century, as Tinctoris repeatedly makes reference to improvised polyphony in his works.[42] Although F-Lad 134 no. 12 has never been discussed in relation to improvised polyphony, its use of mensural notation places it within that tradition. When the Tournai manuscripts and the Cambrai fragment are examined together with other sources from the region, a broader dissemination pattern of chant settings in cantus fractus emerges in relation to specific contexts. I will first discuss the Sanctus and Agnus Dei "Vineux," and then Credo I.

The sources for the Sanctus and Agnus Dei "Vineux" and the differences between their monophonic and polyphonic settings give insight into the creation of the two works and their original context. Table 4.1 shows that monophonic and polyphonic settings of the Sanctus "Vineux" appear in a total of six manuscripts. Table 4.2 reveals that the Agnus Dei "Vineux" is found in fewer sources.

As mentioned at the outset of this chapter, one of the manuscripts in tables 4.1 and 4.2 contains two polyphonic versions of the Sanctus "Vineux," and it also happens to be the largest international compilation of polyphonic works completed between 1420–35 in the Veneto—I-Bc Q 15. This

Table 4.2. Appearances of the Agnus Dei "Vineux" in manuscripts.

Source number	Monophonic (cantus fractus)	Polyphonic	Trope text *Patris filius eterni*	Composer
B-Tc A 58	X			Unknown
I-Bc Q 15		X		Du Fay
F-Dm 2837		X	X	Unknown
F-Pa 204	X		X	Unknown

manuscript includes some pieces composed for the Council of Constance (1414–18), which ended the Western Schism of 1378, and it is an important source for the works of Guillaume Du Fay.[43] The polyphonic Sanctus and Agnus Dei "Vineux" by Du Fay, and the polyphonic Sanctus "Vineux" by Richard Loqueville, are among the earliest and most well-known compositions to use the "Vineux" melody as a tenor. In addition, there is an anonymous three-voice setting of both chants appearing in a fragment from Dijon (F-Dm 2837), dated around 1420.[44]

The monophonic Sanctus "Vineux" circulated in cantus fractus in a total of four sources, two of which indicate that it was connected to religious services that were a result of the schism (see table 4.1). F-Lad 134 no. 12 dates from after 1393, as it includes chants that formed part of the Mass for the Unity of the Church, which was instituted in that year by Pope Clement VII of Avignon.[45] In addition to F-Lad 134 no. 12, the Sanctus also appears in I-AO 15, which is an anthology of polyphonic music from the early fifteenth century that was assembled from elements copied between 1430–46 in Bologna, the Basel-Strasbourg area, and in Innsbruck. Like I-Bc Q 15, I-AO 15 also contains some pieces performed in chapels connected to the Council of Constance (1414–18); in addition, it includes repertoire associated with the Council of Basel (1431–49).[46] Although it is first and foremost a source for polyphonic compositions, I-AO 15 contains only a monophonic version of the Sanctus "Vineux" chant in cantus fractus. The remaining two manuscripts to include the monophonic Sanctus and Agnus Dei "Vineux" are the confraternity sources from Paris and Tournai: B-Tc A 58 and F-Pa 204.

The Sanctus "Vineux" and its use of rhythmic notation are almost identical in the monophonic and polyphonic (as a tenor) versions in all six manuscripts, thereby showing that it was transmitted in a stable manner.[47]

Example 4.3. The Agnus Dei "Vineux."

Transcriptions of the Sanctus from several different sources have been published, allowing for easy comparison.[48] The Agnus Dei, however, is different. The tenors of the two polyphonic settings—one by Du Fay in I-Bc Q 15 and the anonymous version in F-Dm 2837 (see table 4.2)—are both contrafacta created from the Sanctus melody.[49]

The two existing monophonic versions of the Agnus Dei each show different traditions, both of which diverge significantly from each other, from the two polyphonic settings (I-Bc Q 15 and F-Dm 2837), and from the original Sanctus "Vineux" tenor and monophonic versions. These two chants are found only in the confraternity manuscripts B-Tc A 58 and F-Pa 204 (see table 4.2). Brief opening incipits of the Agnus Dei "Vineux" in the two confraternity manuscripts and the tenors of the two polyphonic settings appear in example 4.3. The monophonic versions of the Sanctus "Vineux" along with the tenors of the polyphonic settings are transcribed in example 4.4.[50] Example 4.3 shows that there are similarities between the Agnus Dei versions, as the first articulation of the Agnus Dei is the same in both confraternity manuscripts. Additionally, the contour adheres to the Sanctus model given in example 4.4, establishing it as a source for the initial melodic incipit.

Example 4.3 shows that the version of the Agnus Dei in F-Pa 204 is identical to the one in B-Tc A 58 for the first four notes, but beyond that the two chants are completely different to the end, having little to do with the Sanctus melody in example 4.4. The readings of both Agnus Dei chants may be considered local variants, one from Paris (F-Pa 204), and one from Tournai (B-Tc A 58). One feature that makes a difference is the trope, *Patris filius eterni*, which appears in F-Pa 204 but not in B-Tc A 58. Since more notes are needed to accommodate the lengthy trope text, the Agnus Dei in F-Pa 204 proves considerably longer than the one in B-Tc A 58.[51]

Example 4.4. The Sanctus "Vineux."

When all of the versions of the Sanctus and Agnus Dei "Vineux" are taken into account, we can ascertain that the Sanctus had a more stable transmission than the Agnus Dei, and that the latter was likely a tradition that came out of the polyphonic settings in the fifteenth century. The two melodies have strong connections to polyphonic works from Cambrai, due to their association with composers such as Du Fay and Locqueville, but beyond that they appear to have taken on a life of their own.[52]

It is significant that the Sanctus and Agnus Dei "Vineux" chants circulated in sources not used in the main sanctuaries of cathedrals and parishes, appearing only in manuscript compilations of polyphony and confraternity books. Andrew Kirkman points out that in the course of the fifteenth century, great attention in popular piety was placed on the elevation of the host, which lined up temporally with the Sanctus and Agnus Dei of the Mass.[53] This could account for the prevalence of the Sanctus and Agnus Dei "Vineux" in confraternity devotions and may suggest the specific use of cantus fractus settings as adornments in these sections.

The Credo I in cantus fractus that appears in F-Lad 134 no. 12 shows a different connection between Cambrai and Tournai, one that dates from the fourteenth century. This rhythmicized Credo also appears in the two manuscripts for the Confraternity of the Notaries at the Tournai cathedral mentioned previously (B-Tc A 12 and B-Tc A 27), as well as in B-Tv 13, which is a fourteenth century manuscript used in one of the chapels at the cathedral (see appendix 2). Credo I is one of the earliest settings of the Credo and appears in a number of sources in cantus fractus at the end of the fifteenth century and throughout the sixteenth century. Its popularity is linked to the appearance of Credo IV in cantus fractus around the same time, as well as to an established performance practice in Italy that is thought to have its roots in Avignon and other French territories.[54] While most of the mensurally notated settings of Credo I are found in manuscripts and printed books from the late fifteenth century on, it was not unknown for them to appear in fourteenth-century sources, such as those discussed here.

Example 4.5 highlights certain portions of the beginning of Credo I in the Tournai and Cambrai sources. These versions are all nearly identical, with the exception of the cadences on "et terre" and "invisibilium."[55] In those instances, F-Lad 134 no. 12 and B-Tv 13 are concordant, while the two confraternity manuscripts reveal a slightly different practice. Variants like this are found throughout the chant melody.

Overall, these are very small differences, but what is important here is that evidence of this repertory exists only in confraternity manuscripts and those used in side chapels at the Tournai cathedral.[56] A browse through Miazga's Credo index and other published versions of the fourteenth-century Credo I from different geographical areas shows that various settings of the chant in Italy and elsewhere are similar to this one, making it difficult to ascertain how the rhythmic Credo I came to Cambrai and Tournai.[57] Furthermore, this chant is not written in rhythmic notation in any of the other sources from Tournai, implying that it was used primarily in private devotions there. Aside from F-Lad 134 no. 12, the rhythmicized Credo I is not found in any other Cambrai sources from the fourteenth or fifteenth century, showing that it was not commonly used in that diocese either. Additionally, there is no clear indication of its origins or its intended liturgical use in Cambrai other than the fact that it appears with the Mass for the Unity of the Church and the Sanctus "Vineux." As I stated above for Tournai, this version of the Credo is also linked only to private worship contexts at Cambrai.

The Sanctus and Agnus Dei "Vineux" and the Credo I show different dissemination trajectories, but the larger number of sources containing the "Vineux" settings permit us to say more about how it travelled. The Sanctus and Agnus Dei "Vineux" likely came to the Tournai cathedral by way of the diocese of Cambrai, since four of the six sources for these two works have

Example 4.5. Credo I in cantus fractus.

some connection to that city and composers active there, strengthening the case for its origin in this area.[58] One possible avenue for the transmission of these chants is the contact that the bishops of Cambrai had with Tournai in their role in reunification after the Avignon schism. There were special processions at Cambrai for the unity of the Church, and given the appearance of these two works in manuscripts associated with church council repertories, the Sanctus and Agnus Dei "Vineux" may be specifically tied to these events.[59] Other sources, such as F-Pa 204 and F-Dm 2837, show that these two chants also circulated in locations further south. On the other hand, the Credo I in cantus fractus appears primarily in manuscripts from the Tournai cathedral, which pre-date the sources for the Sanctus and Agnus Dei "Vineux." Such a setting could be tied to an improvised polyphonic practice using the rhythmic plainsong in the tenor, as it was in Italy and other locations. Vestiges of an improvised polyphonic practice at the cathedral appear in other chants in the notary confraternity manuscripts. For instance, B-Tc A 27 contains the sequence *Mittit ad virginem* in cantus fractus, which is clearly documented to have been part of an improvised polyphonic tradition there (see chapter 2).[60]

There are many connections between Cambrai and Tournai, but it is not easy to establish exactly how some of these cantus fractus settings made their way further south to Paris and Dijon. Geographical connections are more easily established through other works in the Tournai confraternity manuscripts. There is also circumstantial evidence of a network of composers that connects Cambrai and Tournai to Paris, a point to which I will return at the end of this chapter.

Interactions of Chant and Polyphony for the Mass Ordinary at the Tournai Cathedral

New Mass ordinary chants and polyphonic canons in B-Tc A 27 were created on the basis of preexisting chant melodies starting in the fourteenth century, much in the same way that the monophonic Agnus Dei "Vineux" was composed from the Sanctus in the early fifteenth. The inventories in appendix 2 show that both rhythmic and non-rhythmic settings of plainchant circulated alongside polyphonic settings of the Mass ordinary in the manuscripts for both confraternities in Tournai.[61] The relationship between chant and polyphony in the notary manuscripts in the first half of the fourteenth century in particular sheds new light on the compositional processes employed in the creation of cantus fractus settings later, in the early part of the fifteenth century. The melodies used as the basis for modelling in these works point us to different geographical locations, as we shall see in the following section on the Tournai Mass.

One of these earlier settings from the late fourteenth or early fifteenth century is a Kyrie in cantus fractus appearing in B-Tc A 12 (example 4.6).[62] This chant is a new composition, possibly based on another Kyrie. Example 4.7 shows that, although transposed, it is very similar in its opening to the Kyrie in *LU* Cycle X. The composer of this work employs a similar method of melodic modelling as those who wrote the new chants for the masses and offices discussed in chapters 2 and 3. Catherine Bradley, in her discussion of polyphonic works from Paris in the twelfth and thirteenth centuries, points out that composers manipulated chant melodies in polyphonic settings.[63] The evidence put forth in the present study shows that this was also the case for plainchant composition several centuries later in northern France.

The use of contrafacta for the Mass ordinary is distinctive because it often involves a cross-reference to other genres. As shown in chapter 3, taking an alleluia verse for St. Louis and creating a new contrafactum for St. Sebastian by adding different texts provides an aural association between the two saints. The genre, however, is still the same—one simply creates another alleluia verse. The Kyrie in cantus fractus discussed above is a type of modeling based on another chant, but again, it is based on another Kyrie melody (so it is not a contrafactum). The genre stays the same. When a composer takes a Mass ordinary chant like the Sanctus "Vineux" and uses it as the basis for an Agnus Dei, the chant then switches genres and becomes an Agnus Dei. The chants are contrafacta in the same sense that some of the Office chants for the Translation of St. Nicholas in chapter 2 were. They use opening thematic

Example 4.6. Kyrie in cantus fractus from B-Tc A 12.

Example 4.7. Kyrie in cantus fractus from B-Tc A 12 compared with *LU* Cycle X.

material going beyond the establishment of a modal formula to provide an aural melodic reference, from which point on they are completely different.

Often overlooked in the Tournai Mass are the monophonic Kyrie in cantus fractus and the Sanctus in cantus fractus with isolated polyphonic sections that were added to the fascicles of B-Tc A 27 with the polyphonic setting (see examples 4.6 and 4.7).[64] These two chants are usually not included in editions of the Tournai Mass, as they are thought to have been extraneous to the cycle.[65] Michael Scott Cuthbert has recently shown that the two works are actually examples of the earliest polyphonic canons, which share compositional features with those found in secular genres in the middle to late fourteenth century. How these melodies are realized in a polyphonic performance has been the subject of a 2019 article by Jason Stoessel and Denis Collins.[66] I argue that in addition, the monophonically notated Kyrie and Sanctus melodies show a process of composition that includes taking widely circulating plainchants as their basis and altering them melodically and rhythmically. The first few notes show similarities to their model and then diverge, reflecting the same compositional approach as that used in the Agnus Dei "Vineux" nearly a century later. Furthermore, the Kyrie and Sanctus appear in the same scribal hand as the Tournai Mass, which I established in chapter 1 and appendix 3. For all of these reasons, I argue that the settings do indeed form part of the Tournai Mass tradition.

The Kyrie and Sanctus were both transcribed in *Polyphonic Music of the Fourteenth Century*, volume 23, and the authors indicate that the Kyrie melody in cantus fractus (example 4.8) is found in the Landwehr-Melnicki index of Kyrie melodies as number 58 (hereafter referred to as Melnicki 58).[67] This is true for the first articulation of the Kyrie eleison, but beyond that the chant is different, being an example of a composition that is inspired by a preexisting melody and then moves beyond it with melodic and rhythmic embellishment through the use of cantus fractus. I have discovered that the original Kyrie melody (Melnicki 58) appears in one other confraternity source from

Example 4.8. Kyrie melody Melnicki 58.

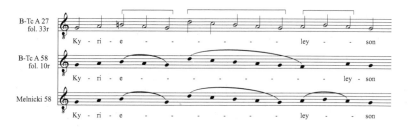

Tournai, for it is also found on fol. 10r of B-Tc A 58, but without rhythm. In addition to this manuscript, it appears in some Parisian books, such as several editions of the *Misse familiares* printed in 1510, 1523, and 1538 (see chapter 5), and the fifteenth-century Ste. Chapelle kyriale (F-Pa 114). These are all later sources, but it is likely that the Kyrie was known in other contexts at the Cathedral of Tournai in the fourteenth century, and documentation of this is now lost. None of these books include the melodic embellishments that occur in the version on the Tournai Mass fascicles in B-Tc A 27, and it is likely that this new setting, which was performed as a canon, came out of an already established tradition of embellishing plainchant in confraternity devotions at the cathedral.

My analysis of the Sanctus reveals that it also shows some similarity to a preexisting melody. The first five-note articulation of the word "Sanctus" matches another Kyrie in the Landwehr-Melnicki catalogue (Melnicki 169) exactly, and from that point on it is completely different (see Example 4.9). Similar to the Melnicki 58 melody discussed above, it is possible that at one time, the Melnicki 169 Kyrie may have been known in other contexts at the cathedral, but the source has not survived. These are two further examples of new Mass ordinary compositions being created at the Tournai cathedral using other plainchant settings as models starting in the middle of the four-teenth century.

The composers' various choices of chants used for modelling usually involved melodies that were not widely known in the geographical area but were used uniquely in confraternity devotions or other private settings. When we take a closer look at the Mass ordinaries in the confraternity man-uscripts from Tournai, we see possible connections to a compositional net-work pointing south to Paris, as I discuss in the following section.

Example 4.9. Kyrie melody Melnicki 169.

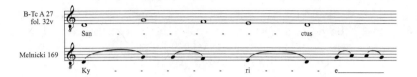

The Tournai Mass

So far, this chapter has focused on the monophonic repertory in the Tournai confraternity manuscripts, but the polyphonic works in these sources go hand in hand with those settings and are part of the same tradition. The polyphonic Tournai Mass in B-Tc A 27 is the one piece in this study that has been cause for the most speculation over the past two hundred years, because it is the first existing polyphonic Mass ordinary organized into a complete cycle. It is also thought to have been the inspiration for the *Messe de Notre Dame* by Guillaume de Machaut.[68] Such polyphonic works marked the beginning of a trend that would continue for centuries—composing all five movements of the Mass ordinary as a thematically organized unit. Among the more important questions surrounding the Tournai Mass are: What connection does the Tournai Mass have to Tournai? Who wrote it and where? For what occasion was it written? Is it connected to a larger network? Nothing has come to light that can answer these questions definitively, but I will speculate anew on the possible patterns of transmission based on the fact that the setting appears in a confraternity manuscript—a context in which it has not been viewed for nearly a century. To understand the place of this Mass cycle in confraternity practices at Tournai, it is necessary to discuss previous scholarship about it in relation to recent discoveries.

Taking as a point of departure the first of the three broad questions posed above, the connection of this Mass to Tournai can be established first and foremost through codicological evidence. The earliest mention of the Tournai Mass in modern scholarship was made by Edmund de Coussemaker, who briefly refers to it as part of the devotions of the Confraternity of the Notaries, and in fact, in late nineteenth- and early twentieth-century French academic literature it is referred to as the "Messe des notaires."[69] At some point in the course of the early twentieth century (around 1920), the connection of B-Tc A 27 to this confraternity fell into obscurity and was not noted by later scholars, as there is no inscription in the manuscript tying it to the organization.[70] My discussion of the scribal hands and contents of the manuscript in chapter 1 showed that B-Tc A 27 was indeed a manuscript used by the confraternity, and it is closely connected to B-Tc A 12 and B-Tc A 13, both of which have internal indicators of their use by the Confraternity of the Notaries. Moreover, Michel Huglo's detailed analysis of the page rulings and structure of B-Tc A 27 also shows that the polyphonic setting was not a later added fascicle to the manuscript; rather, the pages were indeed originally ruled to accommodate the polyphonic setting among the chant contents of the source.[71]

The movements of the Tournai Mass were not all composed at the same time; furthermore, a number of them appear in other manuscripts, and in different notation styles. Table 4.3 shows the concordances for the movements found in other sources, and the types of notation used for each one. The Kyrie, Sanctus, and Agnus Dei are written in thirteenth-century modal notation (Ars Antiqua) and appear uniquely in B-Tc A 27; the Gloria, Credo, and Ite Missa Est motet (*Se grasse/Cum venerint/Ite missa est*) are written in Ars Nova notation and have concordances elsewhere.[72] Some of the sources for the movements known in other locations, like the Codex Las Huelgas and F-Pnm nouv. acq. fr. 23190, have somewhat firm dates, but the others (including B-Tc A 27) do not. This makes it difficult to say in which sources they appeared first. The earliest datable manuscript in table 4.3 is the Codex Las Huelgas, which was produced in the early 1340s.[73]

The most visually prominent feature of the six movements of the Mass is the use of different types of notation, and I propose this has to do with how they arrived in Tournai. The mix of notation styles has been the subject of discussion by several scholars, all of whom try to use it as evidence for when the Mass was compiled. Leo Schrade and Gilbert Reaney give ca. 1330 as the date for the Mass, based on this notational mix.[74] As Irene Guletsky points out, other early fourteenth-century sources contain a combination of these two types of notation, the most notable example being the Roman de Fauvel, but this practice is also found in the Codex Las Huelgas and other manuscripts.[75] Notation, however, is highly variable. Karen Desmond explains that "some motets, extant today only in sources copied in a fully developed Ars Nova notation, were originally conceived in an Ars Antiqua syle of notation like that found in the Roman de Fauvel."[76] She cites the Ite Missa Est motet at the end of the Tournai Mass as an example of one such work based on its similarities to another motet originally written in Ars Antiqua notation, *Se cuers/Rex beatus*.

If we take this mix of polyphonic notation in hand with the different types of chant notation in B-Tc A 12 and B-Tc A 27, which I discussed in chapter 1, the varied styles could simply indicate the preference or skill set of different musicians. An example illustrating this is in B-Tc A 27 on fols. 22v–23r, where there are several Sanctus melodies written in square notation that have been transcribed into Messine notation in the margins, evidently in order to provide clarity for someone more familiar with that style. These types of considerations may also extend to the notation of polyphonic works, as table 4.3 shows that the Credo of the Tournai Mass appears in a total of five sources: in two of these, it is in Ars Antiqua notation; and in the other three it is in Ars Nova. Although the movements of the polyphonic Mass in B-Tc A 27 were written by the same scribe, this individual was not necessarily the one involved in performance of the music; nor do we know if that person had anything to do with the composition of any of the movements. He could have been copying from exemplars given to him that were in different notation styles. Either way, notation does not help much in coming up with a precise date for the different portions of the Mass, but it does give some insight into the preferences of composers, performers, and scribes.

Notable variants occur specifically in the sources for the Credo and Ite Missa Est motet that show how different movements of the Mass were copied and modified in other locations. The most significant of these appear in the Credo, where the Codex Las Huelgas gives only the text in the triplum, while the other voices were possibly to be performed by instruments.[77] This feature of the Las Huelgas version of the Credo, along with its use of thirteenth-century modal notation, has led scholars to believe that it is the oldest of the six Mass ordinary movements. This type of argument is difficult to make, especially given the possible reasons for the variety of different notation styles I discussed above. The Credo is transmitted on its own in all of the sources but B-Tc A 27, showing that it did not circulate as part of a Mass ordinary pair or cycle.[78] Table 4.3 shows that other variations occur in the recently discovered Roman source, which transmits only the triplum, which is transposed down a fifth.[79] The Rome version is reminiscent of the circulation of the monophonic Sanctus and Agnus Dei "Vineux" in different manuscripts outside of its use as a tenor for the Du Fay and Loqueville settings in the fifteenth century. The Ite Missa Est motet, on the other hand, is rather stably transmitted in the manuscripts that include it (see table 4.3), but there is a distinct Picard dialect to the French text in the Tournai version and the Polish fragment that does not appear in the Ivrea manuscript.[80] This could imply northern origins, but it could equally be due to scribal preference or copying from a similar exemplar.

Table 4.3. Concordances for the Tournai Mass movements.

Kyrie	Gloria	Credo	Sanctus	Agnus Dei	Se grasse / Cum venerint / Ite missa est
B-Tc A 27. Ars Antiqua notation.	B-Tc A 27. Ars Nova notation.	B-Tc A 27. Ars Nova notation.	B-Tc A 27. Ars Antiqua notation.	B-Tc A 27. Ars Antiqua notation.	B-Tc A 27. Ars Nova notation.
	CH-HE Codex Chart. 151. Fifteenth-century source with Gloria fragment in the binding. Ars Nova notation.	E-BUlh Codex Las Huelgas. Created in the early 1340s. Ars Antiqua notation. Text appears only in the triplum.			F-Pnm nouv. acq. fr. 23190. Dated 1376. Contains references to the motet in the index, but all that is left are fragments (none of the Ite Missa Est survives, so notation style can't be determined).
	F-CA Inc. B 145. Fourteenth-century fragments from Cambrai. Ars Nova notation.	I-Rsm uncatalogued gradual. Early fourteenth-century (first quarter) gradual from Avignon. The Tournai Credo was a later addition from the second half of the fourteenth century, or early fifteenth century. Ars Nova notation. Only the triplum appears.			I-IV CXV (Ivrea Codex). Fourteenth-century Avignon repertory (1360). Ars Nova notation.

—(continued)

Table 4.3—concluded

Kyrie	Gloria	Credo	Sanctus	Agnus Dei	Se grasse / Cum venerint / Ite missa est
		E-Mn V 21–8. Fourteenth-century Franciscan gradual. Ars Antiqua notation.			PL-WRu AK 1955/KN 195. Fourteenth-century fragments bound into a fifteenth-century Augustinian manuscript from Kłodzko. Ars Nova notation. Contains only the duplum of the motet.
		F-APT Trésor 16 bis (Apt Codex). Choirbook from the Papal residence during the Schism. Mostly fourteenth- century repertoire (some fifteenth-century repertoire). Ars Nova notation.			

The origin and dissemination of the Credo and Ite Missa Est remain unverified, but the appearance of these movements in other sources does show that some parts of the Tournai Mass were widespread and popular, as they are included in large, well-studied repositories of thirteenth and four-teenth-century music—the Apt Codex, the Codex Las Huelgas, and the Ivrea Codex (see table 4.3).[81] That Machaut was likely familiar with the Tournai setting, which others have argued is apparent in the style of the Credo of his Mass, further illustrates the far-reaching influence of this Mass ordinary compilation.[82] The movements that are unica in B-Tc A 27 (Kyrie, Sanctus, and Agnus Dei) are all in modal notation in that source and could indicate that they were local compositions written by someone more familiar with that notation style, but this alone does not allow for an argument concerning their earlier composition.

Musical style as a unifying factor for the Tournai Mass is a theme that has been the source of much debate leading to two predominant viewpoints. Leo Schrade, writing in the 1950s, says the following: "The similarity of the Tenors in the Kyrie, Gloria, Sanctus, and Agnus is, in fact, so great that the Mass of Tournai could well be taken as a cycle musically unified by the ten-ors, were it not for the Credo."[83] Other scholars point out that the Kyrie, Credo, and Sanctus are all written in simultaneous style, while the other three movements are all in motet style, indicating composition over a period of time.[84] The existing evidence seems to point in two different directions. First, as Schrade mentions above, the tenors of four of the movements (Kyrie, Gloria, Sanctus, and Agnus Dei) are somewhat related, but not enough to establish their conception as a unified cycle. The opening statements of the tenor for each of these is similar in contour, but there are not the same types of features based on a model that we saw in chapter 2, or in the monophonic Kyrie and Sanctus copied into the Tournai Mass fascicles in B-Tc A 27, dis-cussed previously.[85] Second, the use of both simultaneous style and motet style, combined with the varied mix of notation, suggests that the move-ments were not all composed by the same person. This is supported by the fact that the Credo, Gloria, and Ite Missa Est clearly have their own histories outside of this cycle, as they are found in other sources. In the end, there is not enough evidence to make an argument for the polyphonic movements being stylistically unified.

We find ourselves on firmer ground when discussing how some of the polyphonic Mass ordinary movements may have ended up in Tournai. One way to determine this is to look at the other contents of B-Tc A 27, in par-ticular the Mass ordinary chants that appear throughout the manuscript,

Example 4.10. Kyrie melody Melnicki 114.

to see if they have concordances elsewhere. One chant especially establishes ties further south to Paris, namely a Kyrie that appears on fol. 34r on the gathering just after the one containing the Tournai Mass (gathering 10, see appendix 3), with the rubric "Item de nostra domina," indicating that it is a chant for the Virgin Mary (see example 4.10). This Kyrie is included in the Landwehr-Melnicki catalogue as number 114 (Melnicki 114), and my study of the Notary Confraternity manuscripts reveals that it appears in them a total of three times: once in B-Tc A 12 and twice in B-Tc A 27 (including the occurrence just after the Tournai Mass mentioned above).[86]

The Melnicki 114 Kyrie melody became very widespread in later centuries and is even included in the *Liber Usualis* (Kyrie 6 from Gregorian Mass XVII for Sundays in Advent), but its absence in other thirteenth- and fourteenth-century sources from areas surrounding Tournai makes it of particular interest that it appears three times in the confraternity manuscripts.[87] This Kyrie was known earlier in Paris, as it is found in a thirteenth-century gradual and sequentiary created around 1242 for use at the Ste. Chapelle (I-BAas Fondo S. Nicola 85).[88] The only other northern source from this time period to contain the chant is a manuscript used at the abbey of Tongerlo in the fourteenth century (B-Br 11396).

Melnicki 114 is related both to the devotions of the Confraternity of the Notaries and to institutions in Paris, which could imply that it and some of the other contents of B-Tc A 27 have origins in the Paris region. For instance, the Ite Missa Est motet for the Tournai Mass is based on the Ite "Joseph" melody, which was known in Paris. This chant was copied into two Notre Dame manuscripts: F-Pnm lat. 1112 (ca. 1225) and F-Pa 110 (fourteenth century), but it appears nowhere in sources from Tournai.[89] Karl Kügle shows that this motet can be directly tied to the French court, as it bears marked musical and textual similarities to another work mentioned earlier in the present chapter in the section on notation, *Se cuers/Rex beatus* from the Roman de Fauvel. *Se cuers/Rex beatus* was composed around 1314 or 1315 by an unnamed musician known as the "Master of the Royal Motets," who was a predecessor of Vitry at the French court in the early fourteenth century.[90]

This setting also at one time appeared in F-Pnm nouv. acq. fr. 23190, which is listed in table 4.3 as one of the sources for the Ite Missa Est motet. One of the characteristics of this composer's style is semibreve-semibreve-minim descending figures, which appear throughout the triplum and tenor of the Ite Missa Est motet of the Tournai Mass.[91]

It is possible that this motet and the Melnicki 114 Kyrie melody came to Tournai through connections the notaries had to Paris. As I showed in chapter 1, notaries in service to the bishop would have been part of his close circle and would have travelled with him to other locations. Notaries were present at all official functions, and due to the interaction of the bishops of Tournai with French, Burgundian, and papal courts (which I will discuss in the following section) they would have come into contact with other individuals in service to these institutions. The discussion of concordances above shows that some of the contents of B-Tc A 27 have connections to repertory at the French court (the Ite Missa Est motet and the Melnicki 114 Kyrie melody), which overlaps in some ways with that of the papal court at Avignon in the fourteenth century as shown in the sources in table 4.3 (the Tournai Mass Credo, and again the Ite Missa Est motet).[92] It is impossible to say with any degree of certainty how this music found its way to Tournai, but the polyphonic works are all products of a courtly clerical culture, which is the same milieu to which the notaries belonged. The three movements of the Tournai Mass that are only found in Tournai—the Kyrie, Sanctus, and Agnus Dei—could easily be local compositions inspired by the three preexisting polyphonic movements that appear in other sources. The use of Ars Antiqua notation for these could be due to personal style preference for that type of notation on the part of the composer. As I showed in chapter 1, there were surely a number of individuals who were capable of writing polyphony, either those employed by the cathedral (including the notaries themselves) or individuals associated with local chambers of rhetoric.[93]

While the full contents of B-Tc A 27 not only allow us to establish ties to other geographical areas, they also permit us to draw more stable conclusions regarding the context for the Tournai Mass. The rubric for the Kyrie melody Melnicki 114 indicates that the chant is for the Virgin Mary, and indeed the Confraternity of the Notaries was devoted to her, as I have established elsewhere.[94] Others have noted the connection of the Tournai Mass to Marian devotions at the Tournai cathedral, most notably Jacques Pycke, who has sought to tie the polyphonic setting to a foundation at the cathedral from May 4, 1349, on which date the bishop of Tournai, Jean des Prés, instituted a Mass for the Virgin Mary "cum nota" to be sung in the main sanctuary.[95]

As I established in chapter 1, the confraternity would have had ready access to the bishop as episcopal notaries in his employ, and he even donated a decorated cloth to the confraternity in the fourteenth century according to the fabric in B-Tc A 12. In an effort to definitively link this polyphonic setting to its original context, Pycke's speculation that the 1349 foundation refers to the first performance of the Tournai Mass has also been cited by other scholars as the occasion for its first performance.[96] It is tempting to relate such a setting to information we already know about a city, especially one with very little existing documentation like Tournai, but there is one important thing to keep in mind. Although the original Kyrie melody and other contents of B-Tc A 27 focus heavily on the Virgin Mary, it does not automatically logically follow that this polyphonic Mass was the one tied to the 1349 foundation. This is especially true in a city like Tournai, the seat of a major bishopric, known to house several famous composers from the fourteenth through sixteenth centuries.[97] The manuscripts used by the notaries feature unique monophonic and polyphonic compositions, so it is clear that the creation of new music was a valued activity in the city as a whole, as well as at the cathedral. The Mass "cum nota" mentioned in the 1349 foundation could have equally been one embellished by improvised polyphony, or a setting that is now lost.

Through this discussion of sources, concordances, and notation, I have sought to recontextualize the polyphonic Tournai Mass by looking at it in relationship to the full contents of B-Tc A 27 and the other liturgical books used by the Confraternity of the Notaries. Handwritten addenda in these manuscripts and in others used by the Confraternity of the Transfiguration show that the chants contained within them were used for centuries, which is proof of their longevity.[98] All of this shows that the creation and performance of both chant and polyphony at the Tournai cathedral was a long-standing part of confraternity devotions at this institution. More importantly, reconsideration of the notary manuscripts in their entirety has opened up new avenues for exploration, and in this case, they point south, to a network of composers working in Paris.

The Movement of Musicians and Networks of Composers

The distinctive plainchant and polyphony in B-Tc A 12, 13, 27, and 58 are all products of a tradition of modeling, either based on preexisting text or music. As shown in chapter 1, confraternities and urban chambers of rhetoric were important places for the creation of works in such a fashion, because they promoted the writing of new music and poetry in cities like Arras and Tournai.[99] The composers of the works in the Tournai confraternity manuscripts may never be accurately identified, but we can be sure that they were part of the clerical culture of poet-composers who functioned as instrumentalists, church choir singers, chaplains, and notaries. They were colleagues and friends, who moved in different overlapping circles. This is the case for both the earlier and later time periods of the present study.[100] These men had many ties to neighboring cities, cathedrals, and courts, and they also had a presence in Paris. Several historians and musicologists have drawn attention to the crossover between courtly and clerical culture, and it is against this backdrop that we must view music composition in confraternities in Tournai during the fourteenth and fifteenth centuries.[101]

There is information about poet-composers working in the vicinity of Tournai in the mid-fourteenth century, right around the time that several of the movements of the Tournai Mass and some of the chants in cantus fractus were created. References to musicians appear in the chronicles of Gilles Li Muisis, who was abbot of the monastery of St. Martin in Tournai. Most notably, in his *Meditations* of 1350 he mentions Philippe de Vitry, Jehan de le Mote, Jehan Campion, Guillaume de Machaut, and Collart Haubiert, lauding their artistic output.[102] Campion and Li Muisis were both based in Tournai, and the other names mentioned above in the chronicles suggests that composers at important courts and ecclesiastical institutions from different cities were also known there.

In addition to the chronicle of Li Muisis, the motet *Appollinis eclipsatur-Zodiacum signis lustrantibus*, found in the Ivrea Codex (also a source for the Ite motet), gives a roster of northern musicians, referring to a "musicorum collegio" in which some of the same composers are mentioned.[103] The list includes Vitry and Johannes de Muris (both of whom were known to have worked in Paris and in Avignon); Guillaume de Machaut; and several composers from Tournai, Douai, Valenciennes, Cambrai, and Arras who ended up working in Avignon, Paris, Cambrai, and Tournai. The motet also references some composers from Soissons and Bruges, such as Pierre de Brugis, who held benefices in Tournai and Liège. It also includes Johannes de Ponte, who was a canon at the Tournai cathedral ca. 1330 and who subsequently moved to Arras and then in 1339 to Thérouanne.[104] The "collegio" here is comprised of musicians from northern centers who all very likely knew each other.[105] Furthermore, Kügle mentions that there are links between Vitry and the composers mentioned in this motet and those responsible for the motet repertory in the Ivrea codex, pointing out that they all worked in administrative positions at the French and ducal courts and at religious institutions that enjoyed royal patronage.[106] It is with this group of poet-composers that sacred and secular compositions meet, just as they represent the overlap between ecclesiastical and courtly circles. While we know they wrote polyphonic secular and sacred compositions, composers associated with this group could have easily also been involved in the composition of plainchant.

The composition of poetry closely parallels music composition in the fourteenth century, especially in the use of preexisting material. One organization that provides fruitful evidence of this is the Goldsmith's confraternity in Paris. This organization promoted the creation of new poetry based on earlier models that had circulated within the confraternity for decades.[107] I have referred to the Tournai Mass and the composition of its various movements as a "tradition." It is possible that in Tournai, there was a similar musical practice of composing plainchant and polyphonic works based on locally known chant melodies (the canonic Kyrie in cantus fractus on the same fascicle as the Tournai Mass, for instance), which ultimately inspired the creation of the three unique movements of the Tournai Mass (Kyrie, Sanctus, and Agnus Dei). Urban *puys* and chambers of rhetoric dedicated to the composition of new music and poetry continued to function well into the late fifteenth and early sixteenth centuries and were responsible for the construction of new liturgical works in nearby cities, such as the Office for the Seven Sorrows of the Virgin Mary in Brussels.[108]

The most detailed information about compositional practice and movement of repertory between Paris and Tournai in relation to the individuals mentioned above exists for the composer Jehan Campion. While he was a chaplain at the Tournai cathedral in 1350, he had much contact with individuals associated with the University of Paris, even though he himself did not hold a degree. Li Muisis and Campion were both part of a group centered around creating music and poetry, which Yolanda Plumley calls "an informal *puy*."[109] This is based on an inscription in F-Pnm lat. 3343, which contains a trouvère poem that was sent to Campion via post from Paris by a notary named Jehan de Savoie. Both Campion and Savoie were associates of Philippe de Vitry, which places them again within the network of musicians discussed here.[110]

In chapter 1, I mentioned Reinhard Strohm's discussion of a "compagnie de le messe Nostre-Dame" (company of the Mass of Our Lady) in Tournai, implying that there was a group of singers who specialized in singing a polyphonic Mass for the Virgin Mary. Jane Hatter has recently explored musician communities in northern France in the fifteenth century, showing that in this same geographical area a century later, singers and composers congregated and took part in activities much like confraternities, but without organizing into such formal communities. These groups were referred to as "companions of music," just like the "compagnie" above. Furthermore, she discusses Rob Wegman's idea that the patron saint of singers was the Virgin Mary, as members of the trade would come together on feasts of the Virgin, much like confraternities would congregate on their patron's feast day.[111] A "compagnie" in Tournai could refer to type of community capable not only of singing but also composing a Mass such as the Tournai Mass (in honor of the Virgin Mary), for these men would have had the proper musical training to do so. It is also feasible that there were a number of such groups of singers and composers in the area. While the extent to which the members of the *puy* above were connected with these loosely organized communities is unclear, exploring such groups could be fertile ground for uncovering a circle of composers in Tournai in the fourteenth century.

While the Tournai Mass comes out of the early Ars Nova and the time of the Avignon popes in the fourteenth century, the Sanctus and Agnus Dei "Vineux" coincided with the end of the Schismatic period in the fifteenth century. The network does not change all that much from before—Paris, Avignon, Cambrai, and Tournai are among the prominent artistic centers of the time. Strohm has indicated that the Schism (1378–1477) isolated churches of Avignonese obedience in France and Spain while strengthening ties between countries of Roman obedience. Clergy moved, and musical clerics received benefices in areas of their own allegiance.[112] Tournai was geographically, dynastically, and ecclesiastically positioned at a crossroads, where musicians and clerics from Burgundian lands (tied to Rome) and French lands (tied to Avignon) met. The city, therefore, was well placed to be a prominent trade and artistic center.

The bishops of Tournai from 1384–1477, although loyal to the French crown, were very politically active in Burgundian territories. They held prominent positions on the Burgundian ducal council, providing contact with that court and its composers. In addition to the presence of two dioceses in the city falling under the jurisdiction of two different political territories (France and Burgundy), two of the diocese of Tournai's most prominent city centers, Ghent and Bruges, were under the control of the Burgundian dukes. Such a strong political presence led to two Tournai bishops, Guillaume Fillastre and his successor Ferry de Clugny, becoming chancellors of the royal Burgundian Order of the Golden Fleece, which was known for its patronage of music.[113]

All of these connections make it likely that composers active at the Burgundian court were also in some ways connected to the Cathedral of Tournai, but we have very few documents from Tournai that give us direct insight into this.[114] There is evidence showing that singers and professional musicians migrated freely and undocumented between neighboring dioceses to cities such as Ghent, Courtrai, Therouanne, Douai, Lille, Tournai, Arras, and Cambrai, and that their employment was rarely permanent.[115] Some of the music in the Tournai confraternity books comes from Cambrai, and such instances of movement imply that it would have been possible for compositions written by composers working at these institutions to travel along similar lines. For example, the fifteenth-century manuscript used by the Confraternity of the Transfiguration illustrates the connections between Cambrai and Tournai, as this confraternity's liturgical practices came from across the ecclesiastical border.

Major events for musical exchange in the early fifteenth century were the Council of Constance (1414–18), which ended the schism, and the Council of Basel (1431–35). As discussed previously, the Sanctus and Agnus Dei "Vineux" may have come out of the context of these councils, as they are both found in I-Bc Q 15, which transmits repertory performed at the Council of Constance. B-Tc A 58 contains vestiges of these traditions from the early to mid-fifteenth century, as well as a later French court repertory from the early sixteenth century, with a motet by Févin. The confraternity could have come by these later works in any number of ways through the movement of new musicians to the cathedral from other areas. The Févin motet could also have been copied from a printed book of motets, which would have been available for sale in a city like Tournai.[116] The practices of this confraternity over nearly two centuries show the effects of movement between the dioceses of Cambrai, Tournai, and possibly beyond.

Conclusion

This chapter began with a discussion of Mass ordinary chants and how they were organized and adorned to reflect the devotional focus of different confraternities. In the course of this exploration, we saw how chants in cantus fractus and polyphonic settings were related to an established tradition of embellishing the liturgy at the Tournai cathedral. The contents of the Tournai manuscripts draw us into a network of cleric-musicians who had ties to other ecclesiastical institutions and courts, inviting us to think in new ways about

the music, how it was created, and the role of confraternities in its circulation. The purpose of this investigation has not been to identify who composed the anonymous plainsong and polyphonic works in these manuscripts,
but instead to more broadly show how music in confraternity devotions was
influenced by local traditions and by the movement of musicians to different
places. Ultimately, we see here that these organizations served as patrons of
new polyphonic composition as early as the fourteenth century. By placing
the Tournai Mass within its context as a work created for a confraternity,
we are able to see it as a product of a network of men who travelled far and
wide and who were committed to artistic innovation in both plainchant and
polyphony.

Chapter Five

The Role of the Parisian Book Production Community in the Perpetuation of Popular Devotions

O Catherine, glorious among virgins, resplendent with laurel: pour out your prayers to the Lord for us, bride of Christ, for whose law you fell by the sword as martyr into the hand of the gentiles.[1]

The text above is an alleluia verse for St. Catherine of Alexandria, which appears in a series of small sixteenth-century printed graduals entitled *Misse familiares*. It refers to St. Catherine's martyrdom and her ability to intercede on behalf of her supplicants, themes that we have seen in confraternity rituals throughout this book. St. Catherine continued to thrive in popular devotional consciousness well into the sixteenth century; in the various editions of the *Misse familiares*, she appears paired with St. Nicholas, showing the continuing relationship that the two saints had to each other. Their connection was widely recognized in Western Europe and is neatly summed up by William Caxton in his 1483 edition of the *Golden Legend* translated into English, where he refers to St. Catherine's virtues and her relationship to other saints:

… she was marvellous in privilege of dignity, for certain special privileges were in some saints when they died, like as the visitation of Jesu Christ was in St. John the Evangelist, the flowing of oil in St. Nicholas, the effusion of milk for blood that was in St. Paul, the preparation of the sepulchre in St. Clement, the hearing and granting of petitions in St. Margaret when she prayed for them remembering her memory. All these things together were in this blessed virgin S. Katherine as it appeareth in her legend.[2]

The advertisements on the title and colophon pages of the *Misse famili-ares* imply that they were produced for a very broad market, which likely included Parisian trade and devotional confraternities, students at the University of Paris, and other types of religious settings. This series of printed graduals, which contain five widespread votive masses and a full kyriale, were produced in Paris during the early decades of the sixteenth century, first by Geoffrey Marnef and later by François Regnault. They were associated with a number of other small liturgical books entitled *Misse solenniores* (which con-tain a dozen Mass ordinaries for major feast days), *Communes prose* (which contain fifteen popular sequences), and *Passiones novissime* (passions accord-ing to Matthew and John).[3] These books have no inscriptions indicating their original function, but their size and contents give us some clues. The same types of variability found in confraternity manuscripts from Paris and Tournai are also present in the different editions of the *Misse familiares, Misse solenniores*, and *Communes prose*.[4] They include all of the same masses of the Temporale and Sanctorale that appear in the confraternity sources discussed thus far (see appendices 2 and 4 ❧ for contents of the confraternity man-uscripts). Although they were sold separately, the books were often bound together in the sixteenth century.[5]

In this chapter, I explore the role of the Parisian book production com-munity in the dissemination of liturgical practices cultivated by confraterni-ties and student groups in Paris and other northern French dioceses. Student groups in particular functioned much like confraternities, forming an important market for such books. Unlike the sources discussed in chapters 1 through 4, these printed editions were produced by people whose names we know, and we can determine a great deal about their lives and working practices. Members of the Parisian book production community wore many hats: they were first and foremost businessmen and women, they sometimes served as editors, and they had much contact with members of other trades, many of whom were active in the confraternities discussed in chapters 2 and 3. Most importantly for the present study, they themselves were members of confraternities, whose liturgical practices are preserved in several manuscript sources. Printers of liturgical books were intimately familiar in a very real sense not only with the religious rituals surrounding them but also those of other dioceses through their movement among different groups of people and their contact with foreign diocesan authorities.

The Origin of the *Misse familiares,*
Misse solenniores, and *Communes prose*

The creation of this series of liturgical books came out of a collaboration between two men who lived in the same neighborhood in Paris, and their relationship represents the myriad personal ties that members of trade communities had with each other. Around 1500, Michel de Toulouze printed an edition of the *Misse solenniores* edited by his neighbor, Guillaume Guerson.[6] Toulouze was a printer who lived in the city's Latin Quarter, otherwise known as the University Quarter, located on the left bank of the Seine. He lived on the rue du Mont St. Hilaire at the sign of the Cornucopia opposite the college of Reims near the abbey of Ste. Geneviève. He also produced the first known printed processional (ca. 1495) containing music for the diocese of Paris while residing at this location.[7] Guerson lived next door to Toulouze at the residence of Master Jean de Fonte.[8] He was a native of the town of Villelongue in the south of France and held a master of arts degree from the University of Paris. Guerson was both a printer and a music teacher and was responsible for editing and compiling a number of liturgical books at the end of the fifteenth century.[9]

The Toulouze/Guerson edition of the *Misse solenniores* became so popular that it was seen as a worthwhile venture for other Parisian printers, which is evident in two subsequent editions, issued in 1510 by Geoffrey Marnef and in 1538 by François Regnault. Regnault in particular is well known for his printing of liturgical books, and especially those produced for sale in England.[10] He first started working in Paris around 1505 and was active there through the late 1530s.[11] By 1510, Regnault was a *libraire juré* (sworn bookseller) for the University of Paris, and until 1523 he resided on the rue St. Jacques at the sign of St. Cloud. From 1523 on his works carry the mark of the rue St. Jacques at the sign of the Elephant across the street from the Trinitarian monastery of the Mathurins.[12]

It is clear in the descriptions below that the *Misse solenniores, Misse familiares,* and *Communes prose* are all related to each other, both through the advertisements on their title pages and through their contents. All three editions of the *Misse solenniores* contain the Proper chants for twelve masses, which appear in calendric order, starting with the three masses for Christmas and continuing through the feast of All Saints on November 1 (see figure 5.1).[13] Most of the masses above are the solemn masses of the Temporale, whereas those for St. John the Baptist, the Assumption of the Virgin, and All Saints are three of the most important feasts of the Sanctorale.

Figure 5.1. Contents of the 1510 and 1538 editions of the *Misse solenniores*.

Missa in gallicantu

Missa in aurora

Mass for the Nativity

Mass for Epiphany

Mass for the Resurrection

Mass for the Ascension

Mass for Pentecost

Mass for the Holy Trinity

Mass for the Holy Sacrament (Corpus Christi)

Mass for St. John the Baptist

Mass for the Assumption of the Virgin

Mass for All Saints

Kyrie, Gloria, Sanctus, Agnus Dei, and Ite Missa Est melodies for duplex and annual feasts

Kyrie *Cunctipotens genitor*

All the editions of the *Misse solenniores* contain marketing slogans on their title pages, lauding them as "new" and "corrected." For instance, the title page of the 1510 edition says: "Solemn masses for the entire year: newly printed and corrected," followed by the device of Geoffrey Marnef.[14] At the end of the volume there is the following text, which goes into a bit more detail about the importance of the source's contents: "Solemn masses that were previously infected with mistakes now elegantly revised. [Printed in] the year one thousand five hundred and ten: on the fourteenth day of the month of October."[15]

The inscription from the title page of the 1538 edition, which includes the same advertisement of recent corrections, also adds that it has newly "reconstituted" psalm intonations:

> Solemn masses for the entire year: recently inspected and perfected. For the most part in the old copies [they were] shortened: in this newly inspected [edition] they have been reconstituted: as can be seen chiefly in the addition of the psalm intonations [Device of François Regnault]. Sold at Paris by Francois Regnault in the street of Saint Jacques residing at the sign of the elephant.[16]

Figure 5.2. Votive masses found in the three editions of the *Misse familiares*.

Mass for the Commemoration of the Virgin

Mass for the Dead

Mass for St. Catherine

Mass for St. Nicholas

Mass for the Holy Spirit

Full kyriale

Credo

Ite Missa Est melodies for the entire year

Salve regina

Ave Maria

On the last page of the edition, it says: "Solemn masses that were previously infected with mistakes now elegantly revised. [Printed in] the year one thousand five hundred [and] thirty eight."[17] Although all the editions of the *Misse solenniores* claim that they are new and improved, a comparison of their chants and texts reveals that they are in fact identical; the psalm intonations were also included in the ca. 1500 and 1510 editions and thus were not new in 1538.

While the *Misse solenniores* contains all the solemn masses of the Temporale, the contents of the *Misse familiares* are a bit more specific and allow for more detailed comparison with other private devotional sources (see figure 5.2). All three editions of the *Misse familiares* contain five masses and a full kyriale, which is the first printed kyriale representing the usage of Parisian communities. Similar to the *Misse solenniores*, the title pages of the three editions of the *Misse familiares* also boast "newly corrected" chants.[18] The musical and textual contents of some of the masses in the ca. 1538 edition differ from those appearing in the 1519 and 1523 editions, but the full psalm intonations are present in all three.

Three of the five masses listed above are the common votive masses found at the end of numerous diocesan manuscripts: for the Commemoration of the Virgin, for the Dead, and for the Holy Spirit. The inclusion of masses for St. Catherine and St. Nicholas is striking, since these are not normally found as votive masses in diocesan sources, but as I established in chapter 2, they appear in confraternity manuscripts from Paris and Tournai.

None of the editions of the *Misse solenniores* or the *Misse familiares* contain the prosas that were to be sung after the alleluia verses in these masses. These appear in a separate volume, a sequentiary entitled *Communes prose*, which contains fifteen prosas used in the Paris region.[19] The two editions of the *Communes prose*, the first one printed in 1509 by Marnef and the second one printed in 1526 by Regnault, have the same text on the title pages and on the last folios.[20] The prosas in these editions and their assignment to feasts of the church year are given in table 5.1.

The two sequentiaries contain only four prosas that do not match up with the masses in the *Misse solenniores* and *Misse familiares*, namely those for the Dedication of a Church, St. Andrew, St. Stephen, and the Annunciation. Furthermore, the two editions are lacking prosas for St. John the Baptist, the Assumption, and All Saints' Day—three masses that do appear in the *Misse solenniores*. Despite this discrepancy, the fact that the editions of the *Communes prose* are found bound together with the editions of the two graduals indicates that they were meant to be used in conjunction with those sources. Neither the texts nor the music of the sequences are different from those that appear in the manuscripts for the diocesan usage.

Of all the printed editions discussed above, the one that shows the most striking affinity with confraternity usages is the *Misse familiares*, and I will focus on the content of that series of graduals in the following sections. Its inclusion of a full kyriale and masses for St. Nicholas and St. Catherine shows a variety of connections to private devotional practices in the Paris region, which are related to a larger network of individuals and communities in the city.

The Kyriale in the *Misse familiares*

The kyriale included at the end of the *Misse familiares* shows on a very practical level how printers worked with preexisting material, for it is related to those in the Parisian diocesan and confraternity manuscripts discussed in chapter 4. Its organization and content firmly place it within the Paris region. Almost all the music in the kyriale that appears in the three editions of the *Misse familiares* is drawn from the diocesan kyriale, but the feasts to which the cycles are assigned differ from those in the kyriale of the cathedral and parish churches. Table 5.2 shows how the cycles in the different editions of the *Misse familiares* match up with each other, and with the diocesan usage of Paris.[21]

Table 5.1. The contents of the *Communes prose* corresponding to feast days of the Temporale and Sanctorale.

Feast days in the *Communes prose* (1510 and 1526)	Prosas (sequences)
Nativity	*Letabundus exultet*
Epiphany	*Epiphania domino*
Easter	*Fulgens preclara*
Octave of Easter through the Ascension	*Agnus redemit oves*
Ascension	*Rex omnipotens*
Pentecost	*Fulgens preclara rutilat*
Trinity	*Profitentes unitatem*
Corpus Christi	*Lauda syon*
Dedication of a Church	*Rex solomon*
St. Andrew	*Exultemus et letemur*
St. Nicholas	*Congaudentes exultemus*
St. Stephen	*Heri mundus exultavit*
Annunciation	*Salve mater salvatoris*
St. Catherine	*Vox sonora nostri chori*
For the Dead	*Dies irae dies illa*

The number of cycles in the editions of the *Misse familiares* varies, as do their connections to the diocesan kyriale. Table 5.2 shows that while the Parisian Kyriale contains fifteen cycles, the kyriale found in the first two editions of the *Misse familiares* only contains twelve, and the one appearing in the ca. 1538 edition has ten. The ten cycles included in the ca. 1538 edition all have musical and textual concordances with the first two editions.[22] The use of trope texts in all three editions of the *Misse familiares* evokes a more antiquated Parisian practice, since by the beginning of the fourteenth century, *Cunctipotens genitor* (*Misse familiares* 1519 and 1523 Cycle 5) and *Fons bonitatis* (*Misse familiares* 1519 and 1523 Cycle 6) had almost disappeared from the Parisian manuscript sources.[23] Nevertheless, their continuation in some instances is evident in their inclusion in the Attaingnant organ Mass.[24]

Although there are melodic concordances between the editions of the *Misse familiares* and the Parisian Kyriale, the assignment of the cycles to specific feast days is not the same. Six of the twelve cycles found in the first

Table 5.2. *Misse familiares* Kyriale Cycles.

Misse familiares 1519 and 1523 cycles	*Misse familiares* ca.1538 cycles (noting concordance with *Misse familiares* 1523 rubrics and melodies)	Parisian Kyriale cycles (noting concordances with *Misse familiares* 1523 rubrics and melodies)
Cycle 1	No concordant cycle	Rubric – Paris Cycle 2 (Not the exact wording) Music – Paris Cycle 2
Cycle 2	Cycle 1	Rubric – No match found Music – Paris Cycle 4 (Without trope text in the *Misse familiares*, Agnus Dei shows no match to the Parisian Kyriale or that of the Ste. Chapelle)
Cycle 3	Cycle 2	Rubric – No match found Music – Paris Cycle 5
Cycle 4	Cycle 3	Rubric – No match found Music – Paris Cycle 9
Cycle 5	No concordant cycle	Rubric – No match found Music – Paris Cycle 2 (The Parisian Kyriale does not contain the trope text, but it does appear in GB-Lbl Add. 16905)
Cycle 6	Cycle 4	Rubric – Paris Cycle 4 (Not the exact wording) Music – Paris Cycle 4 (With trope text in all sources)
Cycle 7	Cycle 5	Rubric – No match found Music – Paris Cycle 6
Cycle 8	Cycle 6	Rubric – No match found Music – Paris Cycle 7
Cycle 9	Cycle 7	Rubric – Paris Cycle 8 (Not the exact wording) Music – Paris Cycle 8

—(*continued*)

Table 5.2—*concluded*

Misse familiares 1519 and 1523 cycles	*Misse familiares* ca.1538 cycles (noting concordance with *Misse familiares* 1523 rubrics and melodies)	Parisian Kyriale cycles (noting concordances with *Misse familiares* 1523 rubrics and melodies)
Cycle 10	Cycle 8	Rubric – Paris Cycle 13 (Not the exact wording) Music – Paris Cycle 13
Cycle 11	Cycle 9	Rubric – Paris Cycle 15 Music – Paris Cycle 15
Cycle 12	Cycle 10	Rubric – Paris Cycle 1 (No rubric in *Misse familiares* 1523) Music – Paris Cycle 1

two editions of the *Misse familiares* have rubrics that match those found in the diocesan usage, but the wording is different. Overall, the rubrics in the printed graduals are simplified in comparison with those in the diocesan manuscript sources.[25] For example, the melodies in *Misse familiares* 1519 and *Misse familiares* 1523 Cycle 10 correspond to Cycle 13 in the Parisian Kyriale, but the diocesan rubric is more specific: "The Kyrie that follows is sung on Sundays of the Temporale from Purification to Easter and from the octave of Trinity Sunday until Advent and in Advent on Sundays without duplex or semiduplex rank, and on [all] Sundays without feasts."[26] The rubric that appears in the three editions of the *Misse familiares* is as follows:

The following is said on Sundays and on feasts of nine lessons from Pentecost to the Nativity. And similarly said from the Purification until Easter unless it is duplex or semiduplex, Gloria, Sanctus, and Agnus, and on Sundays.[27]

The kyriale in the *Misse familiares* shows the same types of similarities and differences in comparison to the diocesan kyriale that I showed in chapter 4, particularly with respect to their reassignment to different feast days, inclusion of new rubrics (discussed above), and incorporation of new chant melodies. The cycles in appendix 6 ❧ and in the Mass ordinary comparison tables in appendix 5 ❧ show that the printed graduals drew melodies from the Parisian Kyriale, many of which were also used in the Ste. Chapelle. Furthermore, half of these cycles carry rubrics similar to those found in diocesan sources. Table 5.2 above illustrates that the printed kyriale includes the melodies from Parisian Cycle 5, Cycle 9, and Cycle 13, which were assigned with some degree of variability in the confraternity manuscripts discussed in chapter 4. One example of a new chant that appears first in Parisian confraternity manuscripts is the Agnus Dei used in *Misse familiares* 1519 and *Misse familiares* 1523 Cycle 2. This chant first arises in Paris in the fifteenth century, as it is found in F-Pa 204 for the Confraternity of the Bourgeois Archers (discussed in chapter 3), and NL-DHk 76 E 18 for the Confraternity of the Doublet Makers (discussed in chapter 2). It was also known as early as the thirteenth century in Tournai, as it is included in B-Tc A 12 and B-Tc A 27. Despite its usage in confraternity devotions, it was not incorporated into the diocesan usage of Paris until 1574, when it appears in the printed *Manuale sacerdotum*.[28] While this is the first printed kyriale reflecting the usage of Parisian churches and confraternities that is known to exist, the overall contents of the *Misse familiares* are also tied further to specific lay communities in the Latin Quarter, as I demonstrate below.

The Place of the Latin Quarter and the University in Parisian Confraternity Devotions

The various editions of the *Misse familiares*, *Misse solenniores*, and *Communes prose* serve as a window into the network of trade communities in Paris and the contact they had with each other, different institutions, and individuals from outside of the city. In particular, they establish a connection to important places in the city's Latin Quarter, on the left bank of the Seine. This area had long been the home of the scribes, illuminators, and other trades people involved in commercial manuscript production since the thirteenth century.[29] As I showed previously, Michel de Toulouze and Guillaume Guerson lived in the heart of this community. Situated in close proximity to the University of Paris and its numerous colleges, this area was ideal for the production and sale of manuscripts, and later, printed books, to be used by university students. The association of members of the book trade in Paris with the university extends back to the thirteenth century, when scribes and booksellers were first required to take an oath of allegiance to the university, thus recognizing its control and protection over all aspects of the trade. This protection served in lieu of a guild at the time, and the oath remained a requirement through the early sixteenth century.[30]

While there are no inscriptions in the various editions of the *Misse familiares*, *Misse solenniores*, and *Communes prose* directly tying them to confraternity devotions, there is a handwritten addendum in another Parisian source that may illustrate the connection of this series of printed liturgical books to confraternity devotions in the University Quarter. The *O katherina* alleluia verse text discussed at the outset of the chapter is written by hand in a copy of a Trinitarian missal printed in 1529 next to the original alleluia verse, *Adducentur regi virgines*, with the indication "La confrerie de Sainte Catherine."[31] This book was likely owned by a Trinitarian house (or an individual from such a house) where there was a St. Catherine confraternity, and the owner had some responsibility for providing the appropriate chant for that organization's services. There is nothing in the Trinitarian book indicating that it was used at the Trinitarian house of the Mathurins in Paris, although St. Catherine was important to this community because it was on her feast day that their monastic order was founded.[32] Other handwritten addenda in the missal show that it was indeed used somewhere in Paris, for many of the prosas have been altered to conform to the diocesan usage.[33] Although the order of service for St. Catherine according to Trinitarian usage shows almost no affinity with the order of service in the *Misse familiares* or the diocesan usage of Paris, the Trinitarian missal, through the handwritten *O katherina* text, shows signs of confraternity usage.

The Trinitarian house of the Mathurins was one of the most influential institutions in the Latin Quarter with close ties to the university—both as a meeting place for university officials and for processions. For instance, there were semimonthly meetings of the Faculty of Theology at the Trinitarian house to discuss curriculum and other matters bearing on academic activity.[34] That such important meetings took place at the house of the Mathurins is due to the active role that its members played in the intellectual life of the university at the beginning of the sixteenth century, for several members of the order taught there.[35] This institution was also the starting point for processions that happened several days before the installation of a new rector of the university.[36] All students were present for these processions, as well as representatives from the other religious orders in the city; the procurators of the different *nationes* (nations) of the university; and the doctors of medicine, law, and theology. At the very end of the procession came, in the following order, the booksellers, paper merchants, bookbinders, parchment makers, illuminators, and scribes.[37]

Since the thirteenth century, the Trinitarian house had been one of only three places in the city that had the right to sell parchment, and it had various financial dealings with members of the book production community.[38] It owned numerous residences in the Latin Quarter that were leased to printers and booksellers, as well as to other members in the community, as dwellings and workshops. One example of this is a June 30, 1529, agreement between the Mathurins and the bookseller Bernard Aubry, in which it is specified that Aubry leased a house owned by the order adjacent to the residence of François Regnault.[39] As mentioned earlier in the chapter, François Regnault's bookshop was directly across the street from the Mathurins' church in the early sixteenth century.

The Trinitarian house served as an important meeting place not only for university officials but also for various confraternities whose members resided in the Latin Quarter. At least five confraternities held their services at this location by the beginning of the seventeenth century, all associated with trades: the Confraternity of the Messengers of the University of Paris met there on the day of St. Charlemagne; the Confraternity of the Papermakers on the day of St. John at the Latin Gate; the Confraternity of the Printers, Booksellers, Bookbinders, Illuminators, and Letter Makers on the day of St. John at the Latin Gate; the Confraternity of the Master Oilers and Candle Makers on the day of St. Nicholas; and the Confraternity of the Velvet Makers on the day of St. Barbara.[40] Two of the five confraternities listed here were made up of members of the book production community.[41]

Those involved with the book trade would have become familiar with the devotional practices of other confraternities in the city through their direct involvement in such communities, and their dealings with practitioners of other trades in these contexts. All members of the book production community belonged to the Confraternity of St. John the Evangelist, who met at the parish church of St. André des Arts in the heart of the Latin quarter.[42] Some members of the Parisian book production community also belonged to other confraternities at the same time. This is best illustrated through the life and business dealings of Geoffrey Marnef, who printed the earliest edition of the *Misse familiares* in 1510. Members of the Marnef family had ties with other individuals involved in the book trade, as they were all members of the Confraternity of St. John the Evangelist, but they also had contact with other artisans.

Marnef's contact with other printers and practitioners of different trades is clear through his place of residence and evidence of his business dealings. He is first mentioned in Paris around 1481, residing in the Latin Quarter at the Sign of the Pelican on the rue St. Jacques until his death in September 1518.[43] His two brothers, Enguilbert I and Jean I, shared this address, although they both also worked as printers in Poitiers and Liège.[44] That printers were financially beholden to each other is shown in a document from March 1524, which indicates that Enguilbert was paying off debts his brother Jean had incurred before his death with the printer Yolande Bonhomme (widow and successor to the master printer Thielmann Kerver) and the master printer Claude Chevallon.[45]

Even though Parisian trades were divided into different banner districts (see introduction), the lines between them were not physically drawn in such a strict manner.[46] The fluidity between the city quarters is evident through a document from 1508, which shows that Marnef bought a house from the oiler and candle maker Jean LeGrenetier, which was adjacent to that of the candle maker Jean Brébion.[47] In this respect, we see that Marnef had contact with practitioners of other trades, which would have been a daily occurrence for people in a medieval or early modern town.

The most compelling bit of information we have about Geoffrey Marnef is that in addition to being a member of the trade Confraternity of St. John the Evangelist, he was also a member of the devotional Confraternity of St. Hubert that met in the chapel of the hospital of St. Julian in Paris. In 1493, Marnef gave a liturgical book containing music to the confraternity (F-Pa 168). An inscription on one of the folios indicates he was a "bastionnaire," or banner holder, for the organization.[48] This piece of evidence tells us quite a bit both about Marnef's place in the Parisian trade community, and his activity in confraternities. First, Marnef, an established Parisian businessman, was a member of several different confraternities and therefore exposed to different musical and liturgical practices. His membership in his trade organization was mandatory, but his membership in the devotional Confraternity of St. Hubert was purely voluntary. Second, Marnef owned a confraternity manuscript containing music, the contents of which reflect the devotional practices of other confraternities in the city. The familiarity of printers with different practices in the city is best illustrated through the masses in the *Misse familiares*.

Masses for St. Nicholas and St. Catherine in the *Misse familiares*

Of all the masses in the *Misse familiares* and *Misse solenniores*, those for St. Nicholas and St. Catherine show the most connections to confraternity practices in the city of Paris and beyond (see appendix 5 ᵛᵈ for comparison tables for these masses). The mixture of specialized and nonspecialized texts in some ways draws our eye to confraternities worshipping at particular institutions, such as the Trinitarian house discussed above. The confraternity sources in chapter 2 included distinctive music and texts for St. Nicholas and St. Catherine. This is not always the case for the editions of the *Misse familiares*. All of the chants in the Mass for St. Nicholas, for instance, came from the Common of Saints in the diocesan usage, and they feature none of the intensely personal pleas that appear in some confraternity sources from Paris and Tournai.[49] The Mass for St. Catherine in both the 1519 and 1523 editions of the *Misse familiares* also uses chants associated with other feasts, such as the gradual *Concupivit rex decorem*, with the verse *Audi filia*. This is concordant with the gradual used in the Mass for the Assumption in the 1538 edition of the *Misse solenniores*. Example 5.1 shows that there are only a few minor variants when the gradual response in the different editions are compared. This melody does not match the one in diocesan manuscripts for the usage of Paris. The version of the Mass for St. Catherine in the ca. 1538 edition of the *Misse familiares* departs from this earlier practice in these editions, adhering instead to the diocesan usage of Paris by using the gradual *Propter veritatem*. Another variation in this edition is the use of the alleluia verse *Veni electa mea*, which has no association with St. Catherine in the other editions of the *Misse familiares* or in the diocesan usage.[50]

As was the case for the masses in chapters 1 through 3, it is the alleluia verses that depart more significantly from the diocesan usage, and those in the *Misse familiares* in particular show connections to confraternity devotions in Paris and Tournai. The *O katherina* alleluia verse given at the outset of the chapter is included in the first two editions of the *Misse familiares* but does not appear in any other Parisian sources aside from the handwritten addendum in the printed Trinitarian missal, discussed earlier. The text is found in only one other source, a fourteenth-century Dominican gradual from Italy, and it is a contrafactum created from the widespread alleluia verse *O consolatrix pauperum*, discussed at length in chapter 2.[51] As I showed there, this chant melody was used to create contrafacta for numerous saints, including St. Catherine, St. Nicholas, the Virgin Mary, St. Barbara, and many others in liturgical books throughout France, Italy, and Germany. *O consolatrix pauperum* also appears numerous times in confraternity sources from Paris and Tournai set with texts for St. Nicholas, St. Catherine, and the Virgin Mary.[52] None of these sources produces an exact melodic match to the version in the 1510 and 1523 editions of the *Misse familiares*, but Karlheinz Schlager's Alleluia index shows a multitude of melodic variants on this chant, both from French dioceses and those outside the realm. The closest parallel to the melody in a northern French source is the Reims version discussed in chapter 2 and transcribed in example 5.2.[53]

Example 5.1. Comparison of the gradual response *Concupivit rex decorum* in the *Misse solenniores* (MS 1538) and *Misse familiares* (MF 1523).

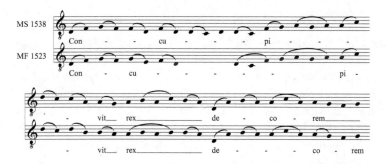

Example 5.2. Alleluia *O katherina* (MF 1523)/*O consolatrix pauperum* (F-RS 264).

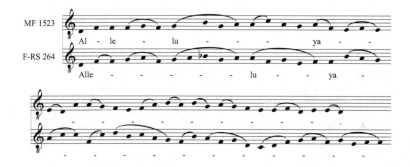

Example 5.2 demonstrates that like several chants for the Office of the Translation of St. Nicholas discussed in chapter 2, the similarities between the Reims and *Misse familiares* 1523 melodies at the outset go beyond the opening formula. Although the *O katherina* chant is only loosely based on *O consolatrix pauperum*, the new melody in the 1510 and 1523 editions of the *Misse familiares* is meant to allude to it, as it circulated widely in northern French confraternity sources and was known to be paired with the *O katherina* text in other locations.

The kyriale and many of the Mass propers show that these printed editions could have been used by private devotional communities in the Paris area. Additionally, they provide keen insight into a network of trades people associated with the university that shows the distinct place of the book production community in the promotion through print of religious practices cultivated by confraternities in Paris, as we shall see in the following section.

The Role of St. Catherine and St. Nicholas at the University

The specific connections of some printers and editors to the University of Paris as students and thus participants in religious services associated with student groups led to an awareness of diverse liturgies, and of new possibilities for the marketing of printed books that could be used by confraternities or in other devotional settings. The persons whose experience gave them intimate knowledge of the spiritual practices of the different foreign student groups at the university were perhaps those known to have edited liturgical books, who themselves were foreigners and had received degrees from the university. Although most students were teenagers when they matriculated (generally fourteen or fifteen years old), everyone in the Faculty of Arts was required to swear an oath to one of four nations, which in the late fifteenth and early sixteenth centuries meant broad geographical areas; this allegiance was seen as a lifelong commitment.[54] The French Nation comprised numerous dioceses within the modern day region of France, as well as Spain, Italy, several Swiss dioceses, and Palestine. The Nation of Picardy was made up of several dioceses in northeastern France, as well as modern day Belgium and the Netherlands; the Nation of Normandy included the dioceses within the modern geographical area of Normandy. The largest was the English-German Nation, which encompassed the dioceses of Poland, Hungary, modern day Germany, Switzerland, Scandinavia, Russia, England, Ireland, and several from the Netherlands.[55] As seen here, the two most culturally varied nations were the French Nation and the English-German Nation.

Just as the trade confraternity devotions discussed in chapters 1 through 3 helped to legitimize and bring about a sense of group solidarity, the same can be said for the practices of the different nations of the university. The nations functioned as confraternal organizations, with their own liturgical practices and important feast days. The specific churches where they met are discussed by William Courtenay, who points out that these institutions included the Trinitarian house of the Mathurins and the church of St. André des Arts. Both of these churches were central meeting places for university officials and the book production community, which I showed previously.[56] One reason for the inclusion of masses in honor of St. Catherine and St. Nicholas in the *Misse familiares* would have been their role as the patron saints of many communities, among them being students and scholars, and the resulting devotional practices surrounding the two saints by all students of the arts as well as students of the English-German nation. As early as the thirteenth century, the feasts of St. Catherine and St. Nicholas were celebrated by all of the nations together.[57] Being the largest student center in Europe, there was great potential for the influx of different liturgical practices, texts, and music to Paris through students who came from afar.[58] As I showed in chapter 1, former choirboys often went to Paris to study at the university when they were of age, so there were certainly some musically literate students within the nations.[59] The inclusion of texts and music with no connection to the diocesan usage, such as the *O katherina* alleluia verse and the different music for the gradual *Concupivit rex decorum* in the various editions of the *Misse familiares* and the *Misse solenniores*, could be attributed to these students.

The university's nations visibly promoted their identities as groups through the use of the visual arts, such as images of their patron saints on seals and in manuscript illuminations, and they also took part in public processions and other ceremonies.[60] In addition to the importance placed on each member's sense of personal pride in his homeland, there are references within the English-German Nation to feeling a sense of group solidarity shared by its members, which focused on the nation as an international fellowship of foreigners within Paris.[61] This is evident in a poem written in 1479 by a student of the English-German Nation, Egidius Delft from the diocese of Utrecht:

> Our Nation. You ask what is our Nation? Certainly it is not I, nor you, not he and he, But a multitude, a multitude forming a unity.[62]

The lifelong commitment that students would make to their nation appears outside of Paris in other cities. For example, a group of clerics residing in Ypres who were trained at the University of Paris met regularly to socialize and establish professional relationships.[63]

Several printers and editors had been students at the university, and thus had been required to swear an oath to one of the four nations. Jean Le Munerat, for instance, was a native of Bourges, and his familiarity with the liturgical practices of other dioceses is evident in his discussion of music performance in his two treatises, *De moderatione et concordia grammatice et musice* (1490) and *Qui precedenti tractatu* (1493). He received a bachelor of arts degree from the university and eventually went on to become its rector. Le Munerat is known to have edited several printed editions of liturgical books, including two breviaries and one missal for Parisian usage.[64] As demonstrated earlier in this chapter, Guillaume Guerson, the editor of the first known edition of the *Misse solenniores* printed ca. 1500 by Michel de Toulouze, had received a master of arts degree from the University of Paris, and he was responsible for editing and compiling liturgical books at the end of the fifteenth century.[65] Furthermore, the printer Berthold Rembolt, who in collaboration with Ulrich Gering printed a psalter for Parisian usage in 1494 (the only printed Parisian psalter known to exist from this period), received a bachelor of arts degree from the university in 1487 and held several high-ranking offices in the English-German Nation.[66] Of course other avenues for the arrival of foreign material in Paris existed, but these men had a direct impact on what appeared in print.[67]

Although we have no surviving music from the nations of the university, we do have vestiges of liturgical practices from one of its colleges. Jean Le Munerat, in the late fifteenth century, refers to the large number of liturgical books representing different usages held by the library of the College of Navarre, and Don Harrán has studied the institution and its liturgical practices in some detail.[68] There is one book relevant to the present study that reflects the unique devotions of the college, and that is a small processional, F-Pnm lat. 1123.[69] This manuscript, produced ca. 1380, was used in the college chapel, which was dedicated in 1373 to St. Louis, St. Catherine, the Virgin Mary, the Holy Trinity, and the Holy Cross.[70] Within its forty-three folios it makes references to all of these feasts, and it contains chants for processions during Holy Week. What is of interest here is that some of its contents have similarities to those of other confraternity manuscripts I have discussed in previous chapters. In particular, it contains a Mass for the feast of St. Louis that includes music and text for the alleluia verse *Felix corona francie*. This comes directly from the diocesan usage, as I showed in chapter 3, but it was also an alleluia verse that was used to create a contrafactum for St. Sebastian in F-Pa 204, for the Confraternity of the Bourgeois Archers. It is not used in the same way here, and the appearance of this melody in both manuscripts does not establish a connection between them, but it does show that the contents of this processional have overlap with both diocesan and confraternity books in Paris.

The Role of the Parisian Book Production Community in the Creation of Liturgical Books

In order to understand the impact of printers on the distribution of liturgical practices such as those found in the *Misse solenniores*, *Misse familiares*, and *Communes prose*, it is important to explore the restrictions that were placed on them as university employees, their relationships with members of the clergy, and the amount of freedom and authority they had in choosing their own business ventures. These printers worked in conjunction with church officials on the production of some diocesan missals, manuals, and breviaries, so we can assume that the clergy regulated these sources to a certain extent. As businessmen and -women, they also worked with other groups and individuals wishing to publish certain works not regulated by church officials. The series of small printed graduals and sequentiaries discussed here fall into this last category.

Understanding the business practices and social connections of the men and women involved in the book trade is key to understanding the dissemination of the diocesan liturgy, as well as the circulation of devotional practices associated with confraternities and the relationship between the two. While the members of the book production community had obligations to the university, this institution appears to have had very little control over the book trade. Essentially, the power struggles between the king and the Faculty of Theology did not affect the production of liturgical books.[71] If anything, swearing an oath to the university came with certain privileges that were not granted to other trades. Writing in the early sixteenth century, Robert Goulet cited the precise number of persons in the book trade listed among the university officials: there were twenty-four sworn booksellers, or *libraires jurés*, "of whom four are termed Great and twenty Small," four parchment makers, four parchment vendors, seven papermakers (three from Troyes, and four from Corbeil and Essones), two book illuminators, two bookbinders, and two scribes (to be understood as scribes who were masters of the trade or heads of scriptoria).[72] These forty-six members of the book trade account for more than half of the perpetual and fiscal officers of the university and are counted among its procurators and advocates.[73] All of them enjoyed special royal privileges, such as exemptions from all taxes. Indeed, it was stated that the king had forbidden "all farmers of revenue and other officers of the King to molest, disturb, or harass in any way the aforesaid officers."[74] As university officers, the members of the book trade also took part in the public university processions, which occurred four times a year at the end of a rectorship.[75]

By all contemporary accounts, members of the book production community were held in very high regard. In addition to their special privileges as university employees, they were also publicly praised by the monarchy. The importance of the printers is outlined in the *Ordonnances* of Privileges given by King Louis XII on April 9, 1513.[76] The following passage speaks of their "means and industry," by which France has benefited in many ways:

> ... by the means and industry of the said Booksellers, by which our holy Catholic faith has been greatly augmented and corroborated, justice better held and administered, and the divine service more honorably and curiously done, said and celebrated, and to the means of which so much of the good and salutary doctrines have been manifested, communicated and published for each and every one, to the means of which our Realm surpasses all others: and other innumerable good things which have preceded it and proceed still every day, to the honor of God and the augmentation of our said Catholic faith as it is said.[77]

While the printers are lauded for their production of liturgical books in the passage above, they were also responsible for numerous other types of books, which ranged from textbooks for use by students at the university to editions of poetry and other books for popular consumption.[78] The affluence of Parisian printers and booksellers can be seen not only through the number of editions that they produced but also through the amount of property that they owned and the number of their employees.[79] An example of the magnitude of these businesses is the print shop of Charlotte Guillard, who owned a bookshop as well as four or five printing presses. For each press, she would have needed three to five workers, as well as additional people to work in the bookshop, an accountant, correctors, editors, and a domestic staff; as part of the pay for her workers she was also required to feed them.[80]

The division of labor in a print shop makes it clear that printers and editors were not the same people, and this gives us a more nuanced view of how printed liturgical books were produced in Paris. The men and women who owned large bookshops with printing presses were considered masters, who had journeymen and apprentices working under them as employees. It was the journeymen who did manual work in the print shop, running the press, etc., but some of them served as correctors, or proofreaders, showing a certain level of education.[81] The editing of music, Greek texts, and mathematical works was done by scholars hired on a periodic basis, as these fields required more specialized knowledge.[82] We can assume that all the music in the various editions of the *Misse solenniores*, *Misse familiares*, and *Communes prose* was edited by a musician or scholar, such as Jean Le Munerat or

Guillaume Guerson. Furthermore, as can be seen on the title pages of liturgical books, printers often collaborated in the production of volumes. There is considerable information regarding the renting of presses, the borrowing of music type and woodcut illustrations, and the practice of hiring out certain portions of the work to be done in different print shops.[83] In some cases, up to three printers were involved in the production of one edition. All of this makes it difficult to identify the exact role that each individual played in the creation of liturgical books containing music.

In a print shop, printers and booksellers were in contact with individuals of various backgrounds who came with works that they wished to be printed, and this type of freedom is what permitted them to take on projects such as the *Misse solenniores* and *Misse familiares*.[84] The ties between the Sorbonne and Parisian printers were established from the outset, but it is also evident that the printers had personal associations with members of the clergy from other dioceses. References to editors and correctors of texts in the workshops of these printers abound, but more important for the present study, there are several references to liturgical books edited by members of the clergy.[85] The Parisian printer Wolfgang Hopyl, for example, produced a missal in 1514 for the usage of Lund that was edited by one of the Lund clergy.[86] And again, in 1519, Hopyl is known to have printed a Sarum antiphoner that was edited by Dr. Sampson of King's College, Cambridge.[87] In 1527, Jean Petit printed a missal for the usage of Evreux that contained changes given to him by clergy of the diocese.[88]

In addition to the examples of clergy being involved in the editing process, we also have evidence that the printers themselves were responsible in some instances for editing the liturgical books they produced. As far as the diocese of Paris is concerned, in 1543, Bernard de Leau, a printer and bookseller in Paris, along with Oudin Petit, Jacques Kerver, and other printers and booksellers, edited a missal for the usage of Paris that was printed by Didier Maheu.[89] This missal was not emended with corrections given to Maheu by clergymen from Paris, but rather by other printers, many of whose fathers had printed earlier missals for the usage of Paris. This may explain many of the similarities among Parisian editions, where older ones were often used as the basis for newer ones. It also contradicts the notion that clergymen from a diocese were always directly involved in the editing process of liturgical books for diocesan usages. All of this shows that to some extent, diocesan usages in the early sixteenth century were not as standardized as we might assume.

There is also evidence for the print runs of editions, primarily in documents concerning François Regnault, Didier Maheu, and Nicholas Prévost, which reveal exactly how large these printing ventures were.[90] The large print run of many editions is evidence that the production of liturgical books could generate a flourishing business. In March of 1522, Regnault paid to acquire two hundred small printed breviaries for the usage of Rome to sell in his shop.[91] Later, in 1524, he produced six hundred manuals for the usage of Toul, a rather small diocese in northeastern France near Nancy, for the merchant Michel Lenglantier. Part of this agreement was that Regnault was forbidden, under penalty of a fine, to print any further editions of the manual.[92]

The most detailed book commission involving the production of liturgical books for communities in Paris is a June 1529 agreement between the printer Nicholas Prévost and Nicolas Musnier, the director general of the Trinitarian house of the Mathurins in Paris.[93] The document states that over the course of the next four months, Prévost would print three hundred copies of a missal on paper, in red and black ink, for the usage of the order. The agreement is highly detailed regarding the number of parchment folios that should be included (the canon of the Mass was normally printed on parchment and inserted among the paper folios after the Temporale), and the paper quality. It also specified that Prévost would print, on the first folio of all the missals, the history of the Trinitarian order, which was to be approved by Musnier. Prévost was also asked to print six or seven copies on parchment in addition to the three hundred that he was to print on paper.[94]

As can be seen in the paragraphs above regarding Regnault, the average print run of an edition of a liturgical book produced for a diocesan usage could be anywhere between two hundred to six hundred copies. Since more than one edition of a missal or breviary from a diocese existed at any given moment, it is likely that well over one thousand copies of the missal and manual circulated in most dioceses by the second and third decades of the sixteenth century. In the cases of the commissions mentioned above, there are several instances when a printer has agreed not to print subsequent editions of the book under penalty of a fine. This type of printing Privilege, which was a commercial monopoly granted to a printer for the sole rights to the production of a specific work, either permanently or for a fixed period of time, was rarely given for liturgical books.[95]

Unlike other types of books, the production of liturgical books for diocesan usages was not regulated by the university or the theologians, and while it can be assumed that diocesan bishops needed at least to be consulted before a liturgical book was printed, it is likely that in many cases they had relatively little to do with the editing process.[96] Furthermore, these editions never appear in the indices of books censored by the Faculty of Theology.[97] The liturgical books printed for the usage of Paris before 1539 lack the uniformity in musical notation that one would expect to see if there were large-scale efforts to adopt a standard in the Paris area.[98] All of this indicates that the Faculty of Theology was much more preoccupied with the regulation of texts, rather than with services involving music at the cathedral and parish churches, thereby giving freedom to printers and booksellers in the production and editing of liturgical books.

Based on the evidence shown above, it is likely that books such as the *Misse familiares*, *Misse solenniores*, and *Communes prose* existed in print runs of anywhere between two hundred to six hundred copies. This sheer number implies that they were not just meant for one specific community or group of people, but instead they were intended to appeal to a variety of student groups, trade confraternities, and other private devotional communities. The existence of these books is a testament to the popularity of the votive masses contained in them and is related to the inclusion of new services in the printed diocesan missals produced for other northern French usages, as we shall see in the following section.

The Role of Printers in the Dissemination of Confraternity Devotions

The evidence above demonstrates that printers could issue specialized liturgical books not intended for regular diocesan use without the obvious supervision of official clergy and that diocesan books also did not necessarily bear explicit indications of clerical control. By the beginning of the sixteenth century most diocesan missals produced by Parisian printers included a list of common votive masses in the table of contents, and then gave the texts of the chants for those masses at the end of the book in a section entitled *Misse familiares*. In chapter 3, I provided a list of those masses from a Parisian missal produced in 1504 (the same one is shown in table 5.3, but here with comparison to printed editions from other dioceses).

Table 5.3 shows that many of the same votive masses that appear at the end of printed liturgical books for the usage of Paris produced by Parisian printers appear in missals that these men and women printed for other dioceses. It is evident above that votive masses for St. Genevieve, St. Roche,

Table 5.3. Votive masses in missals produced by Parisian printers for northern dioceses.

Masses and orations	Parisian Printed Missal, 1504 (F-Psg OEXV 54²)	Tournai Printed Missal, 1498 (B-Ts Inc. 27)	Cambrai Printed Missal, 1507 (F-Lfc 1.M.21)	Amiens Printed Missal, 1529 (F-AM Rés 23 D)	Soissons Printed Missal, 1509 (F-Psg Fol. BB 124 inv. 134)
St. Genevieve	X			X	
St. Sebastian	X		X	X	
All Saints	X				X
Missa pro mortalitate subitanea evitanda	X	X	X	X	X
In the Name of Christ	X				X
For Peace	X	X	X	X	X
For the Sick	X	X	X		X
For the Suffering	X				
The Commendation of the Dead	X				X
For the Dead	X	X	X		X
The Compassion of the Virgin	X		X		X
St. Roche	X		X	X	
St. Claude	X		X		
St. Anthony	X		X	X	
St. Barbara	X			X	
The Five Wounds of Christ	X			X	X

Table 5.3—*continued*

Masses and orations	Parisian Printed Missal	Tournai Printed Missal	Cambrai Printed Missal	Amiens Printed Missal	Soissons Printed Missal
Raphael the Archangel	X				
Sunday. For the Trinity	X	X	X		X
Monday. For the Angels	X	X			X
Tuesday. For the Holy Spirit	X	X	X		X
Wednesday. For the Dead	X				
Thursday. For the Holy Sacrament	X				
Friday. For the Holy Cross	X	X	X		X
Saturday. For the Commemoration of the Virgin	X	X	X	X	X
Against pagans		X			X
Against the Turks					X
For pregnant women			X		
For a Priest Himself		X		X	X
For a Living Friend		X			
For Clear Skies		X			X
For sins		X	X		
For any tribulation		X	X		
Against the power of his enemies, visible and invisible		X			

—(*continued*)

Table 5.3—*concluded*

Masses and orations	Parisian Printed Missal	Tournai Printed Missal	Cambrai Printed Missal	Amiens Printed Missal	Soissons Printed Missal
For giving alms	X				
For an ill person close to death	X	X			
For the congregation		X			
Crown of Thorns				X	
In the name of Jesus				X	X
For friends		X			
Christ's Tears				X	
For the salvation of the living					X
For rain					X
For relatives		X			X
For those who travel					X
The nails and the spear					X
Our lady of piety					X
St. Mary of the Snows					X

St. Anthony, and St. Barbara were included by Parisian printers in liturgical books for the dioceses of Cambrai and Amiens. Other votive masses appearing in books for Parisian usage also show up in Tournai and Soissons, and in some cases, the same order of service is observed in them (see appendix 5 for examples from the St. Sebastian votive masses). All of this indicates that Parisian printers were aware that members of the clergy around the city provided services not just in standard, diocesan situations but also for a variety of other occasions. Therefore, they included in their books non-diocesan material as a convenience for the clergy, who could then carry a single book (or set of books) whether serving in the cathedral or their parish; or for a confraternity, university nation, or a private commemorative Mass. The introduction of non-diocesan feasts by printers has been observed in other dioceses by Barbara Haggh, who shows how the feast of the *Recollectio* celebrated in the diocese of Cambrai was introduced into books that followed usages in which the feast was not normally celebrated.[99] Parisian printers could have come by their material in any number of ways, as their movement in different social circles and contact with individuals from outside of the diocese left them perfectly placed to aid in the transmission of these practices.

Printers exercised a certain amount of power over the production of liturgical books and were partly responsible for disseminating liturgical practices cultivated by confraternities on a broad scale. Table 5.3 shows that the votive masses at the end of diocesan sources are variable, for while one saint is included in one printed edition, the same saint does not always appear in another. Furthermore, in the course of the late fifteenth century, the number of votive masses at the end of diocesan missals expanded from an average of five to an average of twenty-five, but those included at the end of diocesan missals should not be taken as an exhaustive list of all the votive masses celebrated in the diocese. Different communities had different needs, and although St. Catherine and St. Nicholas do not appear in the diocesan *Misse familiares* at the end of liturgical books, I have established in this study that they were two of the most popularly revered saints in Paris generally and in Parisian confraternities specifically. In this way, they may have been seen as deserving inclusion in small, separate volumes, like the editions of the *Misse familiares*, which contained both the music and text of Mass propers and Ordinaries, and could be easily used by communities who celebrated a limited number of masses together. These small printed graduals would likely have served as a supplement to the diocesan missal.[100] I have shown here that their contents share strong connections to religious practices associated with student groups, and they equally would have been appropriate for use in any of the Parisian area trade or devotional confraternities which had either St. Catherine or St. Nicholas as a patron saint. The inclusion of a full kyriale in the *Misse familiares* makes this particular book very versatile, since it could have been purchased for its Mass ordinary chants alone.

Ultimately, these printed liturgical books could have been bought by anyone who either intended to use them in confraternity worship or simply found it a novelty to own a devotional book containing music. Their marketing does not correlate with class distinctions and supports the possibility that the sources were meant for a very broad segment of the population.[101]

If the editions of the *Misse familiares*, for instance, were meant strictly for university students, there would be no guarantee that all of the students would have had the financial means to buy them. For example, according to university records, approximately 65 percent of the students that formed part of the English-German Nation were poor or low-income students.[102] This would make it difficult to envision the production of two hundred copies of a book such as the *Misse familiares* in multiple editions for a single audience. The deliberately phrased description on their title pages of "new and improved"—particularly since not true—is an even further indication that these books were meant to be sold to as wide an audience as possible.

In sum, the editions of the *Misse familiares*, *Communes prose*, and *Misse solenniores* were produced in response to a growing market of consumers, which would have included local confraternities and student groups. The degrees of difference from the liturgical practices of the Parisian cathedral and parish churches, which are commonly found in confraternity manuscripts, are also present in these printed editions. The variations in them when compared to the diocesan usage of Paris show that the books were not forced to be homogeneous by Parisian ecclesiastical authorities, but were planned, produced, and edited autonomously by printers and former university students. Their existence in multiple editions is a testament to their continuing popularity, which by the middle of the sixteenth century extended beyond Paris to the city of Lyon through the reprints of Jacques Moderne.

Conclusion

In the introduction to this book, I broadly explored how the movement of individuals (clerics and the laity) through different physical and social spaces could be related to the circulation of popular devotional practices cultivated by confraternities. In many cases there are no documents or confraternity registers recording the inner workings of these organizations, or information about those who were paid to compile and perform their services. Due to these limitations, I have relied on the contents of their existing liturgical books to investigate how the religious practices of these communities developed. As a result of my focus on the musical and textual contents of these sources, I have demonstrated how decentralized religious and spiritual authority was during the time period under study. As individuals, confraternity members were people who worked as merchants and artisans, clerics, and students. As communities, they had the power to develop their own corporate identities. I do not mean to imply that the laity directly challenged ecclesiastical authority. Instead, it is evident that lay authority and ecclesiastical authority were two different things, and that popular devotions, such as those promoted by confraternities, occupied a different space altogether from that of larger ecclesiastical and monastic institutions.

Confraternity liturgies were created and mediated by individuals and communities and were heavily influenced by contact between different networks. The various types of interactions between these entities could have been responsible for the dissemination of religious ideas, and particularly in times of plague, widespread beliefs concerning the healing attributes of certain saints. Those most commonly revered at the time were the fourteen holy helpers, which in northern France included St. Barbara, St. Catherine, and St. Nicholas. The popular devotional practices in this study did not travel in direct, easily traceable lines, but instead through constellations of individuals and communities, all of which were marked by movement—physical, social, and spiritual—resulting in the formation of different identities, with music playing a central role. While my interest has been northern France, looking at these types of movement would be a useful tool for investigations into other geographical areas further north in the Low Countries, east in the Hapsburg lands, and south in Italy. Below, I recap some of the examples from the present work that illustrate each type of movement.

The physical movement of individuals to different institutions in Paris and Tournai had a hand in shaping the music and liturgical practices of confraternities in these two cities. This is seen most directly through the Confraternity of the Spice Dealers and Apothecaries in Paris, who moved to a variety of parishes and monastic communities in the sixteenth century. At each institution that housed them, they would have hired clergy to perform their services. Some of the later handwritten addenda in their existing liturgical book (F-Pm 464)—such as the *O nicholae* alleluia verse that was added on the opening flyleaf, and the prosas added at different points (see chapter 2)— show the role that these individuals had in shaping the practices of the confraternity. The Confraternity of the Transfiguration also celebrated their services at different institutions in Tournai, crossing the diocesan border into parishes under the jurisdiction of the diocese of Cambrai. As a result, the two existing manuscripts from this confraternity show a mixture of monophonic and polyphonic musical practices from both dioceses.

The travel of individuals and communities to other institutions and geographical areas also accounts for the influx of new practices into a diocese, which was evident in the case of St. Barbara. My codicological analysis of the notaries' liturgical books and their contents showed how popular devotions to her were promoted by the confraternity and eventually made their way into the liturgical books used in the main sanctuary of the Tournai cathedral. The transformation of widely recognized saints such as St. Nicholas, St. Catherine, and St. Sebastian into local protectors via a focus on relics and their translation shows another aspect of this process.

Social movement, or the contact that individuals had with each other, is more difficult to trace, but the power of these connections is implied throughout this study. The Confraternity of the Notaries, for instance, had ready access to the bishop of Tournai, who was a powerful political figure. Their presence at official functions would have put them into contact with others who held similar clerical positions at the French court, and at other royal households. Since some notaries were renowned composers in these establishments, such as Philippe de Vitry and Guillaume de Machaut, the notaries in service to the bishop of Tournai could have come into contact with new compositions. As educated, literate men, the notaries of Tournai themselves also could have been responsible for the creation of new monophonic and polyphonic compositions found in their manuscripts.

Other vestiges of social movement have to do with physical proximity, and we have the most evidence of this in the city of Paris. I have shown through data recorded in notarial registers that tradespeople in Paris were connected to each other as neighbors and through marriage. These documents also reveal that members of different trades took part in confraternity services together. This type of social movement was inherent in the Confraternity of the Bourgeois Archers, who were all members of different trades. Their job guarding the various trade quarters of the city was secondary to their main occupations. Because they were active practitioners of different trades, they were required to be members of those guilds, which did not preclude them from joining this particular confraternity. Spiritual movement indicates the individual transformation that one undergoes in the process of confraternity devotions, and at the heart of this is receiving divine protection from sickness. The connections between relics, contact relics, and healing powers transcended physical objects, and led to new specialized rituals celebrating the acts of *Translatio* and *Inventio*. References to contact relics, like healing oils, are central to these narratives, and in the absence of physical objects, music takes on a new role in healing and procuring the divine protection of a patron saint by dwelling on the acts surrounding them. In *Translatio* and *Inventio* texts, healing is embodied in moving objects—in these instances relics—from one place to another, and it was on this that the laity was meant to meditate in order to receive the favor of the community's patron saint. This process is mirrored in popular devotional literature, such as Books of Hours and guides for virtual pilgrimage that were produced starting in the fifteenth century.

Musical practices may have travelled through physical and social movement, but new chant and polyphonic compositions were meant to be spiritually moving and transformative. On a most basic level, it is apparent through the examples put forth in this study that the primary mode of composition for the Mass proper, hymns, and prosas (and to a lesser extent, the Office) was textual, through the creation of contrafacta. While this compositional technique was used to establish connections between different saints, the Virgin Mary, and Christ, there may also have been a civic element. Parisian institutions such as Notre Dame and the Sainte Chapelle had public altars, and this was also the case at Notre Dame in Tournai (see chapters 1, 2, and 3). In chapters 2 and 3, I discussed indulgences to visit pilgrimage sites, and one that held public masses and offices was the lower level of the Ste. Chapelle. The melodic references to the Crown of Thorns in chapter 2, and to the feast of St. Louis in chapter 3, could be related to this. In this way, these musical and textual pairings reflect a sense of pride in the city of Paris. In this study, I have explored nonpublic aspects of confraternity devotions, studying the masses and offices attended exclusively by members; at the same time, these organizations existed as official public entities who took part in processions and other displays for which there is no musical record.

Spiritual protection took different forms based on the attributes of each community's patron saint, and music was used to reinforce this. The subject matter of some offices and masses newly constructed for confraternities in the fourteenth century is martyrdom, which was the case for the Office of St. Barbara in chapter 1. In the fifteenth century the object of worship becomes healing, and ways to make this personal and immediate were through *Translatio* and *Inventio* narratives, celebrating the saint's movement to different geographical locations. The process of *Translatio* and *Inventio* is to create a social place, focused on the action of presentation. Certain chant genres played an important part in reinforcing a confraternity's devotions to their patron saint—alleluia verses, sequences, and hymns are among the most popular for all the saints discussed here. The offices for St. Barbara, St. Nicholas, and St. Catherine also showed the specific events of these saints' lives that were important to each community, and in the case of Paris, *Translatio* was a pivotal theme. It was through the act of *Translatio* that the relics of St. Nicholas and St. Catherine made their way to northern France, enabling them to become local protectors, and from that point on, they were thought to carry healing properties in times of sickness and death.

The act of *Translatio* is also how St. Sebastian attained importance in northern France, and efforts were made by local composers to also refashion him as a local protector. Masses for St. Sebastian reference geography and Gallo-Roman history, all in an attempt to ground his relics on French soil in order to procure divine protection. In *Translatio* and *Inventio* narratives for St. Catherine and St. Nicholas, the liminal space of contact relics makes them accessible. For liturgies focused on the actual relics of a saint, the presence of objects and their rightful place makes them powerful. This implies a type of temporal mobility in confraternity devotions, where the saints are immediately present, instead of remaining merely historical figures in the past. In this respect, history is telescoped in the confraternity's liturgical calendar.

These types of spiritual connections also extend to monophonic and polyphonic settings of the Mass ordinary, which were created as a high form of devotion in honor of a community's patron saint. The composition of monophonic and polyphonic Mass ordinaries in Tournai shows the possible role of confraternities in the creation of new practices on the cutting edge of musical innovation at the time. The Mass ordinary chants found in the Tournai books in particular show links between old and new practices, much in the same way links between old and new were made in liturgies for St. Catherine and St. Nicholas through the use of contrafacta. The only polyphony in the sources for this study comes from confraternity books in Tournai, but chants in cantus fractus that came out of polyphonic settings are also found in the manuscript F-Pa 204 for the Bourgeois Archers in Paris, which includes the Sanctus and Agnus Dei "Vineux." Polyphony and plainchant in cantus fractus were likely a part of other trade confraternity rituals as well. Ultimately, confraternity books in Paris and Tournai show patterns in how liturgies were constructed (drawing on well-known chants and using contrafacta carrying popular devotional ideas), links between older and newer repertories, movement of liturgical practices across and within dioceses, and the possible roles of members of different trades and confraternities in the dissemination of those practices.

If we reconsider the role of lay communities as patrons of new Mass and Office composition, we unlock new ways of looking at musical production. While work on polyphony in the sixteenth century naturally ventures into these issues by discussing the influence of the printing press, I have shown that this type of lay involvement predates the advent of this medium. Through this lens, we could reconsider the repertoire of confraternities in the Low Countries with royal patronage, especially the masses in the Alamire court complex of manuscripts. Among the more compelling examples in those sources are the inclusion of cantus firmus chant and chanson texts in polyphonic Mass settings that could have been performed during the Mass.[1] This is but one example of the different ways we can view new repertories as part of the devotional ethos of confraternities in this region. It is clear here that the laity played a prominent role in the cultivation of plainchant and polyphony, and this practice has its roots in the fourteenth century, and possibly before.

The case studies that I have put forth show how confraternity devotions to specific saints acted to construct and reinforce corporate identities. This works on multiple levels, but those that are the most important here are geographical area and trade. For instance, as I showed in chapter 5, student identities in Paris were bound to the places they came from, and they had intense loyalty to their specific "nation" within the university, which involved adoration of specific saints. Notions of geography are also present in the *Translatio* and *Inventio* narratives, and in the St. Sebastian liturgies that focus on place. Places have power, and a sense of belonging based on common geography was very strong at this time period. Liturgical texts—especially for St. Sebastian—reflect this. This likely intensified during France's war with Britain (the Hundred Years War), which ended in 1453, for at this time devotions to local saints promoted as national protectors took on special importance.

Trade identities were also reinforced through devotions to specific patron saints. The Confraternity of the Spice Dealers and Apothecaries and their celebration of the act of *Translatio* is a good example of this. Spice dealers and apothecaries sold oils that were used for healing, a fact reflected in their choice of St. Nicholas as a patron saint and adoration of his healing oil. The vernacular sequence text *Previst le createur* invites us to examine the role of congregational singing, which had an increasingly important place in the royal devotional confraternities of the late sixteenth century.[2]

In the late fifteenth and early sixteenth centuries, those men and women in control of book production in Paris had an important part in the distribution of the specialized practices promoted by confraternities. Printers cannot only be seen as university employees and entrepreneurs, and editors of books containing music cannot only be viewed as musicians and redactors of chant. These persons were also educated and were aware of the liturgical practices of institutions surrounding them. This extends to trade and devotional confraternities, student groups, and practices from other dioceses. The printers themselves were responsible for disseminating many of the votive masses that also appeared in confraternity manuscripts by adding them at the end of printed missals for Tournai, Cambrai, Amiens, and Soissons. It is not clear where they obtained these masses, but their similarity to those used in confraternity books implies that they likely had similar origins. The estimated print runs of the editions of liturgical books, in each case far in excess of the number of parish churches and confraternities in these cities, suggests that the printed diocesan missals and the editions of the *Misse familiares*, *Misse solenniores*, and *Communes prosa* could easily have been sold not only to churches and confraternities but also to individuals. It would not at all be surprising if every one of the thousands of priests in the city of Paris owned a missal, and this is true for other geographical areas as well. Furthermore, the very small format of these printed books also strongly suggests preparation for purchase by individuals.[3] Identical editions were printed in the middle of the century in Lyon by Jacques Moderne, demonstrating their wide appeal.

Confraternities were central to life in urban centers at this time, and this continued well into the seventeenth and eighteenth centuries. For example, interest in knowing which confraternities worshipped at which institutions in Paris is evident through the publication in 1621 of Le Masson's guide to different confraternities, their patron saints, and their sheltering houses in Paris.[4] The importance placed on comprehension of liturgical texts continues to increase in the centuries after, resulting in confraternities having texts for the Mass and Office translated into French and printed by local printers. One such example is a book printed in 1717 in Paris by Gilles Paulus-Du-Mesnil, entitled *Les Offices Propres de S. Nicolas Evesque de Myre*. The title page indicates that it was printed for the Confraternity of the Wine Merchants in Paris, who worshipped at the Church of St. Jacques de l'Hôpital on the rue St. Denis. Among the contents of the book are masses and offices for the Feast of St. Nicholas on December 6, and his Translation on May 9. There is no music in the book, nor do the texts share any of the unique references discussed in the present study, but this printed edition shows a later manifestation of a process that commenced in the fifteenth century with F-Pm 464 and continued into the sixteenth century with the printed editions of the *Misse familiares*. All of this shows that confraternities were central in shaping local lay devotional and musical practices in ways that were equally important to the major ecclesiastical and monastic institutions and courts that have received notable scholarly attention.

Appendix I:

Sources

This appendix records all the manuscript and printed liturgical books referred to in this study. Each source is assigned a number that corresponds to those used in the comparison tables throughout the chapters and appendices. This appendix only includes liturgical books and others that contain texts, or chant and polyphony for the Mass and Office. It does not include the confraternity registers, chronicles, hagiographical works, and other archival collections referenced throughout the study.

1   B-Br Inc. A 545—*Misse solempniores*. Printed in Paris by Michel de Toulouze, ca. 1500.
2   B-Br 3782—Missal from the diocese of Liège with music only for the Mass ordinary, early sixteenth century.
3   B-Br 6434—Antiphoner for a Franciscan community, diocese of Liège, sixteenth century.
4   B-Br 11396—Gradual from the Abbey of Tongerlo, fourteenth century.
5   B-Gu 15—Antiphoner from the Abbey of St. Bavo in Ghent, fifteenth century.
6   B-Lsc 1—Antiphoner (winter) for the Church of Ste. Croix in Liège, 1333–34.
7   B-Lsc 2—Antiphoner (summer) for the Church of Ste. Croix in Liège, 1333–34.
8   B-Tc A 10—Notated missal for the usage of the Tournai cathedral (before ca. 1265).
9   B-Tc A 11—Notated missal for the usage of Tournai cathedral ca. 1265.
10 B-Tc A 12—Antiphoner and gradual used by the Confraternity of the Notaries at the Cathedral of Tournai, thirteenth through sixteenth centuries.
11 B-Tc A 13—Gradual used by the Confraternity of the Notaries at the Cathedral of Tournai, thirteenth through sixteenth centuries.
12 B-Tc A 27—Gradual used by the Confraternity of the Notaries at the Cathedral of Tournai, thirteenth through sixteenth centuries.
13 B-Tc A 28—Tonary for the usage of the Tournai cathedral, fourteenth and fifteenth centuries.

14   B-Tc A 58—Antiphoner, gradual, and processional used by the Confraternity of the Notaries at the Cathedral of Tournai, fifteenth through seventeenth centuries.

15   B-TOb 63—Antiphoner for the Onze-Lieve-Vrouwekerk in Tongeren, ca. 1375–1400.

16   B-TOb 64—Antiphoner for the Onze-Lieve-Vrouwekerk in Tongeren, ca. 1375–1400.

17   B-Ts Inc. 27—*Missale insignis ecclesie Tornacensis.* Printed in Paris by Johannes Higman, 1498.

18   B-Tv 12—Notated missal used in a chapel at the Tournai cathedral, early fourteenth century.

19   B-Tv 13—Missal and ritual used in a chapel at the Tournai cathedral, early fourteenth century.

20   B-Tv 21—Breviary from Tournai (no music), late fourteenth century.

21   B-Tv 22—Breviary from Tournai (no music), middle of the fifteenth century.

22   CH-HE Codex Chart. 151—Fifteenth-century book containing Ars Nova fragment of the Tournai Mass Gloria in the binding.

23   D-Mbs Mus. 66—Manuscript containing polyphonic masses, produced ca. 1515.

24   D-Mbs Mus. 1536—Series of partbooks containing polyphonic liturgical compositions, produced in 1583.

25   D-TRb 480—Antiphoner from the Cathedral of St. Peter in Trier, middle of the fourteenth century.

26   D-TRb 486—Antiphoner from Koblenz, late fourteenth century.

27   D-TRb 488a—Antiphoner from Dietkirchen, fifteenth century.

28   D-TRb 498a—Antiphoner from the Cathedral of St. Peter in Trier, fifteenth century.

29   D-TRsb 427/1250—Breviary from the Church of St. Simeon in Trier, fourteenth century.

30   E-BUlh Codex Las Huelgas—Manuscript containing polyphonic works, includes the Tournai Mass Credo, produced in the early 1340s.

31   E-Mn V 21–8—Fourteenth-century gradual containing the Tournai Credo.

32   F-AM 162 D—Liturgical book containing chant and polyphony for the Confraternity of St. Barbara at the Abbey of Corbie, sixteenth century.

33   F-AM 165 F—Gradual for the usage of Amiens, late fifteenth or early sixteenth century.

34   F-AM Rés 23 D—*Missal ad usum et consuetudinem insignis ecclesie Ambiansis.* Printed by Jean Petit in Paris, 1529.

35   F-APT Trésor 16 bis (Apt Codex)—Choirbook from the papal residence in Avignon during the Avignon schism, containing the Credo of the Tournai Mass.

36   F-CA 38—Cambrai cathedral antiphoner, middle of the thirteenth century.

37   F-CA 69—Antiphoner and gradual used in the bishop's chapel at the Cambrai cathedral, fourteenth century.

38   F-CA 104—Tournai cathedral breviary, middle of the fifteenth century.

39   F-CA 158—Missal containing votive masses for Cambrai, fifteenth century (no music).

40   F-CA 406—Portions of a missal, thirteenth or fourteenth century (no music).

41   F-CA Inc. B 145—Fourteenth-century fragments from Cambrai containing the Tournai Mass Gloria.

42   F-CA Impr. XVI C 4—*Antiphonale secundum usum Cameracensis ecclesie.* Published by Simon Vostre in Paris, ca. 1508–18.

43   F-Dm 2837—Incunabulum containing a manuscript fragment with a polyphonic setting of the Sanctus and Agnus Dei "Vineux."

44   F-Lad 134 no. 12—Fragment from Cambrai containing the Credo I and Sanctus "Vineux" in cantus fractus.

45   F-Lfc 1.M.21—*Missale parvum secundum usum venerabilis ecclesie Cameracensis.* Published by Henri Estienne I in Paris, 1507.

46   F-Lm 23 (502)—Notated missal from the Church of St. Amé in Douai, thirteenth century.

47   F-MOf H 196 (Montpellier Codex)—Manuscript containing polyphonic works, produced in the late thirteenth century and early fourteenth century.

48   F-Pa 110—Gradual from Paris, fourteenth century

49   F-Pa 114—Ordinal from the Ste. Chapelle in Paris, fifteenth century.

50   F-Pa 168—Antiphoner and gradual used by the Confraternity of St. Hubert at the Hospital of St. Julian in Paris, fifteenth century.

51   F-Pa 204—Notated missal used by the Confraternity of the Bourgeois Archers in Paris, fifteenth through seventeenth centuries.

52   F-Pa 611—Missal for an unknown confraternity containing votive masses without music, produced in the late fifteenth or early sixteenth century.

53   F-Pa 620—Notated missal from Paris, fifteenth century.

54   F-Pm 390—Liturgical book from Bruges containing music for the Mass, sixteenth century.

55   F-Pm 411—Notated missal from the College of Navarre in Paris, ca. 1380.

56   F-Pm 461—Notated missal and breviary for the Confraternity of St. John the Evangelist for the book production community in Paris, fifteenth century.

57   F-Pm 462—Notated breviary and missal for the Confraternity of the Oilers and Candle Makers in Paris, fifteenth and sixteenth centuries.

58   F-Pm 464—Notated breviary and missal for the Confraternity of St. Nicholas for the spice dealers of Paris, fifteenth and sixteenth centuries.

59   F-Pm 502—Book of hours for the usage of Rome, fifteenth century.

60   F-Pm 511—Book of hours for the usage of Troyes, sixteenth century.

61   F-Pm 527—Missal for the usage of St. Victor, fifteenth through seventeenth centuries.

62 F-Pm 8° 90939 Rés—Sens Missal, *Missale ad consuetudinem senonensis ecclesiae.* Printed in Paris in 1506 by Simon Vostre.

63 F-Pnlr Microfilm M–10268—*Graduale Cenomanense.* Printed in Paris in 1515 by Thielmann Kerver I.

64 F-Pnlr Rés B. 27695 (part 1 of a bound volume, cited throughout this study as MS 1510)—*Misse solenniores.* Printed in Paris in 1510 by Geoffrey Marnef.

65 F-Pnlr Rés. B 27695 (part 2 of a bound volume, cited throughout this study as MF 1519)—*Misse familiares.* Printed in Paris in 1519 by Geoffrey Marnef.

66 F-Pnlr Rés. B 27695 (part 3 of a bound volume, cited throughout this study as CP 1509)—*Communes prose.* Printed in Paris in 1509 by Geoffrey Marnef.

67 F-Pnlr Rés. B 27695 (part 4 of a bound volume)—*Passiones novissime.* Printed in Paris at an undetermined date by François Regnault.

68 F-Pnlr Rés. B 27762—*Misse familiares.* Printed in Rouen in 1523 to be sold in Paris by François Regnault. Cited throughout this study as MF 1523.

69 F-Pnm fr. 819–20—Manuscript containing miracle plays for the Confraternity of the Goldsmiths in Paris from 1339–82.

70 F-Pnm lat. 830—Notated missal from St. Germain l'Auxerrois in Paris, thirteenth century (second half).

71 F-Pnm lat. 859—Missal from Paris, fifteenth century (second half).

72 F-Pnm lat. 860—Missal for the usage of Bruges, altered for Parisian usage for the "Grande Confrérie de Notre Dame aux prêtres et bourgeois de Paris," fourteenth century.

73 F-Pnm lat. 861—Notated missal from Paris (Confraternity of the Burghers at Ste. Marie-Madeleine-en-la-Cité), fourteenth century.

74 F-Pnm lat. 862—Missal for the usage of Paris, used by a confraternity at the Church of Ste. Marie-Madeleine-en-la-Cité, thirteenth century.

75 F-Pnm lat. 1051—Notated breviary for the Confraternity of St. James in Paris, fifteenth century.

76 F-Pnm lat. 1112—Notated missal from Notre Dame in Paris, ca. 1225.

77 F-Pnm lat. 1123—Notated processional from the College of Navarre in Paris, ca. 1380.

78 F-Pnm lat. 1337—Gradual from Paris, late thirteenth or early fourteenth century.

79 F-Pnm lat. 3461—Parisian manuscript from the thirteenth century containing the *Speculum ecclesiae* and a vernacular hymn for St. Nicholas.

80 F-Pnm lat. 8884—Missal for Dominican usage, adapted for the chapel of St. Louis de Marseille at Notre Dame, thirteenth century.

81 F-Pnm lat. 9441—Notated missal from the Chapel of St. Aignan (Notre Dame) in Paris, thirteenth century.

82 F-Pnm lat. 10506—Gradual and antiphoner used by the Confraternity of the Coopers in Paris, fifteenth century.

83 F-Pnm lat. 12065—Missal from Paris, fifteenth century.

84   F-Pnm lat. 14282—Missal from Paris, fifteenth century.

85   F-Pnm lat. 15181—Notated breviary from Notre Dame in Paris, ca. 1300 (winter).

86   F-Pnm lat. 15182—Notated breviary from Notre Dame in Paris, ca. 1300 (summer).

87   F-Pnm lat. 15280—Missal for the usage of Paris (Church of St. Marcel), fifteenth century.

88   F-Pnm lat. 15614—Missal for the usage of St. Médard in Soissons, twelfth century.

89   F-Pnm lat. 15615—Notated missal from the Sorbonne in Paris, thirteenth century.

90   F-Pnm lat. 15616—Notated missal from Evreux (adapted to Parisian usage), thirteenth century.

91   F-Pnm lat. 17311—Notated missal from Cambrai (Confraternity of Notre Dame de Cambrai, altered for Parisian usage), 1300–25.

92   F-Pnm lat. 17314—Missal from Paris (Confraternity of the Holy Sacrament at St. Nicholas-des-Champs), fifteenth century.

93   F-Pnm nouv. acq. lat. 2649—Notated missal from Paris, first quarter of the fourteenth century.

94   F-Pnm nouv. acq. fr. 23190—Collection of Ars Nova fragments, ca. 1376.

95   F-Psg 97—Missal for the usage of Paris, fourteenth century.

96   F-Psg 4º BB 138 inv. 351 Rés—*Missale ad usum ecclesiae Cenomanensis*. Printed in Paris in 1530 by Wolfgang Hopyl.

97   F-Psg 8 BB 533 inv. 717—*Missale ad consuetudinem ecclesiae Romane*. Printed in Paris in 1511 by Guillaume Eustace.

98   F-Psg Fol. BB 97 INV 102 Rés—*Missale ad usum fratrum ordinis Sancte Trinitate de Redemptione*. Printed in Paris in 1529 by Nicolas Prévost.

99   F-Psg Fol. BB 124 inv. 134 Rés—*Missale secundum usum ecclesiae Suessoniensis*. Printed in Paris in 1509 by Simon Vostre.

100 F-Psg OEXV 54²—*Missale ad consuetudinem insignis ecclesiae Parisien*. Printed in Paris in 1504 by Simon Vostre.

101 F-Psg OEXV 828 (3) Rés—*Breviarium Tornacense* (pars hyemalis). Printed in Paris in 1497 by Jean Higman.

102 F-RS 264—Gradual for the usage of the Abbey of St. Thierry near Reims, twelfth century.

103 F-VAL 122—Missal containing votive masses, music only for prefaces, fifteenth century.

104 GB-Lbl Add. 16905—Notated missal from Notre Dame in Paris, fourteenth century.

105 GB-Lbl Add. 38723—Notated missal from Notre Dame in Paris, thirteenth century (middle).

106 I-AO 15—Anthology of polyphonic music compiled in Bologna, the Basel-Strasbourg area, and Innsbruck between 1430–46.

107 I-BAas Fondo S. Nicola 85—Gradual and sequentiary created around 1242 for the Ste. Chapelle in Paris.

108 I-Bc Q 15—Anthology of polyphonic works compiled in the Veneto, Padua, and Vicenza between 1420–35.

109 I-CFm LVI—Dominican gradual from Italy, fourteenth century.

110 I-IV CXV (Ivrea Codex)—Anthology of fourteenth-century Avignon repertory (1360).

111 I-Rsm uncatalogued gradual—Fourteenth-century gradual used at the papal chapel in Avignon, which contains the Credo of the Tournai Mass.

112 NL-DHk 71 A 13—Ordinal without music notation for the Onze-Lieve-Vrouwekerk in Maastricht, 1354–73.

113 NL-DHk 76 E 18—Antiphoner and gradual used by the Confraternity of the Doublet Makers at the Hospital of Ste. Catherine in Paris, fifteenth century.

114 P-Cug M.2—Manuscript containing polyphonic masses produced in the middle of the sixteenth century.

115 PL-WRu AK 1955/KN 195—Fourteenth-century fragments containing the Ite Missa Est of the Tournai Mass.

116 US-BAw 302—Notated missal from Paris (unidentified ducal chapel), fifteenth century.

117 US-Bp *M.149a.47 (part 1 of a bound volume, cited throughout this study as MF ca. 1538)—*Misse familiares*. Printed at an unknown location ca. 1538 and sold in Paris by François Regnault.

118 US-Bp *M.149a.47 (part 2 of a bound volume, cited throughout this study as MS 1538)—*Misse solenniores*. Printed in Paris in 1538 by François Regnault.

119 US-Bp *M.149a.47 (part 3 of a bound volume, cited throughout this study as CP 1536)—*Communes prose*. Printed in Paris in 1536 by François Regnault.

120 US-Cn Inc. 9344.5—*Breviarium leodiense*. Printed in 1484 in Brussels by the Frères de la vie commune.

121 US-ELmsu 2—Book of hours from northern France (possibly Paris region), fifteenth century.

Appendix 2:

Inventories of Sources from Tournai

This appendix records all the manuscript and printed liturgical books containing music that were used by confraternities at various institutions in Tournai through the end of the sixteenth century.[1] Because musical sources from Tournai have not been the object of an in-depth study, sources used in the main sanctuary of the cathedral, as well as those used in other chapels at this institution, are included in the appendix with truncated descriptions. Within the inventories, all Mass ordinary chants are listed in the order in which they appear in the manuscript or printed book, along with a "C" number that has been assigned solely for the purposes of the present study.[2] The appendix also takes special care to indicate sequences appearing outside of the Mass in these sources. The numbering system in this appendix corresponds to the numbers assigned to the sources in appendix 1, which are used for all comparison tables in the chapters and appendices throughout the present study.

---

1   Less detailed versions of the following inventories of the Tournai manuscripts (used in both confraternity and parish/cathedral settings) are published in Long, "Les devotions des confréries." They have been modified here to highlight the Mass ordinary chants, to which I have assigned numbers corresponding to those given in the tables in appendix 5 ⌖. I provide descriptions of all Tournai sources here because a cohesive list of the manuscripts and printed books containing music that were used at institutions in the city is not found elsewhere.

2   CK (Confraternity Kyrie), CG (Confraternity Gloria), CC (Confraternity Credo), CS (Confraternity Sanctus), CA (Confraternity Agnus Dei). This numbering system has no relationship to those used in other published or online chant indices.

Liturgical Books Used by Confraternities in Tournai[3]

10. Archives et Bibliothèque de la Cathédrale de Tournai, Manuscript 12 (B-Tc A 12).[4] 270 x 185 mm. Late fourteenth- or early fifteenth-century binding (a date determined based on the index of the source's contents, discussed in chapter 1), consisting of brown leather over wooden boards, with evidence of missing clasps. 1 unnumbered parchment flyleaf + 216 numbered parchment folios. Foliation in a modern hand beginning on the second parchment folio in pencil, using Arabic numerals written only on the recto of each leaf in the lower right-hand margin. Penwork initials, and use of red, blue, and yellow throughout. No illuminations. The music notation, which appears on red four-lined staves, consists primarily of a hybrid form commonly found in the southern Low Countries, which mixes elements of French and German neumes.[5] There is also square chant notation on four-lined red staves throughout.

Antiphoner and gradual used by the Confraternity of the Notaries at the Cathedral of Tournai, with original contents and later additions dating from the thirteenth through sixteenth centuries.[6] There is a card glued to the front of the book in the nineteenth century indicating the source's place of origin,

3   Truncated versions of the inventories for B-Tc A 12, B-Tc A 13, and B-Tc A 27 are published in Long, "La musique et la liturgie."

4   For a basic description of the source, see Dumoulin, "Livre de choeur." There is also a rudimentary description of the manuscript in an unpublished inventory held at the Cathedral Archives. See the unpublished inventory by Van Cranenbroeck, "Analyse codicologique de l'antiphonaire A 12." A more detailed description in French appears in the 2016 edition of the Tournai Mass with more information on the binding, but without special attention to the use of notation and chant contents. See the preface to *La Messe de Tournai*, eds. Dumoulin et al., 9–12.

5   De Loos calls this type of notation "Notation of the Low Countries" or "Dutch notation" in *Duitse en Nederlandse Muzieknotaties*, 373. A visual reproduction of the music appears in the 2016 edition of the Tournai Mass (from fol. 48r); see the preface to *La Messe de Tournai*, eds. Dumoulin et al., 12.

6   Jacques Pycke has indicated that the manuscript was produced ca. 1280, in "Matériaux pour l'histoire de la bibliothèque capitulaire," 80. A discussion of the inventory of the confraternity's holdings appears in Derolez, *Corpus Catalogorum Belgii*, vol. 4, 307–8; and Voisin, "Drames liturgiques de Tournai."

"Cathedral de Tournay" [*sic*]. Written in pen on the recto of the first unnumbered flyleaf is the old code from the previous numbering system, written in an early twentieth-century hand, "474."[7] Contains masses and offices for all the Marian services throughout the year as well as those for St. Barbara, St. Catherine, St. Nicholas, and St. Vincent. In addition to the offices, this manuscript contains masses for the main feasts of the Temporale, and Mass ordinary chants. At the beginning of the book there is a fabric listing the holdings of the confraternity, and an index of the book's contents.

[i]v	"Incipit ordo Officiorum in isto libro existencium" (includes original foliation)
1r	"Ista sunt ornamenta spectantia ad confraternitatem notariorum pro capella" (not found in the "Incipit ordo")
2v	*Regina celi letare* (not found in the "Incipit ordo")
3r	Office for St. Barbara (not found in the "Incipit ordo")
11v	Mass for St. Barbara (not found in the "Incipit ordo")
14v	*Alleluya. Inclita virgo barbara* (not found in the "Incipit ordo")
15r	Mass for the Commemoration of the Virgin; Kyrie (CK 2), Gloria (CG 6)
16v	Kyrie (CK 1); sequence *Preter rerum* (sequence not found in the "Incipit ordo")
17r	Credo (CC 2)
18r	Kyrie (CK 14), Kyrie (CK 9); Sanctus (CS 3); Agnus Dei (CA 5)
18v	Kyrie in cantus fractus (CK 19)
19r	Office for St. Vincent
20r	Office for the Purification of the Virgin
36r	Office for the Annunciation
48r	Office for the Assumption
59r	Office for the Nativity of the Virgin
67v	Office for St. Catherine
81r	Office for St. Nicholas
94v	Office for the Nativity
115r	Mass for St. Vincent
118r	Mass for All Saints
121v	Mass for the Nativity (in *Gallicantu*)
123r	Mass for the Nativity (in *Aurora*)
124v	Mass for the Nativity (main Mass)
128r	Mass for Epiphany

---

7   Most musicological literature referring to this book uses the code from the old numbering system, whereas I have adopted the new numbering system throughout this book for all of the holdings at the Cathedral Archives of Tournai.

131v   Sanctus (CS 4) (not found in the "Incipit ordo")
132r   Mass for the Assumption
136r   Mass for the Nativity of the Virgin
140r   Mass for the Purification
142v   Mass for the Annunciation
145r   Mass for St. Catherine
147v   Mass for St. Nicholas
152v   Kyrie *Fons bonitatis* (CK 4)
154r   Kyrie (CK 6); Sanctus (CS 5)
154v   Kyrie (CK 7); Gloria (CG 3)
156r   Sequences
    156r   *Marie preconio servat cum gaudio*
    157r   *Inviolata intacta et casta es maria*
    157v   *Verbum bonum et suave*
    158v   *Ave stella marium, maria spes tristium*
    159v   *Alma redemptoris mater quem de celis misit pater*
    161r   *Ave virgo virginum, ave lumen luminum*
    162r   *Ave maria gratia plena*
    163v   *Ave mundi spes maria*
    165r   *Epythalamica dic sponsa cantica*
    167r   *Hodierne lux diei*
    168r   *Benedicta es celorum*
    169r   *Letabundus exultet fidelis*
    170r   *Virginis marie* (not found in "Incipit ordo")
171r   Mass for the Holy Spirit
175r   Requiem
178r   Gloria (CG 4)
179r   Gloria (CG 1)
179v   Gloria (CG 2)
181r   Sanctus (CS 1); Sanctus (CS 2)
181v   Agnus Dei (CA 6); Agnus Dei (CA 1)
182r   Agnus Dei (CA 2)
182v   Alleluias for the Mass (not found in "Incipit ordo")
185r   Chants for the feast of the Purification
189v   Hymn *Ave maris stella*; antiphon *Salve regina*
190v   Antiphon *Ave regina celorum*
191r   Hymn *Te deum laudamus*
194r   Kyrie (CK 10); Sanctus (CS 15)
195r   Office for Corpus Christi
209r   Mass for Corpus Christi
213r   Sanctus (CS 6); Sanctus (CS 7)
214v   Mass for the Resurrection (ends on fol. 216)

11. Archives et Bibliothèque de la Cathédrale de Tournai, Manuscript 13 (B-Tc A 13).[8] 250 x 185 mm. Brown leather binding over wooden boards with clasps, possibly dating from the thirteenth or fourteenth century. 1 unnumbered parchment flyleaf + 33 unnumbered parchment folios (the foliation given below is my own, using brackets). Penwork initials, and use of red, blue, and yellow throughout. No illuminations. The music notation, which appears on red four-lined staves, consists primarily of a hybrid form commonly found in the southern Low Countries, which mixes elements of French and German neumes.[9] There is also some black square chant notation on four-lined red staves.

Gradual used by the Confraternity of the Notaries at the Cathedral of Tournai, with original contents and later additions dating from the thirteenth through sixteenth centuries. On the recto of the first unnumbered parchment flyleaf is a pastedown with the code from the old numbering system (475) and written in pen in a twentieth-century hand is the new code (A 13). There are also handwritten addenda on fol. [i]r containing the names of eight notaries and the date "46," "notarii anno xlvi, magister Johannes de la Forge, Dominus Johannes Corvillain, Dominus Jacobus Cerier, Dominus Alardus Bourdiau, Dominus Gerardus Maresquiau, Dominus, Cornelius Steenkist, Dominus Straten, Dominus Nicholaus." Jacques Pycke has traced Jean Corvillain and Gerardus Maresquiau to documents from the mid-to-late sixteenth century, indicating that this date possibly refers to 1546.[10] A pastedown on the end binding includes a handwritten addendum specifying the introit, readings, gradual, sequence, offertory, and communion chants

8   See Long, "La musique et la liturgie." A preliminary description of the manuscript appears in the unpublished inventory by Arboit and Ledèque, "Manuscrit A 13." The manuscript is also described in the 2016 edition of the Tournai Mass without special attention to the chant notation and musical contents, but with added details about the binding. See the preface to Dumoulin et al., *La Messe de Tournai*, 13–15.

9   It is the same type of hybrid notation described in the inventory for B-Tc A 12 and discussed by De Loos in *Duitse en Nederlandse Muzieknotaties*, 373. A reproduction of this type of notation from the manuscript (on fol. 17r) appears in the 2016 edition of the Tournai Mass. See the preface to Dumoulin et al., *La Messe de Tournai*, 14.

10   Pycke has also transcribed the names and included reference to documents where the names are found. See the preface to Dumoulin et al., *La Messe de Tournai*, 13–15.

to be done on the feast of the Conception of the Virgin Mary.[11] Contains masses for the Virgin Mary, St. Catherine, and St. Nicholas.

[i]r   List of notaries from the year 1546
[1]r   Chants for the office of the Purification
[3]r   Mass for the Purification
[5]r   Mass for the Annunciation
[8]r   Mass for the Assumption
[12]r   Mass for the Nativity of the Virgin
[16]r   Kyrie (CK 5)
[17]r   Mass for St. Catherine
[19]v   Mass for St. Nicholas
[25]r   Readings for various masses in hands dating from the fourteenth through sixteenth centuries (Holy Sacrament, Purification, Requiem, Annunciation, Assumption, Nativity of the Virgin, Conception of the Virgin, St. Nicholas, and St. Catherine) (ends on fol. 33v).

12. Archives et Bibliothèque de la Cathédrale de Tournai, Manuscript 27 (B-Tc A 27).[12] 350 x 225 mm. Binding of wood boards with leather spine and missing clasps, possibly dating from the fourteenth century, based on the contents of the book. 1 unnumbered parchment flyleaf (fragment of a charter) + 40 numbered parchment folios. Foliation in a modern hand beginning on the second parchment folio in pencil, using Arabic numerals written only on the recto of each leaf in the upper right-hand margin. Penwork initials, and use of red, blue, and yellow throughout. No illuminations. The music notation, which appears on red four-lined staves, consists primarily of a hybrid form commonly found in the southern Low Countries, which mixes

11   "Finis in conceptione beate marie ad missam gaudeamus epistola ego quasi iuris graduale audi filia alleluya nobilis sequentia stella maris o maria evangelii liber offertorium ave maria communio diffusa est" (For the Conception of Holy Mary at Mass, *Gaudeamus*, epistle *Ego quasi iuris*, Graduale *Audi filia*, *Alleluya nobilis*, Sequence *Stella Maris o Maria*, gospels, Offertory *Ave Maria*, Communion *Diffusa est*).

12   Of all the confraternity sources in the Cathedral Archives, this one has received the most attention starting in the nineteenth century. See Coussemaker, "Messe du XIIIe siècle"; Dumoulin, "Messe de Tournai," 55–56; Pycke, "Matériaux pour l'histoire de la bibliothèque capitulaire," 80; Huglo, "La Messe de Tournai"; Dumoulin et al., *La Messe de Tournai*; and Guletsky, "The Four 14th-Century Anonymous Masses." For a preliminary study of the chant contents of this source, see Long, "La musique et la liturgie."

elements of French and German neumes.[13] There is also some square chant notation on four-lined red staves.

Gradual used by the Confraternity of the Notaries at the Cathedral of Tournai, with original contents and later additions dating from the thirteenth through sixteenth centuries. On the recto of the first numbered parchment leaf is a pastedown with the code from the old numbering system (476) and written in pen in a twentieth-century hand is the new code (A 27). Contains select masses in honor of the Virgin Mary, chants for St. Catherine and St. Nicholas, and select feasts from the Temporale. This manuscript contains the polyphonic Tournai Mass (fol. 28r–33v).

[i]	fragment of a charter
1r	Mass for Resurrection
2v	Mass for the Nativity
3v	Sequence *Veni costi filia* (St. Catherine); *Alleluya. O gratiarum balsamo referta*
4r	Mass for the Commemoration of the Virgin; Kyrie (CK 6); Kyrie (CK 7); Gloria (CG 3)
5v	Credo (CC 1)
6v	Sanctus (CS 2); Sanctus (CS 11); Agnus Dei (CA 1); Agnus Dei (CA 7); Mass for the Annunciation (during Advent)
7r	Requiem; Kyrie (CK 15)
7v	Kyrie (no music)
8v	Sanctus (CS 8); Agnus Dei (CA 9)
9r	Sequences[14]

9r	*Marie preconio servat cum gaudio*
9v	*Gaude mater virgo christi que per aurem concepisti*
9v	*Gratuletur orbis totus*
10r	*Inviolata intacta et casta es maria*
10v	*Verbum bonum et suave*
11r	*Ave stella marium maria spes tristium*
11v	*Alma redemptoris mater quem de celis misit pater*
12r	*Ave virgo virginum, ave lumen luminum*
12r	*Ave maria gratia plena*
13r	*Ave mundi spes maria*

---

13   See the inventory of B-Tc A 12 for a description of this type of notation, and the work of de Loos.

14   There is a rubric in the manuscript indicating that these are "Sequences for the Blessed Virgin Mary" (Sequentiae de beata virgine maria). Although more or less the same series of sequences appears in B-Tc A 12, they are not introduced with a rubric.

13v   *Epythalamica dic sponsa cantica*
14v   *Hodierne lux diei*
15r   *Benedicta es celorum*
15v   *Letabundus exultet fidelis*
16r   *Alleluya. Ave maria gratia plena*; sequence *Mittit ad virginem*
17r   Mass for the Holy Cross
19r   Sequence *Post partum virgo maria*
19v   Sequence *Hac clara die*
20r   Offertory *Letare mater que virginitate*
20v   *Sancta maria succurre*; Sanctus (CS 16)
21r   Readings for the Nativity
22r   Sanctus (CS 12)
22v   Sanctus (CS 10); Sanctus (CS 13); Sanctus (CS 6)
23r   Sanctus (CS 4); Sanctus (CS 3)
23v   Agnus Dei (CA 5); Agnus Dei (CA 6); Agnus Dei (CA 7)
24r   Agnus Dei (CA 2); Mass for the Holy Spirit
27v   Gradual *Propter veritatem*; *Ecce dominus veniet*
28r   Polyphonic Tournai Mass
34r   Kyrie *Cunctipotens genitor* (CK 1); Kyrie *Fons bonitatis* (CK 4); Kyrie (CK 16); Kyrie (CK 6)
34v   Kyrie (CK 7); Kyrie (CK 9); Gloria (CG 4)
35r   Gloria (CG 1)
35v   Gloria (CG 3)
36r   Gloria (CG 2)
36v   *Virginis marie laudes*
37r   *Ave virgo gloriosa mater*
37v   Offertory *Regina celi letare*; Credo (CC 2)
38v   Sanctus (CS 7); Agnus Dei (CA 3)
39r   Kyrie (CK 8); Kyrie (CK 2); Kyrie (CK 10)
39v   *Alleluya. Orietur stella ex iacob*; Kyrie (CK 5); communion *Diffusa est gratia*
40r   *Alleluya. Benedictus es domine deus*; *Alleluya. Inter natos mulierum*; sequence *Gaude virgo mater cristi*; *Alleluya. Tumba sancti nicholai*
40v   *Alleluya. Dulce trium glorium*; *Alleluya. In te domini speravit*; Kyrie (CK 8)

14. Archives et Bibliothèque de la Cathédrale de Tournai, Manuscript 58 (B-Tc A 58).[15] 290 x 220 mm. The book is bound using a parchment folio

---

15   A very detailed codicological inventory of the source and its contents appears in Pycke, "La confrérie de la Transfiguration." Here I present a truncated version of that inventory, with a primary focus on the musical contents. Also see Ceulemans, "Le manuscrit musical Tournai B.C.T. A 58"; Ceulemans, "Une 'Missa Sancta Trinitas' anonyme"; and Ceulemans, "Le manuscrit BCT A 58."

as its outer cover, attached with leather. 49 numbered parchment folios. Foliation in a modern hand beginning on the second parchment folio in pencil, using Arabic numerals written only on the recto of each leaf in the upper right-hand margin. Penwork initials and use of red and blue throughout. No illuminations. Square chant notation on red four-lined staves is used throughout, as well as rhythmic chant notation for the chants appearing on fol. 15r–21v, and white mensural notation for the polyphonic Mass, motet, and sequence.

Antiphoner, gradual, and processional used by the Confraternity of the Transfiguration at the Church of Mont-Saint-Aubert in Tournai (and later, the Cathedral of Tournai). Chant contents dating from the early fifteenth century, with additions through 1602. On folio 49r is a handwritten addendum indicating ownership by the Confraternity of the Transfiguration. On the recto of the first numbered parchment leaf is a pastedown with the code from the old numbering system (471). The book contains select masses, readings, and office chants for the Transfiguration, St. Aubert, and the Trinity. At the end of the manuscript, there is a sixteenth-century polyphonic Mass setting in honor of the Transfiguration, a polyphonic motet for the Trinity (Févin), and an anonymous late sixteenth-century polyphonic setting of the sequence *Thabor superficie.*

2r	Vigil of the Transfiguration
4v	Suffrage for the Trinity *Te deum patrem ingenitum*
5r	Antiphon for the Virgin Mary *Ave templum castitatis*
6r	Antiphon for St. Aubert *Sancte audeberte tu dulcedo*
6v	Antiphon for All Saints *Beati estis sancti dei omnes*
7r	Procession before the Mass of the Transfiguration
8v	Mass for the Transfiguration (I)
10r	Kyrie (CK 11)
10v	Gloria (CG 4)
15r	Sequence for the Transfiguration, *Thabor superficie verbi dei gloria* in cantus fractus
18v	Offertory *Deus enim omnium in cantus fractus*
19v	Sanctus "Vineux" in cantus fractus (with trope "Qui vertice thabor affuisti") (CS 9)
20v	Agnus Dei "Vineux" in cantus fractus (CA 8)
21v	Sanctus (CS 1)
22r	Agnus Dei (CA 10)

An older discussion of the confraternity comes from Voisin, "Notice sur la confrérie de la Transfiguration."

23r	Communion *Revelabitur gloria domini*
24r	Antiphon for the Trinity *Benedicta sit creatrix*
25r	Readings
27v	Polyphonic *Missa sancta Trinitas* (Anonymous sixteenth-century)
40v	Motet *Sancta Trinitas* (Févin)
42v	Polyphonic sequence for the Transfiguration, *Thabor superficie verbi dei gloria* (Anonymous late sixteenth-century, added in 1602)
47r	Mass for the Transfiguration (II) (added in 1602)
49r	"Ordo confratrum [Transfigurationis] renovatum anno 1573" (handwritten addendum)

Liturgical Books Used at the Cathedral and Parishes of Tournai (brief descriptions)

8. Archives et Bibliothèque de la Cathédrale de Tournai, Manuscript 10 (B-Tc A 10).[16] 350 x 240 mm. 240 parchment folios (both modern and original foliation present). The music notation, which appears on red four-lined staves, consists of a hybrid form commonly found in the southern Low Countries, which mixes elements of French and German neumes.[17] There are decorated gold champie initials with filigrane throughout the volume marking the main feasts of the Temporale, which bear a resemblance in style to other sources from Cambrai and Namur.[18]

Notated missal for the usage of the Tournai cathedral (before ca. 1265). Contains a calendar reflecting the cathedral usage, the only original part of which is for December (the previous months are all fifteenth-century additions). The source also is missing the masses of Christmas and the text of the canon. Masses added at the end in a late fifteenth- or early sixteenth-century hand starting on folio 266r for St. Barbara, the Conception of the Virgin, St.

---

16 This manuscript is described by Jean Dumoulin in "Missel de la Cathédrale de Tournai," 49; and Jacques Pycke, "Matériaux pour l'histoire de la bibliothèque capitulaire," 79.

17 See the inventory of B-Tc A 12 for a description of this type of notation and the work of de Loos.

18 In particular, Namur, Musée diocésain, MS 516, which is a notated missal from the secular chapter of noble canonesses in Andenne, produced ca. 1260. See Long, "The Sanctorale of Andenne," 72.

Anthony, the Visitation, Corpus Christi, St. Anne, the Transfiguration, and
St. Hubert.

9. Archives et Bibliothèque de la Cathédrale de Tournai, Manuscript 11
(B-Tc A 11).[19] 380 x 260 mm. 324 parchment folios (both modern and
original foliation are present). The music notation, which appears on red
four-lined staves, consists of a hybrid form commonly found in the southern Low Countries, which mixes elements of French and German neumes.[20]
This source contains a full-page illumination before the canon, and eight
historiated initials in the temporale, all of which resemble a style of illumination found in other books from Tournai and Cambrai.[21]

Notated missal for the usage of the Tournai cathedral ca. 1265. Contains
a calendar reflecting the cathedral usage. Messine notation on four lines
throughout. In 1367, the missal was given to the capitulary hospital, and
there are many handwritten addenda at the end of the source pertaining to
the administration of that institution.

13. Archives et Bibliothèque de la Cathédrale de Tournai, Manuscript A
28 (B-Tc A 28). 340 x 260 mm. 2 paper flyleaves + 17 parchment folios
+ 2 paper flyleaves. Black square chant notation on black four-lined staves
throughout. Red and blue initials throughout, but no illuminations.

Tonary for the usage of the Tournai cathedral, fourteenth through fifteenth centuries. Contains an incomplete calendar missing the months of
March through June reflecting the cathedral usage. Numerous lacunae
throughout. Contains nine settings of the hymn *Venite exultemus*.

17. Bibliothèque du Grande Seminaire du Tournai, Inc. 27, *Missale insignis
ecclesie Tornacensis*. Printed in Paris by Johannes Higman: 1498 (B-Ts Inc.
27).[22] 320 x 220 mm. 259 paper folios. Black square music notation on red
four-lined staves. There is music only for the incipits of the Gloria, Credo,
Ite Missa Est, Benedicamus Domino, and the Prefaces.

---

19   For a general description of the source and its contents see Pycke, "Matériaux
     pour l'histoire de la bibliothèque capitulaire," 79.
20   See the inventory of B-Tc A 12 for a description of this type of notation and
     the work of de Loos.
21   For a detailed discussion of the illuminations, see Stones, "Missel de la cathe-
     drale de Tournai."
22   See Polain, *Catalogue des livres imprimés*, vol. 2, 222–24, no. 2743.

This is the very first printed edition of the missal for the usage of Tournai, printed in Paris by Johannes Higman. The calendar reflects the usage of the Tournai cathedral.

18. Tournai, Bibliothèque de la Ville, Manuscript 12 (B-Tv 12).[23] 324 x 220 mm.
135 parchment folios. The music notation, which appears on red four-lined staves, consists of a hybrid form commonly found in the southern Low Countries, that mixes elements of French and German neumes.[24] The only parts that are notated in the source are the Prefaces. There is a full-page illumination for the Prefaces on fol. 76r that represents Christ on the cross surrounded by the four Evangelists.[25]
Notated missal used in a chapel at the Tournai cathedral, with contents dating from the early fourteenth century. There is no calendar in the source, but there is a table of contents on fol. 1v–3r outlining the contents of the source, which mentions the main masses of the Temporale, the Virgin Mary, and collects for several saints, such as St. Peter, St. James, St. Mary Magdalene, St. Nicholas, St. Quentin, St. Piat, St. Martin, St. Nichasius, St. Catherine, and St. Agatha. The manuscript at one time resided in the collection at the Cathedral of Tournai, which is evident based on a stamp on fol. 1r "Bibliothecae ecclesiae Cathedralis Torn." [sic]. There is no indication that the source was used by a confraternity, but due to its limited contents, it was likely used in a private devotional setting.

19. Tournai, Bibliothèque de la Ville, Manuscript 13 (B-Tv 13).[26] 325 x 220 mm.
186 parchment folios. The music notation is of two types. Black square notation on four-lined red staves; and a hybrid form commonly found in the Southern Low Countries, which mixes elements of French and German

23 In Pycke, "Matériaux pour l'histoire de la bibliothèque capitulaire" (80) he confuses this manuscript, listed as "ca. 1326," with B-Tv 13, discussed below. For a general discussion of the book and its contents, see Faider, *Catalogue des Manuscrits Conservés a Tournai*, 40–42.

24 See the inventory of B-Tc A 12 for a discussion of this type of notation and the work of de Loos.

25 For a general discussion of the book and its contents, see Faider, *Catalogue des Manuscrits Conservés à Tournai*, 40–42.

26 For a general discussion of the book and its contents, see Faider, *Catalogue des Manuscrits Conservés à Tournai*, 42–44.

neumes, also black on red four-lined staves.[27] The square notation is used for several hymns and sequences, and the masses for Easter, Ascension, Pentecost, the Holy Trinity, the Holy Sacrament, Commons, the Virgin Mary, the Holy Cross, the Annunciation, the Requiem, Pro Pace, St. Nichasius, and the Credo in cantus fractus on fol. 181v–182r (the same as that found in B-Tc A 12 and B-Tc A 27); while the Low Countries notation is used for the Genealogies of Matthew and Luke, the Exsultet, and Prefaces. One full-page illumination of Christ on the cross on fol. 62v. Decorated initials throughout.

Missal and Ritual used in a chapel at the Tournai cathedral dating from the early fourteenth century, with additions well into the fifteenth century. Marks of ownership consist of several coats of arms, painted on fol. 1r in the large penwork initial "R." These have been identified as the coats of arms of Gui de Boulogne, bishop of Tournai from 1301–26, and his successor, Guillaume de Vantadour (1329–33).[28] There is no calendar in the source, but a survey of its musical contents (see paragraph above) includes the main feasts of the Temporale, as well as some from the sanctorale. The manuscript at one time resided in the collection at the Cathedral of Tournai, which is evident based on a pastedown on fol. 1r "Bibliothecae ecclesiae Cathedralis Torn." [sic]. Further evidence of its usage at the cathedral is the appearance of the same rare Credo in cantus fractus found in other Tournai books. In addition, there is a Mass for St. Nichasius, which may indicate some connection to B-Tv 12. There is no indication that the source was used by a confraternity, but due to its limited contents and ownership, it was used in a private devotional setting.

---

27   See the inventory of B-Tc A 12 for a discussion of this type of notation and the work of de Loos.

28   For the most recent discussion of the coats of arms, see Fourez, "Missel début XIVe siècle," 130. For an earlier discussion of the manuscript, see Faider, *Catalogue des Manuscrits Conservés à Tournai*, 42–44.

Appendix 3:

Scribal Hands and Gatherings in the Tournai Notary Confraternity Manuscripts

The following images and tables show the gathering structures for the three manuscripts used by the Confraternity of the Notaries at the Cathedral of Tournai. Each hand has been given a name such as Scribe A, Scribe B, etc., based on the order in which they appear in each book. Therefore, scribes that are common among all three sources will be called something different in all three inventories.

Appendix 3 Figure 1. Gathering structure for B-Tc A 12.

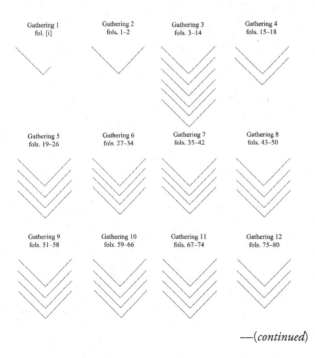

—(continued)

Appendix 3 Figure 1—*continued*

Gathering 13
fols. 81–88
Gathering 14
fols. 89–96
Gathering 15
fols. 97–104
Gathering 16
fols. 105–114
Gathering 17
fols. 115–122
Gathering 18
fols. 123–131
Gathering 19
fols. 132–139
Gathering 20
fols. 140–147
Gathering 21
fols. 148–155
Gathering 22
fols. 156–163
Gathering 23
fols. 164–171
Gathering 24
fols. 172–180
Gathering 25
fols. 181–184
Gathering 26
fols. 185–188
Gathering 27
fols. 189–194
Gathering 28
fols. 195–202
Gathering 29
fols. 203–210
Gathering 30
fols. 211–216

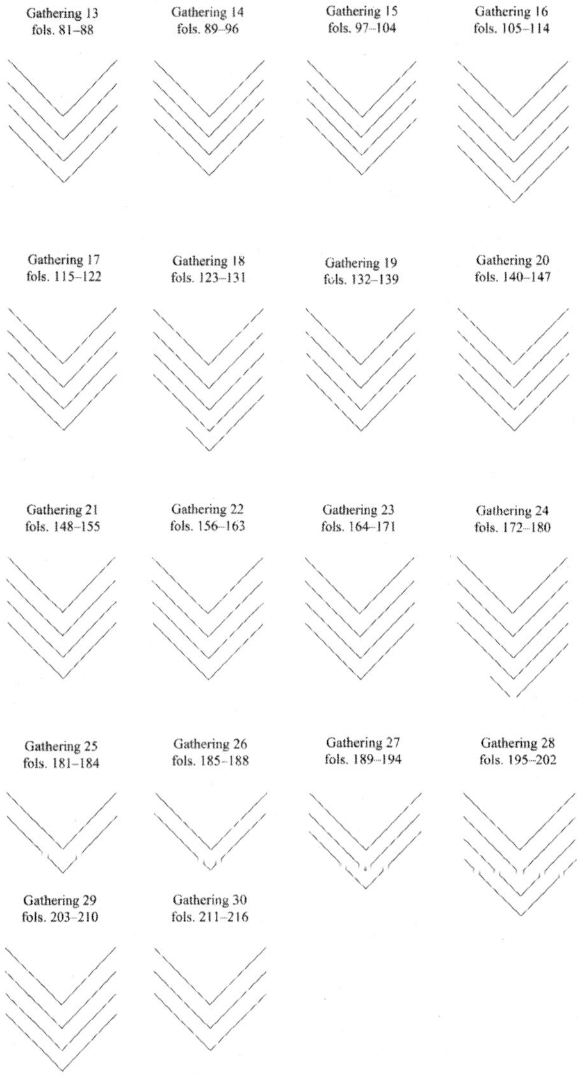

Appendix 3 Table 1. Gatherings, scribes, folio numbers, and contents of B-Tc A 12.

B-Tc A 12 scribes (20 total)	Gatherings	Folio numbers	Contents
Scribe A	1 (1 folio)	[i]	Index
Scribe B	2 (2 folios)	1r–v	Fabric
Scribe C	2	1v	Later addenda to the fabric
Scribe D	2	2v	Alleluia (square notation)
Scribe E	2	2v	*Regina celi letare* (square notation)
Scribe F	3 (12 folios)	3r–14v	Office for St. Barbara (square notation)
Scribe G	4 (4 folios)	15r–17r	Mass for the Commemoration of Virgin; Kyrie; and *Preter rerum* (Messine notation)
Scribe H	4	17r–v	Credo in cantus fractus
Scribe I	4	18r	Kyrie and Sanctus (square notation)
Scribe J	4	18v	Kyrie in cantus fractus
Scribe K	5–18; 22–24; 25–26	19r–131v; 156r–180v; 184r–188v	Offices for the Virgin Mary (several), St. Vincent, St. Catherine, St. Nicholas, Nativity (Christmas); Masses for St. Vincent, Christmas, Epiphany, All Saints (Messine notation)
Scribe L	18	131v	Partially written Sanctus (square notation)
Scribe M	19–21; 25	132r–155v; 181r–184r	Masses for the Assumption, Nativity of the Virgin, Purification, Annunciation, St. Catherine, St. Nicholas; Kyries; and a Gloria (square notation)
Scribe N	23	171r	Handwritten addendum at the bottom of the Mass for the Holy Spirit

—*(continued)*

Appendix 3 Table 1—*concluded*

B-Tc A 12 scribes (20 total)	Gatherings	Folio numbers	Contents
Scribe O	27	189r–194v	Middle of the Purification Mass; hymns; and Mass ordinary. The scribe uses Messine notation in the beginning, but then changes to square notation on 189v. *This scribe appears in all three books for the Confraternity of the Notaries (B-Tc A 13, Scribe C; and B-Tc A 27 Scribe K).*
Scribe P	28–30	195r–212v	Office and Mass for Corpus Christi (Messine notation)
Scribe Q	30	213r	Sanctus
Scribe R	30	213r	Sanctus
Scribe S	30	214r	Sanctus
Scribe T	30	214v–216r	Mass for the Resurrection

Appendix 3 Figure 2. Gathering structure for B-Tc A 13.

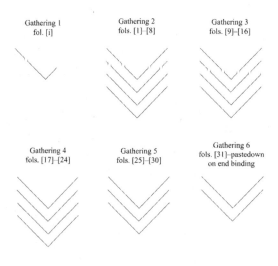

Gathering 1
fol. [i]

Gathering 2
fols. [1]–[8]

Gathering 3
fols. [9]–[16]

Gathering 4
fols. [17]–[24]

Gathering 5
fols. [25]–[30]

Gathering 6
fols. [31]–pastedown
on end binding

Appendix 3 Table 2. Gatherings, scribes, folio numbers, and contents of B-Tc A 13.

B-Tc A 13 scribes (11 total)	Gatherings	Folio numbers	Contents
Scribe A	Flyleaf	[i]r	List of names of members
Scribe B	1 (fols. [1]–[8])	[1]r–[4]v	Office for the Purification of the Virgin (Messine notation)
Scribe C	1 and 2 (fols. [9]–[16]); 3 (fols. [17]r–[24]v)	[5]r (it starts with the rubric on [4]v)–[16]r; [17]r–[24]r	Mass for the Annunciation (Messine notation). *This scribe appears in all three books for the Confraternity of the Notaries (B-Tc A 12, Scribe O; and B-Tc A 27, Scribe K).*
Scribe D	2	[16]r	Kyries (square notation)
Scribe E	3	[24]r	Text rubric as an addendum
Scribe F	4	[25]r–[26]v	Readings
Scribe G	4	[26]v–[30]v	Readings
Scribe H	5	[31]r–[32]v	Readings
Scribe I	5	[32]v	Addendum (one line)
Scribe J	5	[32]v–[33]v	Readings
Scribe K	Pastedown on end binding		Mass for the Conception of the Virgin Mary; and an Ite Missa Est melody

Appendix 3 Figure 3. Gathering structure for B-Tc A 27.

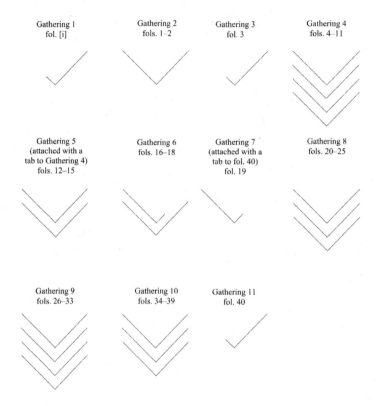

Gathering 1
fol. [i]

Gathering 2
fols. 1–2

Gathering 3
fol. 3

Gathering 4
fols. 4–11

Gathering 5
(attached with a
tab to Gathering 4)
fols. 12–15

Gathering 6
fols. 16–18

Gathering 7
(attached with a
tab to fol. 40)
fol. 19

Gathering 8
fols. 20–25

Gathering 9
fols. 26–33

Gathering 10
fols. 34–39

Gathering 11
fol. 40

Appendix 3 Table 3. Gatherings, scribes, folio numbers, and contents of B-Tc A 27.

B-Tc A 27 scribes (13 total)	Gatherings	Folio numbers	Contents
Scribe A	1	[i]	Charter on flyleaf
Scribe B	2	1r–2r	Mass for the Resurrection (later hand in square notation)
Scribe C	2–3	2v–3v	Mass for the Nativity; sequence *Veni costi filia*; *Alleluya. O gratiarum balsamo referta* (Messine notation)
Scribe D	4	4r–11v	Mass for the Commemoration of the Virgin, Mass for the Annunciation, Requiem; Mass ordinary chants; sequences (mostly square notation, but the scribe also uses some Messine notation)
Scribe E	5–6	12r–17r	Sequences (square notation)
Scribe F	6	16r–17r	*Alleluya. Ave maria gratia plena*; sequence *Mittit ad virginem* (square notation)
Scribe G	6	17r–18r	Mass for the Holy Cross (square notation)
Scribe H	7–9	19r–27v	Sequences; Marian Mass propers; Mass ordinary chants; Readings for the Nativity (square notation)
Scribe I	9	27v	*Ecce dominus veniet* (square notation)
Scribe J	9	28r–33v	Polyphonic Tournai Mass
Scribe K	10	34r–39v	Mass ordinary chants; miscellaneous Mass proper chants (mostly square notation, but the scribe also uses Messine notation for *Orietur stella ex iacob*). *This scribe appears in all three books for the Confraternity of the Notaries (B-Tc A 12, Scribe O; and B-Tc A 13, Scribe C).*
Scribe L	11	40r	Alleluia chants (Messine notation)
Scribe M	11	40v	Alleluia chants; Kyrie (Messine notation)

Notes

Introduction

1   Cessat morbus cessat pestis altari edificato. Sancte martir christi testis pro
    nobis deum orato. Ut cesset epidimia qua flagellatur patria, et cum misericor-
    dia currat dei sententia, finitaque miseria huius labentis saeculi, tecum simus
    in gloria; Dicamus Amen singuli. The prosa is transcribed in *AH*, vol. 37,
    256–57 (the Latin spelling here is retained from *AH*). *AH* refers to F-Pa 204
    as the only source for this text, where it appears attached to the end of the
    prosa *Adest Dies*. It also appears on its own at the end of the diocesan notated
    missal F-Pa 620, on fol. 570r-v. Most Parisian manuscripts use the word
    "prosa" for sequence, and I have retained that usage here.
2   See Gabriel, *Foreign Students* (6) for statistics on the plague in Paris.
3   See Chiu, *Plague and Music*, who, throughout his book discusses responses to
    the plague in the fifteenth and sixteenth centuries.
4   See Giffords, who indicates that this group of saints, with a collective feast day
    of August 8, was variable, with twenty-three different saints being included
    interchangeably in the list depending on geographical location [*Sanctuaries of
    Earth, Stone, and Light* (388).]
5   For the important place of popular devotions in confraternities, see two works
    by Vincent, *Des charités bien ordonnées* and *Les confréries médiévales*, where this
    theme is discussed throughout.
6   Women in Paris also had the power to inherit and run businesses as masters.
    See Beech, "Charlotte Guillard," 351–52. The letters of enfranchisement for
    Parisian trade confraternities were transcribed and published in the nineteenth
    century; they give details on the composition of these organizations with mas-
    ters, journeymen, and apprentices. For transcriptions of these documents, see
    Lespinasse, *Métiers et corporations de la ville de Paris*.
7   This study joins a growing bibliography of monographs focused on music in
    civic communities and urban contexts, such as Peters, *The Musical Sounds*,
    and Saucier, *A Paradise of Priests*. Its treatment of individual saints is related
    to other recent works, particularly by Maurey and Anderson. See Maurey,
    Medieval Music, Legend, and the Cult of St. Martin; and Anderson, *St. Anne*.
    My discussion of relics is also related to the work of Brand, *Holy Treasure and*

Sacred Song. Since confraternities are the focus of this work, it also intersects with earlier studies of lay communities in Italy, such as Wilson, *Music and Merchants*, and Glixon, *Honoring God and the City.*

8   Anderson gives a good overview of the rise of popular devotions in this region during the fifteenth and sixteenth centuries as a result of the laity's feelings of uncertainty about their salvation. See Anderson, *St. Anne*, 2.

9   These books were produced from the fourteenth through sixteenth centuries. I have included the *Misse familiares*, *Misse solenniores*, and *Communes prosa* once in this number, although they appear in different editions. These printed books were not marketed specifically to confraternities, but their contents coincide in some respects with confraternity manuscripts. This number includes only books containing music, and those that are central to my study are the following: F-Pa 204; Paris, Bibliothèque Mazarine MS 464 (F-Pm 464); Den Haag, Koninklijke Bibliotheek MS 76 E 18 (NL-DHk 76 E 18); F-Pm 461; F-Pm 462; F-Pa 168; Paris, Bibliothèque nationale de France, MS lat. 10506 (F-Pnm lat. 10506); Tournai, Bibliothèque et Archives de la Cathédral, MS 12 (B-Tc A 12); B-Tc A 13; B-Tc A 27; and B-Tc A 58. Confraternity statute books and registers have not been counted in this number, but I refer to them throughout the study. Wright briefly mentions F-Pa 204, listing the masses present in the manuscript and discussing some of the Mass ordinary material, but a detailed study of confraternity practices at Notre Dame or in Paris as a whole fell outside of the scope of his study. See Wright, *Music and Ceremony at Notre Dame*, 134–39. There are several known confraternity liturgical books containing music that fall outside the scope of my study, such as Amiens, Bibliothèque Centrale Louis Aragon, MS 162 D, for the Confraternity of St. Barbara at the Abbey of Corbie. This manuscript is the focus of two works by Christoffersen, *Songs for Funerals and Intercession* and "L'Abbaye de Corbie, sainte Barbe." In addition, there is F-Pnm lat. 1051, a fifteenth-century notated breviary discussed in detail in Wolinski, "Music for the Confraternity of St. James." There are also two liturgical books containing no music that are not included in the list above: F-Pa 611, which is a confraternity missal; and F-Pnm fr. 819–20, which contains texts for the Miracle Plays of the Confraternity of the Goldsmiths in Paris from 1339–82. On this last source, see Plumley, *The Art of Grafted Song* (170–72) and Clark and Sheingorn, "'Visible Words.'"

10   Detailed inventories of the confraternity sources and their contents appear in appendix 2 for Tournai, and appendix 4 ❧ for Paris.

11   Confraternities were housed in the chapels of cathedrals, parish churches, monasteries, and convents.

12   Several influential studies dealing with Parisian ecclesiastical and monastic institutions are Wright, *Music and Ceremony at Notre Dame*; Guyon, *Les écoliers du Christ*; Bermès, "Le couvent des Mathurins"; and Fassler, *Gothic Song.*

13 See Wright, *Music and Ceremony at Notre Dame*, 139.

14 Among the important works on the patronage of polyphony in north-
ern confraternities (especially those that did not have royal patronage) see
Wegman, "Music and Musicians at the Guild of Our Lady" (Bergen Op
Zoom); Forney, "Music, Ritual and Patronage" (Antwerp); Haggh, "Music,
Liturgy, and Ceremony" (Brussels); and Bloxam, "A Survey of Late Medieval
Service Books" ('s-Hertogenbosch). One corpus of manuscripts from the
Confraternity of Our Lady at Den Bosch includes both chant and polyphony.
The chant has not been studied in detail, but there is much on the poly-
phonic works, such as Roelvink, *Gegeven den sangeren* and *Gheerkin de Hondt*.
For royal Burgundian patronage of confraternities and music, see Snow,
"The Lady of Sorrows." On patronage in general, see Haggh, "Itinerancy
to Residency." For an overview of confraternities in the Netherlands and
Flanders, see Mannaerts, "Die Bruderschaften und Zünfte."

15 On the role of chambers of rhetoric and urban *puys* in the creation of the
Seven Sorrows liturgy in one of these manuscripts in the late fifteenth century,
Brussels, Bibliothèque Royale, MS 215–16, see Snow, "The Lady of Sorrows";
Thelen, "The Feast of the Seven Sorrows," and *The Seven Sorrows Confraternity
of Brussels*; and Sutch and van Bruaene, "The Seven Sorrows of the Virgin
Mary." For other aspects of the creative output of chambers of rhetoric, see
Dumolyn, "I Thought of It at Work, in Ostend." On the creative output of
urban *puys* in northern France, see Plumley, *The Art of Grafted Song*, 176–90.

16 See Roelvink, who focuses on the polyphonic works in manuscripts from
the confraternity in 's-Hertogenbosch (*Gegeven den sangeren* and *Gheerkin de
Hondt*).

17 See Wegman, "Music and Musicians"; Forney, "Music, Ritual and Patronage";
Haggh and Trio, "The Archives of Confraternities in Ghent and Music";
Gushee, "Two Central Places"; and Slocum, "Confrerie, Bruderschaft, and
Guild.".

18 This is the case for Vincent, *Des charités bien ordonnées* and *Les confréries
médiévales*; Dieterich, "Confraternities and Lay Leadership"; George, "Les
confraternités de l'abbaye de Stavelot-Malmedy"; Trio, "Les confréries des
Pays-Bas"; Desmette, *Les brefs d'Indulgences*; and Desmette, "Les confréries
religieuses à Tournai."

19 Paris is where many northern French liturgical books were produced. For
a comprehensive study of book production in Paris, see Rouse and Rouse,
Manuscripts and Their Makers.

20 I use the term "trade confraternity" here instead of guild, because in some
cases, use of the word guild is inaccurate. For instance, the Confraternity of St.
John the Evangelist for the book production community in Paris is organized
around the trade, as its members consisted solely of men and women involved
in the book trade, but the confraternity did not regulate the everyday aspects

of the trade (wages, prices, etc.). Guilds were distinguished from other types of confraternities by their role in trade regulation. In this case, the book producers were regulated by the University of Paris, putting this confraternity in a slightly different category and thus necessitating a different use of terminology.

21   The functional and spiritual roles of confraternities are explained throughout Vincent, *Des charités bien ordonnées*, and Rosser, "Crafts, Guilds, and the Negotiation of Work." Rosser indicates that in addition to status, there was a concern for personal reputation among medieval artisans, and piety and confraternity membership was a part of this. Furthermore, he theorizes that voluntary membership in these organizations added a moral component: "The voluntary basis of participation in the fictional kinship of a fraternity lent a moral force to the declarations of mutual respect sworn between 'brothers' and 'sisters.' These declarations reinforced high standards of sobriety and Christian charity imposed by fraternity statutes on all members; ideal qualities which helped to provide a basis for collaboration in the complex environment of work in the medieval town" (9–10). That these organizations were voluntary could be questioned, since practicing members of the trade would have been more or less required by their peers to be registered members.

22   Symes, *A Common Stage*, 169.

23   Notions of cultural permeability and cultural exchange have been a fixture of the work of Davis, who holds that there was no impermeable "official culture" imposing criteria on popular culture; rather, the interaction of members of different groups resulted in an exchange of practices and ideas. See Diefendorf and Hesse, "Introduction: Culture and Identity." This is the underlying premise of three works by Davis: *Culture and Society in Early Modern France*; "A Trade Union in 16th Century France"; and "Women in the Crafts in Sixteenth-Century Lyon." The introduction to her Festschrift focuses on Zemon Davis's view that "cultural life [is] the infrastructure of a given social order rather than as its superstructure." Her basic approach is to study how societies order themselves. See Diefendorf and Hesse, "Introduction: Culture and Identity," 1.

24   A list of the sixty-one banners may be found in Favier, *Nouvelle histoire de Paris*, 433–34. The confraternity statutes, parliamentary, and royal decrees are all transcribed in Lespinasse, *Métiers et corporations de la ville de Paris*. Interest in tracking the number of confraternities in the city extends back into the seventeenth century. See, for instance, LeMasson, *Le Calendrier des confréries de Paris*, which was originally printed in 1621 and issued in a critical edition in the nineteenth century.

25   See Slocum, "Confrerie, Bruderschaft, and Guild," 262–63, who mentions that this is indicated in the statutes for the Confraternity of St. Julien des Menestriers, formed in 1321 for the musicians in Paris.

26 See Small, "Centre and Periphery in Late Medieval France" (148) on trades-people moving to learn trades in other towns. Symes also mentions how news of confraternity practices travelled to other cities, citing a case where actors from Bruges went to Arras to observe the practices of the actors' guild there. See Symes, *A Common Stage*, 122–23, 218–19.

27 Composers like Guillaume Du Fay were known to have written both plain-chant and polyphony. See Haggh, "The Celebration of the 'Recollectio.'"

28 The common of saints was a section in liturgical books that had chants appropriate for a number of feast days, as they did not contain texts specific to certain saints and holidays.

29 Wright also makes note of this in his study on Notre Dame. He lists a number of these masses and sums up the situation by saying "that the vast majority of these supernumerary services were celebrated outside the walls of the chancel and sanctuary shows their somewhat suspect lineage." See Wright, *Music and Ceremony at Notre Dame*, 128–29.

30 See Wright's statement above.

31 Honisch, "Drowning Winter, Burning Bones," 566–67. In her discussion she draws ideas about popular devotions more broadly from the work of Duffy, *The Stripping of the Altars*; Burke, *Popular Culture in Early Modern Europe*; and Schribner, *Popular Culture and Popular Movements*.

32 Williamson, in "Sensory Experience in Medieval Devotion" (1) discusses the problems with what she refers to as the "binary opposition" of liturgy versus devotion in modern scholarship. Gaposchkin, in *Invisible Weapons* (23) describes how liturgy was not a medieval term and is now more widely used by historians to include the devotions of lay communities, vernacular religious works, and other types of rituals performed outside of the church. On the obscured line between sacred and secular piety, see Haggh, "The Meeting of Sacred Ritual and Secular Piety," 60; and Rubin, *Emotion and Devotion*, 5–44.

33 Fassler, in *Gothic Song* (161–62) discusses the importance and complexity of the method of contrafactum to liturgical poets and composers, as well as those writing in the vernacular. She also discusses the theological implications of sequence texts (3–78). The importance of contrafacta is articulated in Long, "In Praise of St. Nicholas," 60–78.

34 Small, "Centre and Periphery in Late Medieval France" (145–47) indicates that Tournai is not well studied due to a lack of documents after a 1940 German raid destroyed the municipal archives. On Tournai's history of occupation by and fidelity to France, see Grange, "Sur la politique des Rois de France," 307–10.

35 The organization of the city of Tournai into two dioceses (Tournai and Cambrai) and how this functioned is discussed in Dumoulin, "L'organisation paroissiale de Tournai aux XIIe et XIIIe siècles" and "Les églises paroissiales de Tournai"; Dumoulin and Pycke, "Introduction à l'histoire paroissiale de la

ville de Tournai"; Dumoulin and Pycke, "Topographie chrétienne de Tournai"; and Desnoyers, "Topographie Ecclesiastique de la France".

36 Small, "Centre and Periphery in Late Medieval France," 160.

37 See Geremeck, *Les Marginaux Parisiens* (147) about Paris as a student center.

38 In the late fifteenth and early sixteenth centuries, the word *nationes* simply meant broad geographical areas based on one's land of birth. Beaune points out that the word "nation" was used, for example, in the context of the "natio of Bretons" (Breton nation). See Beaune, *The Birth of an Ideology*, 4–5. See also Courtenay, *Rituals for the Dead* (37–51) on student nations as confraternities.

39 See Vincent, *Les confréries médiévales*, 38–39. She refers to confraternities associated with the different nations of the University of Paris.

40 Brand has also studied the development of new liturgical practices surrounding relic cults in *Holy Treasure and Sacred Song*.

41 Beaune devotes a considerable portion of the first half of her book to a discussion of the emergence of these saints as national saints of the French people and the construction of French identity as the Most Christian Kingdom united by the Most Christian King. See Beaune, *The Birth of an Ideology*. See also Smith, *Chosen Peoples*, 95–130, whose discussion of this process in medieval France is derived directly from Beaune. He categorizes the French at the time as a "Missionary People," whose sense of national identity was built on the divine right to rule and the conquest of heathens for the purpose of conversion to Christianity.

42 Notarial registers for the city of Paris are published in three works by Renouard (*Imprimeurs parisiens*, *Documents sur les imprimeurs*, and *Répertoire des Imprimeurs Parisiens*) and Coyecque, *Recueil d'actes notariés*. The documents published by Renouard and Coyecque include financial contracts that offer a wide range of information about the domestic and professional lives of trades people in the late fifteenth and early sixteenth centuries. Many of these documents have been lost, thus the transcriptions of these two authors are paramount.

Chapter One

1 O decoris viola paradisi planta te duplex aureola virgo martir sancta barbara cum aurea coronavit insigni fac ut celi laurea nos reddamur digni. B-Tc A 12, fol. 11r. Translation by Kerry McCarthy.

2 Boulton discusses this in the introduction to her book *Sacred Fictions of Medieval France*, 4–5. She has coined the term "emotional imagination" to describe the process and provides an early fifteenth-century example from Jean Gerson's Passion sermon *Ad Deum vadit*. Dillon also describes what she calls

"the paradox of people committed to violent religious symbols" in her book *The Sense of Sound* (9).

3   For a description of devotional responses to the plague in Tournai, see Pycke, "La 'Messe de Tournai'" (59–66), which gives detail about the siege and how it led to Marian devotions at the Cathedral. This is a reprint of the first edition from 1988, and it includes an additional introduction.

4   See the introduction to this book for a brief discussion of the fourteen holy helpers.

5   On St. Barbara's role as patron saint of coal miners and artillery makers, see Dumay, "Sainte Barbe." Wolf, in *The Old Norse-Icelandic Legend of Saint Barbara* (29–44, 156–60), embarks on a detailed discussion of St. Barbara's popularity in northern France and provides a transcription of the life of St. Barbara in Latin from F-DOU MS 838.

6   See Pycke, "La 'Messe de Tournai,'" 45–58.

7   See Pycke, "La 'Messe de Tournai,'" 59–66.

8   See Leach, *Guillaume de Machaut* (13–14) on the roles of notaries, secretaries, and almoners in service to political figures in the fourteenth century.

9   The Confraternity of the Transfiguration, discussed in chapter 4, is the other organization. See Desmette, "Les confréries religieuses à Tournai," 87–90, 98–107. Desmette does not include the Confraternity of the Notaries in this list. He says that there were eleven Marian confraternities, seven in honor of particular saints, and three for divine cults (the Holy Sacrament, the Trinity, and the Transfiguration), and indicates that some of the organizations were open (both men and women) and others were closed (only men). For confraternities in later centuries, see Desmette, *Les Brefs d'Indulgences*.

10   See Haggh, "The Meeting of Sacred Ritual" (60–61) on the prominent role of the laity serving as patrons of devotional practices through obits. See Nys, "Les Confréries de Devotion" (53–62), for references to organs, obits, and choristers for the Confraternity of Notre Dame de la Gésine; (66–82) for the Confraternity of Notre Dame du Choeur; and (83–102) for the parish of Ste. Marie Magdalene. In annex 1 of her thesis (II–VI) she transcribes the 1459 rules for Notre Dame de la Gésine, showing that there were many masses observed by the confraternity. Use of instruments in confraternity devotions in the Low Countries is better documented for other cities, such as Antwerp. See Forney, "Music, Ritual and Patronage," 13–14.

11   See Nys, "Les Confréries de Devotion," 83–102, and annex 1, II–VI.

12   For more on this community, see the article by Grange, "Obituaire de la paroisse de Saint-Piat," 13, 45–46, 48–49, 62–67; and Strohm, *Music in Late Medieval Bruges*, 102.

13   On the prominence of musicians from Tournai, see Peters, *The Musical Sounds*, 132–37, 151–71; and Peters, "Urban Minstrels," 220. Wright

mentions musicians from Tournai who worked as organists at Notre Dame in *Music and Ceremony at Notre Dame*, 145.

14 There is no record of this confraternity by 1400, and it does not appear in Van Bruaene, "Repertorium van rederijkerskamers in de Zuidelijke Nederlanden." On the *puy* in Tournai, see Symes, *A Common Stage*, 218–19.

15 See Symes, *A Common Stage*, 132, 159–65, 219.

16 Notaries and their organization are the focus of the work of Vleeschouwers-Van Melkebeek, *De Officialiteit van Doornik*; and Murray, "Notaries Public in Flanders." Although this was an office held by clerics, some, at least, were married laymen. This is evident in article 4 of an act from the cathedral chapter from 1347 or 1348, which refers to several notaries by name, and in one case the wife of a notary: "Odardus Dassegni, notarius curie Tornacensis et Maria dicta Li loutre, eius uxor, Jacobus Li Cordewaniers et Johanna eius uxor, et Jacobus dictus Platiaus, notarius curie Tornacensis et plures alii" (Odard Dassegni, notary of the Curia of Tournai and Maria, dubbed the otter, his wife, Jacob the cobbler and Johanna his wife, and Jacob, dubbed Platiaus, notary of the Curia of Tournai and many others). For a transcription of the document, see Pycke, *Les documents du Trésor*, 286.

17 For the location of the chapel of St. Vincent at the cathedral, see Pycke, *Sons, couleurs, odeurs*, 168–69. As the notaries were clerics in service to the bishop of Tournai, it is likely that they had ready access to the chapel.

18 See Pycke, "Matériaux pour l'histoire de la bibliothèque capitulaire" for the dating of this manuscript.

19 See the transcription in appendix 2.

20 Pycke, in "Deux manuscrits apparentés au manuscrit A 27" (15), indicates that Jean Corvillain was a member of the church tribune in 1526, which carried out the laws of the diocese under the bishop of Tournai. Gerardus Maresquiau is also listed in 1570 as a great vicar in the obituary of the Confraternity of Notre-Dame (for which there are no surviving liturgical books). This last detail mentioned by Pycke makes reference to Tournai, Archives de la Cathédrale, Fonds du Chapitre, Registre 526, fol. 6v.

21 This is also the case for the feast of the Conception of the Virgin Mary, for which there are fleeting references in the oldest layers of the confraternity service books. This feast was included only later in the cathedral sources. See Long, "Les devotions des confréries."

22 For the first study of all three books together, see Long, "La musique et la liturgie." Brief descriptions of many of the manuscripts appear in Pycke, "Matériaux pour l'histoire de la bibliothèque capitulaire". In addition, there are several unpublished inventories held at the cathedral archives that give rudimentary descriptions of some of the sources. For example, see Arboit and Ledèque, "Manuscrit A 13"; and Van Cranenbroeck, "Analyse codicologique de l'antiphonaire A 12." Pycke mentions the aforementioned published and

unpublished inventories as the basis for his description of all three manuscripts in Pycke, "Deux manuscrits apparentés au manuscrit A 27."

23 Huglo discusses the gathering structure of B-Tc A 27 in "Le manuscrit de la Messe de Tournai," but he does not discuss the scribal hands. The gathering structures of B-Tc A 12 and 13, although described in a rudimentary way in the unpublished inventories in the archive, are given for the first time in appendix 3 of this book, along with a drawing of the gathering structure for B-Tc A 27. How the composition of B-Tc A 27 matches up with the scribal hands in the manuscript, and how they, in turn, relate to the hands in B-Tc A 12 and 13, appears for the first time in appendix 3. Each hand has been given a name such as Scribe A, Scribe B, etc., based on the order in which they appear in each book. This practice is followed for each manuscript. Therefore, scribes that are common among all three sources will be called something different in all three inventories, but there are indications in appendix 3 showing how they correlate.

24 Among the most important are Coussemaker, "Messe du XIII siècle"; Huglo, "La Messe de Tournai"; Dumoulin, Huglo, Mercier, and Pycke, *La Messe de Tournai*; Guletsky, "The Four 14th-Century Anonymous Masses"; and Stoessel and Collins, "New Light."

25 This nineteenth-century view (and reinvention) of the polyphonic Mass repertory is the subject of Kirkman's study, "The Invention of the Cyclic Mass," where he gives a good overview of the situation (16–22, 28). As a case in point, he cites Ambros's view on the Tournai Mass in his 1868 tome, *Geschichte der Musik*, 40.

26 There are thirteen sequences in B-Tc A 12, but the one at the end of the series, *Virginis marie*, does not appear in B-Tc A 27 or in the incipit ordo. B-Tc A 27 has a series of fourteen sequences, with *Gaude mater virgo christi* and *Gratuletur orbis totus* not appearing at all in B-Tc A 12.

27 See Long, "La musique et la liturgie" and "Les devotions des confréries"; and Arboit and Ledèque, "Manuscrit A 13."

28 Lectio libri machabeorum. In anniversariis confraternitatis notariorum.

29 Incipit ordo Officiorum in isto libro existencium.

30 See Voisin, "Drames liturgiques de Tournai."

31 See Voisin, "Drames liturgiques de Tournai" (277) for the fabric. He served as episcopal archivist starting in 1837 before becoming the vicar general in 1844. For the life and works of Canon Voisin, see Huguet, "Esquisse sur la vie et les oeuvres de Mgr Voisin."

32 Complete transcriptions of this booklist and inventory of the confraternity's holdings are not given in appendix 2, for they appear in Derolez, *Corpus Catalogorum Belgii*, vol. 4, 307–8; and Voisin, "Drames liturgiques de Tournai."

33 Long, "La musique et la liturgie."

34 See Derolez, *Corpus Catalogorum Belgii*, vol. 4, 307–8; and Voisin, "Drames liturgiques de Tournai," 277.

35 Primo quatuor psalteria.

Item duo libri rubei et unus platus pro missis communibus.

Item unus quaternus ad cooperturas pilosas in quo continentur officia sanctorum Nicolai, Katerine et Purificationis.

Item quidam alius quaternus coristarum, in fine cuius continentur plene officium Nativitatis Domini.

Item duo quaterni officiorum beate Virginis ["de Conceptione" added in a later hand before "beate Virginis"].

Item unus quaternus continens officium Dedicationis, vesperarum, matutinarum et misse.

Item tres quaterni officium Conceptionis notatum continentes.

Item unus quaternus legendarum Conceptionis et Nativitatis Domini.

Item quatuor paria vigiliarum.

Item unus liber continens solum officia missarum totius anni.

36 Voisin, "Drames liturgiques de Tournai," 277.

37 In general, feast days carry different ceremonial ranks, with "duplex" or "annual" designated as the highest ("triplex" is also found in some books as a feast rank above "duplex"), and then in progressive descending order "semiduplex," "9 lessons," "3 lessons," with the lowest rank being "memorial."

38 This is also evident in other manuscripts and printed sources from Tournai. For example, sources 25, 26, and 42 in appendix 1 are all manuscript breviaries from Tournai produced in the late fourteenth and early fifteenth centuries. These books show that the feast of St. Barbara was celebrated at the low rank of three lessons. A calendar in the printed missal for Tournai, produced in 1498 (appendix 1, source 17) shows her feast celebrated at duplex rank. At other institutions in the city St. Barbara is hardly mentioned, although there is a 1476 reference to a Confraternity of St. Barbara at the parish of St. Brice in Tournai, making it likely that there was an altar for her there. For more on the confraternity at the parish of St. Brice, see Cloquet, "Bulle accordée à la confrérie Notre Dame," 337. See also Nys, "Les confréries de devotion," 104–5.

39 B-Tc A 10, fols. 266r–276v. Masses for St. Barbara, the Conception of the Virgin, St. Anthony the Abbot, the Conversion of St. Paul, the Visitation of the Virgin, Corpus Christi, the Transfiguration, and St. Hubert (Bishop of Liège), all appear together on these folios. The Mass for the Transfiguration, discussed in chapter 4, also appears first in confraternity sources used by communities at the cathedral.

40 See Nys, "Les confréries de devotion" (36) for the Confraternity of Notre Dame de la Gésine at the Parish of St. Jacques. She gives details from a document indicating that obits were to be entered into the missal, which says the following: "ces choses seront escriptes au missel comme sont les aultres obis de

ladite église" (these things will be written in the missal as are the other obits of
the said church). This was also likely the practice at the cathedral.

41 Appendix 5 ❧ shows a comparison of all of the texts of the Mass proper for
St. Barbara appearing in B-Tc A 12 and B-Tc A 10, and in B-Tc A 11. The
1498 printed missal for the usage of Tournai also has different chants. B-Tc
A 12 contains music and text for all of the chants of the Mass proper for St.
Barbara. The cathedral manuscript B-Tc A 10 only provides music for the
alleluia, offertory, and communion of the St. Barbara Mass.

42 Ave barbara celorum, virgo regis angelorum, post mariam flos virginum, velud
rosa vel lilium, funde preces ad dominum, pro salute fidelium. B-Tc A 10, fol.
266r-v.

43 The Lateran council of 1215 required every Christian to participate in, be
taught, and understand these concepts. See Camille, "The Book of Signs,"
134. For more information on the use of images in devotional contexts, and
medieval visual literacy, see Camille, "Seeing and Reading"; and Chazelle,
"Pictures, Books, and the Illiterate."

44 See Rothenberg, *The Flower of Paradise* (225–32) on devotions appealing to
the laity.

45 See Brown, "The Mirror of Man's Salvation," 764–65.

46 On the meaning of prayer and literacy, as well as the concept of "charisma,"
see Zieman, *Singing the New Song*, 83. On the sounds of prayer, see Dillon,
The Sense of Sound, 195–96.

47 There are several studies on the ownership of devotional books in the late fifteenth and early sixteenth centuries. Among them see Bell, "Medieval Women
Book Owners," 742–67; Saenger, "Books of Hours," 239–69. In Wieck,
Time Sanctified (40), he explains that even if they had never studied Latin,
the familiarity of the laity with the liturgy and sacraments of the Church gave
them a practical education in Latin that would be foreign to us. On literacy
rates in Arras and surrounding areas, see Symes, *A Common Stage*, 181.

48 Many prayer books and other literature focused on the lives of the saints
that were destined for the diocese of Tournai were produced in Paris, and the
importance of that center in disseminating local legends is discussed in chapter 5.

49 See Young, *The Drama of the Medieval Church*, vol. 2, 245–46; and
Robertson, "Remembering the Annunciation."

50 Symes, *A Common Stage*, 159.

51 For cities in France, see Peters, *The Musical Sounds*, 151–81, "Urban
Minstrels," 205–6, and "Urban Musical Culture," 403–10; Bowles, "Musical
Instruments in Civic Processions"; and Symes, "The Appearance of Early
Vernacular Plays." There are also a number of studies focusing on Italy and the
role of street performers in popular devotions. See Rospocher, "From Orality
to Print," 27–28; and Salzberg, "The Word on the Street," 337–40.

52 Wolf, *Old Norse-Icelandic Legend*, 1–3.

53 Wolf, *Old Norse-Icelandic Legend*, 22. The Constantinople-Torcello-Venice route is described in *BHL* 922–24. *BHL* 918, 920, and 926, written in the fourteenth century, describes their movement to Rome. I have not tried to account for the placement of all of her relics, as some ended up in Kiev and other locations. An Office for St. Barbara appears in a fifteenth-century manuscript from the abbey of St. Bavo in Ghent, currently held at the University library in Ghent (appendix 1, source 5), but it differs from the ones discussed here. See Long and Behrendt, eds., *Catalogue of Notated Office Manuscripts Preserved in Flanders (c.1100–c.1800)*, 82–86.

54 See Gaiffier, "La Légende de sainte Barbe." The thirteenth-century Latin text from Douai is transcribed in Wolf, *The Old Norse-Icelandic Legend*, 156–60. Caxton's 1483 version of the *Golden Legend* differs in its narration of St. Barbara's life in comparison with other editions. See Jacobus de Voragine, *The Golden Legend … by William Caxton*, vol. 6, 91–93. A truncated version of St. Barbara's *passio* (which focuses on the act of her martyrdom) was printed by Vérard: see Jacobus de Voragine, *La légende dorée en françois*, fol. 294v.

55 For the French poetic version copied by Vagus, see Denomy, "An Old French Life of Saint Barbara," 157–75.

56 See Rudy, "A Play Built for One" (56–65) for devotions to St. Barbara in the Netherlands.

57 See Dunn-Lardeau, *Jacques de Voragine* (9) on the importance of this work. Seybolt, "Fifteenth-Century Editions of the Legenda Aurea" (328–34) shows that by the end of the fifteenth century, there were already nine French editions of this work issued by Parisian printers. Most of these were produced by Vérard, as well as two by Du Pré, and one by Nicole de la Barre. Considering that editions of books of this type ran to an average of four hundred or five hundred copies (see chapter 5), there could have been at least two or three thousand copies of the *Golden Legend* in French circulating in the Paris area alone by the beginning of the sixteenth century, a testament to the book's popularity.

58 This is clear in fifteenth-century additions to liturgical books in Cambrai, Amiens, and Lille (see appendix 1, sources 33, 40, and 46), just as she was a later addition to B-Tc A 10, discussed at the outset of the chapter. These three manuscripts are all compared with the Mass in B-Tc A 12 in appendix 5 ❧. There is also an early sixteenth-century confraternity manuscript containing vespers for St. Barbara from the abbey of St. Pierre in Corbie, which is the focus of Christoffersen, *Songs for Funerals and Intercession*, and "L'Abbaye de Corbie, sainte Barbe." Also see Meyer, *Collections du Nord-Pas-de-Calais et de Picardie*, 39–40.

59 On the creation of the first French translation of the *Golden Legend* by Jean de Vignay in the fourteenth century, and its subsequent revision in the fifteenth

century by the Dominican Jean Batallier, see Dunn-Lardeau, "La contribution de J. Batallier," 183. Vérard's edition was marketed as the 1476 translation of Batallier and makes no mention of added vitae.

60 See Jacobus de Voragine, *The Golden Legend ... by William Caxton*, vol. 6, 91–93.

61 Jacobus de Voragine, *La légende dorée en françois*, fol. 294v.

62 There is considerable difference among the versions of St. Barbara's vita about whether the bath was built in Barbara's tower, or elsewhere, but all sources agree on the three windows and their Trinity symbolism.

63 Both versions of the story paraphrased here, as well as the Vérard edition, make reference to the pool of Siloe from the story of the blind man bathing in sacred waters and receiving sight in the Gospel of John 9:7.

64 This figure of seventeen comes from Frisque, "Les manuscrits liturgiques notés" (176), but he does not list these offices, nor mention which ones correspond to those found in *AH*. Brink, in her dissertation "Historiae Trevirenses" (419), mentions that according to *CANTUS*, and *AH* volumes 18 and 25, there are around fourteen St. Barbara offices. The number of offices is variable, but what is important here is that there were many in circulation. The only portion of this Office listed in *AH* is Vespers (*AH* vol. 18, 34).

65 For recent work on historiae, see Hankeln, "Kingship and Sanctity"; and Hiley, "Gens, laudum titulis concrepet Anglica." Haggh-Huglo gives a good definition of the genre, and a description of how the texts are in rhymed, or verse ("versified") form. See Haggh-Huglo, "Proper Offices for Saints," 24–25.

66 Offices were often borrowed from elsewhere and adapted locally; see Haggh-Huglo, "Proper Offices for Saints," 37–38.

67 On the history and use of the term "contrafactum," see Falck, "Parody and Contrafactum," 14–16.

68 Haggh-Huglo describes different methods of Office composition in the fifteenth century and indicates that the primary ones include "processes of compilation, borrowing, or contrafacting." Her discussion seeks to determine how medieval authors viewed composing chant and composing polyphony, particularly in regard to the use of the terms "facere" and "compilare." Haggh-Huglo highlights the different types of adaptations that local composers would make, such as changing the order of responsories, etc. See "Proper Offices for Saints," 26, 35–37. The examples of contrafactum that I gave previously in the Mass for St. Barbara are only one manifestation of that compositional technique, where the source melody remains unchanged. Chapter 2 shows how melodies of contrafacta were also changed, which truly does make them new compositions.

69 Two recent edited volumes that include a wealth of information about chant composition at this time are *Music, Liturgy, and the Veneration of Saints*, ed.

Buckley; and *Medieval Cantors and Their Craft*, eds. Bugyis, Kraebel, and Fassler.

70   Appendix 5 ◌ offers textual comparisons of all the chants of the Office in sources 3, 6, 10, 15, 16, 25, 42, 112, and 120 in figure 1.2. Sources 26–29 are not compared here, as they have been discussed in detail in Brink's dissertation, "Historiae Trevirenses," 419–42. Source 101 is mentioned as a source for the Office in *AH* vol. 18, no. 11 (pg. 37), but upon consultation, Matins and Lauds are different. Vespers was likely the same, as the responsory and verse match, but there are no antiphons listed in the 1497 Tournai print.

71   The chant texts (incipits only) without music were included in a fourteenth-century ordinal from the Onze-Lieve-Vrouwekerk in Maastricht (NL-DHk 71 A 13), copied between 1354 and 1373 (source 112 in figure 1.2). See the transcription of the ordinal in Tagage, *De Ordinarius van de Collegiale Onze Lieve Vrouwekerk*, 129–30.

72   See Saucier, "Sacred Music and Musicians," 192–204; and Frisque, "Les manuscrits liturgiques notés," 176–200.

73   This is the main source for Brink's discussion of the Trier Office. See Brink, "Historiae Trevirenses," 419–42.

74   See Brink, "Historiae Trevirenses," 419–42. At the time of her study, she was unaware of the existence of B-Tc A 12, and the work of Saucier and Frisque.

75   See Saucier, "Sacred Music and Musicians," 192–204; Frisque, "Les manuscrits liturgiques notés," 176–200; and Brink, "Historiae Trevirenses," 419–42. *Dulci voce resonet* is also a contrafactum constructed with the *Salve Regina* melody in Tournai—one of the only places where that Office is melodically similar to the others. An English translation of the entire Office was circulated in a handout by Brink and is part of a work in progress entitled "The Portrayal of Female Sanctity in the Local Offices from the Diocese of Trier," which she presented at the 2016 International Musicological Society's Cantus Planus Study Group conference in Dublin (Ireland), August 2–7. English translations of chants in the present study will only be given for those texts not translated by Brink.

76   "Ecclesia Treverensis tenet antiphonas nocturnales." See Brink, "Historiae Trevirenses," 421.

77   See Brink, "Historiae Trevirenses," 419–42.

78   Figure 1.2 shows that the Cambrai printed antiphoner only contains Vespers, and the Trier manuscripts do not contain Vespers at all. That is why I have separated the music of Vespers from my discussion of Matins and Lauds.

79   While Trier is an important comparison, Brink's discussion of the chant melodies for the Office in those sources is well treated in "Historiae Trevirenses," 419–42.

80   This reflects what Hughes observes in *The Versified Office* (vol. 1, 15), where he discusses how items in rhymed and versified offices can easily be moved to different sections, even though it interferes with the rhyme scheme.

81   As mentioned previously, Vespers does not appear in Trier, which is why there is no comparison in table 1.3 and why it does not appear in Brink's translation of the Office. The table in appendix 5 ⁀θ gives the same information, but without the full chant texts and English translations. Translations by Kerry McCarthy.

82   The translations in figure 1.3 are by Kerry McCarthy. The original Latin text for antiphon 1 is "Iratus preses in responsis barbare gloriose martyris latera eius truciter discerpi et lampades ardentes iubet ei applicari." The text for antiphon 2 is "Iubet preses tondi malleo caput virginis et eius mamillas gladio amputari."

83   On the rearrangement of responsories, see Boynton *Shaping a Monastic Identity*, 62–80; Hughes, *The Versified Office* (15); and Hughes, "Modal Order and Disorder in the Rhymed Office."

84   Appendix 5 ⁀θ shows that the third responsory and verse for nocturn 3 in B-Tc A 12 also differs from Trier, but the Trier version, *Precepto presulis christi virgo*, is found elsewhere. The unique third responsory and verse in B-Tc A 12 is: "R. Honor deo pro tropheo dato barbare per quem adiuta est et consecuta celi thronum et summum bonum. Signis splendens et virtutum iubare" (Honor be to God for the victory given to Barbara; by him she was helped and she achieved the throne of heaven and the highest good, gleaming with miracles and with the radiance of mighty works); "V. Celi leta mensa freta debriata divino nectare" (Supported by the joyful table of heaven, intoxicated with divine nectar). Translations for this Office in appendix 5 ⁀θ and table 1.4 were done by Kerry McCarthy.

85   These are all translated by Brink in "The Portrayal of Female Sanctity."

86   See Hughes, "Late Midieval Plainchant," vol. 3, 34–44. For offices and chant composition before the fifteenth century, see Bain, "Hildegard, Hermannus, and Late Chant Style"; Hankeln, "Kingship and Sanctity"; Hiley, "Gens, laudum titulis concrepet Anglica"; and Parkes, "St. Edmund between Liturgy and Hagiography," 131–59.

87   See Hughes, "Late Medieval Plainchant," vol. 3, 34–44; and Hankeln, "St. Olav's Augustine-Responsories."

88   On modal order and disruption in other offices, see Hughes, "Modal Order and Disorder." Many late medieval offices are not in modal order, and Hughes mentions that responsories and verses are the most unstable portions modally as they were likely to be shuffled around to accommodate readings. See also Boyce, "The Carmelite Feast of the Presentation of the Virgin," 490; and Slocum, *Liturgies in Honour of Thomas Becket*, 149.

89   In Frisque's analysis of the cadential formulae in the Ste. Croix antiphoner, he indicates that through a series of complicated transpositions, both the antiphons and responsories of the St. Barbara Office for Matins and Lauds proceed in modal order. For this to be true for the responsories, a series of unlikely transpositions at the 2nd and 3rd would have to take place rather than more likely ones at the 4th and 5th. See Frisque, "Les manuscrits liturgiques notés," 183–84.

90   The modal order of the responsories in Trier is given in Brink, "Historiae Trevirenses," 5.

91   This chant text is not unique to Tournai, as it also appears in the confraternity manuscript F-AM 162 D (appendix 1, source 32) with a very different chant melody.

92   Haggh-Huglo, "Proper Offices for Saints" (37–38) mentions an Office for St. Juliana that was sent by post with a letter, and the Recollectio Office by Du Fay that was sent in similar fashion to Cambrai. On the Office for St. Juliana, see Mannaerts, "A Collegiate Church on the Divide," 108.

93   Saucier has done a considerable amount of work on the text of the Cathedral Office, but this Office has no relation to the one discussed here. See Saucier, "Sacred Music and Musicians," 194–95.

94   B-Br 3782 (appendix 1, source 2), is a handwritten missal with music only for the Mass ordinary and prefaces; and B-Br 6434 (appendix 1, source 3) is an antiphoner.

95   B-La, St. Barbara Register 12. Both Saucier and Dieterich mention this confraternity but do not go into detail about its devotional practices. See Saucier, "Sacred Music and Musicians," 198; and Dieterich, "Brotherhood and Community," 102–3. Dieterich also discusses the power of confraternities in Liège and their performance of weekly masses in "Confraternities and Lay Leadership," 20–21.

96   Haggh and Downey, *Two Cambrai Antiphoners*, xxix.

97   See Gaiffier, "La Légende de sainte Barbe."

98   See Haggh and Downey, *Two Cambrai Antiphoners*, xxix; and *AH* vol. 18, 34–37. Beyond Vespers, the offices of Matins and Lauds in the 1497 printed source cited in *AH* differ from those discussed here.

99   See Li Muisis, *Poésies de Gilles Li Muisis*, vol. 1, 88–89.

100   See Plumley, *The Art of Grafted Song*, 265.

101   See Dupont, "Le chant dans l'espace," 75; and Wright, *Music and Ceremony at Notre Dame*, 318.

102   See Dupont, "Le chant dans l'espace," 84–91.

103   Saucier highlights the important place of Liège for musical instruction, in *A Paradise of Priests*, 5. On music instruction in northern France, see Kirkman, "The Seeds of Medieval Music," 115–16; and Planchart, "Choirboys in Cambrai in the Fifteenth Century," 124–25.

104 See Wright, *Music and Ceremony at Notre Dame*, 175–77.

105 See Symes, *A Common Stage*, 156. Evidence of adult singers working as free-lance musicians in both sacred and secular contexts in Paris is discussed in Page, *The Owl and the Nightingale*, 144–54.

106 See Wright, *Music and Ceremony at Notre Dame* (300) on Vitry as a notary and maître des requêtes for Charles IV, Philip VI, and John II. On Machaut's role as an almoner, notary, and secretary to John of Luxembourg, see Leach, *Guillaume de Machaut*, 13–14.

107 Haggh, "Composers-Secretaries and Notaries." She lists both Vitry and Machaut as notaries (32–33). On Machaut serving as a notary, and for detailed information on what a notary did, see Earp, *Guillaume de Machaut*, 21.

108 See Symes, *A Common Stage*, 156.

Chapter Two

1 Alleluya. O nicholae tumulus tuus distillat oleum cuius servatur rivulus ad infirmorum curam serva presentem cuneum a febribus causantibus mortem non defecturam. F-Pm 464, fol. 1r. English translation by Kerry McCarthy.

2 In F-Pm 464, the chant is added on the opening flyleaf in an early to mid-sixteenth-century hand. It appears in the main scribal hand for the Mass in B-Tc A 13.

3 While there were many devotional confraternities that focused specifically on the veneration of relics, trade confraternities were not organized with this in mind, as their function was not only spiritual but also practical—they regulated different aspects of the trade (see Introduction).

4 The Translation of St. Nicholas does not appear in the diocesan calendar of Tournai until the late fifteenth century, when it was included in the printed missal for the usage of Tournai in 1498 (B-Ts Inc. 27). The feast appears as early as the thirteenth century in Parisian sources, as it is included in the calendar of the notated breviary F-Pnm lat. 15181. The Finding of the Relics of St. Catherine on May 13 is given only brief mention in the *AASS*, vol. 3, 186. It appears to only be indicated in one manuscript from Italy.

5 On the role of confraternities in solidifying corporate identity through both public and private displays, see Black, "The Development of Confraternity Studies." On private devotions of the laity, see Williamson, "Sensory Experience in Medieval Devotion."

6 Public processions and banquets on a patron saint's feast day were common events for Parisian confraternities, and the letters of enfranchisement for the city's trade guilds give details on these activities. These were transcribed and

published in the nineteenth century by Lespinasse, *Métiers et corporations de la ville de Paris.*

7   Wright outlines the responsibilities of the clergy at Notre Dame in perform-ing confraternity services in *Music and Ceremony at Notre Dame*, 134–39. This gives a good indication of how this worked at other institutions at the time. See also the discussion of confraternity devotions in the city of Tournai in chapter 1.

8   Marks of ownership appear in both books. The inscription on the title page of F-Pm 464 is "Incipit liber confratrie sancti nicholai ad speciarios" (Incipit book of the confraternity of Saint Nicholas for the spice dealers). The term "speciarios" can mean grocers (in French, "épiciers"), but based on the items sold by the members of the trade, the more appropriate term would be spice dealers. On the very last folio of NL-DHk 76 E 18 (119r), there is the follow-ing inscription, "Ce livre est a laconfrairie de saincte katherine fondee par les pourpaintiers de paris" (This book is for the Confraternity of St. Catherine founded by the doublet makers of Paris).

9   On the popularity of St. Nicholas, see Clare, *Saint Nicholas*, 114; and Thiriet, "Essai sur la géographie du culte de Saint Nicolas."

10 Among them are the parish of St. Nicholas at Tournai, the parish of St. Nicholas des Champs in Paris; and numerous St. Nicholas chapels, such as the chapel of St. Nicholas at the Hospital of Ste. Catherine in Paris. For the foun-dation of the St. Nicholas church in Tournai, see Voisin, "Note sur l'église de Saint-Nicolas à Tournai," 173–210.

11 See Wright, *Music and Ceremony at Notre Dame,* 192; and Fassler, "The Feast of Fools and Danielis Ludus," 95. For a discussion of St. Nicholas plays and their widespread popularity, and a fulsome bibliography on the subject, see Caldwell, "Singing, Dancing, and Rejoicing," 406–526.

12 On *Le Jeu de Saint Nicolas* written between 1191–1202 by Jehan Bodel, see Henry, *Jehan Bodel: Le Jeu de Saint Nicolas*; and Symes, "The Appearance of Early Vernacular Plays," 780. On Robert Wace, see Blacker, Burgess, and Ogden, *Wace, The Hagiographical Works.* Symes also refers to a play about the Translation of St. Nicholas in Arras in *A Common Stage*, 271. Symes (171) also discusses music for the liturgy on the feast day of St. Nicholas, and an account from a local prior on secular elements in the liturgy, referring to "jonglerie" in the alleluia verse.

13 See Warichez, *La cathédrale de Tournai et son chapitre*, 358.

14 See Walsh, *The Cult of St. Katherine of Alexandria* (63–96) on St. Catherine and other female saints in Normandy. Walsh (173–83) transcribes the Norman miracles from Rouen and gives an analytical table (89).

15 See Walsh, *The Cult of St. Katherine of Alexandria*, 67–74.

16 See Courtenay, *Rituals for the Dead*, 94–95; and Harrán, *In Defense of Music* (33) for information on the College of Navarre. On the Augustinian house

of Val des Ecoliers, see Guyon, *Les écoliers du Christ*. For the Hospital of Ste. Catherine in Paris, see Warolin, "L'hôpital et la chapelle Sainte-Catherine"; Cheymol, "L'hôpital Sainte-Catherine à Paris"; and Brièle, *L'Hôpital de Sainte-Catherine*.

17 See Nys, "Les Confréries de Devotion," 108. The parish of Ste. Catherine, built in 1261, has since been destroyed. See Bozière, *Tournai ancien et moderne*, 29–30.

18 Masses and offices for both St. Catherine and St. Nicholas are included in the oldest layers of all three books for the Confraternity of the Notaries at Tournai, showing strong devotions to them at the organization's inception (see appendix 2). Services for St. Nicholas and St. Catherine also appear in a wide variety of other liturgical sources used in private devotions in northern France. See, for instance, the liturgical book used by the Confraternity of St. Barbara at the Abbey of Corbie that is the focus of Christoffersen, *Songs for Funerals and Intercession* and "L'Abbaye de Corbie, sainte Barbe." F-CA 69, which was used in a private chapel of the bishop in the fourteenth century, contains full masses and offices for both saints. These are but two examples of liturgical books where both saints appear together in private devotions.

19 Head, *Hagiography and the Cult of Saints*, 153.

20 Oils were also kept as relics at churches, which I will explore later in the chapter. On the different classes of relics and the plenitude of oils and other contact relics, see Taylor, ed., *Encyclopedia of Medieval Pilgrimage*, 597–99. Accounts of contact relics being produced for consumption by pilgrims are discussed in Crook, *English Medieval Shrines*, 16–17.

21 Archeological evidence of this practice is discussed in Brazinski and Fryxell, "The Smell of Relics."

22 Geary focuses on this in *Furta Sacra*, 3–27.

23 See Goodson, *The Rome of Pope Paschal I*, 221–22.

24 See Vanderputten, "Itinerant Lordship," 143–45. Hermann-Mascard, *Les reliques des saints* (103–105) discusses papal decrees since the twelfth or thirteenth century that indicate relic translation ought to be celebrated at a high rank.

25 See Caroli, "Bringing Saints to Cities and Monasteries," 260.

26 See Karsallah, "Un subsitutut original au pèlerinage au Saint-Sépulcre" (419–20) on indulgenced images.

27 See Cheymol, "L'hôpital Sainte-Catherine à Paris" (240–41) for the history of the community. Harding, *The Dead and the Living in Paris and London* (106–7) discusses the community's role in burial.

28 This is according to the Confraternity Register for the Spice Dealers discussed below, B-Br 17939, fol. 80r.

29 See Cheymol, "L'hôpital Sainte-Catherine à Paris," 244–45. For more details on the institution at large, see Brièle, *L'hôpital de Sainte-Catherine*.

30 For more on this institution, see Brièle, *L'Hôpital de Sainte-Catherine*; and Bouvet, *La confrérie de Saint-Nicolas,* 34–38. According to LeMasson, writing in the early seventeenth century, by that time only the Doublet Makers were still worshiping at the institution. The reasons for this will be discussed below. See LeMasson, *Le calendrier des confréries de Paris,* 87.

31 The only previous study of this community was published in 1950 by Bouvet, who was the president of the Société d'Histoire de la Pharmacie. See Bouvet, *La confrérie de Saint-Nicolas.* Bouvet wrote prolifically on the history of pharmaceutical studies in France, which has its roots in the Middle Ages with the apothecary trade. In his work on the confraternity, he draws extensively from the confraternity register. Bouvet's study is not at all concerned with music or liturgy, but in the course of writing about this organization, he is the only author to mention F-Pm 464 in relation to the Confraternity of the Spice Dealers and Apothecaries, giving the inscription on the title page of the manuscript as proof of the organization's ownership. The connection of this confraternity book to the Spice Dealers and Apothecaries of Paris was first made by Bouvet in his book, and he even includes a reproduction of the title page (35) but does not go into any liturgical detail. I was unaware of Bouvet's work and the confraternity register in 2009, when I published my article entitled "In Praise of St. Nicholas."

32 See Franklin, *Dictionnaire historique des arts, métiers et professions* (307) for more information on these distinctions. Both apothecaries and spice dealers had the right to sell wax and make candles, which is why they were also associated with the candle makers, as mentioned previously. Their statutes are published in Lespinasse, *Métiers et corporations de la ville de Paris,* vol. 1, 496–539.

33 See Bouvet, *La confrérie de Saint-Nicolas* (35–37), where it is transcribed. Also see B-Br 17939, fol. 15r. "Cest le service qui se faict en lan pour les freres et soeurs de la confrairie monsieur sainct nycolas aux maistres espiciers et apothicaires de la ville de paris en lesglise de lospital sainte katherine en la grant rue sainct denis à paris Et premierement tous les dimanches de lan eaue beniste une haulte messe a diacre et soulz diacre pain benist et apres ung de profundis pour les trespasses en la maniere accoustumee Item les deux jours de monsieur sainct nycolas pareil service et doubles vespres Item trois aultres messes de la sepmaine; cest assavoir le lundi le mardi et le jeudi Et de augmentacion faicte lan mil cinq cens et deux Item les deux journees sainct nicolas matines a IX pseaulmes et IX lecons Item les deux journees de landemain sainct nicolas vigilles et recommandasses a IX pseaulmes et IX lecons avecques une haulte messe de requiem et libera pour les trespasses Item le jour des trespasses pareil service Et tout ce moyennant la somme de trente deux livres tournoys a paier pour chacun an."

34 On this, see Maddox and Sturm-Maddox, *Parisian Confraternity Drama,* 19. They discuss the Goldsmith's Guild manuscript, F-Pnm fr. 819–20 (see

introduction to the present study) and mention the fact that large trades, like the Goldsmiths, supported more than one confraternity. See also Runnalls, "Medieval Trade Guilds and the *Miracles de Nostre Dame par personnages*" (29–65) in the same volume.

35 See Bouvet, *La confrérie de Saint-Nicolas*, 37–38. The document is F-Pan Minutier Centrale XCI, 2.

36 See Warolin, "L'hôpital et la chapelle Sainte-Catherine," 420. The original document is transcribed in *Collection de documents inédits sur l'histoire de France*, 547–53.

37 See Sauval, *Histoire et recherches des antiquités*, 473.

38 See Bouvet, *La confrérie de Saint-Nicolas* (39–52), who cites F-Pan Minutier Centrale LXI, 78. According to this document, all of the masters of the confraternity had to vote (their votes are recorded in this document) for which institution to move to, and Ste. Opportune won. Then, the parish voted. The church of Ste. Opportune is not to be confused with the Augustinian abbey founded in honor of the saint, which eventually became the Hospital of Ste. Catherine.

39 See Bouvet, *La confrérie de Saint-Nicolas* (51–52), and F-Pan Minutier Centrale XVIII, 113, fol. 289.

40 See LeMasson, *Le calendrier des confréries de Paris*, 72.

41 See Huisman, *Notes sur un registre*, 245.

42 See Huisman, *Notes sur un registre*, 245.

43 See Lespinasse, *Métiers et corporations de la ville de Paris*, vol. 3, 205–6.

44 See Beaune, *The Birth of an Ideology* (129–32), who outlines this development in the legends of St. Catherine by Pierre de Natali, Saint Vincent Ferrier, and Jean Miélot.

45 See Lespinasse, *Métiers et corporations de la ville de Paris*, vol. 3, 205–6, and their statutes (207–16).

46 See Franklin, *Dictionnaire historique des arts, métiers et professions*, 595.

47 The original French and an English translation appear in appendix 4 ❧.

48 My comparisons show that Vespers for St. Catherine is the same as what appears in the Notre Dame Breviary, F-Pnm lat. 15181 and 15182.

49 This is evident for most of the confraternities whose statutes are published in Lespinasse, *Métiers et corporations de la ville de Paris*. They indicate that members would have been required to be in attendance on these occasions.

50 There are considerably fewer diocesan sources from Tournai than there are from Paris. All of the existing Tournai sources are given in appendix 2. The select sources used for comparison from Paris are all listed in appendix 1.

51 According to legend, this took place between 940 and 1000. For a full discussion of the finding of her relics on Mount Sinai between 940 and 1000, see Walsh, *The Cult of St. Katherine of Alexandria*, 39–40, 73. Walsh explains that the monastery on Mount Sinai was founded by the emperor Justinian in

the middle of the sixth century and dedicated to the Virgin Mary, and it was referred to as such for several centuries. She also indicates that the story of the discovery of St. Catherine's bones originated much later than 800, and the retroactive date given in these accounts was an attempt to explain the acquisition of the relics, for there is no evidence of her on Mount Sinai until the late tenth century. Blasina has also recently shown that this account was fabricated in "Music and Gender," 36.

52   See Walsh, *The Cult of St. Katherine of Alexandria*, 96.

53   See Blasina, "Music and Gender," 4, 21; Jenkins and Lewis, "Introduction," 6; and Lewis, *The Cult of St. Katherine*, 46.

54   According to Walsh, *The Cult of St. Katherine of Alexandria* (158–59), Jacobus used the Latin Vulgate *passio* of St. Catherine. The retelling of the legend here is a paraphrase in English (translation mine) of what appears in the 1476 French version by Batallier. See Dunn-Lardeau, *Jacques de Voragine*, 1105–16, legend 167. I have also consulted the 1483 version by Caxton, see Jacobus de Voragine, *The Golden Legend ... by William Caxton.* vol.7, 3–12.

55   See Voragine, *The Golden Legend ... by William Caxton*, vol. 7, 10–11. Batallier's 1476 French version says something similar: "je suys donnee a Jhesucrist a espouse: c'est ma gloire, c'est m'amour, c'est ma doulceur" (I am given over to Jesus Christ as his wife: It is my glory, my love, and my sweetness). See Dunn-Lardeau, *Jacques de Voragine* (1110) for the Batallier version.

56   See Walsh, *The Cult of St. Katherine*, 39–40, for the change of the monastery's name on Mount Sinai.

57   English translations by Kerry McCarthy.

58   I would like to thank Kerry McCarthy for her input on Latin poetic styles.

59   As shown in the inventory, the book does not contain the Vigil or a feast, but only the music for this Vespers Office.

60   See Leahy, "Some Musical Elaborations" (81–91), who discusses these chants for St. Nicholas in detail.

61   Many St. Nicholas and St. Catherine texts also appear in F-AM 162 D, for the Confraternity of St. Barbara at Corbie.

62   See Hughes, "Late Medieval Plainchant," vol. 3, 73–78; Hankeln, "Kingship and Sanctity"; Hiley, "Gens, laudum titulis concrepet Anglica"; Hankeln, "St. Olav's Augustine-Responsories"; and Hankeln, "Reflections of War and Violence."

63   On the importance of contrafacta and their symbolic meanings, see Fassler, *Gothic Song*, 161–62.

64   For a comparison of Paris and Tournai liturgies for St. Nicholas, see Long, "La musique et la liturgie," who discusses the variability of the alleluia verse as a genre. See also Hughes, "The Paschal Alleluia in Medieval France," 11–12.

65   The alleluia verse *Summe dei* appears in the Tournai manuscripts instead of *Egregie christi*, which appears only in F-Pm 464. For a detailed discussion of

the alleluia verses for St. Nicholas in F-Pm 464, see Long, "In Praise of St. Nicholas," 63–64.

66   The first place to record accounts of his restorative power is the Vita Nicolai composed by the Neapolitan John the Deacon around 880, which is discussed more fully later in the chapter. The story of the healing oil is among the oldest legends of his miracles and formed the basis for Jacobus's Life of St. Nicholas in the *Golden Legend*. See Jones, *The St. Nicholas Liturgy*, 42. For a translation of the text by Nicephorus, see Jones, *Saint Nicholas of Myra*, 172–202.

67   The Translation story in F-Pm 464 conforms to *BHL* 6179, which is the same version Jones used for his translation of the text. What follows is a paraphrased version of the story based on Jones's translation.

68   On saints choosing their own resting place, see Caroli, "Bringing Saints to Cities and Monasteries," 262–63.

69   Alleluya. Egregie christi confessor nicholae pro nobis tui mirabilem corporis translationem venerantibus quesumus intercede. English translation by Kerry McCarthy.

70   It appears in B-Tc A 10, 11, and the 1498 printed missal (B-Ts Inc. 27).

71   Alleluya. Summe dei confessor nycholae te venerantes protege namque credimus tuis precibus nos posse salvari. English translation by Kerry McCarthy.

72   Alleluya. Iustus germinabit sicut lylium et florebit in eternum ante dominum.

73   It appears twice in different Parisian books (F-Pm 464; and there was a newly composed chant using this one as a model in the printed *Misse familiares* of 1523, which is discussed in chapter 5), and four times in the Tournai notary manuscripts (three times in B-Tc A 12 and once in B-Tc A 13). It also is found without music in the missal F-Pnm lat. 861 as a fifteenth century addendum with texts similar to those for a Marian votive Mass.

74   See Schlager, *Alleluia-Melodien II*, 709, 887. This verse is found in at least sixty sources throughout Western Europe, with numerous textual and melodic variants.

75   The St. Nicholas text is not found in Schlager, but the Reims version of the chant is. The transcriptions from the Reims source are taken from Schlager, *Alleluia-Melodien II*, 315, 703–11.

76   Alleluya. O consolatrix pauperum / barbara virgo preclara / fraglans odore virtutum / tuos famulos conserva / fac ut post vite decursum / ad gaudia permansura / tecum perveniamus. The Latin text is transcribed in Schlager, *Alleluia Melodien II*, 315.

77   See Long, "La musique et la liturgie," 63–65. Alleluya. Dulcis martir dulcis virgo diversa ferens verbera exora pro nobis clemens katerina regem celorum et dominum. This verse appears on fols. 145v–146r. English translation by Kerry McCarthy.

78   B-Tc A 12 fols. 182r–182v. Alleluya. Dulcis mater dulcis virgo dulcia ferens ubera que sola fuisti digna lactare regem celorum et dominum.

79   Schlager mentions this text and melody in *Alleluia-Melodien II* (710) and says
it appears in F-Pnm lat. 17313, which is a missal from 1480–1520, used at an
unidentified institution. See Leroquais, *Les sacramentaires et les missels manuscrits*, Vol. 3, 188–89; and Leroquais, *Les Pontificaux manuscrits*, vol. 2, 438.

80   Several scholars have noted the importance of the contrafactum method in
new Office and Mass compositions. This is a theme throughout Fassler, *Gothic
Song*; Hankeln, "Kingship and Sanctity"; Hankeln, "St. Olav's Augustine-
Responsories" and Hankeln, "Reflections of War and Violence."

81   Figure 2.1 shows that Translation Office 1 appears on fols. 35r–47r, the
Office for the Feast of St. Nicholas appears on fols. 69r–114v, and Translation
Office 2 appears at the very end of the manuscript. Portions of the following
discussion of the Translation Office appeared earlier as Long, "The Office of
the Translation of St. Nicholas." In addition to F-Pm 464, the manuscript
F-Pnm lat. 10506, for the Confraternity of the Barrel Makers in Paris, contains Vespers for the feast of St. Nicholas. Both sources have the same order
of service for the Feast of St. Nicholas as that found in the late thirteenth-
early fourteenth-century diocesan noted breviary from Notre Dame, F-Pnm
lat. 15181. See Long, "La musique et la liturgie." The Tournai confraternity
manuscript B-Tc A 12 has one Office for the feast of St. Nicholas, which
textually conforms to a breviary reflecting the usage of Tournai, B-Tv 21.
Unfortunately, there are no known sources containing music for the Office
reflecting the usage of the Cathedral of Tournai.

82   The same fifteenth-century scribal hand was responsible for both offices in
F-Pm 464, and there is nothing about the gathering structure of the manuscript that would indicate that Translation Office 2 was a later addition. Thus,
both offices appear to be part of this confraternity's devotional practice in the
fifteenth century.

83   I have published detailed comparison tables of Translation Offices 1 and
2 with the offices for the Feast of St. Nicholas and the Translation of St.
Nicholas in diocesan usage, so these will not be reproduced here. See Long,
"The Office of the Translation of St. Nicholas"; and Long, "In Praise of St.
Nicholas."

84   In secular religious usages (meaning diocesan, not monastic) Matins normally
has three nocturns, which was the case in the office for St. Barbara in chapter
1. It was not unknown in private devotional settings for offices to be truncated
in this way and include only one Matins nocturn.

85   I would like to thank Kerry McCarthy for drawing my attention to the fact
that the Responsory and verse are found almost word for word in Surius, *De
probatis Sanctorum*, 400. The text is as follows: "Expositis autem membris
caeteris confuse ac temere, caput adhuc deerat. Quo nondum reperto, tristes
aliquantulum sunt effecti" (Whereas the other members were set out in a confused and rash way, the head was still missing. As it had not yet been found,

they became somewhat sad). The portions of it that are found in the responsory in table 2.3 are highlighted in italics. The missing head is not recounted
in Nicephorus of Bari's translation story. See Jones, *Saint Nicholas of Myra*
(172–202) on different versions of the translation story.

86 This is described in great detail by Nicephorus. See Jones, *Saint Nicholas of
Myra*, 184–85.

87 The dramatic aspects of this particular office are reminiscent of others that
have been studied by Benjamin Brand, most notably the office of St. Ansanus
in Italy, which uses similar language, "The entire Sienese populace, men and
women of every age and condition, who had remained [in the city] hurried to
meet the most holy relics." See Brand, *Holy Treasure and Sacred Song*, 129. He
describes translation narratives as "post mortem drama."

88 This number does not include the connections of three of the chants that
are marked "tenuous" in table 2.6. In some cases, there are multiple texts set
to the same melody in the diocesan usage, which is true for *Tecum princi-
pium* and *Ave maria gratia plena*, as well as *Postquam domi puerilem* and *Reges
intellegite*.

89 The contrafacta for the alleluia verses were not written by the same person,
but instead different texts were added to the repertory over time.

90 A formula can be easily established through two or three notes at the opening
of a melody. Wright discusses this in *The Maze and the Warrior*, 159–205.

91 I have compared these chants to all of the antiphons and responsories in the
Parisian notated breviary F-Pnm lat. 15181–15182, and no other chants have
these same openings. This implies that the similarities between Translation
Office 2 in F-Pm 464 and chants from the Parisian breviary are significant and
deliberate. Modeling in the antiphons and responsories of the office have been
noted in other locations. See Hankeln, "Reflections on War and Violence," 21;
and Hankeln, "St. Olav's Augustine-Responsories," 171–77. Some liturgies
are entirely modeled on preexisting sources, such as the Seven Sorrows of the
Virgin, which was based on an office for the Compassion of the Virgin. See
Snow, "The Feast of the Seven Sorrows." Fassler's discussion of contrafacta and
the methods used for sequences reflect what we find in the antiphons here.
The beginning and ends of the chants are the same, while the internal sections
maintain a similar melodic shape. See Fassler, *Gothic Song*, 161–66.

92 For a discussion of the event, and the feast in thirteenth- and fourteenth-
century calendars, see Baltzer, "The Sources and the Sactorale," 124. She indicates that August 11 is the day the relics were received at the Cathedral of St.
Etienne in Sens, before they arrived in Paris.

93 See Cohen, *The Sainte-Chapelle and the Construction of Sacral Monarchy* (166)
for a full description of the arrival of the relics in Paris, as well as of Louis IX's
construction of the Ste. Chapelle to legitimize his reign.

94 See Cohen, "An Indulgence for the Visitor." For works focused on the Crown of Thorns liturgy, see May, "Rhymed Offices at the Sainte-Chapelle"; and Blezzard, Ryle, and Alexander, "New Perspectives on the Feast of the Crown of Thorns."

95 Hymns that are not set to music or carry nonspecific texts, such as the *Cum quidem*, which was sung during lauds; and *Iste confessor*, which was sung before Translation Office 2, are not given in tables 2.7 and 2.8. Prosas that appear regularly in the diocesan usage for the Mass and Office for St. Nicholas, such as *Congaudentes* and *Sospitati*, and the *Dies irae* (which was not part of the diocesan usage) are also not recorded here. None of them have textual concordances with the only notated breviaries for the usage of Paris produced before 1550, F-Pnm lat. 15181 and 15182 (the two Notre Dame notated breviaries), or F-Pnm lat. 1051 for the Confraternity of St. James in Paris. I provide the *AH* volume number and assigned hymn number in tables 2.7 and 2.8.

96 See *AH*, vol. 12. This is the case for *Presulis sancti gesta nicholai*, *Nicholay preconia*, and *Adest nunc dies*, where *AH* lists F-Pm 464 as the only source for these hymns. See also Chevalier, *Repertorium Hymnologicum*, vol. 2, 290 (Chevalier cites *AH* for most of his information); and Mone, *Lateinische Hymnen des Mittelalters*, vol. 3, 463. My comparisons with hundreds of manuscripts in northern France and the Low Countries has revealed no textual concordances.

97 I have discussed these hymns and prosas, their connections to the diocesan usage, and the relationship of the texts to the Life of St. Nicholas by Jacobus de Voragine in detail in "In Praise of St. Nicholas." Table 2.8 above is a revised version of the prosa table of that article (55), as the previous version lacks *Clemens fotor pauperum*. This chant is based on the very popular prosa tune *Veni sancte spiritus* for Pentecost. This source melody only appears in one manuscript from Paris, and that is F-Pnm lat. 10506 for the Confraternity of the Barrel Makers, where *Veni sancte spiritus* is listed as the prosa for Pentecost Sunday. The prosa for Pentecost Sunday in the diocesan usage of Paris was *Fulgens preclara*, according to Notre Dame sources such as GB-Lbl Add. 16905.

98 There is much literature on the nature of these chant genres and their variability within the Mass and Office. For hymns and prosas, see Hughes, "Late Medieval Plainchant" (32–4), who highlights the two genres as outlets for personal expressieon on the part of composers of texts, and he notes the vast repertory of chants with new texts set to preexisting melodies. See also Boynton, "Orality, Literacy, and the Early Notation"; Crocker, *The Early Medieval Sequence*; Kruckenberg, "Neumatizing the Sequence"; Bower, "From Alleluia to Sequence," 351–99; and Van Deusen, "Songs of Exile, Songs of Pilgrimage"

on the peripheral role of these two genres in the Mass and Office. See Bakker, "A Life in Hours" (331) on hymns as memory aids.

99   See *AH*, vol. 12 (379–80) for these two hymn texts.

100 Laus tibi sit domine regum rex eterne. Qui regnas in ethere cum patre et matre. Tecum sancti gaudent nicholausque. Quem barrenses receperunt hodie. Gaudentes de tam sancto pontifice. Quem disposueras eis donare. Certantes in qua locaretur parte. Et eorum lis cum discensione. In duas est partes divisa. Alleluya. Translation by Kerry McCarthy.

101 *Mittit ad virginem* appears in countless sources, including some used in private devotional settings. For use of this chant in Parisian sources, see Long, "In Praise of St. Nicholas." Scattered references are in Roelvink, *Gegeven den sangeren*, 148–49; *AH*, vol. 54, 296–98; Cuyler, "The Sequences of Isaac's 'Choralis Constantinus,'" 5; and Van Deusen, "Songs of Exile, Songs of Pilgrimage." For the alternatim polyphonic setting of this prosa attributed to Du Fay, see Hamm, "Dating a Group of Dufay Works," 71. For other polyphonic settings, see Robertson, "Remembering the Annunciation," 282–83. For Josquin's polyphonic setting, see Elders, "Plainchant in the Motets, Hymns, and Magnificat."

102 This prosa was normally transmitted in mensural notation, and it appears as such in the Parisian manuscript F-Pa 620 and in the Notary Confraternity manuscript from Tournai, B-Tc A 27. For more on the use of mensural notation in monophonic hymns and sequences, see Turner, "Spanish Liturgical Hymns"; Ward, "Polyphonic Settings," 332–33; and Sherr, "The Performance of Chant," 190–93.

103 The folios containing the vernacular prosa and Latin incipit in F-Pm 464 (fols. 66v–68v) are reproduced in Long, "In Praise of St. Nicholas," 73–77.

104 In F-Pa 620, the sequence appears with the rubric "De beata maria Prosa in tempore adventus. Et in annunciatione." On the significance of the Annunciation, see Boulton, *Sacred Fictions of Medieval France*, 8.

105 See Robertson, "Remembering the Annunciation"; and Young, *The Drama of the Medieval Church*, vol. 2, 225–58. The feast is March 25, but due to Lent, it is celebrated in the liturgy for Advent.

106 Young gives a full transcription of the ceremony in *The Drama of the Medieval Church*, vol. 2, 480–82. It ends with the following instructions: "Item fiet Missa per omnia, ut in die Annunciationis Dominice cum sequentia sive prosa *Mittit ad virginem*, cum organis et discantu prout in triplicibus." See also Gozzi, "La sequenza *Mittit ad virginem* ricostruita da Tr 92," who includes a transcription of an alternatim setting in I-Bc Q 15, which shows connections between the repertory in this source and the confraternity manuscripts discussed here (this is explored in chapter 4).

107 For a recent discussion of the educational nature of such vernacular literature, see Rubin, *Mother of God*, 217–42.

108 See Baltzer, "The Little Office of the Virgin"; and Reinburg, "Praying to
    Saints in the Late Middle Ages" for a discussion of the ways in which the laity
    prayed to their patron saints to intercede for them.
109 This was not unknown in other Parisian contexts, for as early as the thirteenth
    century, there is a vernacular hymn appearing in the manuscript F-Pnm lat.
    3461 A, which contains the *Speculum ecclesiae*. See Jeanroy, "Une hymne
    bilingue à Saint Nicolas," 107–9. See also Caldwell, "Singing, Dancing, and
    Rejoicing," 406–526.
110 This is the only source for the text I have found, and the only source listed in
    Rézeau, *Répertoire d'incipit des prières françaises*, 369.
111 Previst le createur du ciel le firmament le vray dispositeur bien convenable-
    ment de foy le champion. Je qui suis debiteur impugnant fermement du
    deable lauditeur loe admirablement vray religion. Translation by Valerie
    Wilhite.
112 The setting of nonliturgical, religious vernacular texts to preexisting chant
    melodies, popular songs, and dances, was fairly widespread in the English
    carol repertory, and at the end of the fifteenth century, the French noël. When
    viewed in light of these two genres, the appearance of a prosa in the vernacular
    follows a preexisting, and widespread, trend. For more on French song for St.
    Nicholas, see Caldwell, "Singing, Dancing, and Rejoicing," 584–91. For car-
    ols, see Harrison, "Benedicamus, Conductus, Carol." For the noël repertory,
    which emerged at the end of the fifteenth century, see Adrienne Fried Block,
    "Timbre, texte et air." See Wilson, *Music and Merchants*, which focuses on the
    lauda repertory in Florence. Venetian confraternities and the participation of
    members in communal singing is one of the main themes of Glixon, *Honoring
    God and the City*. Forney, "Music, Ritual and Patronage" (21–22) mentions
    a document from 1376 indicating that the members of the Confraternity of
    the Holy Cross in Antwerp would "sing the Mass themselves" at the altar of
    the Holy Cross in the Church of Our Lady. Although this was not done in
    the vernacular, it does show active participation on the part of confraternity
    members.
113 See Huisman, *Notes sur un Registre* (247) on the high honor placed on carrying
    the canopy.
114 On confraternity members participating in singing in public in Italy, see
    Wilson, *Music and Merchants*, 113, 124; and Hatter, *Composing Community in
    Late Medieval Music*, 106–7.
115 The June 1467 proclamation stated that the main reason for the division
    of the trades into sixty-one "banners" was to maintain order in the city and
    to conduct work more efficiently. See the transcription of this document in
    Lespinasse, *Metiers et corporations de la ville de Paris*, vol. 1, 53–60. Also see
    Rouse and Rouse, *Manuscripts and Their Makers*, 12. Some references to per-
    sons in other trades living there in the late sixteenth century appear in notarial

documents published by Renouard, *Documents sur les imprimeurs*, 23–24. For instance, in a 1571 census, among the booksellers and printers residing on the rue St. Jean de Lateran, there were also several people practicing other trades, such as coopers. In some tax records from the same year, one finds that among the inhabitants of the rue St. Jacques, rue des Mathurins, and the rue des Poirées there were wine merchants, spice dealers, and members of scattered other occupations residing among the printers, booksellers, scribes, book binders, etc. Also see Favier, *Nouvelle histoire de Paris*, 74. These documents prove that while the banner districts may have been to some extent enforced, members of other trades were not excluded from residence in the Latin Quarter.

116 See the transcribed documents in Renouard, *Imprimeurs parisiens*, *Documents sur les imprimeurs*, and *Répertoire des Imprimeurs Parisiens*; and Coyecque, *Recueil d'actes notariés*.

117 See Coyecque, *Recueil d'actes notariés*, vol. 1, 73, 184–85. The printer Charlotte Guillard was a parishioner there as well. See Beech, "Charlotte Guillard," 356.

118 See Coyecque, *Recueil d'actes notariés*, vol. 1, 73.

119 See Coyecque, *Recueil d'actes notariés*, vol. 1, 73.

120 Dodier and Kerver are the only ones mentioned by trade in the document transcribed by Coyecque. The names of the other men and their trades are found in the index of Renouard, *Documents sur les imprimeurs*, 321–65.

121 According to the index in Coyecque, *Recueil d'actes notariés*, vol. 1 (877) this institution was the home of numerous chapels: St. James, the Virgin, St. John the Evangelist, St. Nicholas, St. Peter and St. Paul, St. Genevieve, and St. Sebastian—one could speculate that confraternity devotions took place in them.

122 Public displays were an important part of confraternity devotions, but my intent here is to explore those services that took place privately.

Chapter Three

1 Martir egregie decus milicie athleta fidei ora natum dei ut avertat a nobis indignationem suam. Martir suffragia effunde pia. Ut epydeimia non sit noxia. In hac patria aut in alia. Que subsidia poscit tua. Audi talia tu preconia. Hic precepia dantur premia miles eya nobis. Alleluya. F-Pa 204, fol. 27r. F-Pnm lat. 859 says "miles eya ergo a nobis," on fol. 400r.

2 The confraternity likely met in the chapel of St. Sebastian at Notre Dame Cathedral. See Wright, *Music and Ceremony at Notre Dame*, 134–39.

3 See the introduction to this book on the fourteen holy helpers and their variability.

4   St. Genevieve was patron saint of Paris because she saved the city from sickness. The importance of St. Genevieve to the city of Paris is the primary subject of Sluhovsky, *Patroness of Paris*.

5   See Barker, "The Making of a Plague Saint," 93–94.

6   See Barker, "The Making of a Plague Saint," 93–94.

7   See Chiu, *Plague and Music*, 144. Also see Ressouni-Demigneux, "La personalité de saint Sébastien," 569; and Gecser, "Sermons on St. Sebastian after the Black Death," 264. The exact date of the translation of these relics to St. Victor is unclear, nor are there any details concerning the amount of relics that were moved to St. Victor.

8   This is the focus of the work of Gaposchkin, *The Making of Saint Louis*. See also Beaune, *The Birth of an Ideology*, 90–125; and Smith, *Chosen Peoples*, 108, 111, 116.

9   Several articles in the volume *Medieval Cantors and Their Craft*, eds. Bugyis, Kraebel, and Fassler, explore historical narratives and reference to location, as well as how an institution's history is presented in the liturgy through hagiographic construction (see the essays by Fassler, McKitterick, and Witnah).

10   This is the only confraternity manuscript referred to by Wright in his six-page discussion of confraternities in *Music and Ceremony at Notre Dame*, 134–39. He lists the masses in the manuscript and mentions that confraternity usages differed in some ways from the diocesan usage. His work does not go into detail concerning this confraternity or its liturgical practices, as they fell outside the scope of his study.

11   Pour la confrairie de Mr. St. Sebastien des archers bourgeois de Paris 1658.

12   This is clear throughout the documents published in Renouard, *Imprimeurs parisiens, Documents sur les imprimeurs*, and *Répertoire des Imprimeurs Parisiens*; and Coyecque, *Recueil d'actes notariés*. Also see the section entitled "Citizenship in Ancient and Medieval Cities," in Weber's famous *General Economic History* (43–49), which is based on his work from 1919–20.

13   See Price, *A Concise History of France*, 99.

14   See Garsonnin, *Le guet et les compagnies du guet d'Orleans*, 12–16, 18. He discusses the artisans who formed the citizen's guard but does not mention a confraternity.

15   See van Bruaene, "In Principio Erat Verbum" (64–68) on St. Sebastian guilds for the longbow.

16   See Wright, *Music and Ceremony at Notre Dame*, 135. He says that the "archers of Paris" started worshipping at the chapel of St. Sebastian in 1434. According to F-Pan LL 289, 136, there is an entry dated April 5, 1434, saying that the "Missa confratriae St. Sebastiani" is celebrated there, but with no mention of the corporation of the archers. An entry from January 18, 1433, in F-Pan LL 253, fol. 29v also refers to the Confraternity of St. Sebastian but says nothing about the archers.

17   On Pope Clement VI's Mass, which is variable in most sources, see Macklin, "Plague, Performance"; and Macklin, "Stability and Change." The feasts in figure 3.1 appear in different combinations in other northern French manuscripts. For example, F-AM 165 has a Mass with music for St. Genevieve and one for St. Anthony; and F-VAL 122 has services for St. Anthony and the *Missa pro evitanda mortalitate.*

18   St. Anthony's life and miracles appear in the *Golden Legend.* See Dunn-Lardeau, *Jacques de Voragine,* 222–27, Legend 22. See also Larson, "Odilon Redon's Temptation of Saint Anthony Lithographs," 47–49.

19   On St. Anthony's Fire and its relationship to the fires of hell and purgatory, see Wegman, "For Whom the Bell Tolls," 125–26.

20   On the life of St. Roche, see Boecki, *Images of Plague and Pestilence,* 57–58; Terry-Fritsch, "Proof in Pierced Flesh," 24–26; and Marshall, "A Plague Saint for Venice." Although he does not appear in the French translation of the *Golden Legend* in 1476, he does appear in Vérard's printed edition of the *Golden Legend.* See Jacobus de Voragine, *La légende dorée en François,* fol. 297r.

21   See Sluhovsky, *Patroness of Paris,* 11–17, 32–35. She does not appear in the French version of the *Golden Legend* produced in 1476, nor is she included in Vérard's printed edition of 1496, but she does appear in Caxton's printed version of 1483. See Jacobus de Voragine, *The Golden Legend … by William Caxton,* vol. 3, 149.

22   See Sluhovsky, *Patroness of Paris,* 22–23.

23   See Dunn-Lardeau, *Jacques de Voragine* (229–35) and also the printed edition by Vérard discussed above. This life is also the same in the English version printed by Caxton. The following description of St. Sebastian's life comes from the Batallier version, edited by Dunn-Lardeau. The sources used by Jacobus in constructing St. Sebastian's life are discussed in Jacobus de Voragine, *The Golden Legend of Jacobus de Voragine,* 104–9.

24   Dunn-Lardeau, *Jacques de Voragine* (230): "la carone perdurable."

25   Dunn-Lardeau, *Jacques de Voragine* (233): "Nostre Sire m'a ressucité pour vous preprendre des maulx que vous faictes aux crestiens serviteurs de Jhesu crist."

26   St. Lucina is St. Lucy.

27   See Marshall, "Manipulating the Sacred," 495. Also see Hall and Uhr, "*Aureola super Auream,*" 573.

28   See Barker, "The Making of a Plague Saint," 95–96; and Marshall, "Manipulating the Sacred," 489.

29   On plague imagery and the arrow, see Chiu, *Plague and Music,* 146–51; and Marshall, "Manipulating the Sacred," 493–500.

30   Marshall, "Manipulating the Sacred" (493–500) discusses this in detail, and it is also a theme throughout Barker, "The Making of a Plague Saint" and an article in the same volume by Berger, "Mice, Arrows, and Tumors."

31 See Marshall, "Manipulating the Sacred" (493), who quotes all of these biblical texts as evidence for arrow imagery.

32 See Marshall, "Manipulating the Sacred," 495. The panel is also discussed in Barker, "The Making of a Plague Saint," 113.

33 See Marshall, "Manipulating the Sacred," 495–96.

34 Manuscript sources 51, 53, 71, 82, and 95 are all discussed in Leroquais, *Les sacramentaires et les missels manuscrits*, vol. 2, 313; vol. 3, 24, 39, 149, 151.

35 I have also included comparisons to Amiens and Soissons, which are discussed later in the chapter.

36 St. Sebastian was not central to any of the northern French diocesan usages, with the exception of Soissons. He does appear in a confraternity source from Corbie, F-AM 162 D.

37 F-Pnm lat. 1112 includes this feast without rank. It is also found in F-Pnm lat. 9441, and F-Pnm lat. 15181 as a feast of 9 lessons. All printed liturgical books produced after 1504 also say it is a feast of 9 lessons.

38 The Amiens missal (source 34 in table 3.2) was printed in 1529 in Paris by Jean Petit, and it contains no music for this Mass, which appears at the end with the weekly round of votive masses. The Mass 2 chants are highlighted with an asterisk in this table.

39 The alleluia verse for Mass 2 in F-Pa 620 and several other sources is "O sancte Sebastiane militie presidium exaudi sero et mane voces ad te clamantium" (O Saint Sebastian, guard in the field, hear the voices in the morning and evening crying out to you.)

40 See Marshall, "Manipulating the Sacred" (495) on St. Sebastian's Christlike role and representations of St. Sebastian at the column.

41 US-ELmsu MS 2, fol. [178]v. This manuscript's northern French provenance is discussed in LaPonsey, "Michigan State University Library MS. 2," 103–6. This type of depiction appears in countless other books of hours from other locations, for instance, F-Pm 511, which is a sixteenth-century book for the usage of Troyes (fol. 266r), and F-Pm 502, which is a book of hours for the usage of Rome, also has such an image.

42 Table 3.4 gives the only sources containing music for these prosas, thus they are the only ones that allow for source melody comparison.

43 See Fassler, *Gothic Song*, 163–74.

44 Latin spelling and capitalization for this prosa are according to *AH*, vol. 37, 258.

45 On David's portrayal in courtly literature and Christianity as a "noble service," see Boulton, *Sacred Fictions of Medieval France*, 73–74. Boulton indicates that this is especially present in Venette's *L'Histoire des Trois Maries*, written around 1357.

46 Bozoky, *La Politique des reliques* (41–42) discusses the idea that the loss of a saint from French soil was a loss for the French realm. See Beaune, *The*

Birth of an Ideology (90–125), who discusses St. Louis in French identity and nationhood in the fourteenth and fifteenth centuries. And most recently, St. Louis's role in French national identity is discussed in Gaposchkin, *The Making of Saint Louis*, 4–5. See also Gaposchkin, "Political Ideas in Liturgical Offices."

47 Ressouni-Demigneux, "La personalité de saint Sébastien" (571–72), gives a good example of texts praising him as a champion of Christ but does not discuss liturgical texts. The implications are clear in the opening text of the prosa *Athleta sebastianus* in F-Pnm lat. 10506.

48 Latin spelling and capitalization for this prosa are according to *AH*, vol. 37, 257. English translation by Kerry McCarthy.

49 Latin spelling and capitalization for this prosa are according to *AH*, vol. 37, 256–57. English translation by Kerry McCarthy.

50 See Riess, *Narbonne and Its Territory*, 2.

51 Latin spelling and capitalization for this prosa are according to *AH*, vol. 37, 258. English translation by Kerry McCarthy.

52 For other examples of geography in liturgical texts for local saints, see Saucier, *A Paradise of Priests*, 49–93.

53 See Barker, "The Making of a Plague Saint," 93–94.

54 On giving relics as gifts, see Chiu, *Plague and Music*, 141–42; and Geary, *Living with the Dead*, 208–10.

55 On St. Genevieve's role in the conversion of Clovis, see Périn, "The Undiscovered Grave of King Clovis," 256. On Chlothair at Soissons, see Kaiser, "Aspects de l'histoire de la civitas suessionum," 115–22. For Soissons as a royal coronation site, see Enright, *Iona, Tara, and Soissons*, 79–154.

56 See Barker, "The Making of a Plague Saint," 93–94.

57 See Ressouni-Demigneux, "La personalité de Saint-Sebastian," 559. He indicates that the feast is found in a missal from Soissons, F-Pnm lat. 15614. There is no surviving music for the feast.

58 This is source 99 in appendix 1, *Missale secundum usum ecclesiae Suessoniensis*. The texts for the Mass are the same as Votive Mass 4 (see appendix 5 ❧), with a few exceptions. All the chants for this service come from the Common of Saints. There is also a votive Mass for St. Sebastian without music in this source, and it is an exact match to the one in the printed missal for the Usage of Paris.

59 See *AH*, vol. 37, 258.

60 See Byrne, *Daily Life during the Black Death*, 204. The plague was a problem for the citizens of Tournai as well, as discussed in chapter 1. An illuminated copy of the chronicles of Gilles Li Muisis (1350) currently held at the Bibliothèque Royale in Brussels (B-Br 13076–77) shows the citizens of Tournai burying plague victims on fol. 24v.

61 The date of the relic translation is unclear, but the abbots of St. Médard promoted the relics in their possession by sending pieces to other monasteries and constructing collections of miracles. See Gecser, "Sermons on St. Sebastian," 264.

62 Gecser, "Sermons on St. Sebastian," 264–65. Also see Chiu, *Plague and Music*, 144.

63 This is according to F-Pm 527, which is a missal for the usage of St. Victor dating from the fifteenth through seventeenth centuries. This source does not mention a St. Sebastian altar at St. Victor.

64 Felix corona francie ludovici virtutibus cuius corona glorie refulget in celestibus. The St. Sebastian text is given in table 3.3. US-BAw 302 is a notated missal for the usage of Paris produced in the fifteenth century for an unidentified institution.

65 Pater sancte ludovice fusa deo precum vice solve reos a sagena peccatorum et apena. English translation by Kerry McCarthy.

66 The exception to this is example 3.1, where the verse *O sancte sebastiane imploramus* diverges significantly from the chant model. The opening statement, however, is enough to establish a link to the model.

67 See Gaposchkin, *The Making of Saint Louis*, 2–4; and Beaune, *The Birth of an Ideology*, 90–125. Hankeln, in "Reflections of War and Violence" (6), remarks that "Saints manifest religious and political ideals."

68 The designation of royal saints as Christlike and champions of Christ appear in offices from other locations. See Hankeln, "Kingship and Sanctity"; and Hiley, "Gens, laudum titulis concrepet Anglica."

69 The translations of these texts comprise the main content of Gaposchkin, Field, and Field, *The Sanctity of Louis IX*.

70 See Farmer, *Surviving Poverty in Medieval Paris* (7–9) who shows how well into the fifteenth century St. Louis is seen as a healer, which is evident through new hospital foundations in his honor.

71 On the ability of the French kings to heal illness, see Enright, *Iona, Tara, and Soissons*, 159–62. This is also the theme throughout Bloch, *The Royal Touch*.

72 See Beaune, *The Birth of an Ideology*, 117–21. There are no liturgical books that survive from these organizations.

73 Antoni pastor inclite qui cruciatos reficis morbos sanas et estruis ignis calorem extinguis pie pater ad dominum ora pro nobis miseris. F-Pa 204, fol. 13r. English translation by Kerry McCarthy.

74 Ora pro nobis miseris sancta virgo genouefa que nunc gaudes in superis miraculis innumeris fulgens virtute divina. F-Pa 204, fol. 16v. English translation by Kerry McCarthy.

75 O beate confessor sancte roche quam magna apud deum sunt merita tua quibus credimus nos a morbo epidimie posse liberari et aeris temperiem concede. F-Pa 204, fol. 30r-v. English translation by Kerry McCarthy.

76 A votive Mass for St. Genevieve starts to appear at the end of printed missals for the usage of Paris starting in 1504, as shown in figure 3.4 earlier in the chapter.

77 In Freeman, *Holy Bones Holy Dust* (2–3), he discusses a "community of the supernatural": "The tribulations of life, combined with the very specific burden of dread laid by the medieval conception of the afterlife, drove the helpless masses into a world 'between heaven and earth,' the only part of their lives that they could fashion for themselves."

78 According to Chiu, *Plague and Music* (125), during a plague epidemic in Milan in 1576, Carlo Borromeo advised people to "go to church in spirit."

79 On virtual pilgrimage books, see Taylor, ed., *Encyclopedia of Medieval Pilgrimage*, 693–95; and Rudy, *Virtual Pilgrimages in the Convent*, 35–37, 97, 240–45.

80 Chapters 1 and 2 give multiple sources for the vitae of St. Barbara, St. Catherine, and St. Nicholas.

81 See Chiu, *Plague and Music*, 144; and Gecser, "Sermons on St. Sebastian," 264.

82 Wright, *Music and Ceremony at Notre Dame*, 220.

83 On royal processions in Paris, see Bryant, "La ceremonie de l'entrée à Paris." Parallels to other urban centers where the monarchy used saints and other religious topoi while interacting with the populace may be found in the Burgundian court. See Sutch and van Bruaene, "The Seven Sorrows," 254.

84 Symes, "The Lordship of jongleurs" (238), describes how the confraternity of the jongleurs in Arras "developed a vocabulary of power based on and in texts." On confraternities and identity, see Black, "The Development of Confraternity Studies," 17. See also Trio, "Lay Persons in Power," 54.

Chapter Four

1 Sanctus, sanctus, sanctus, Dominus Deus sabaoth. *Qui vertice thabor affuisti et clarior sole micuisti.* Pleni sunt celi et terra Gloria tua. *Quia hac die pie revelasti discipulis quos mire pasti.* Osanna in exelsis. Benedictus qui venit in nomine Domini. *Redimere peccata seculi quem precamur supplices servuli.* Osanna in excelsis. The original Latin was translated into French by Anne-Emmanuelle Ceulemans, in "Le manuscrit BCT A 58," 22. The translation into English here was also done by Ceulemans.

2 For more on the confraternity's membership and devotions to the Transfiguration at Tournai, see Pycke, "La confrérie de la Transfiguration."

3 The word "Vineux" is also written in the margins of the manuscript Aosta, Seminario Maggiore, MS 15 (I-AO 15); and in the fragment F-Lad 134 no.

12, it is called "Pie vineux." See Fallows, "Dufay and Nouvion-le-Vineux" (44–50) on the "Vineux" phenomenon.

4   This is clear through the appearance of countless Kyrie tropes, among the most popular being *Fons bonitatis*, *Clemens rector*, and *Cunctipotens genitor*. Tropes are not included in settings of the Credo.

5   See Kirkman, *The Cultural Life of the Early Polyphonic Mass*, 169–73.

6   There are examples of this throughout the confraternity sources in Paris and Tournai, such as B-Tc A 12, B-Tc A 27, F-Pm 461, and F-Pnm lat. 10506.

7   Wright has fully discussed the Parisian Kyriale, using primarily fourteenth-century sources, and he has transcribed their melodies. See Wright, *Music and Ceremony at Notre Dame*, 81–97. Wright's study of the fourteenth-century diocesan manuscripts will be used as a control study in the discussion of the Mass ordinary material found in the confraternity manuscripts and printed sources. Haggh has also discussed the kyriale of the Ste. Chapelle, which differs from that of Notre Dame and other Parisian secular churches. See Haggh, "An Ordinal of Ockeghem's Time," 60, 62–67. The indices used to trace the foreign melodies of the Mass ordinary are Hiley, "Ordinary of Mass Chants"; Landwehr-Melnicki, *Das Einstimmige Kyrie*; Bosse, *Untersuchung einstimmiger mittelalterlicher Melodien*; Schildbach, *Das einstimmige Agnus Dei*; and Thannabaur, *Das einstimmige Sanctus*. All of these publications are referred to in the Mass ordinary tables in appendix 5 ❧.

8   This is based on the assumption that they would celebrate their patron saint's feast day with highest ceremony. Chapter 1 describes feast ranks.

9   The examples from the diocesan sources for this cycle appear in Wright, *Music and Ceremony at Notre Dame*, 83. The incipits that Wright gives throughout his discussion of the Parisian Kyriale are not reproduced in this chapter; only the incipits from the confraternity manuscripts are given. This is the only Mass ordinary music to appear in F-Pm 461, for the Confraternity of St. John the Evangelist for the book production community. On very rare occasions, the word "annual" is used in place of "duplex."

10   See Wright, *Music and Ceremony at Notre Dame* (89) for Cycle 15 in the diocesan usage.

11   See Wright, *Music and Ceremony at Notre Dame* (85) for the corresponding melody and rubric for Cycle 5 in the diocesan usage.

12   See Wright, *Music and Ceremony at Notre Dame* (86–87) for Cycles 8 and 9 in the diocesan usage. The rubric in the diocesan sources indicates that this melody is to be used "on any other Saturday when the Office of the Virgin is sung." This rubric can only be understood in relationship to the rubric for Cycle 8 preceding it, where there is a Kyrie and a Gloria that are to be sung on certain feast days for the Virgin but not others.

13   See Wright, *Music and Ceremony at Notre Dame* (85) for music and the full text of the rubrics for Cycles 2 and 5.

14   Those other feast days include the following: the third day of the octaves of Easter, Pentecost, and Christmas; the feasts of Apostles and Evangelists; the feasts of saints celebrated at the rank of nine lessons; the feasts of nine lessons occurring on Sundays when no duplex or semiduplex feast falls; the Octave of the Nativity; Transfiguration; Sundays within the octaves and on the octaves of St. John the Baptist, Peter and Paul, St. Marcel and St. Martin; and on days of the Temporale between Christmas and Purification, or Septuagesima when it precedes the Purification. This is a paraphrase of Wright, *Music and Ceremony at Notre Dame*, 85.

15   Other appearances of Mass ordinary chants in F-Pnm lat. 10506 that seem to be disconnected from their function in the diocese can be seen on fol. 168v, where a Kyrie appears directly after the Mass for St. Sebastian. The music for this Kyrie corresponds to Cycle 13 in the diocesan manuscripts for the cathedral and parish usage. In these sources, it is indicated that this Kyrie is sung from the Octave of Trinity Sunday until Advent, on Sundays in Advent without duplex or semiduplex rank, on all Sundays without feasts, and on Sundays of the Temporale from the Purification until Easter. Similar to Cycle 5 above, this particular melody was associated with a wide variety of services. Since there was no Mass for St. Sebastian in the diocese of Paris, this confraternity chose another melody its members saw to be fitting for their devotions on that day. See Wright, *Music and Ceremony at Notre Dame* (88–89), for a translation of the rubric for diocesan Cycle 13, and the melody.

16   They are organized in pairs with the two Kyries together, followed by the two Glorias, the two Sanctus melodies, and the two Agnus Dei chants.

17   See Wright, *Music and Ceremony at Notre Dame* (87) for Parisian Cycle 9. Other than this, there is no match for this melody in Haggh, "An Ordinal of Ockeghem's Time," 62–67; Hiley, "Ordinary of Mass Chants"; or Landwehr-Melnicki, *Das Einstimmige Kyrie*. As mentioned previously, Cycle 9 was for Saturdays when the Office of the Virgin was celebrated.

18   This melody has no match in Wright, *Music and Ceremony at Notre Dame*; Haggh, "An Ordinal of Ockeghem's Time," 62–67; Hiley, "Ordinary of Mass Chants"; or Landwehr-Melnicki, *Das Einstimmige Kyrie*.

19   See Wright, *Music and Ceremony at Notre Dame* (84–85), for Gloria Cycles 4 and 5. The rubric in the diocesan sources for Cycle 4 is just as specific as that for Cycle 5, which was paraphrased previously. Cycle 4 indicates that the material is to be sung on the second day of the octaves of Easter, Pentecost and Christmas; on semiduplex feasts in alternation with that of Cycle 3; the Kyrie is to be sung with Cycle 2 on Christmas and Epiphany; and on Sundays within the octaves of the Assumption, Nativity of the Virgin, and St. Denis. This is a paraphrase of Wright's translation.

20   These two settings have no counterparts within the diocesan usage, nor were they used at the Ste. Chapelle. However, the first Sanctus and Agnus Dei do

have concordances in other northern French usages, such as a Benedictine
manuscript from Douai, as well as a Dominican source from Paris ca. 1260.
See Hiley, "Ordinary of Mass Chants" (107, 5, 111), melody A34. This melody is also found in later printed sources and will be discussed in more detail
in the following chapter.

21 Sequences in cantus fractus appeared in one of the confraternity manuscripts
discussed in chapter 2 (F-Pm 464), and there is a Credo in cantus fractus in
a diocesan notated missal discussed in chapter 3 (F-Pa 620). On the whole,
though, there are more from Cambrai and Tournai.

22 See appendix 2 for an inventory of B-Tc A 58, which is a truncated version of
that given in Pycke, "La confrérie de la Transfiguration." A full inventory and
transcription of B-Tc B 29 (not in appendix 1) also appears in Pycke's article.

23 Refer to the introduction of this study for a discussion of the division of
Tournai along the Escaut river between the dioceses of Tournai and Cambrai.
For information on the confraternity's membership, its founding, and its his-
tory see Pycke, "La confrérie de la Transfiguration."

24 Charles Van den Borren published an inventory of the source in 1934,
and it was apparently still in the Cathedral Archive collection by 1948, as
Walter Rubsamen was able to view it. By the time of the publication of the
Census Catalogue (1979–88) the manuscript had disappeared from the
Cathedral Archive collection, and in this work it is listed as no longer extant.
See Van den Borren, "Inventaire des manuscrits de musique"; Rubsamen,
"Musicological Notes from Belgium, Switzerland, and England," 55; and
Hamm and Kellman, Census Catalogue, vol. 3, 218.

25 The following discussion of the community, its membership, its foundation,
and its movement within the city of Tournai comes in large part from Pycke,
"La confrérie de la Transfiguration." Descriptions of the liturgical practices
and music represented in B-Tc A 58 are found in Ceulemans, "Le manuscrit
musical Tournai B.C.T. A 58"; Ceulemans, "Une 'Missa Sancta Trinitas'
anonyme"; and Ceulemans, "Le manuscrit BCT A 58." An older discussion of the confraternity comes from Voisin, "Notice sur la confrérie de la
Transfiguration"; and Warichez, La cathédrale de Tournai et son chapitre, 275–
76. This organization is also discussed in Dupont, "Le chant dans l'espace,"
84–87; and Desmette, "Les confréries religieuses à Tournai."

26 Refer to the introduction of this study for a discussion of the division of the
city of Tournai along the Escaut river between the dioceses of Tournai and
Cambrai.

27 Ceulemans discusses the appearance of the feast of the Transfiguration in the
calendar of B-Tc A 11 at the rank of duplex, and as a fifteenth-century addition in Cambrai, as seen in the antiphoner F-CA 38. See Ceulemans, "Le
manuscrit BCT A 58," 17.

28 Pycke, in "La confrérie de la Transfiguration" (134), mentions the possible connection to the Taborites, who were disciples of Jean Hus, and the possible affinity for this doctrine among the textile community in Tournai and Lille. He says that one of the early members of the confraternity was canon Paschasius Grenier, who could be the son of the celebrated Tournaisien tapestry maker Pasquier Grenier, who worked for the dukes of Burgundy. On the Hussites in Lille and Tournai and their connection to the tapestry trade, see Kaminsky, *A History of the Hussite Revolution*, 357. Ceulemans discusses Taborite sympathies and their implications in "Le manuscrit BCT A 58," 18–22.

29 See Soil, "Les tapisseries tournaisiennes," 96–101. Some of the most famous political figures of the fifteenth century were clients of the tapestry makers of Tournai. The tapestry makers also had strong relations with those of the same trade in Lille.

30 The Transfiguration evidently played an important role in popular devotions in the city of Tournai during the fifteenth century, and this was established after the circulation of Taborite doctrine in the area. It was also at this time that devotions to the Transfiguration spread to Cambrai, which is reflected in similarities between the liturgies for that day in the two dioceses. The feast of the Transfiguration was also known in other cities in the diocese of Tournai, such as Bruges, although the same order of service was not observed. It appears in F-Pm 390, a manuscript from Bruges, but the only chant in common with the B-Tc A 58 version is the offertory, *Deus enim firmavit*.

31 For more information on the connection between the Holy Trinity and the Transfiguration, see Pycke, "La confrérie de la Transfiguration"; and Ceulemans, "Le manuscrit BCT A 58." For a transcription of the Kyrie of the anonymous Mass, see Ceulemans, "Une 'Missa Sancta Trinitas' anonyme." She indicates that this Mass is based on the motet *Sancta Trinitas* by Févin, but it is compositionally different and therefore unlikely that it is by Févin. My own survey of other manuscript sources containing polyphonic settings of masses in honor of the Trinity, such as the *Missa Sancta Trinitas* by Mouton/Févin found in P-Cug M.2 (fol. 87v–103r); and the anonymous settings in D-Mbs Mus. 66 (fols. 133v–156r); and D-Mbs Mus. 1536 (piece number 113), all yield no concordances. Although the Mass appears only in B-Tc A 58, the Févin motet, *Sancta Trinitas* is found in numerous sources, among them the Zheghere van Male partbooks from Bruges, owned by a layman. See Diehl, "The Partbooks of a Renaissance Merchant," 627–28; and Gabriëls, "Bourgeois Music Collecting in Mid Sixteenth-Century Bruges," 265.

32 See Pycke's transcription in "La confrérie de la Transfiguration," 142–43.

33 For a transcription of the items in the register, see Pycke, "La confrérie de la Transfiguration," 143. *O nata lux* was done at Matins and Vespers at the Cambrai cathedral, according to a search on Cantus, where it appears in a

cathedral manuscript (F-CA 38) and a printed antiphoner produced by Simon Vostre (F-CA Impr. XVI C 4). See *CANTUS*.

34   See the transcription of the item in Pycke, "La confrérie de la Transfiguration," 143. The text of the *De Profundis* is found in B-Tc B 29 (not in appendix 1) without music.

35   Pycke noted the appearance of the antiphon and its possible connection to Item 19. See Pycke, "La confrérie de la Transfiguration," 147.

36   See Long, "Les dévotions des confréries." The Agnus Dei "Vineux" is not included. I would like to thank the late Alejandro Planchart for sharing his unpublished inventory of this fragment with me. A brief inventory appears in Long, "Les dévotions des confréries."

37   See appendix 2 for inventories of all three manuscripts. Long, "Les dévotions des confréries," includes a full inventory of the source. This manuscript contains additions well into the fifteenth century and includes the main feasts of the Temporale, as well as some from the Sanctorale. The manuscript at one time resided in the collection at the Cathedral of Tournai, which is evident based on a pastedown on fol. 1r: "Bibliothecae ecclesiae Cathedralis Torn. [sic]." There is no indication that the source was used by a confraternity, but due to its limited contents, it was likely used in a private devotional setting.

38   Fallows, "Dufay and Nouvion-le-Vineux"; and Planchart, "The Early Career of Guillaume Du Fay."

39   The practice of notating chants in cantus fractus was particularly prevalent in Cambrai, as existing manuscripts attest. For example, the Médiathèque municipale in Cambrai has many sources containing chants in cantus fractus, among the most important being manuscripts 11 and 12. See Bouckaert, ed., *Cantus 21*, 92–94, 130. For general studies of hymns in cantus fractus and polyphonic settings, see Ward, *The Polyphonic Office Hymn*; and Ward, "Polyphonic Settings." See also Sherr, "The Performance of Chant."

40   Nicola Tangari mentions that three liturgical genres are most likely to employ rhythm: hymns, sequences, and the Credo. See Tangari, "Mensural and Polyphonic Music," 52. Examples from each of these genres appear in cantus fractus in the confraternity books discussed in the present study.

41   For transcriptions of mensural Credos, refer to Miazga, *Die Melodien der einstimmigen Credo*. See also Sherr, "The Performance of Chant"; Gozzi, "Il canto fratto"; and Gabrielli, "Il manoscritto 327." Other important works are Gozzi, "Alle origini del canto fratto"; Gozzi, "I prototipi del canto fratto"; and Kügle, *The Manuscript Ivrea*, 182–85, 199–200.

42   See Stäblein-Harder, *Fourteenth-Century Mass Music … Critical Text*, 15.

43   For a facsimile of the manuscript and a full bibliography, see Bent, *Bologna Q 15*.

44   This is a series of fragments (ca. 1420) that were used to reinforce the binding of a late fifteenth-century incunabulum. It contains an anonymous three-voice

setting of the polyphonic Sanctus and Agnus Dei "Vineux." Only the superius and final portion of the tenor of the Sanctus are preserved, and the Agnus Dei is poorly transmitted. Due to this, I have not reproduced it here. See Wright, "A Fragmentary Manuscript."

45 See Amiet, "La messe pour l'unité des chrétiens."

46 See Hamm and Kellman, *Census Catalogue*, vol. 1, 6–7. Planchart has speculated that the polyphonic settings of the Sanctus and Agnus Dei "Vineux"
by Du Fay and Loqueville were composed for performance at the Council of
Constance. See Planchart, "The Early Career of Guillaume Du Fay," 359–60.

47 The tenor of the Loqueville setting in I-Bc Q 15 and the monophonic version
in I-AO 15 have the same pitches, but they use slightly different ligatures.

48 A complete transcription of the Sanctus in B-Tc A 58 appears in Ceulemans,
"Le manuscrit BCT A 58," 15–16. The legible parts of the polyphonic setting
in F-Dm 2837 are transcribed in Wright, "A Fragmentary Manuscript." The
polyphonic settings by Du Fay and Loqueville in I-Bc Q 15 are published in
Du Fay, *Fragmenta Missarum*, 9–10; and Du Fay, *Compositiones Liturgicae
Minores,* 155–56. The monophonic versions in I-AO 15, F-Pa 204, and F-Lad
134 no. 12 are the same as the tenors of the polyphonic settings in I-Bc Q 15
and the monophonic chant in B-Tc A 58.

49 See tables 4.1 and 4.2 for a breakdown of the sources containing the Sanctus
and Agnus Dei, and which ones include monophonic and polyphonic versions, and tropes. Wright was the first to note that the Agnus Dei is a contrafactum of the Sanctus ("A Fragmentary Manuscript").

50 All rests in the music examples for the Sanctus and Agnus Dei "Vineux" are
intentional.

51 This trope also appears in F-Dm 2837, but the tenor voice is too damaged to
ascertain whether or not it matches F-Pa 204. The other voices of the Agnus
Dei are no match.

52 It is not necessarily certain that this monophonic tenor was composed by Du
Fay, but he did write the polyphonic version based on it in I-Bc Q 15. It was
at least possibly composed after 1393 and used as inspiration for a piece in
F-Dm 2837 dated around 1420.

53 See Kirkman, *The Cultural Life of the Early Polyphonic Mass*, 203. On what it
means for the laity to participate and focus on the Mass, see Filippi, "'Audire
missam est verba missae intelligere …,'" 11–21. On the elevation of the
host in place of communion for the laity, see Pavanello, "The Elevation as
Liturgical Climax," 34–39.

54 Gozzi, "Alle origini del canto fratto," 245–46. See also Glixon, *Honoring God
and the City*, 82.

55 Although these two words appear together in the transcription, they do not
appear in succession in the Credo. This is indicated in the musical example by
a short line break.

56   As shown in the introduction and chapter 1, few sources survive containing music performed in the main sanctuary, and those that do have no Mass ordinary chants.

57   See Gozzi, "Il canto fratto," 25; and Gabrielli, "Il manoscritto 327," 107.

58   These four sources are F-Lad 134 no. 12, B-Tc A 58, I-Bc Q 15, and F-Dm 2837. See table 4.1.

59   See Luypaert, "Des assemblées capitulaires aux assemblées conciliaires"; and Moreau, "Un évêque de Tournai au XIVe siècle" on processions for the Unity of the Church. Neither author mentions music at all.

60   Young, *The Drama of the Medieval Church* (vol. 2, 480–82), gives a full transcription of the ceremony. It ends with the following instructions: "Item fiet Missa per omnia, ut in die Annunciationis Dominice cum sequentia sive prosa *Mittit ad virginem*, cum organis et discantu prout in triplicibus." Gozzi, "La sequenza *Mittit ad virginem* recostruita da Tr 92" includes a transcription of an alternatim setting of *Mittit ad virginem* in I-Bc Q 15, which shows even further connections between the repertory in this source and the confraternity manuscripts discussed here.

61   Kügle, *The Manusript Ivrea* (182–85, 199–200), also notes that this was the case in French sources of the Avignon school.

62   A reproduction of the Kyrie from B-Tc A 12 appears in Long, "Les dévotions des confréries."

63   See Bradley, *Polyphony in Medieval Paris*, 11–12.

64   The Sanctus appears directly after the Benedictus in the bottom margins of fol. 32v. The Kyrie appears directly after the Agnus Dei in the bottom margins of fol. 33r.

65   Editions that do not include them are Van den Borren, *Missa Tornacensis*; Dumoulin, Huglo, Mercier, and Pycke, *La Messe de Tournai*; and Schrade, *Polyphonic Music of the Fourteenth Century … Critical Text* (123), who indicates in the commentary that the Kyrie is a three-voice work. In Stäblein-Harder, *Fourteenth-Century Mass Music … Critical Text* (33–34) she discusses how Ludwig, in "Die Quellen der Motetten ältesten Stils" (221) originally established that the Kyrie added at the end of the cycle is in three voices. Ludwig says this in passing mention in a footnote, without going into detail. Stäblein-Harder transcribes this as a polyphonic work in *Fourteenth-Century Mass Music … Music Score* (20), but it is dissonant and does not resemble other works in that volume. Furthermore, the way the chant is written in the manuscript does not imply at all that it was a polyphonic work; instead, it is written exactly as one would expect for a monophonic Kyrie in cantus fractus.

66   See Cuthbert, "The (Other) Tournai Mass"; and Stoessel and Collins, "New Light."

67   See Cattin and Facchin, *Polyphonic Music of the Fourteenth Century* (vol. 23 A, 348, 393), where the Kyrie and Sanctus are both transcribed as monophonic

chants in cantus fractus. The critical commentary (vol. 23 B, 503) discusses the Kyrie briefly: "The well known melody (of which the incipit is found, with a variant, in *Landwehr-Mel*, no 58) occurs in the T range in the Tournai MS; the question therefore remains whether one or more voices would have accompanied it. For this reason we decided to include this purely monodic piece in the present edition." The editors make no mention of Ludwig, Schrade, or Stäblein-Harder's assertions that it is a polyphonic piece.

68 Gomez, "Quelques remarques sur le repertoire sacré."

69 See Coussemaker, "Messe du XIII siècle." In that article he refers to the fabric published by Voisin. See Voisin, "Drames liturgiques de Tournai."

70 Van den Borren, *Missa Tornacensis* (vol. 3) traces this to information given to Friedrich Ludwig in 1915 by the archivist at the Cathedral, Canon Warichez, who indicates that Coussemaker confused B-Tc A 27 with B-Tc A 12. See also Ludwig, "Die Quellen der Motetten ältesten stils," 220.

71 See Huglo, "Le manuscrit de la Messe de Tournai" for the manuscript's gathering structure.

72 The appearance of the Gloria in CH-HE Codex Chart. 151 was first discussed on *Musicologie Médievale* on November 11, 2016. See Gatté, "A New Concordance of Tournai Gloria." This manuscript is digitized on *E-codices*. For the appearance of the Credo in the I-Rsm uncatalogued gradual, see Tangari, "Mensural and Polyphonic Music," 44–51.

73 The date for the Codex Las Huelgas has recently been reevaluated by David Catalunya, whose detailed analysis of the scribal hands and other physical attributes of the collection allow for a new date, early in the 1340s (it was previously thought to have been created around 1325). Catalunya, "Music, Space and Ritual in Medieval Castille," 106–8. I would like to thank David for sharing his dissertation with me.

74 See Schrade, *Polyphonic Music of the Fourteenth Century ... Critical Text*, 123. See also Reaney, *Manuscripts of Polyphonic Music*, 49; and Guletsky, "The Four 14th-Century Anonymous Masses," 177–80. Guletsky believes that the notation styles can be tied to the individual musical form of each movement.

75 See Guletsky, "The Four 14th-Century Anonymous Masses," 177–80.

76 See Desmond, *Music and the Moderni*, 146.

77 See Anglés, "Una Nueva Version del Credo de Tournai," 97–99.

78 See Tomasello on the dating and transmission of the Credo in "The Transmission of the Las Huelgas Credo," 505–7.

79 See Tangari, "Mensural and Polyphonic Music," 48.

80 Huglo mentions the Picard dialect in B-Tc A 27. See Huglo, "Le manuscrit de la Messe de Tournai," 27. On the Polish fragment, see Brewer, "A Fourteenth-Century Polyphonic Manuscript Rediscovered," 8.

81　The Ivrea Codex is the primary focus of Kügle, *The Manuscript Ivrea*. See also Tomasello, "Scribal Design"; and Anglés, "Una Nueva Version del Credo de Tournai."

82　See Leech-Wilkinson, *Machaut's Mass*, 38–41.

83　See Schrade, *Polyphonic Music of the Fourteenth Century … Critical Text*, 126; Guletsky also makes a case for this based on the formal structures of the movements, but her evidence is inconclusive. See Guletsky, "The Four 14th-Century Anonymous Masses," 177–80.

84　See Guletsky, "The Four 14th-Century Anonymous Masses," 177–80; and Bain and McGrady, *A Companion to Guillaume de Machaut*, 151.

85　Modern transcriptions of this Mass are easily available and were mentioned in the section on the Kyrie and Sanctus in cantus fractus in B-Tc A 27.

86　Guletsky indicates that the polyphonic Sanctus and Agnus Dei of the Tournai Mass are based on the Kyrie melody Melnicki 114. She provides detailed musical transcriptions of this Kyrie melody and its relationship to the two polyphonic movements. The connection that Guletsky makes is tenuous, as it is based on a stepwise rising and falling scale on F that appears in the Kyrie melody, and in the polyphonic Sanctus and Agnus Dei. This figure is found in many other stepwise Mode 6 melodies, which weakens Guletsky's hypothesis. Furthermore, Guletsky picks and chooses notes from the polyphonic version as examples of how they relate to the chant, making her argument based primarily on contour rather than pitches. See Guletsky, "The Four 14th-Century Anonymous Masses," 222–27.

87　My own comparison of chants from sources in Lille, Cambrai, Arras, Douai, and Valenciennes yielded no results. There are also manuscripts from these geographical areas compared in Hiley, "Ordinary of Mass Chants," none of which contain this melody.

88　Elsa De Luca recently wrote about this manuscript in her dissertation. She renumbers the sources, calls it MS 5, and gives a good bibliography of other authors who have discussed this source. Most notable among these works are Branner, "Two Parisian Capella Books"; Huglo, "Notated Performance Practices"; and Hesbert, *Le Prosaire de la Sainte-Chapelle*. These authors all call this source MS 1. For a more detailed discussion, see De Luca, "I manoscritti musicali dell' Archivio di San Nicola a Bari," 47–51.

89　See Robertson, "Remembering the Annunciation," 295–304.

90　See Kügle, *The Manuscript Ivrea*, 163–69.

91　On the Master of the Royal French Motets and his style, see Leech-Wilkinson, *Machaut's Mass*, 38–41.

92　Table 4.3 shows that the Credo is found in two sources from Avignon, and the Ite Missa Est motet is found in one source containing Avignonese repertory. On the connections between the Avginon and French court repertories more broadly, see Tomasello, "Scribal Design."

93 On chambers of rhetoric in the fourteenth century, see Plumley, *The Art of Grafted Song*, 176–90.

94 See Long, "Les dévotions des confréries."

95 See Pycke, "La 'Messe de Tournai,'" (59–66) for a reference to the foundation of 1349. This is a reprint of an earlier edition from 1988, so for the past thirty years scholars have cited this as evidence of the original context of the Mass.

96 See Strohm, *Music in Late Medieval Bruges*, 102. See Robertson, "Remembering the Annunciation" (295–304), who cites Pycke. See also Stoessel and Collins, "New Light," 1, 5.

97 On composition at Tournai, see Coussemaker's discussion of the motet text from the Montpellier Codex MS 196, *Quant se depart*. Coussemaker speculates that the author is a trouvère from Tournai, because the text has the following passage: "que je les aportai de mon païs, ce endroit de Tornoi" (that I brought from my country, that place, Tournai). See Coussemaker, "Messe du XIII siècle," 102–3. The word "Tornoi" could mean "Tournai" in this context, although it is more often translated as "tournament" (which makes no sense here). Plumley discusses the compositional network associated with Tournai in the fourteenth century in *The Art of Grafted Song*, 178–90, 265. Other composers of the fourteenth, fifteenth, and sixteenth centuries who worked at the cathedral are Johannes Cuvelier, Petrus de Domarto, Pierre de Manchicourt, and Nicolas Gombert. Thomas Crequillon also wrote a song about Tournai, *Dedans Tournay*.

98 Stäblein-Harder, *Fourteenth-Century Mass Music … Critical Text* (15) mentions that some of the Parisian Notre Dame polyphonic Mass propers written in the twelfth and thirteenth centuries were still copied into manuscripts at that institution well into the fourteenth century.

99 Modeling is a theme throughout Symes, *A Common Stage*. Plumley discusses compositional procedures and modeling in such contexts, which I noted is certainly present in the Kyrie and Sanctus chants in cantus fractus attached to the Tournai Mass. If the other three polyphonic movements of the Tournai Mass found uniquely in B-Tc A 27 (Kyrie, Sanctus, Agnus) were local compositions, they could have been part of the tradition of modeling out of which came liturgical drama and other compositions. See Plumley, *The Art of Grafted Song*, 178–90.

100 Mark Everist discusses what he calls "confraternity motets" in the Montpellier Codex, which are pieces that include rosters of musicians. In particular, he discusses works that refer to composer networks in Paris. See Everist, "Montpellier 8," 24–28. For the fifteenth and sixteenth centuries, we see this is the case in places like Cambrai, where group identity was reinforced in musician circles, as Jane Hatter points out in *Composing Community in Late Medieval Music*, 19–52.

101 In addition to the discussion of this throughout the work of Symes, *A Common Stage*, and Plumley, *The Art of Grafted Song*, see Saltzstein, *The Refrain and the Rise of the Vernacular*, 39–43; and Jaeger, *Scholars and Courtiers*, vii. The city of Tournai had a group of men residing in Paris, "le conseil de la ville à Paris," who facilitated the city's interests and handled affairs at court. There was also a sizeable Tournaisien presence in the later fourteenth century at the literary society of the cour amoreuse of Charles VI. See Small, "Centre and Periphery in Late Medieval France," 154, 156–57.
102 See Li Muisis, *Poésies de Gilles Li Muisis*, vol. 1, 88–89.
103 See Hoppin and Clercx, "Notes biographiques."
104 See Hoppin and Clercx, "Notes biographiques," 72–73.
105 See Plumley, *The Art of Grafted Song*, 265.
106 See Kügle, *The Manuscript Ivrea*, 139.
107 See Plumley, *The Art of Grafted Song*, 184.
108 This is the main theme of Thelen, "The Feast of the Seven Sorrows" and *The Seven Sorrows Confraternity of Brussels*.
109 See Plumley, *The Art of Grafted Song*, 178–90, and 265.
110 See Plumley, *The Art of Grafted Song*, 262.
111 See Hatter, *Composing Community in Late Medieval Music*, 13–16; and Wegman, "From Maker to Composer," 471–73.
112 See Strohm, "The Ars Nova Fragments of Gent," 120–21.
113 See Small, "Centre and Periphery in Late Medieval France," 149–50; Warichez, *La cathédrale de Tournai et son chapitre*, 138–39; and Pycke, "De Louis de la Trémoille à Ferry de Clugny" on the political action of the bishops. See Haggh, "The Archives of the Order of the Golden Fleece and Music," 1–3.
114 See Nosow, *Ritual Meanings in the Fifteenth-Century Motet*, 108–9. He mentions a document from 1457 concerning the musician Waghe Feustrier who was in the service of Charles of Charolais (Duke Philip the Good's son) as well as a chaplain at the Tournai cathedral.
115 See Wegman, "Mensural Intertextuality in Busnoys," 190–91. On the details of musicians moving to different locations with the diocese of Tournai, see Verroken, "Gaspar van Weerbeke."
116 The motet circulated in a number of printed editions, among them being the *Motetti de la Corona*.

Chapter Five

1 O katherina virginum precelsa fulgens laurea: funde preces ad dominum pro nobis sponsa Christi pro cuius lege romphea in manum gentilium martyr occubuisti.

2   See Voragine, *The Golden Legend ... by William Caxton*, vol. 7, 13–14.

3   *Misse solenniores* (solemn masses) printed ca. 1500 (Michel de Toulouze), 1510 (Marnef), and 1538 (Regnault); *Misse familiares* (votive masses) printed in 1519 (Marnef), 1523 (Regnault), and ca. 1538 (Regnault); and *Communes prose* (common prosas) printed in 1519 (Marnef) and 1526 (Regnault). The alleluia verse above appears in the 1519 and 1523 editions of the *Misse familiares*.

4   There is only one edition of the *Passiones novissime*.

5   There are three different bound volumes, two already bound together in the sixteenth century, that will form the basis of the following discussion: F-Pnlr Rés. B 27695, which includes four books—*Misse solenniores* (1510), *Misse familiares* (1519), *Communes prose* (1509), and *Passiones novissime* (n.d.). The first three books were printed by Marnef, and the *Passiones* was printed by Regnault. F-Pnlr Rés. B 27762 is a single volume of the *Misse familiares* (1523) printed by Regnault. A nineteenth-century handwritten addendum on the opening flyleaf indicates that this bound volume was owned at the time of the revolution by a Cistercian convent in Burgundy, Notre Dame de Reconfort de Saizy. US-Bp *M. 149a.47 consists of three books bound together—*Misse solenniores* (1538), *Misse familiares* (ca. 1538), and *Communes prose* (1526), all of which were printed by Regnault. To date there has not been an in-depth study of these editions. Jean Duchamp has devoted a fifteen-page annex (without page numbers) in his dissertation to the editions of the *Misse familiares* printed by Jacques Moderne in the 1550s in Lyon. See Duchamp, "Motteti del Fiore." He discusses the connection of Moderne's editions to the earlier Parisian ones, indicating that they were copied almost entirely from the Regnault edition of 1523. He concludes that Moderne's editions were produced for Parisian usage since the important Parisian saint, St. Denis, is mentioned in one of the kyriale rubrics. He hypothesizes that these sources may have been produced for young priests learning how to sing plainchant. Duchamp is more concerned with how the Moderne editions were produced, and issues of typography, than the themes addressed in the present study.

6   Kathi Meyer-Baer asserts that it was supposedly produced for the sisterhood of penitents at St. Magloire, founded in Paris in 1492, although there is no inscription in the book indicating this. Copies of the books were probably sold in Guerson's or Toulouze's bookshop for anyone to buy. See Meyer-Baer, "Michel de Toulouze"; and Polain, *Catalogue des livres imprimés* (vol. 2, 336–38) for a discussion of the edition produced by Guerson and Toulouze.

7   See the published documents in Renouard, *Imprimeurs parisiens*, 351, for the addresses of Toulouze and Guerson. For more information on the connection of Guerson to Toulouze, see Meyer-Baer, "Michel de Toulouze," 179–81. Guerson has been the subject of musicological interest primarily due to his

publication of a book of *Noëls*. See Block, "Timbre, text et air." The processional printed by Toulouze is mentioned in Meyer-Baer, *Liturgical Music Incunabula*, 57; and Molin and Aussedat-Minvielle, *Répertoire de rituels et processionnaux*, 218. This source has apparently passed into private ownership. The last record of its location is found in *Bulletin mensuel de la Librairie Damascène Morgand*, no. 9, 122. Toulouze was also known to have produced one of the first books of printed instrumental music in 1496, *L'art et instruction de bien dancer*. See Kelly, *Early Music*, 42.

8   See Renouard, *Imprimeurs parisiens* (166–67) for Guerson's address.

9   See Meyer-Baer, "Michel de Toulouze," 180. She mentions that Guerson had a small print shop next to that of Michel de Toulouze, where he also taught music.

10   Aside from the documents and biographies published by Renouard that mention Regnault, there is a thesis by Jaulme, *Etude sur François Regnault*, for which only a detailed abstract is available. More recent studies have been concerned with his printing of a Bible in English and the controversy surrounding that. See Slavin, "The Rochepot Affair."

11   See Renouard, *Imprimeurs parisiens*, 311–14; and Jaulme, *Etude sur François Regnault*, 1–2. Slavin, "The Rochepot Affaire" cites the work of Duff on Regnault's biography. See Duff, *London and Westminster Printers* (205–209), which mentions the existence of two printers named François Regnault. There has been considerable disagreement among scholars concerning his life and business. Renouard, for example, was under the impression that there were two printers in Paris named François Regnault, a father and son. However, André Jaulme points out that all documents pertaining to a printer by that name indicate that there was indeed only one François Regnault.

12   See Renouard, *Imprimeurs parisiens*, 311–14.

13   The Kyrie *Cunctipotens genitor* does not appear in the Toulouze edition ca. 1500.

14   Misse solenniores totius anni: noviter impresse et emendate.

15   Misse solenniores que antea mendis infecte errant nunc ad limam sunt polite. Anno domini millesimo quingentesimo decimono: die vero. xiiii. Mensis Octobris.

16   Misse solenniores totius anni: nuperrime ad unguem recognite: Nam pleraque in vetustioribus exemplaribus truncata: in hac novissima recognitione redintegrata sunt / sicuti precipue in intonationibus Psalmorum videre est. [Device of François Regnault] Venumdantur Parisiis apud Franciscum regnault in vico divi Jacobi ad intersignium Elephantis commorantem.

17   Misse solenniores que antea mendis infecte erant / Nunc ad limam sunt polite. Anno dominice incarnationis millesimo quingentesimo. xxxviii.

18   The title page of the 1519 edition by Geoffrey Marnef is missing. The following is the text from the 1523 title page of the *Misse familiares*: "Misse

familiares cum suis cantibus angelicis recenter emendate" (Votive masses
recently corrected with their angelic chants). [Device of François Regnault]
"Venundantur Parisius in vico sancti Jacobi sub signo elephantis a Francisco
Regnault ibidem commorantem" (Sold at Paris by François Regnault in the
neighborhood of Saint Jacques residing under the sign of the elephant). The
following text appears on the last folio: "Finissent les Messes familieres. nou-
vellement Imprimes a Rouen Pour Francoys Regnault libraire iure de luni-
versite de Paris demourant en la rue saint Jacques a lenseigne de Lelephant"
(Here ends the *Misse familiares* newly printed in Rouen for François Regnault,
sworn bookseller for the University of Paris residing in the rue saint Jacques
at the sign of the elephant). Although no date is indicated in the print, this
edition can be dated 1523 through Regnault's device and address. Some have
speculated that this edition was printed by Martin Morin, a printer in Rouen
who is known to have had connections with Regnault and is known as well
to have been involved in the printing of confraternity books. See Duchamp,
"Motteti del Fiore," annex, 12. The ca. 1538 edition of the *Misse familiares* by
Regnault contains almost exactly the same advertisement as the one appearing
in the 1538 edition of the *Misse solenniores* (there is no text on the last page
of this edition): "Misse familiares cum suis cantibus angelicis / nuperrime ad
unguem recognite. Nam pleraqe in vetustioribus exemplaribus truncata: in
hac novissima recognitione reintegrata sunt: sicuti precipue in intonationibus Psalmorum videre est" (Votive masses with their angelic chants recently
inspected and perfected. For the most part in the old copies [they were] short-
ened: in this newly inspected [edition] they have been reconstituted: as can
be seen chiefly in the addition of the psalm intonations). [Regnault's device]
"Venumdantur parisiis apud Franciscum Reganault in vico divi Jacobi ad
intersignium Elephantis commorantem" (Sold in Paris by Francois Regnault
in the street of Saint Jacques residing at the sign of the elephant). For further
information regarding Regnault's device and dating, see Renouard, *Imprimeurs
parisiens*, 313.

19   See Fassler, "Who was Adam of St. Victor," 233–69; and Fassler, "The Role of
the Parisian Sequence" (345–74) for more information on the sequences used
in Paris.

20   The following is a transcription from the title page of the 1519 edition:
"Communes prose totius anni novissime emendate" (Common prosas for
the entire year newly corrected) [Printer's device]. The text on the last folio:
"Prosarum correctarum finis" (The end of the corrected prosas).

21   Full transcriptions and translations of the rubrics from the three editions of
the *Misse familiares* are given in appendix 6 ✍. The *Misse solenniores* also
includes Cycle 1 corresponding to *Misse familiares* 1523 for all duplex feasts,
and it has the troped Kyrie *Cunctipotens genitor*, which is *Misse familiares* 1523
Cycle 5 (the same Kyrie melody as *Misse familiares* 1523 Cycle 1, but with

a trope text). As was the case in chapter 4, my comparisons to the diocesan kyriale are based on the kyriale in Wright, *Music and Ceremony at Notre Dame*, 81–97.

22 *Misse familiares* ca. 1538 is missing a cycle for all duplex feasts, which is Cycle 1 in the first two editions, and Cycle 2 in the Parisian Kyriale. In addition to this, *Misse familiares* ca. 1538 also lacks the troped Kyrie *Cunctipotens genitor*, which is Cycle 5 in the first two editions.

23 They are still found in GB-Lbl Add. 16905. See Wright, *Music and Ceremony at Notre Dame*, 92.

24 A modern edition of the organ Mass was published in Rokseth, *Deux Livres d'Orgue*.

25 See figure 5.2 for these indications.

26 Wright, *Music and Ceremony at Notre Dame*, 88.

27 See appendix 6 ⌐ for the Latin text.

28 See Wright, *Music and Ceremony at Notre Dame*, 91. He does not discuss the full contents of the manual, but only indicates that there was an additional Agnus Dei chant in this book that does not appear in any of the earlier sources. My comparisons here show its use a century earlier in confraternity manuscripts, and in the early decades of the sixteenth century in the *Misse familiares*.

29 This is the theme of Rouse and Rouse, *Manuscripts and Their Makers*, which is the most authoritative work on book production in Paris through the end of the fifteenth century. Also see De Hamel, *Glossed Books of the Bible*, which also focuses on book production in the Latin Quarter. The connections of the University to the book production community at large have been well explored by numerous other scholars. Among them are Farge, *Orthodoxy and Reform in Early Reformation France*; Charon, *Les métiers du livre à Paris au XVIe siècle*; Updike, *Printing Types*; Gabriel, *Petrus Cesaris Wagner and Johannes Stoll*; and Severin, "Universities and Early Printing," 83–123. There is no comprehensive study of their production of liturgical books produced in Paris that contain music, which is the focus here.

30 See Rouse and Rouse, *Manuscripts and Their Makers*, 75.

31 F-Psg Fol. BB 97 INV 102 rés.

32 See Bermès, "Le couvent des Mathurins," 81, 171.

33 Since this is one of the copies of the missal printed on paper, it is not the same copy held in the library of the Augustinian house of St. Victor (printed on vellum), which Jean de la Caille refers to in his 1689 monograph on the history of printing and bookselling in Paris, *Histoire de l'imprimerie et de la librairie à Paris*, 101. The prosas for Trinity Sunday, the Dedication of the Church, St. Vincent, the Purification, and St. Michael have all been altered to conform to the diocesan usage of Paris on these days.

34 See Farge, *Registre des conclusions de la Faculté de Théologie*, 20–21. Other works focusing on the University and its various colleges and structure are Bourrelier, *La vie du Quartier latin, des origines à la Cité universitaire*; Boyce, *The English-German Nation*; Gabriel, *Student Life in Ave Maria College*; Gabriel, *Les Étudiants étrangers a l'Université de Paris*; Gabriel, *Foreign Students*; and Bauer, "Visual Constructions of Corporate Identity." The four faculties of the university in order of descending rank were the Faculty of Theology, the Faculty of Decrees, the Faculty of Medicine, and the Faculty of Arts. This last faculty was the largest of all. See Goulet, *Compendium Universitatis Parisiensis*, 38–41.

35 See Bermès, "Le couvent des Mathurins," 71.

36 These solemn processions took place "at some sacred church or religious cloister to offer thanks to God at the end of a Rectorship." Goulet, *Compendium Universitatis Parisiensis*, 77. Goulet is ambiguous as to the destination of these processions. According to Bermès, however, the house of the Mathurins was the most common place to begin these processions. See Bermès, "Le couvent des Mathurins," 73.

37 See Goulet, *Compendium Universitatis Parisiensis*, 79. Bermès, "Le couvent des Mathurins" (71) mentions that the general minister of the order, Robert Gaguin, was an admirer of Guillaume Fichet, who was instrumental in bringing the first printers to Paris from Germany.

38 See Bermès, "Le couvent des Mathurins," 75. The sale of parchment at the Trinitarian house was regulated by the rector of the university, who received a tax on all parchment brought to Paris, and confiscated it if it was found anywhere before being brought to this location. See Goulet, *Compendium Universitatis Parisiensis*, 54–55.

39 See Coyecque, *Recueil d'actes notariés*, vol. 1, 220.

40 See Bermès, "Le couvent des Mathurins," 75; and LeMasson, *Le calendrier des confréries de Paris*, 71–72.

41 The surviving liturgical book used by the Confraternity of the Book Production Community, F-Pm 461, indicates signs of its usage at St. André-des-Arts, before the confraternity was divided and moved to the Trinitarian house. The book contains music and texts following Parisian liturgical usage. See the inventory in appendix 4 ❧.

42 On the importance of parish churches in Paris and their role in community, see Van Orden, *Music, Discipline, and Arms*, 148.

43 See Renouard, *Imprimeurs parisiens*, 260.

44 See Renouard, *Imprimeurs parisiens*, 261.

45 See Coyecque, *Recueil d'actes notariés*, vol. 1, 96.

46 The June 1467 proclamation stated that the main reason for the division of the trades into sixty-one "banners" was to maintain order in the city and to conduct work more efficiently. See the transcription of this document in

Lespinasse, *Metiers et corporations de la ville de Paris*, 53–60. Also see Rouse and Rouse, *Manuscripts and Their Makers*, 12. Some references to persons in other trades living there in the late sixteenth century appear in notarial documents published by Renouard, *Documents sur les imprimeurs*, 23–24. For instance, in a 1571 census, among the booksellers and printers residing on the rue St. Jean de Lateran, there were also several people practicing other trades, such as coopers. In some tax records from the same year, one finds that among the inhabitants of the rue St. Jacques, rue des Mathurins, and the rue des Poirées there were wine merchants, spice dealers, and members of scattered other occupations residing among the printers, booksellers, scribes, book binders, etc. Also see Favier, *Nouvelle histoire de Paris*, 74. These documents prove that while the banner districts may have been to some extent enforced, members of other trades were not excluded from residence in the Latin Quarter.

47 Renouard, *Documents sur les imprimeurs*, 141, 185.

48 All of this is written on fol. 63v of F-Pa 168. The inscription states that the confraternity met in the chapel of the hospital of St. Julian. See appendix 4 ᪥ for an inventory of the manuscript. The role of the "bastionnaire" in confraternities in the sixteenth century is described in Simiz, *Confréries urbaines* (89), who explains that the banner holder was responsible for carrying the emblem of the confraternity's patron saint in processions.

49 As I have shown in each chapter, the comparison tables in appendix 5 ᪥ reveal that in some cases, confraternity devotions drew from diocesan usages and did not include special texts.

50 The chant *Veni electa mea* appears in the Common of Virgins in Parisian diocesan sources, but it was not assigned to the feast of St. Catherine.

51 The Dominican source is I-CFm LVI. See Schlager, *Alleluia-Melodien II*, 709, 887.

52 The *O nicholae* verse, discussed in chapter 2, was set to a version of the *O consolatrix pauperum* melody closely matching the one used in Reims.

53 The Reims version is similar to those found in other northern French sources from Autun and Troyes. See Schlager, *Alleluia-Melodien II* (310–15) for transcriptions of these melodies.

54 Bauer, "Visual Constructions of Corporate Identity," 55, 84.

55 See Goulet, *Compendium Universitatis Parisiensis*, 41–49. Writing in 1517, Goulet gives a very detailed account of all the different geographical areas making up the four nations. Also see Bauer, "Visual Constructions of Corporate Identity," 55.

56 On the nations as confraternities, see Courtenay, *Rituals for the Dead*, 37–51. Others who briefly mention students celebrating services together are Vincent, *Les confréries médiévales*, 38–39; and Pirro, "L'enseignement de musique aux universités françaises," 47.

57 I am grateful to Charlotte Bauer for pointing out to me that the two saints on the university seal have long been thought to be St. Catherine and St. Nicholas, though this identification is not without problems. See Bauer, "Visual Constructions of Corporate Identity," 28–53. The principal feasts celebrated by the English-German Nation were those in honor of the Virgin Mary: the Purification, the Annunciation, the Visitation, the Assumption, the Nativity, and the Conception; and the feasts for St. Catherine, St. Nicholas, and St. Edmund. See Boyce, *The English-German Nation*, 150–55.

58 See Geremeck, *Les marginaux parisiens* (147) about Paris as a student center.

59 See Kirkman, "The Seeds of Medieval Music."

60 See Bauer, "Visual Constructions of Corporate Identity," 55–56.

61 See Gabriel, *Foreign Students*, 20. He discusses the importance of these geo- graphical affiliations within the English-German Nation. Devotional groups and confraternities provided kinship ties in new places, as discussed in Lynch, *Individuals, Families and Communities*, 62, 87, 94–99. On confraternities and corporate behavior, and the power of these communities to provide a sense of community, see Black, "The Development of Confraternity Studies," 17.

62 See Gabriel, *Foreign Students*, 20.

63 See Trio, "A Medieval Students' Confraternity at Ypres," 14–53.

64 See Harrán, *In Defense of Music* (3–8), for information on Le Munerat. He also includes English translations of the two treatises. According to Lebeuf, Le Munerat supervised the publication of most of the liturgical books for the usage of Paris in the late fifteenth century. See Lebeuf, *Traité historique et pra- tique sur le chant*, 112–15.

65 See Meyer-Baer, "Michel de Toulouze," 180. She mentions that he had a small print shop next to that of Michel de Toulouze where he also taught music.

66 See Renouard, *Imprimeurs parisiens*, 317. He mentions that Rembolt was an associate of Gering's but does not discuss the existence of the psalter. I believe this may be the first printed psalter containing music printed for Parisian usage. It appears in the bibliography of Berry, "The Performance of Plainsong" (421), but she does not discuss it. On the English-German Nation, see Gabriel, *Foreign Students*, 19.

67 See Harrán, *In Defense of Music*, 44. References to chapels in Paris that adhered to different diocesan usages appear in several fifteenth- and sixteenth- century accounts. For instance, there was a chapel following the usage of Sens, as well as one following the usage of Bourges.

68 Le Munerat and the College of Navarre is one of the underlying themes of Harrán, *In Defense of Music*.

69 See Harrán, *In Defense of Music* (31–32, 44) for references to the holdings of the College of Navarre library.

70 See Harrán, *In Defense of Music*, 33. For the dating and contents of the manu- script, see Huglo, *Les manuscrits du processional*, vol. 2, 110–11.

71 University control over the trade has been the subject of some controversy
    among scholars. Earlier authors, such as Updike, believed that the control of
    the book trade by the university and the monarchy was very rigid, and that
    every aspect of the trade was affected. See Updike, *Printing Types*, 266–70.
    However, the Rouses have found that based on the overall output of the
    scribes and printers, university control was ineffectual. They indicate that
    a large part of the income of a bookseller or printer came from outside the
    university. As long as the bookmen and women fulfilled their oath to the uni-
    versity and produced books commissioned by masters and scholars, they were
    free to do whatever they wanted. See Rouse and Rouse, "The Booktrade at
    the University of Paris," 47–48; and Rouse and Rouse, *Manuscripts and Their
    Makers*, 75, 81, 285–302.

72 This is outlined in Goulet, *Compendium Universitatis Parisiensis*, 72–73. The
    sworn booksellers are referred to as *libraires jurés* in documents, and some
    of them were also printers and bookbinders. There is a possibility that there
    were more than twenty-four booksellers in Paris at any given time. There are
    fourteenth-century references to booksellers who did not swear an oath to the
    university, and because of this they could only sell books valued at ten solidi
    or less and were not permitted to own a shop. See Rouse and Rouse, "The
    Booktrade at the University of Paris," 47–48. One could speculate that these
    booksellers most likely sold their books in stalls set up at marketplaces or other
    locations in Paris. The conclusions for the sixteenth century are that all mem-
    bers of the trade had to swear an oath to the university, but it is more than
    likely that some of them did not own shops and were not counted as members
    of the twenty-four above.

73 See Goulet, *Compendium Universitatis Parisiensis*, 71–72.

74 Goulet, *Compendium Universitatis Parisiensis*, 54, 73–74. I have understood
    "farmers of revenue" to be tax collectors. Along with these privileges, there was
    a certain amount of monetary control that the university exercised over the
    trade. For instance, Goulet mentions that the rector of the university levied a
    tax on parchment that was brought to Paris and confiscated any such materi-
    als sold in the city if they were found elsewhere before coming to the monas-
    tic house of the Mathurins, which was the official parchment house for the
    university.

75 Goulet, *Compendium Universitatis Parisiensis*, 78–79.

76 F-Pan M68 no.93.

77 F-Pan M68 no.93, page 5: "... .par le moyen & industrie desdits Libraires,
    par laquelle nostre saincte foy Catholique a esté grandement augmentée &
    corroborée, Iustice mieux entendue administrée, le divin service ply hon-
    orablement & curieusement fait, dit & celebré, & au moyen dequoy tant de
    bonnes & salutaires doctrines ont esté manifestées, cómuniquées, & publiées à
    tout chacun, au moyen dequoy nostre Royaume precelle tous autres: & autres

innumerables biens qui en sont procedés & procedent encores chacun jour, à l'honneur de Dieu & augmentation de nostredicte foy Catholique, comme dict est."

78   A look at the lists of books censored by the Faculty of Theology reveals that these printers were also responsible for a great number of humanist works and texts in Greek. Their printed editions appear throughout the published booklists of Bujanda, *Index des livres interdits*; Higman, *Censorship and the Sorbonne*; and Thijssen, *Censure and Heresy at the University of Paris*.

79   The diplomatic transcriptions of documents published by Philippe Renouard and Ernst Coyecque give many indications of this throughout. See Renouard, *Imprimeurs parisiens*; Renouard, *Documents sur les imprimeurs*; Renouard, *Répertoire des imprimeurs parisiens*; and Coyecque, *Recueil d'actes notariés*. See Davis, "A Trade Union in 16th Century France" for a case study involving print shop employees. There are numerous scattered references in Renouard as to how many houses the printers owned, to whom they rented, from whom they rented, etc.

80   See Beech, "Charlotte Guillard," 351–52. Davis discusses trade unions in Lyon, and some of the abuses of printers toward their employees, and in particular, feeding them poor quality food. Davis, "A Trade Union in 16th Century France," 51. There is no evidence of this in the case of Guillard. Note that journeymen at this time were skilled workers who did not own their own businesses, and who had not yet graduated to the level of master within the trade.

81   See Davis, "A Trade Union in 16th Century France," 54–55. Some of them were limited in their literacy but were still able to perform the tasks of proof reading or correcting.

82   See Davis, "A Trade Union in 16th Century France" (54–59), for more on the education of correctors or proofreaders. Also see Charon, *Les métiers du livre*, 124. She indicates that in the workshops of music printers, musicians were available to look over texts and music. As evidence, she discusses the editing of Nicholas Du Chemin's chanson, Mass, and motet volumes and his employment of the composer Nicolas Regues as an editor.

83   There are references to this in the business of Pierre Attaingnant in the sixteenth century. A contract between Attaingnant and the printer Jean de la Roche from 1514 shows that Attaingnant rented the use of a printing press from la Roche and was "for hire" upon commission. See Heartz, *Pierre Attaingnant*, 38. For a focused study on Attaingnant's early prints and typography, see Heartz, "Typography and Format in Early Music Printing." Henri Stein has also produced two focused studies on Wolfgang Hopyl, showing his connections to other printers through the exchange of materials. See Stein, *L'atelier typographique de Wolfgang Hopyl*; and Stein, *Nouveaux documents sur Wolfgang Hopyl*. The borrowing of woodcut illustrations in the numerous

editions of Books of Hours produced by these printers, particularly those printed by Simon Vostre and Philippe Pigouchet, have been the subject of studies by a number of art historians, as have bookbindings. See Chatelain, "Reliures parisiennes de l'atelier de Simon Vostre"; Reid, "The Hours of the Usage of Landres"; Renouvier, *Des gravures sur bois*; Richard, "Les livres d'heures imprimés poitevins"; and Suau, "Les Vertus des Heures imprimées."

84   Beech discusses Charlotte Guillard's connection to various Parisian humanist circles, which resulted in the production of several books. See Beech, "Charlotte Guillard," 356–57.

85   Renouard lists numerous names of editors and correctors throughout his three works, but the editors of liturgical books containing music are almost never mentioned. Those documents that do give some information regarding the editing of liturgical books appear in relation to books produced for dioceses outside of Paris. See Renouard, *Imprimeurs parisiens*, *Documents sur les imprimeurs*, and *Répertoire des Imprimeurs Parisiens*.

86   See Armstrong, *Before Copyright*, 1–20.

87   See Berry, "The Performance of Plainsong," 121. According to her, Sampson was a fellow and vice provost of King's College. Stanley Boorman also refers to this volume in Boorman, "Early Music Printing," 231. This two-volume antiphoner is the subject of a recent study by Williamson, "Affordable Splendour."

88   See Armstrong, *Before Copyright*, 56.

89   See Renouard, *Imprimeurs Parisiens*, 216.

90   The following are selected accounts of printing arrangements, since many exist. For more information from notarial documents, see Coyecque, *Recueil d'actes notariés*, vol. 1, 92–93.

91   See Coyecque, *Recueil d'actes notariés*, vol. 1, 47.

92   See Coyecque, *Recueil d'actes notariés*, vol. 1, 107.

93   I present here a paraphrased description of the document transcribed by Coyecque in *Recueil d'actes notariés*, vol. 1, 218. For more information on Nicolas Musnier, see Bermès, "Le couvent des Mathurins," 66, 71. She mentions money donated to the Trinitarian order in 1550 under Musnier's leadership, given by Yolande Bonhomme. There were numerous ties between the order and the book production community.

94   One of these parchment books from the 1529 edition is mentioned in Jean de La Caille, *Histoire de l'imprimerie et de la librairie à Paris* (101), as being held at the Augustinian house of St. Victor by the end of the seventeenth century.

95   Armstrong, *Before Copyright*, 57.

96   In some cases described above, there is evidence that the bishop of a given diocese was involved in the editing, but others simply mention members of the clergy or even other printers as editors. See Armstrong, *Before Copyright*

(56–60, 197–98), for more on permission regarding the printing of liturgical books.

97 These editions are absent from Higman, *Censorship and the Sorbonne*; and Bujanda, *Index des livres interdits*.

98 Between 1539 and 1540 printed editions of the Parisian missal carried the name of the Bishop of Paris as editor, and from that point on in the 1540s there was much more standardization in both music and text.

99 See Haggh, "The Medium Transforms the Message," 78. Many Parisian printers were responsible for printing this material in books for dioceses other than Cambrai. Among them were Regnault and Kerver.

100 Diocesan printed missals did not contain the chant melodies for votive masses, only the chant texts.

101 There are records from bookselling firms in Italy that indicate that customs officers as well as leather workers were customers in the Morosi book shop in Florence. See Carter, "Music Selling in Late Sixteenth-Century Florence," 483–504. In the sense that these books were available to anyone, Duchamp's speculation in "Motteti del Fiore" that part of this market was formed by young priests learning to sing plainchant (mentioned at the outset of the present chapter) is also accurate.

102 See Gabriel, *Foreign Students*, 13. He goes into great detail about the financial status of the students of the English-German Nation in the fifteenth century and demonstrates that contrary to current popular belief, over half of the university students were not of the upper classes.

Conclusion

1 For studies of this repertoire, see Snow, "The Lady of Sorrows," 131–77; Planchart, "Parts with Words and without Words"; Bloxam, "In Praise of Spurious Saints," 163–220; Bloxam, "Plainsong and Polyphony for the Blessed Virgin"; and Curtis, "Brussels Bibliothèque Royale MS. 5557."

2 See Bazinet, "The Musical Encart of the Royal Printers."

3 The number of textually literate persons was increasing appreciably, as can be seen in the production of different types of popular books in French, such as the *Golden Legend*. It is possible, of course, that persons who were not musically or textually literate bought service books for reasons of their own, such as their religious devotion, or for the novelty of owning a printed book.

4 LeMasson, *Le Calendrier des confréries de Paris*. Originally printed in 1621, this source was transcribed with an introduction by Valentin Dufour in 1875.

Bibliography

Ambros, August Wilhelm. *Geschichte der Musik*. 5 vols. Leipzig: Leuckart 1868. Reprint, Otto Kade, 1893.

Amiet, Robert. "La messe pour l'unité des chrétiens." *Revue des Sciences Religieuses* 28 (1954): 1–35.

Anderson, Michael. *St. Anne in Renaissance Music*. Cambridge: Cambridge University Press, 2014.

Anglés, Higinio. "Una Nueva Version del Credo de Tournai." *Revue Belge de Musicologie* 8 (1954): 97–99.

Arboit, Fabienne, and Laurent Ledèque. Manuscrit A 13 (475) conservé aux Archives de la Cathédrale de Tournai. Unpublished description of the manuscript. 2005. Archives de la Cathédrale de Tournai, Tournai.

Armstrong, Elizabeth. *Before Copyright: The French Book-Privilege System 1498–1526*. Cambridge: Cambridge University Press, 1990.

Bain, Jennifer. "Hildegard, Hermannus, and Late Chant Style." *Journal of Music Theory* 52 (2008): 123–49.

Bain, Jennifer, and Deborah McGrady. *A Companion to Guillaume de Machaut*. Leiden: Brill, 2012.

Bakker, Anna de. "A Life in Hours: Goswin of Bossut's Office for Arnulf of Villers." In *Medieval Cantors and Their Craft: Music, Liturgy and the Shaping of History, 800–1500*, edited by Katie Ann-Marie Bugyis, A. B. Kraebel, and Margot Fassler, 326–39. York: York Medieval Press, 2017.

Baltzer, Rebecca. "The Little Office of the Virgin and Mary's Role at Paris." In *The Divine Office in the Latin Middle Ages*, edited by Margot Fassler and Rebecca Baltzer, 463–84. Oxford: Oxford University Press, 2000.

———. "The Sources and the Sactorale: Dating by the Decade in Thirteenth-Century Paris." In *Music and Culture in the Middle Ages and Beyond: Liturgy, Sources, Symbolism*, edited by Benjamin Brand and David J. Rothenberg, 111–41. Cambridge: Cambridge University Press, 2016.

Barker, Sheila. "The Making of a Plague Saint: Saint Sebastian's Imagery and Cult before the Counter-Reformatio." In *Piety and the Plague: From Byzantium to the Baroque*, edited by Franco Mormando and Thomas Worcester, 90–131. Kirksville, MO: Truman State University Press, 2007.

Bauer, Charlotte. "Visual Constructions of Corporate Identity for the University of Paris 1200–1500." PhD diss., University of Illinois at Urbana-Champaign, 2007.

Bazinet, Geneviève. "The Musical Encart of the Royal Printers Le Roy & Ballard in the 1583 Hours of Jamet Mettayer Held in the Musée de l'Amérique francophone in Quebec City." *Renaissance and Reformation* 39 (2016): 253–83.

Beaune, Colette. *The Birth of an Ideology: Myths and Symbols of Nation in Late-Medieval France.* Berkeley: University of California Press, 1991.

Beech, Beatrice. "Charlotte Guillard: A Sixteenth-Century Business Woman." *Renaissance Quarterly* 36, no. 3 (1983): 345–67.

Bell, Susan Groag. "Medieval Women Book Owners: Arbiters of Lay Piety and Ambassadors of Culture." *Signs: Journal of Women in Culture and Society* 7, no.4 (1982): 742–68.

Bent, Margaret. *Bologna Q 15: The Making and Remaking of a Musical Manuscript.* Lucca: LIM Editrice, 2008.

Berger, Pamela. "Mice, Arrows, and Tumors: Medieval Plague Iconography North of the Alps." In *Piety and the Plague: From Byzantium to the Baroque,* edited by Franco Mormando and Thomas Worcester, 23–63. Kirksville, MO: Truman State University Press, 2007.

Bermès, Emmanuelle. "Le couvent des Mathurins de Paris et L'Estampe au XVIIe siècle." Thèse pour le diplôme d'archiviste paléographe, École nationale des Chartes, 2001.

Berry, Mary (Mother Thomas More). "The Performance of Plainsong in the Later Middle Ages and the Sixteenth Century." PhD diss., Cambridge University, 1968.

Black, Christopher F. "The Development of Confraternity Studies Over the Past Thirty Years." In *The Politics of Ritual Kinship: Confraternities and Social Order in Early Modern Italy,* edited by Nicholas Terpstra, 9–29. Cambridge: Cambridge University Press, 1999.

Blacker, Jean, Glyn S. Burgess, and Amy Ogden. *Wace, the Hagiographical Works.* Leiden: Brill, 2013.

Blasina, James. "Music and Gender in the Medieval Cult of St. Katherine of Alexandria, c.1050–1300." PhD diss., Harvard University, 2015.

Blezzard, Judith, Stephen Ryle, and Jonathan Alexander. "New Perspectives on the Feast of the Crown of Thorns." *Journal of the Plainsong and Medieval Music Society* 10 (1987): 23–47.

Bloch, Marc Léopold Benjamin. *The Royal Touch: Sacred Monarchy and Scrofula in England and France.* Montreal: McGill-Queen's University Press, 1973.

Block, Adrienne Fried. "Timbre, texte et air; ou: comment le noël—parodie peut aider à l'étude de la chanson du XVIe siècle." *Revue de musicologie* 69, no. 1 (1983): 21–54.

Bloxam, M. Jennifer. "In Praise of Spurious Saints: The 'Missa Floruit egregiis' by Pipelare and LaRue." *Journal of the American Musicological Society* 44 no. 2 (1991): 163-220.

————. "Plainsong and Polyphony for the Blessed Virgin: Notes on Two Masses by Jacob Obrecht." *Journal of Musicology* 12 (1994): 51–75.

————. "A Survey of Late Medieval Service Books from the Low Countries: Implications for Sacred Polyphony 1460–1520." PhD diss., Yale University, 1987.

Boecki, Christine M. *Images of Plague and Pestilence: Iconography and Iconology.* Kirksville, MO: Truman State University, 2000.

Bookseller Catalogue, Damascène Morgand. "504. Processionale Parisiense." *Bulletin mensuel de la Librairie Damascène Morgand* 9 (1909): 122.

Boorman, Stanley. "Early Music Printing: Working for a Specialized Market." In *Print and Culture in the Renaissance*, edited by Gerald P. Tyson and Sylvia S. Wagonheim, 222–45. Newark: University of Delaware Press, 1986.

Bosse, Detlev. *Untersuchung einstimmiger mittelalterlicher Melodien zum "Gloria in excelsis Deo."* Forschungsbeiträge zur Musikwissenschaft, Bd. 2. Regensburg: G. Bosse, 1955.

Bouckaert, Bruno, ed. *Cantus 21. Mémoires du chant. Le livre de musique d'Isidore de Séville à Edmond de Coussemaker.* Neerpelt: Editions Alamire, 2007.

Boulton, Maureen. *Sacred Fictions of Medieval France: Narrative Theology in the Lives of Christ and the Virgin, 1150–1500.* London: Boydell & Brewer, 2017.

Bourrelier, Henri. *La vie du Quartier latin, des origines à la Cité universitaire.* Paris: Impr. Labor, 1936.

Bouvet, Maurice. *La confrérie de Saint-Nicolas des apothicaires et des épiciers de Paris.* Paris: Le Noeud de Vipères, 1950.

Bower, Calvin. "From Alleluia to Sequence: Some Definitions of Relations." In *Western Plainchant in the First Millennium: Studies in the Medieval Liturgy and its Music*, edited by Sean Gallagher, James Haar, John Nádas, and Timothy Striplin, 351–98. Aldershot, UK: Ashgate, 2003.

Bowles, Edmund. "Musical Instruments in Civic Processions During the Middle Ages." *Acta Musicologica* 33 (1961): 147–61.

Boyce, Gray Cowan. *The English-German Nation in the University of Paris during the Middle Ages.* Bruges: The Saint Catherine Press, Ltd., 1927.

Boyce, James John. "The Carmelite Feast of the Presentation of the Virgin." In *The Divine Office in the Latin Middle Ages*, edited by Margot Fassler and Rebecca Baltzer, 485–516. Oxford: Oxford University Press, 2000.

Boynton, Susan. "Orality, Literacy, and the Early Notation of the Office Hymns." *Journal of the American Musicological Society* 56 no. 1 (2003): 99–168.

————. *Shaping a Monastic Identity: Liturgy and History at the Imperial Abbey of Farfa, 1000–1125.* Ithaca, NY: Cornell University Press, 2006.

Bozière, Aime François Joseph. *Tournai Ancien et Moderne.* Tournai: Typographie D'Adophe Delmée, 1864.

Bozoky, Edina. *La politique des reliques de Constantin à Saint Louis.* Paris: Editions Beauchesne, 2007.

Bradley, Catherine. *Polyphony in Medieval Paris: The Art of Composing with Plainchant.* Cambridge: Cambridge University Press, 2018.

Brand, Benjamin. *Holy Treasure and Sacred Song: Relic Cults and their Liturgies in Medieval Tuscany.* New York: Oxford University Press, 2014.

Branner, Robert. "Two Parisian Capella Books in Bari." *Gesta* 8, no. 2 (1969): 14–19.

Brazinski, Paul Anthony, and Allegra R. P. Fryxell. "The Smell of Relics: Authenticating Saints, Bones and the Role of Scent in the Sensory Experience of Medieval Christian Veneration." *Papers from the Institute of Archaeology* 23, no. 1 (2013): 11. https://doi.org/10.5334/pia.430.

Breviarium Tornacense (Pars hyemalis). Paris: Jean Higman, 1497. *The Internet Archive.* https://archive.org/details/OEXV828_3a.

Brewer, Charles. "A Fourteenth-Century Polyphonic Manuscript Rediscovered." *Studia Musicologica Academiae Scientiarum Hungaricae* 24 (1982): 5–19.

Brièle, Léon. *L'Hôpital de Sainte-Catherine en la rue Saint-Denis (1184–1790).* Paris: Imprimerie nationale, 1890.

Brink, Danette. "Historiae Trevirenses: The Medieval Office Chants for the Saints of Trier." PhD diss., University of Regensburg, 2014.

———. "The Portrayal of Female Sanctity in the Local Offices from the Diocese of Trier." Paper presented at the International Musicological Society's Cantus Planus Study Group Conference, Dublin (Ireland), August 2–7, 2016.

Brown, Howard Mayer. "The Mirror of Man's Salvation: Music in Devotional Life about 1500." *Renaissance Quarterly* 43, no. 4 (1990): 744–73.

Bryant, Lawrence. "La ceremonie de l'entrée à Paris au Moyen Age." *Annales. Economies, societies, civilisations* 41 (1986): 513–42.

Buckley, Ann, ed. *Music, Liturgy, and the Veneration of Saints of the Medieval Irish Church in a European Context.* Turnhout: Brepols, 2017.

Bugyis, Katie Ann-Marie, A. B. Kraebel, and Margot Fassler, eds. *Medieval Cantors and Their Craft: Music, Liturgy and the Shaping of History, 800–1500.* York: York Medieval Press, 2017.

Bujanda, Jesus Martinez de. *Index des livres interdits.* 11 vols. Geneva: Librairie Droz, 1985.

Burke, Peter. *Popular Culture in Early Modern Europe.* Burlington, VT: Ashgate, 2009.

Byrne, Joseph Patrick. *Daily Life during the Black Death.* London: Greenwood Press, 2006.

Caille, Jean de la. *Histoire de l'imprimerie et de la librairie à Paris, où l'on voit son origine et ses progrès jusqu'en 1689.* Paris: Chez Jean de la Caille, 1689.

Caldwell, Mary Channen. "Singing, Dancing, and Rejoicing in the Round: Latin Sacred Songs with Refrains, Circa 1000–1582." PhD diss., University of Chicago, 2013.

Camille, Michael. "The Book of Signs: Writing and Visual Difference in Gothic Manuscript Illumination." *Word & Image* 1 (1985): 133–48.

———. "Seeing and Reading: Some Visual Implications of Medieval Literacy and Illiteracy." *Art History* 8, no.1 (1985): 26–49.

Caroli, Martina. "Bringing Saints to Cities and Monasteries: *Translationes* in the Making of a Sacred Geography (Ninth-Tenth Centuries)." In *Towns and Their Territories between Late Antiquity and the Early Middle Ages*, edited by Gian Pietro Brogiolo, Nancy Gauthier, and Neil Christie, 259–74. Leiden: Brill, 2000.

Carter, Tim. "Music Selling in Late Sixteenth-Century Florence: The Bookshop of Piero Di Giuliano Morosi." *Music and Letters* 70 (1989): 483–504.

Catalunya, David. "Music, Space and Ritual in Medieval Castille, 1221–1350." PhD diss., Universität Würzburg, 2016.

Cattin, Giulio, and Francesco Facchin. *Polyphonic Music of the Fourteenth Century.* Vol. 23 A-B. Monaco: Editions de L'Oiseau-Lyre, 1991.

Ceulemans, Anne-Emmanuelle. "Le manuscrit BTC A 58 de la cathédrale de Tournai et le plain-chant pour la confrérie de la Transfiguration." *Revue Belge de Musicologie* LXIII (2009): 5–29.

———. "Le manuscrit musical Tournai B.C.T. A58 et les deux versions de la séquence *Thabor superficie.*" In *Archives et manuscrits précieux tournaisiens* 1. Tournai—Art et Histoire, Instruments de travail 6, edited by Jacques Pycke, 153–68. Louvain-la-Neuve: Université Catholique de Louvain, 2007.

———. "Une 'Missa Sancta Trinitas' anonyme du 16e siècle conservée aux Archives et Bibliothèque de la cathédrale de Tournai (B.C.T., A58)." In *Archives et manuscrits précieux tournaisiens* 3. Tournai—Art et Histoire, Instruments de travail 11, edited by Jacques Pycke, 95–103. Tournai-Louvain-la-Neuve: Université Catholique de Louvain, 2009.

Charon, Annie. *Les métiers du livre à Paris au XVIe siècle: 1535–1560.* Geneva: Droz, 1974.

Chatelain, Jean-Marc. "Reliures parisiennes de l'atelier de Simon Vostre." *Bulletin du bibliophile* 1 (1993): 99–111.

Chazelle, Celia M. "Pictures, Books, and the Illiterate: Pope Gregory I's Letters to Serenus of Marseilles." *Word & Image* 6, no. 2 (1990): 138–53.

Chevalier, Cyr Ulysse. *Repertorium Hymnologicum.* 6 vols. Leuven: Imprimerie Polleunis & Ceuterick, 1892–1920.

Cheymol, Jean. "L'hôpital Sainte-Catherine à Paris (1181–1794)." *Histoire des sciences médicales* 16 (1982): 239–51.

Chiu, Remi. *Plague and Music in the Renaissance.* Cambridge: Cambridge University Press, 2017.

Christoffersen, Peter Woetmann. "L'Abbaye de Corbie, sainte Barbe et le manuscrit Amiens 162." In *La musique en Picardie du xiveme au xviieme siècle*, edited by Camilla Cavicchi, Marie-Alexis Colin, and Philippe Vendrix, 257–61. Turnhout: Brepols, 2012.

———. *Songs for Funerals and Intercession: A Collection of Polyphony for the Confraternity of St. Barbara at the Corbie Abbey. Amiens, Bibliothèque Centrale Louis Aragon, MS 162 D.* Copenhagen: University of Copenhagen, 2016.

Clare, Edward G. *Saint Nicholas: His Legends and Iconography.* Firenze: L. S. Olschki, 1985.

Clark, Robert L. A., and Pamela Sheingorn. "'Visible Words': Gesture and Performance in the Miniatures of BNF, MS fr. 819–20." In *Parisian Confraternity Drama of the Fourteenth Century: The "Miracles de Nostre Dame par personnages,"* edited by Donald Maddox and Sara Sturm-Maddox, 193–218. Turnhout: Brepols, 2008.

Cloquet, Louis. "Bulle accordée à la confrérie Notre Dame." *Bulletin de la société d'histoire et de littérature à Tournai* 20 (1884): 288–92.

Cohen, Meredith. "An Indulgence for the Visitor: The Public at the Sainte-Chapelle of Paris." *Speculum* 83 (2008): 840–83.

———. *The Sainte-Chapelle and the Construction of Sacral Monarchy: Royal Architecture in Thirteenth-Century Paris.* Cambridge: Cambridge University Press, 2014.

Collection de documents inédits sur l'histoire de France publiés par les soins du Ministre de l'Instruction publique. Paris: Imprimerie nationale, 1880.

Courtenay, William J. *Rituals for the Dead: Religion and Community in the Medieval University of Paris.* Notre Dame, IN: University of Notre Dame Press, 2019.

Coussemaker, Edmond de. "Messe du XIIIᵉ siècle." *Bulletins de la Société historique et littéraire de Tournai* 8 (1862): 100–10.

Coyecque, Ernst. *Recueil d'actes notariés relatifs à la histoire de Paris au XVIe siècle.* 2 vols. Paris: Imprimerie nationale, 1905.

Crocker, Richard L. *The Early Medieval Sequence.* Berkeley: University of California Press, 1977.

Crook, John. *English Medieval Shrines.* Woodbridge, UK: The Boydell Press, 2011.

Curtis, Gareth. "Brussels Bibliothèque Royale MS. 5557, and the Texting of Dufay's *Ecce Ancilla Domini* and *Ave Regina Celorum* Masses." *Acta Musicologica* 51 (1979): 73–86.

Cuthbert, Michael S. "The (Other) Tournai Mass." *Prolatio: Michael Scott Cuthbert Research Blog.* Posted 11 June 2014. http://prolatio.blogspot.com/2014/06/the-other-tournai-kyrie.html.

Cuyler, Louise E. "The Sequences of Isaac's 'Choralis Constantinus." *Journal of the American Musicological Society* 3, no.1 (1950): 3–16.

Davis, Natalie Zemon. *Culture and Society in Early Modern France.* Stanford, CA: Stanford University Press, 1975.

————. "A Trade Union in 16th Century France." *The Economic History Review* 19, no. 1 (1966): 48–69.

————. "Women in the Crafts in Sixteenth-Century Lyon." *Feminist Studies* 8, no. 1 (1982): 46–80.

De Hamel, Christopher. *Glossed Books of the Bible and the Origins of the Paris Book-trade*. Woodbridge, Suffolk: D. S. Brewer, 1984.

De Luca, Elsa. "I manoscritti musicali dell' Archivio di San Nicola a Bari: Elementi francesi nella musica e nella liturgia." PhD diss., Università del Salento, 2011.

Denomy, Alexander Joseph. "An Old French Life of Saint Barbara." *Mediaeval Studies* 1 (1939): 148–78.

Derolez, Albert. *Corpus Catalogorum Belgii. The Medieval Booklists of the Southern Low Countries. Provinces of Brabant and Hainault*, vol. 4. Brussels: Palais des Académies, 2001.

Desmette, Philippe. *Les brefs d'indulgences pour les confréries des diocèses de Cambrai et de Tournai aux XVIIe et XVIIIe siècles*. Brussels: Institut historique belge de Rome, 2002.

————. "Les confréries religieuses à Tournai aux XVe et XVIe siècles." In *De Pise à Trente; la réforme de l'Eglise en gestation. Regards croisés entre Escaut et Meuse. Actes du colloque international de Tournai, 19–20 mars 2004*, edited by Monique Maillard-Luypaert and Jean-Maries Cauchies, 85–125. Brussels: Facultes Universitaires Saint-Louis, 2004.

Desmond, Karen. *Music and the Moderni, 1300–1350: The Ars Nova in Theory and Practice*. Cambridge: Cambridge University Press, 2018.

Desnoyers, Jules. "Topographie ecclesiastique de la France pendant le Moyen Age, et dans les temps modernes jusqu'en 1790." *La Société de l'Histoire de France* 27 (1861–62): 1–640.

Diefendorf, Barbara B., and Carla Hesse. "Introduction: Culture and Identity." In *Culture and Identity in Early Modern Europe (1500–1800): Essays in Honor of Natalie Zemon Davis*, edited by Barbara B. Diefendorf and Carla Hesse, 1–15. Ann Arbor: University of Michigan Press, 1994.

Diehl, George Karl. "The Partbooks of a Renaissance Merchant, Cambrai: Bibliothèque Municipale, Mss 125–28." PhD diss., University of Pennsylvania, 1974.

Dieterich, David. "Brotherhood and Community on the Eve of the Reformation: Confraternities and Parish Life in Liège, 1450–1540." PhD diss., University of Michigan, 1982.

————. "Confraternities and Lay Leadership in Sixteenth-Century Liège." *Renaissance and Reformation* 13 (1989): 15–34.

Dillon, Emma. *The Sense of Sound: Musical Meaning in France, 1260–1330*. New York: Oxford University Press, 2012.

Duchamp, Jean. "Mottetti del Fiore: Une etude des huit livres de motets édites à Lyon par Jacques Moderne (1532—1543) avec la transcription des pieces inédites." PhD diss., Université François Rabelais de Tours, 2000.

Du Fay, Guillaume. *Compositiones Liturgicae Minores,* ed. Heinrich Besseler. Rome: American Institute of Musicology, 1966.

———. *Fragmenta Missarum,* ed. Heinrich Besseler. Rome: American Institute of Musicology, 1962.

Duff, Edward Gordon. *London and Westminster Printers, 1476–1535.* Cambridge: The University Press, 1906.

Duffy, Eamon. *The Stripping of the Altars: Traditional Religion in England, 1400–1580.* New Haven: Yale University Press, 2005.

Dumay, Raymond. "Sainte Barbe et tous les saints protecteurs des métiers des armes." In *Les saints patrons des métiers de France,* edited by Jérôme Tharaud, 205–24. Avignon: Maison Aubanel Père, 1942.

Dumolyn, Jan. "'I Thought of It at Work, in Ostend': Urban Artisan Labour and Guild Ideology in the Later Medieval Low Countries." *International Review of Social History* 62 (2017): 389–419.

Dumoulin, Jean. "Les églises paroissiales de Tournai au 15e siècle. Art et histoire." In *Les grands siècles de Tournai (XIIe–XVe siècles),* edited by Jean Dumoulin and Jacques Pycke, 257–78. Tournai/Louvain-la-Neuve: Université Catholique de Louvain, 1993.

———. "Livre de choeur." In *Trésors sacrés des églises et couvents de Tournai. Cathédrale Notre-Dame de Tournai, 9 mai-1er août 1971,* Exhibition Catalogue, 54–55. Tournai: Publication du Trésor de la Cathédrale et du Musée d'Histoire et d'Archéologie du Tournai, 1971.

———. "L'organisation paroissiale de Tournai aux XIIe et XIIIe siècles." In *Horae Tornacensis: Recueil d'études d'histoire publiées à l'occasion du VIIIe centenaire de la consécration de la Cathédrale de Tournai,* 28–47. Tournai: Archives de la Cathédrale, 1971.

———. "Missel de la Cathédrale de Tournai." In *Trésors sacrés des églises et couvents de Tournai. Cathédrale Notre-Dame de Tournai, 9 mai-1er août 1971,* Exhibition Catalogue, 49. Tournai: Publication du Trésor de la Cathédrale et du Musée d'Histoire et d'Archéologie du Tournai, 1971.

Dumoulin, Jean, Michel Huglo, Philippe Mercier, and Jacques Pycke, eds. *La Messe de Tournai. Une messe polyphonique en l'honneur de Notre-Dame à la Cathédrale de Tournai au XIVe siècle. Étude et nouvelle transcription.* Tornacum 4 and Musicologica Neolovaniensia. Musica Sacra 2. Tournai and Louvain-la-Neuve: Archives du Chapitre Cathédral/Université Catholique de Louvain, 1988. Reprint, 2016.

Dumoulin, Jean, and Jacques Pycke. "Introduction à l'histoire paroissiale de la ville de Tournai." In *Trésors sacrés des églises et couvents de Tournai. Cathédrale Notre-Dame de Tournai, 31 août-22 octobre 1973,* Exhibition Catalogue, 13–42. Tournai: Publication du Trésor de la Cathédrale et des Archives de la Cathédrale, 1973.

———. "Topographie chrétienne de Tournai des origines au milieu du XIIe siècle. Problématique nouvelle." *Sacris Erudiri* 26 (1983): 1–50.

Dunn-Lardeau, Brenda. "La contribution de J. Batallier à la traduction Française de Jean de Vignay de la Legenda Aurea." In *Legenda Aurea, Sept Siècles de Diffusion: Actes du Colloque international sur la Legenda aura, texte latin et branches vernaculaires à l'Université du Québec à Montréal, 11–12 mai 1983*, edited by Brenda Dunn-Lardeau, 183–96. Montréal: Université du Québec, 1983.

Dunn-Lardeau, Brenda, ed. *Jacques de Voragine: La Légende dorée. Edition critique, dans la révision de 1476 par Jean Batallier, d'après la traduction de Jean de Vignay (1333–1348) de la Legenda aurea (c.1261–1266)*. Paris: Honoré Champion, 1997.

Dupont, Anne. "Le chant dans l'espace: La cathédrale de Tournai au XVe siècle." *Revue de la Société Liégeoise de Musicologie* 28 (2009): 73–92.

Earp, Lawrence. *Guillaume de Machaut: A Guide to Research*. London: Routledge, 1995.

Elders, Willem. "Plainchant in the Motets, Hymns, and Magnificat of Josquin des Prez." In *Josquin des Prez. Proceedings of the International Josquin Festival-Conference*, edited by Edward E. Lowinsky and Bonnie J. Blackburn, 523–42. Oxford: Oxford University Press, 1976.

Enright, Michael. *Iona, Tara, and Soissons: The Origin of the Royal Anointing Ritual*. Boston: De Gruyter, 2011.

Everist, Mark. "Montpellier 8: Anatomy of …" In *The Montpellier Codex, The Final Fascicle: Contents, Contexts, Chronologies*, edited by Catherine Bradley and Karen Desmond, 13–31. Woodbridge, UK: The Boydell Press, 2018.

Faider, Paul. *Catalogue des manuscrits conservés a Tournai (Bibliothèques de la ville et du séminaire)*. Catalogue Général des Manuscrits des Bibliothèques de Belgique. Vol. 4. Gembloux: Imprimerie J. Duculot, 1950.

Falck, Robert. "Parody and Contrafactum: A Terminological Clarification." *The Musical Quarterly* 65 (1979): 1–21.

Fallows, David. "Dufay and Nouvion-le-Vineux: Some Details and a Thought." *Acta Musicologica* 48 (1976): 44–50.

Farge, James K. *Orthodoxy and Reform in Early Reformation France: The Faculty of Theology of Paris, 1500–1543*. Leiden: Brill, 1985.

———. *Registre des conclusions de la Faculté de théologie de l'Université de Paris: 1533–1550*. Paris: Klincksieck, 1994.

Farmer, Sharon. *Surviving Poverty in Medieval Paris*. Ithaca: Cornell University Press, 2002.

Fassler, Margot. *Gothic Song: Victorine Sequences and Augustinian Reform in Twelfth-Century Paris*. Cambridge: Cambridge University Press, 1993.

———. "The Feast of Fools and Danielis Ludus: Popular Tradition in a Medieval Cathedral Play." In *Plainsong in the Age of Polyphony*, edited by Thomas Forrest Kelly, 65–99. Cambridge: Cambridge University Press, 1992.

———. "The Role of the Parisian Sequence in the Evolution of Notre Dame Polyphony." *Speculum* 62, no. 2 (1987): 345–74.

———. "Who was Adam of St. Victor? The Evidence of the Sequence Manuscripts." *Journal of the American Musicological Society* 37, no. 2 (1984): 233–69.

Favier, Jean. *Nouvelle histoire de Paris: Paris au XVe siècle 1380–1500*. Paris: Diffusion Hachette, 1997.

Filippi, Daniele. "'Audire missam est verba missae intelligere …': The Low Mass and the *Motetti* missales in Sforza Milan." *Journal of the Alamire Foundation* 9 (2017): 11–32.

Forney, Kristine K. "Music, Ritual and Patronage at the Church of Our Lady, Antwerp." *Early Music History* 7 (1987): 1–57.

Fourez, Lucien. "Missel début XIVe siècle." *Trésors sacrés des églises et couvents de Tournai. Cathédrale Notre-Dame de Tournai, 9 mai-1er août 1971*, Exhibition Catalogue, 130. Tournai: Publication du Trésor de la Cathédrale et du Musée d'Histoire et d'Archéologie du Tournai, 1971.

Franklin, Alfred. *Dictionnaire historique des arts, métiers et professions exercés dans Paris depuis le treizième siècle*. Paris: H. Welter, 1906.

Freeman, Charles. *Holy Bones Holy Dust: How Relics Shaped the History of Medieval Europe*. New Haven: Yale University Press, 2011.

Frisque, Xavier. "Les manuscrits liturgiques notés du XIVe siècle de la collegiale Sainte-Croix à Liège." PhD diss., Université Catholique de Louvain, 1989.

Gabriel, Astrik. *Les Étudiants étrangers a l'Université de Paris au XVe siècle*. Paris: Imp. Administrative Centrale, 1959.

———. *Foreign Students, Members of the English-German Nation, at the University of Paris in the Fifteenth Century*. Modeno: S.T.E.M. Mucchi, 1966.

———. *Petrus Cesaris Wagner and Johannes Stoll: Fifteenth-Century Printers at the University of Paris*. Notre Dame: International Commission for the History of Universities, the Medieval Institute, 1978.

———. *Student Life in Ave Maria College, Mediaeval Paris*. Notre Dame: University of Notre Dame Press, 1955.

Gabrielli, Giulia. "Il manoscritto 327 della Fondazione Biblioteca San Bernardino di Trento." In *Il canto fratto: l'altro gregoriano: Atti del convegno internazionale di studi, Parma-Arezzo, 3–6 dicembre 2003 Il canto fratto*, edited by Marco Gozzi and Francesco Luisi, 93–120. Rome: Torre d'Orfeo, 2005.

Gabriëls, Nele. "Bourgeois Music Collecting in Mid Sixteenth-Century Bruges: The Creation of the Zeghere van Male Partbooks (Cambrai, Médiathèque Municipale, MSS 125–28)." PhD diss., Katholieke Universiteit Leuven, 2010.

———. "Mis-en officieboek van de broedershap van de heilige Catharina (Vesperae et Missae Confraternitatis S. Catharinae Parisiensis)." In *Liefde en Devotie. Het Gruutehuse handschrift: Kunst en cultuur omstreeks 1400*, edited by Jos Koldewij, Inge Geysen, and Eva Tahon, 140. Antwerp: Ludion, 2013.

Gaiffier, Baudoin de. "La Légende de sainte Barbe par Jean de Wackerzeele." *Analecta Bollandiana* 77 (1959): 5–41.

Gaposchkin, Cecilia. *Invisible Weapons: Liturgy and the Making of Crusade Ideology.* Ithaca: Cornell University Press, 2017.

———. *The Making of Saint Louis: Kingship, Sanctity, and Crusade in the Later Middle Ages.* Ithaca, NY: Cornell University Press, 2008.

———. "Political Ideas in Liturgical Offices of Saint Louis." In *Political Plainchant? Music, Text and Historical Context in Medieval Saints' Offices,* edited by Roman Hankeln, 59–80. Ottawa: Institute of Medieval Music, 2004.

Gaposchkin, Cecilia, Larry Field, and Sean Field. *The Sanctity of Louis IX: Early Lives of Saint Louis by Geoffrey of Beaulieu and William of Chartres.* Ithaca: Cornell University Press, 2014.

Garsonnin, Maurice. *Le guet et les compagnies du guet d'Orleans: Etude historique.* Orléans: H. Herluison, 1898.

Gatté, Dominique. "A New Concordance of Tournai Gloria." *Musicologie Médievale.* Posted 11 November 2016. https://gregorian-chant.ning.com/group/arsnovaetarssubtilior/forum/topics/a-new-source-of-ars-nova-glora.

Geary, Patrick. *Furta Sacra: Thefts of Relics in the Central Middle Ages.* Princeton: Princeton University Press, 2011.

———. *Living with the Dead in the Middle Ages.* Ithaca: Cornell University Press, 1994.

Gecser, Ottó. "Sermons on St. Sebastian after the Black Death (1348–ca.1500)." In *Promoting the Saints: Cults and Their Contexts from Late Antiquity until the Early Modern Period,* edited by Ottó Gecser, József Laszlovszky, Balázs Nagy, Marcell Sebok, and Katalin Szende, 261–72. Budapest: Central European University Press, 2011.

George, Philippe. "Les confraternités de l'abbaye de Stavelot-Malmedy." *Bulletin de la Commission royale d'Histoire* 161 (1995): 105–69.

Geremeck, Bronislaw. *Les marginaux parisiens aux XIVe et XVe siècles.* Paris: Flammarion, 1976.

Giffords, Gloria Fraser. *Sanctuaries of Earth, Stone, and Light: The Churches of Northern New Spain, 1530–1821.* Tucson: University of Arizona Press, 2007.

Glixon, Jonathan. *Honoring God and the City: Music at the Venetian Confraternities, 1260–1807.* New York: Oxford University Press, 2003.

Gomez, Maria del Carmen. "Quelques remarques sur le repertoire sacré de l'Ars nova provenant de l'ancien royaume d'Aragon." *Acta Musicologica* 57 (1985): 166–79.

Goodson, Caroline. *The Rome of Pope Paschal I: Papal Power, Urban Renovation, Church Rebuilding and Relic Translation, 817–824.* Cambridge: Cambridge University Press, 2010.

Goulet, Robert. *Compendium Universitatis Parisiensis: (Compendium on the magnificence, dignity, and excellence of the University of Paris in the year of grace 1517. Lately done into English by Robert Belle Burke for Josiah Harmar Penniman),* trans. Robert Belle Burke. Philadelphia: University of Pennsylvania Press, 1928.

Gozzi, Marco. "Alle origini del canto fratto: il Credo Cardinalis." *Musica e storia* 14 (2006): 245–302.

———. "I prototipi del canto fratto: Credo regis e Credo cardinalis." In *Cantus fractus italiano: un'antologia*, edited by Marco Gozzi, 137–54. Hildesheim: Georg Olms Verlag, 2012.

———. "Il canto fratto: Prima classificazione dei fenomeni e primi esiti del progetto RAPHAEL." In *Il canto fratto: l'altro gregoriano: atti del convegno internazionale di studi, Parma-Arezzo, 3–6 dicembre 2003 Il canto fratto*, edited by Marco Gozzi and Francesco Luisi, 7–58. Rome: Torre d'Orfeo, 2005.

———. "La sequenza Mittit ad Virginem recostruita da Tr 92." In *Cantus fractus italiano: un'antologia*, edited by Marco Gozzi, 259–64. Hildesheim: Georg Olms Verlag, 2012.

Grange, Amaury de la. "Obituaire de la paroisse de Saint-Piat." *Bulletin de la Société Historique et Littéraire de Tournai* 23 (1890): 11–105.

———. "Sur la politique des Rois de France, à Tournai au début du XVe siècle." *Annales de la Société Historique et Archéologique de Tournai* 5 (1900): 5–33.

Guletsky, Irene. "The Four 14th-Century Anonymous Masses: Their Form; the Restoration of Incomplete Cycles; and the Identification of Some Authors." *Acta Musicologica* 81 (2009): 167–228.

Gushee, Lawrence. "Two Central Places: Paris and the French Court in the Early 14th Century." In *Bericht über den Internationalen Musikwissenschaftlichen Kongress Berlin 1974*, edited by H. Kühn and P. Nitsche, 135–57. Kassel: Bärenreiter, 1980.

Guyon, Catherine. *Les écoliers du Christ: L'Ordre canonial du Val-des-Écoliers 1201–1539*. Saint-Étienne: Publications de l'Université de Saint-Étienne, 1998.

Haggh, Barbara. "The Archives of the Order of the Golden Fleece and Music." *Journal of the Royal Musical Association* 120, no. 1 (1995): 1–43.

———. "The Celebration of the 'Recollectio Festorum Beatae Mariae Virginis,' 1457–1987." *Studia Musicologica Academiae Scientiarum Hungaricae* 30 (1988): 361–73.

———. "Composers-Secretaries and Notaries of the Middle Ages and Renaissance: Did They Write?" In *Music, Space, Chord, Image: Festschrift for Dorothea Baumann's 65th Birthday*, edited by Antonio Baldassarre, 27–42. Bern: Peter Lang, 2012.

———. "Itinerancy to Residency: Professional Careers and Performance Practices in 15th-Century Sacred Music." *Early Music* 17 (1989): 359–66.

———. "The Medium Transforms the Message? Conflicting Evidence from the Printed Sources of the 'Officium recollectionis festorum Beatae Mariae Virginis.'" In *Il canto piano nell'era della stampa: Atti del convegno internazionale di studi sul canto liturgico nei secoli XV–XVII*, edited by Giulio Cattin, 73–80. Trent: Provincia Autonoma di Trento, 1999.

———. "The Meeting of Sacred Ritual and Secular Piety: Endowments for Music." In *Companion to Medieval and Renaissance Music,* edited by Tess Knighton and David Fallows, 60–68. London: Dent, 1992.

———. "Music, Liturgy, and Ceremony in Brussels, 1350–1550." PhD diss., University of Illinois at Urbana-Champaign, 1988.

———. "An Ordinal of Ockeghem's Time from the Sainte-Chapelle of Paris: Paris Bibliothèque de l'Arsenal, MS 114." *Tijdschrift van de Koninklijke Vereniging voor Nederlandse Muziekgeschiedenis* 47, no.1/2 (1997): 33–71.

Haggh, Barbara, and Charles Downey. *Two Cambrai Antiphoners: Cambrai Médiathèque Municipale, 38 and Impr. XVI C 4.* Ottawa: The Institute of Mediaeval Music, 1995.

Haggh, Barbara, and Paul Trio. "The Archives of Confraternities in Ghent and Music." In *Musicology and Archival Research,* edited by Barbara Haggh, Frank Daelmans, and André Vanrie, 44–90. Brussels: Archives et Bibliothèques de Belgique, 1994.

Haggh-Huglo, Barbara. "Proper Offices for Saints and the *Historia*: Their History and Historiography, and the Case of the *Historia* for St. Livinus." In *Music, Liturgy, and the Veneration of Saints of the Medieval Irish Church in a European Context,* edited by Ann Buckley, 23–50. Turnhout: Brepols, 2017.

Hall, Edwin, and Horst Uhr. "*Aureola super Auream*: Crowns and Related Symbols of Special Distinction for Saints in Late Gothic and Renaissance Iconography." *The Art Bulletin* 67 (1985): 567–603.

Hamm, Charles. "Dating a Group of Dufay Works." *Journal of the American Musicological Society* 15, no. 1 (1962): 65–71.

Hamm, Charles, and Herbert Kellman. *Census Catalogue of Manuscript Sources of Polyphonic Music, 1400–1550.* 5 vols. Rome: American Institute of Musicology, 1979–88.

Hankeln, Roman. "Kingship and Sanctity in the Historia in Honour of St. Canutus Rex." In *Of Chronicles and Kings: National Saints and the Emergence of Nation States in the High Middle Ages,* edited by John Bergsagel, David Hiley, and Thomas Riis, 159–92. Copenhagen: Museum Tusculanum Press, the Royal Library of Copenhagen, 2015.

———. "Reflections of War and Violence in Early and High Medieval Saints' Offices." *Plainsong and Medieval Music* 23 (2014): 5–30.

———. "St. Olav's Augustine-Responsories: Contrafactum Technique and Political Message." In *Political Plainchant? Music, Text and Historical Context of Medieval Saints' Offices,* edited by Roman Hankeln, 171–99. Ottawa: Institute of Mediaeval Music, 2009.

Harding, Vanessa. *The Dead and the Living in Paris and London, 1500–1670.* Cambridge: Cambridge University Press, 2002.

Harràn, Don. *In Defense of Music: The Case for Music as Argued by a Singer and Scholar of the Late Fifteenth Century.* Lincoln: University of Nebraska Press, 1989.

Harrison, Frank Lloyd. "Benedicamus, Conductus, Carol: A Newly-Discovered Source." *Acta Musicologica* 37 (1965): 35–48.

Hatter, Jane. *Composing Community in Late Medieval Music.* Cambridge: Cambridge University Press, 2019.

Head, Thomas. *Hagiography and the Cult of Saints: The Diocese of Orléans, 800–1200.* Cambridge: Cambridge University Press, 1990.

Heartz, Daniel. *Pierre Attaingnant: Royal Printer of Music.* Berkeley: University of California Press, 1969.

———. "Typography and Format in Early Music Printing: With Particular Reference to Attaingnant's First Publications." *Notes* 23 (1967): 702–6.

Henry, Albert. *Jehan Bodel: Le Jeu de Saint Nicolas.* Geneva: Librairie Droz, 2008.

Hermann-Mascard, Nicole. *Les reliques des saints: Formation coutumière d'un droit.* Collection d'histoire institutionnelle et sociale 6. Paris: Klincksieck, 1975.

Hesbert, Rene-Jean. *Le Prosaire de la Sainte-Chapelle. Manuscrit du chapitre de Saint-Nicolas de Bari (vers 1250).* Mâcon: Protat frères, 1952.

Higman, Francis M. *Censorship and the Sorbonne: A Bibliographical Study of Books in French Censured by the Faculty of Theology of the University of Paris, 1520–1551.* Geneva: Librairie Droz, 1979.

Hiley, David. "Gens, laudum titulis concrepet Anglica: The Proper Office for St. Oswin, King of Deira." In *Of Chronicles and Kings: National Saints and the Emergence of Nation States in the High Middle Ages*, edited by John Bergsagel, David Hiley, and Thomas Riis, 251–70. Copenhagen: Museum Tusculanum Press, the Royal Library of Copenhagen, 2015.

———. "Ordinary of Mass Chants in English, North French, and Sicilian Manuscripts." *Journal of the Plainsong and Medieval Music Society* 9 (1986): 1–128.

Honisch, Erika. "Drowning Winter, Burning Bones, Singing Songs: Representations of Popular Devotion in a Central European Motet Cycle." *Journal of Musicology* 34 (2017): 559–609.

Hoppin, Richard, and Suzanne Clercx. "Notes biographiques sur quelques musiciens français du XIVe siècle." *Les Colloques de Wégimont II: 1955, L'ars nova—Recueil d'études sur la musique du XIVe siècle.* Bibliothèque de la Faculté de Philosophie et Lettres de L'Université de Liège, edited by Paul Collaer, 63–92. Paris: Belles Lettres, 1959.

Huglo, Michel. "Le manuscrit de la Messe de Tournai." In *La Messe de Tournai. Une messe polyphonique en l'honneur de Notre-Dame à la Cathédrale de Tournai au XIVe siècle. Étude et nouvelle transcription.* Tornacum 4 and Musicologica Neo-lovaniensia. Musica Sacra 2, edited by Jean Dumoulin, Michel Huglo, Philippe Mercier, and Jacques Pycke, 18–30. Tournai et Louvain-la-Neuve: Archives du Chapitre Cathédral/Université Catholique de Louvain, 1988. Reprinted with added chapter on confraternity manuscripts, 2016. Page references are to the 2016 edition.

———. *Les manuscrits du processional.* Vol. 2. RISM B XIV / 1–2. Munich: G. Henle, 1999, 2004.

———. "La Messe de Tournai et la Messe de Toulouse." In *Aspects de la musique liturgique au Moyen Age*, edited by Michel Huglo, Marcel Pérès, and Christian Meyer, 221–28. Paris: Créaphis, 1991.

———. "Notated Performance Practices in Parisian Chant Manuscripts of the Thirteenth Century." In *Plainsong in the Age of Polyphony*, edited by Thomas Forrest Kelly, 32–44. Cambridge: Cambridge University Press, 1992.

Hughes, Andrew. "Late Medieval Plainchant for the Divine Office." In *Music as Concept and Practice in the Late Middle Ages*, edited by Reinhard Strohm and Bonnie J. Blackburn, 45–96. Oxford: Oxford University Press, 2001.

———. "Modal Order and Disorder in the Rhymed Office." *Musica Disciplina* 37 (1983): 29–51.

———. *The Versified Office: Sources, Poetry, and Chants.* Vol. 1. Lions Bay, ON: The Institute of Mediaeval Music, 2011.

Hughes, David. "The Paschal Alleluia in Medieval France." *Plainsong and Medieval Music* 14, no.1 (2005): 11–57.

Huguet, Léon. "Esquisse sur la vie et les oeuvres de Mgr Voisin." *Bulletins de la Société historique et littéraire de Tournai* 16 (1874): 5–46.

Huisman, Georges. *Notes sur un registre des apothicaires et epiciers parisiens conservé à la Bibliothèque de Bruxelles (1311–1534).* Paris: Imprimerie de Daupeley-Gouverneur, 1912.

Jaeger, C. Stephen. *Scholars and Courtiers: Intellectuals and Society in the Medieval West.* Aldershot, UK: Ashgate, 2002.

Jaulme, André. *Etude sur François Regnault, libraire et imprimeur à Paris (1500–1541), suivi d'un catalogue de ses éditions.* Ecole Nationale des Chartes, positions de thèses soutenues par les élèves de la promotion de 1924 pour obtenir le diplôme d'archiviste paléographe. Paris: Librairie Alphonse Picard et Fils, 1924.

Jeanroy, Alfred. "Une hymne bilingue à Saint Nicolas." *Speculum* 6, no. 1 (1931): 107–9.

Jenkins, Jacqueline, and Katherine J. Lewis. "Introduction." In *St. Katherine of Alexandria: Texts and Contexts in Western Medieval Europe*, edited by Jacqueline Jenkins and Katherine J. Lewis, 1–18. Turnhout: Brepols, 2003.

Jones, Charles. *Saint Nicholas of Myra, Bari, and Manhattan: Biography of a Legend.* Chicago: University of Chicago Press, 1978.

———. *The St. Nicholas Liturgy and Its Literary Relationships (Ninth to Twelfth Centuries).* Berkeley: University of California Press, 1963.

Kaiser, Reinhold. "Aspects de l'histoire de la civitas suessionum et du diocèse de Soissons aux époques romaine et Mérovingienne." *Cahiers archeologiques de Picardie* 1 (1974): 115–22.

Kaminsky, Howard. *A History of the Hussite Revolution.* Los Angeles: University of California Press, 1967.

Karsallah, Elsa. "Un substitut original au pèlerinage au Saint-Sépulcre: Les Mises au tombeau monumentales du Christ en France (XVe–XVIe siècles)." *Reti Medievali Rivista* 17 (2016): 417–28.

Kelly, Thomas Forrest. *Early Music: A Very Short Introduction.* New York: Oxford University Press, 2011.

Kirkman, Andrew. *The Cultural Life of the Early Polyphonic Mass: Medieval Context to Modern Revival.* Cambridge: Cambridge University Press, 2010.

———. "The Invention of the Cyclic Mass." *Journal of the American Musicological Society* 54 (2001): 1–47.

———. "The Seeds of Medieval Music: Choirboys and Musical Training in a Late-Medieval Maitrise." In *Young Choristers: 650–1700,* edited by Susan Boynton and Eric Rice, 104–22. London: Boydell & Brewer, 2008.

Korteweg, Anne S. *Splendour, Gravity and Emotion: French Medieval Manuscripts in Dutch Collections.* Zwolle: Waanders Publishers, 2004.

Kruckenberg, Lori. "Neumatizing the Sequence: Special Performances of Sequences in the Central Middle Ages." *Journal of the American Musicological Society* 59 (2006): 243–317.

Kügle, Karl. *The Manuscript Ivrea, Biblioteca Capitolare 115: Studies in the Transmission and Composition of Ars Nova Polyphony.* Ottawa: The Institute of Mediaeval Music, 1997.

La Caille, Jean de. *Histoire de l'imprimerie et de la librairie à Paris, où l'on voit son origine et ses progrès jusqu'en 1689.* Paris: Chez Jean de la Caille, 1689.

Landwehr-Melnicki, Margaretha. *Das Einstimmige Kyrie des lateinischen Mittelalters.* Regensburg: G. Bosse, 1955.

LaPonsey, Mary Haynes. "Michigan State University Library MS. 2: A Late-Fifteenth Century Book of Hours." Master's thesis, Michigan State University, 1991.

Larson, Barbara. "Odilon Redon's Temptation of Saint Anthony Lithographs." In *Medieval Saints in Late Nineteenth-Century French Culture: Eight Essays,* edited by Elizabeth Emery and Laurie Postlewate, 47–81. London: McFarland, 2004.

Leach, Elizabeth Eva. *Guillaume de Machaut: Secretary, Poet, Musician.* Ithaca, NY: Cornell University Press, 2014.

Leahy, Eugene. "Some Musical Elaborations in the Office of St. Nicholas." In *Music in Performance and Society: Essays in Honor of Roland Jackson*, edited by Malcome Cole and John Koegel, 81–91. Warren, MI: Harmonie Park Press, 1997.

Lebeuf, Jean. *Traité historique et pratique sur le chant ecclésiastique*. Paris: J. B. et J. T. Hérissant, 1741. Reprint, Geneva: Minkoff, 1972.

Leech-Wilkinson, Daniel. *Machaut's Mass: An Introduction*. Oxford: Clarendon Press, 1990.

LeMasson, Jean Baptiste. *Le Calendrier des confréries de Paris, par J. B. LeMasson / précédé d'une introduction avec des notes par l'abbé Valentin Dufour*. Collection de Documents rares ou inédits relatifs à l'histoire de Paris. Paris: Léon Willem, 1875.

Leroquais, Victor. *Les Pontificaux manuscrits des bibliothèques de France*. 3 vols. Mâcon: Protat frères, 1937.

———. *Les sacramentaires et les missels manuscrits des bibliothèques publiques de France*. 4 vols. Mâcon: Protat frères, 1924.

Lespinasse, René de. *Métiers et corporations de la ville de Paris, XIVe–XVIIIe siècles*. 3 vols. Paris: Imprimerie nationale, 1886–97.

Lewis, Katherine J. *The Cult of Saint Katherine of Alexandria in Late Medieval England*. London: Boydell & Brewer, 2000.

Li Muisis, Gilles. *Poésies de Gilles Li Muisis. Publiées pour la première fois d'après le manuscrit de Lord Ashburnham*. 2 vols. Edited by Baron Kervyn de Lettenhove. Louvain: Imprimerie de J. Lefevre, 1882.

Long, Sarah Ann. "The Chanted Mass in Parisian Ecclesiastical and Civic Communities, 1480–1540: Local Liturgical Practices in Manuscripts and Early Printed Service Books." PhD diss., University of Illinois at Urbana Champaign, 2008.

———. "In Praise of St. Nicholas: Music, Text, and Spirituality in the Masses and Offices of Parisian Trade Confraternity Manuscripts." *Journal of the Alamire Foundation* 1, no. 1 (2009): 50–78.

———. "La musique et la liturgie de la confrérie des notaires à la cathédrale de Tournai à la fin du Moyen Age." In *Archives et Manuscrits précieux tournaisiens* 4. Tournai—Art et Histoire: Instruments de travail 15, edited by Jacques Pycke, 45–66. Louvain-la-Neuve: Université catholique de Louvain, 2011.

———. "Les dévotions des confréries à la cathédrale de Tournai du XIVe au XVIe siècle." In *Le Hainaut et la musique de la Renaissance*, edited by Camilla Cavicchi and Marie-Alexis Colin. Tournhout: Brepols, in press 2020.

———. "Saint Jean l'évangeliste, patron des chandeliers et huiliers de Paris." In *Notre-Dame de Paris: 1163–2013. Actes du colloque scientifique tenu au Collège des Bernardins, à Paris, du 12 au 15 décembre 2012*, edited by Cédric Giraud, 597–99. Turnhout: Brepols, 2013.

———. "The Office of the Translation of St. Nicholas in Fifteenth-Century Parisian Confraternity Manuscripts." In *Papers Read at the 15th Meeting of the IMS Study Group CANTUS PLANUS, Dobogóko, Hungary, 2009*, edited by Barbara Haggh-Huglo and Debra Lacoste, 715–35. Ottawa: The Institute of Mediaeval Music.

———. "The Sanctorale of Andenne: A Description and Analysis of Liturgical Manuscripts for the Secular Chapter of Noble Canonesses." *Révue Belge de musicologie* 67 (2013): 63–81.

Long, Sarah Ann, and Inga Behrendt eds. *Catalogue of Notated Office Manuscripts Preserved in Flanders (c.1100–c.1800)*. Volume 1. Antiphonaria: A Catalogue of Notated Office Manuscripts (c.1100–c.1800). Turnhout: Brepols, 2015.

Loos, Ike de. "Duitse en Nederlandse Muzieknotaties in de 12e en 13e eeuw." PhD diss., Universiteit Utrecht, 1996.

Ludwig, Friedrich. "Die Quellen der Motetten ältesten Stils." *Archiv für Musikwissenschaft* 5 (1923): 185–222.

Luypaert, Monique Maillard. "Des assemblées capitulaires aux assemblées conciliaires: La contribution du chapitre cathedral de Cambrai à l'unité de l'Eglise d'Occident (1378–1417)." In *Eglise et Etat, Eglise ou Etat? Les clercs et langenèse de l'Etat modern*, edited by Christine Barralis, Jean-Patrice Boudet, Fabrice Delivré, and Jean-Philippe Genet, 281–92. Paris: Editions de la Sorbonne, 2015.

Lynch, Katherine. *Individuals, Families and Communities in Europe, 1200–1800: The Urban Foundations of Western Society*. Cambridge: Cambridge University Press, 2002.

Macklin, Chris. "Plague, Performance and the Elusive History of the *Stella Celi Extirpavit*." *Early Music History* 29 (2010): 1–31.

———. "Stability and Change in the Composition of a 'Plague Mass' in the Wake of the Black Death." *Plainsong and Medieval Music* 25, no. 2 (2016): 167–89.

Maddox, Donald, and Sara Sturm-Maddox. *Parisian Confraternity Drama of the Fourteenth Century: The Miracles de Nostre Dame par Personnages*. Medieval Texts and Cultures of Northern Europe 22. Turnhout: Brepols, 2008.

Mannaerts, Pieter. "Die Bruderschaften und Zünfte und die kirchenmusikalische Praxis in den Niederlanden (14–16. Jahrhundert)." In *Kirchenmusikalische Berufe, Institutionen, Wirkungsfelder—Geschichtliche Dimensionen und Aktualität*, edited by Matthias Schneider and Wolfgang Bretschneider, 101–22. Laaber: Laaber, 2015.

———. "A Collegiate Church on the Divide: Chant and Liturgy at the Church of Our Lady in Tongeren, 10th–15th Centuries." PhD diss., Katholieke Universiteit Leuven, 2008.

Marshall, Louise. "Manipulating the Sacred: Image and Plague in Renaissance Italy." *Renaissance Quarterly* 47, no. 3 (1994): 485–532.

———. "A Plague Saint for Venice: Tintoretto at the Chiesa di San Rocco." *Artibus et Historiae* 33, no. 66 (2012): 153–87.

Maurey, Yossi. *Medieval Music, Legend, and the Cult of St. Martin: The Local Foundations of a Universal Saint*. Cambridge: Cambridge University Press, 2014.

May, Judith Louis. "Rhymed Offices at the Sainte-Chapelle in the Thirteenth-Century: Historical, Political, and Liturgical Contexts." PhD diss., University of Texas, Austin, 1994.

Meyer, Christian. *Collections du Nord-Pas-de-Calais et de Picardie: Abbeville, Amiens, Arras, Bergues, Boulogne-sur-mer, Cambrai*. Catalogue des Manuscrits notes du Moyen Age conservés dans les Bibliothèques publiques de France. Turnhout: Brepols, 2014.

Meyer-Baer, Kathi. *Liturgical Music Incunabula: A Descriptive Catalogue*. London: The Bibliographical Society, 1962.

———. "Michel de Toulouze." *Music Review* 7 (1946): 178–82.

Miazga, Tadeusz. *Die Melodien der einstimmigen Credo der römisch-katholischen lateinischen Kirche*. Graz: Akademische Druck- und Verlagsanstalt, 1976.

Molin, Jean-Baptiste, and Annik Aussedat-Minvielle. *Répertoire de rituels et processionnaux imprimés conservés en France*. Paris: CNRS, 1984.

Mone, Franz Joseph. *Lateinische Hymnen des Mittelalters*. 3 vols. Freiburg: Herder'sche Verlagshandlung, 1853–55.

Moreau, Edouard de. "Un évêque de Tournai au XIVe siècle: Philippe d'Arbois (1378)." *Revue belge de philologie et d'histoire* 2, no. 1 (1923): 23–60.

Motetti de la Corona. Libro Primo. Venice: Ottaviano Petrucci, 1514.

Murray, James M. "Notaries Public in Flanders in the Late Middle Ages." PhD diss., Northwestern University, 1983.

Nosow, Robert. *Ritual Meanings in the Fifteenth-Century Motet*. Cambridge: Cambridge University Press, 2012.

Nys, Agathe. "Les Confréries de Devotion dans les Paroisses de Tournai au XVe Siècle." Master's thesis, Université Catholique de Louvain-la-Neuve, 1987.

Page, Christopher. *The Owl and the Nightingale: Musical Life and Ideas in France 1100–1300*. Oxford: Oxford University Press, 1990.

Pallier, Denis. "La confrérie Saint-Jean-l'Evangeliste, confrérie des métiers du livre à Paris. Jalons historiques (XVIe–XVIIe siècle)." *Bulletin du bibliophile* (2014): 78–120.

———. "Piété et sociabilité. La vie de la confrérie Saint-Jean-l'Evangéliste à la fin du XVIe siècle et au XVIIe siècle." *Bulletin du bibliophile* (2017): 40–98.

Parkes, Henry. "St. Edmund between Liturgy and Hagiography." In *Bury St. Edmunds and the Norman Conquest*, edited by Tom Licence, 131–69. Woodbridge, UK: The Boydell Press, 2014.

Pavanello, Agnese. "The Elevation as Liturgical Climax in Gesture and Sound: Milanese Elevation Motets in Context." *Journal of the Alamire Foundation* 9 (2017): 33–59.

Périn, Patrick. "The Undiscovered Grave of King Clovis." In *The Age of Sutton Hoo: The Seventh Century in North-Western Europe*, edited by M. O. H. Carver, 255–64. Woodbridge, Suffolk: Boydell Press, 1992.

Peters, Gretchen. *The Musical Sounds of Medieval French Cities: Players, Patrons, and Politics*. Cambridge: Cambridge University Press, 2012.

———. "Urban Minstrels in Late Medieval Southern France: Opportunities, Status and Professional Relationships." *Early Music History* 19 (2000): 201–35.

———. "Urban Musical culture in Late Medieval Southern France: Evidence from Private Notarial Contracts." *Early Music* 25 (1997): 403–10.

Pirro, André. "L'enseignement de musique aux universités françaises." *Bulletin de la Société internationale de Musicologie* 2 (1930): 45–56.

Planchart, Alejandro. "Choirboys in Cambrai in the Fifteenth Century." In *Young Choristers: 650–1700*, edited by Susan Boynton and Eric Rice, 123–45. London: Boydell & Brewer, 2008.

———. "The Early Career of Guillaume Du Fay." *Journal of the American Musicological Society* 46 (1993): 341–68.

———. "Parts with Words and without Words: The Evidence for Multiple Texts in 15th Century Masses." In *Studies in the Performance of Late Medieval Music*, edited by Stanley Boorman, 227–51. Cambridge: Cambridge University Press, 1983.

Plumley, Yolanda. *The Art of Grafted Song: Citation and Allusion in the Age of Machaut*. Oxford: Oxford University Press, 2013.

Polain, Louis. *Catalogue des livres imprimés au quinzième siècle des bibliothèques de Belgique*. 4 vols. Brussels: Société des bibliophiles et iconophiles de Belgique, 1932.

Poulle, Emmanuel. *La Bibliothèque Scientifique d'un Imprimeur Humaniste au XVe siècle: Catalogue des Manuscrits d'Arnaud de Bruxelles a la Bibliothèque Nationale de Paris*. Geneva: Librairie Droz S.A., 1963.

Price, Roger. *A Concise History of France*. Cambridge: Cambridge University Press, 2014.

Pycke, Jacques. "La confrérie de la Transfiguration au Mont-Saint-Aubert puis à la cathédrale de Tournai du 15e au 18e siècle." *Archives et manuscrits précieux tournaisiens* 1. Tournai—Art et Histoire, Instruments de travail 6, edited by Jacques Pycke, 123–51. Louvain-la-Neuve: Université Catholique de Louvain, 2007.

———. "Deux manuscrits apparentés au manuscrit A 27 (Messe de Tournai)." In *La Messe de Tournai. Une messe polyphonique en l'honneur de Notre-Dame à la cathédrale de Tournai au XIVe siècle. Étude et nouvelle transcription*. Tornacum 4 and Musicologica Neolovaniensia. Musica Sacra 2, edited by Jean Dumoulin, Michel Huglo, Philippe Mercier, and Jacques Pycke, 9–17. Tournai and Louvain-la-Neuve: Archives du Chapitre Cathédral/Université Catholique de Louvain, 1988. Reprinted with this chapter added, 2016. Page references are to the 2016 edition.

————. *Les documents du Trésor des chartes de la cathédrale de Tournai relatifs aux relations économiques, commerciales et juridiques avec la Ville de Tournai au Moyen Age.* Tournai: Archives et Bibliothèque de la Cathédrale, 2012.

————. "De Louis de la Trémoille à Ferry de Clugny: Cinq évéques tournaisiens au service des ducs de Bourgogne (1388–1483)." In *Les grands siècles de Tournai (XIIe–XVe siècles),* edited by Jean Dumoulin and Jacques Pycke, 209–38. Tournai/Louvain-la-Neuve: Université Catholique de Louvain, 1993.

————. "Matériaux pour l'histoire de la bibliothèque capitulaire de Tournai au Moyen Âge." *Scriptorium* 33 (1979): 76–83.

————. "La 'Messe de Tournai' et le culte de Sainte Marie à la cathédrale de Tournai." In *La Messe de Tournai* 45–66.

————. *Sons, couleurs, odeurs dans la cathédrale de Tournai au 15e siècle.* Louvain-la-Neuve: Université catholique de Louvain, 2003.

Reaney, Gilbert. *Manuscripts of Polyphonic Music (c. 1320–1400).* RISM B IV/2. Munich: G. Henle, 1969.

Reid, Donna Karen. "The Hours of the Usage of Landres, c.1502, Printed by Philippe Pigouchet for Simon Vostre." PhD diss., University of California, 1974.

Reinburg, Virginia. "Praying to Saints in the Late Middle Ages." In *Saints: Studies in Hagiography,* edited by Sandro Sticca, 269–82. Binghamton, NY: Center for Medieval and Early Renaissance Studies, 1996.

Renouard, Philippe. *Documents sur les imprimeurs, libraires, cartiers, graveurs fondeurs de lettres, relieurs, doreurs de livres, faiseurs de fermoirs, enlumineurs, parcheminiers et papetiers ayant exercé à Paris de 1450 à 1600.* Paris: H. Champion, 1901.

————. *Imprimeurs parisiens, libraires, fondeurs de caractères et correcteurs d'imprimerie: depuis l'introduction de l'imprimerie à Paris (1470) jusqu'à la fin du XVIe siècle.* Paris: Librairie A. Claudin, 1898.

————. *Répertoire des Imprimeurs Parisiens (libraries, fondeurs de caractères et correcteurs d'imprimerie) depuis l'introduction de l'imprimerie à Paris (1470) jusqu'à la fin du seizième siècle avec un plan de Paris sous Henri II.* Paris: Lettres Modernes, 1965.

Renouvier, Jules. *Des gravures sur bois dans les livres de Simon Vostre, libraire d'heures, avec un avant-propos par Georges Duplessis.* Paris: A. Aubry, 1862.

Ressouni-Demigneux, Karim. "La personalité de saint Sébastien: Exploration du fonds euchologique médiéval et renaissant, du IV au XVI siècle." *Mélanges de l'Ecole française de Rome. Moyen Age* 114, 1 (2002): 557–79.

Rézeau, Pierre. *Répertoire d'incipit des prières françaises à la fin du Moyen Age: Addenda et corrigenda aux repertoires de Sonet et Sinclair: nouveaux incipit.* Geneva: Librairie Droz, 1986.

Richard, Hélène. "Les livres d'heures imprimés poitevins conservés a la Bibliothèque Municipale de Poitiers." *Bulletin de la Société des antiquaires de l'Ouest et des musées de Poitiers* 16, no. 1 (1982): 343–58.

Riess, Frank. *Narbonne and Its Territory in Late Antiquity: From the Visigoths to the Arabs*. New York: Routledge, 2016.

Robertson, Anne Walters. "Remembering the Annunciation in Medieval Polyphony." *Speculum* 70, no. 2 (1995): 275–304.

Roelvink, Veronique. *Gegeven den sangeren: meerstemmige muziek bij de Illustre Lieve Vrouwe Broederschap te 's-Hertogenbosch in de zestiende eeuw*. 's-Hertogenbosch: Heinen, 2002.

———. *Gheerkin de Hondt: A Singer-Composer in the Sixteenth-Century Low Countries*. Utrecht: Donaas Projecten, 2015.

Rokseth, Yvonne. *Deux Livres d'Orgue parus chez Pierre Attaingnant en 1531, transcrits et publiés avec une introduction par Yvonne Rokseth*. Geneva: Librairie Droz, 1925.

Rospocher, Massimo. "From Orality to Print. Revolution or Transition? Street Singers in the Renaissance Multi-Media System." In *The Historiography of Transition: Critical Phases in the Development of Modernity (1494–1973)*, edited by Paolo Pombeni, 23–39. New York: Routledge, 2016.

Rosser, Gervase. "Crafts, Guilds, and the Negotiation of Work in the Medieval Town." *Past and Present* 154 (1997): 3–31.

Rothenberg, David. *The Flower of Paradise: Marian Devotion and Secular Song in Medieval and Renaissance Music*. New York: Oxford University Press, 2011.

Rouse, Richard H., and Mary A. Rouse. "The Booktrade at the University of Paris, ca.1250–ca.1350." In *La Production du livre universitaire au Moyen Age*, edited by Louis J. Bataillon, Bertrand G. Guyot, and Richard H. Rouse, 41–114. Paris: Éditions du CNRS, 1988.

———. *Manuscripts and Their Makers: Commercial Book Producers in Medieval Paris 1200–1500*. 2 vols. Turnhout: Harvey Miller Publishers, 2000.

Rubin, Miri. *Emotion and Devotion: The Meaning of Mary in Medieval Religious Cultures*. Budapest: Central European Press, 2009.

———. *Mother of God, A History of the Virgin Mary*. New Haven: Yale University Press, 2009.

Rubsamen, Walter. "Musicological Notes from Belgium, Switzerland, and England." *Journal of the American Musicological Society* 1 (1948): 55–58.

Rudy, Kathryn. "A Play Built for One: The Passion of Saint Barbara." In *The Sides of the North: An Anthology in Honor of Professor Yona Pinson*, edited by Tamar Cholcman and Assaf Pinkus, 56–82. Newcastle-upon-Tyne: Cambridge Scholars Publishing, 2015.

———. *Virtual Pilgrimages in the Convent: Imagining Jerusalem in the Late Middle Ages*. Turnhout: Brepols, 2011.

Runnalls, Graham A. "Medieval Trade Guilds and the *Miracles de Nostre Dames par personnages*." In *Parisian Confraternity Drama of the Fourteenth Century*, edited by Donald Maddox and Sara Sturm-Maddox, 29–65. Turnhout: Brepols, 2008.

Saenger, Paul. "Books of Hours and the Reading Habits of the Later Middle Ages." *Scrittura e civiltà* 9 (1985): 239–70.

Saltzstein, Jennifer. *The Refrain and the Rise of the Vernacular in Medieval French Music and Poetry.* Woodbridge, Suffolk: D. S. Brewer, 2013.

Salzberg, Rosa. "The Word on the Street: Street Performers and Devotional Texts in Italian Renaissance Cities." *The Italianist* 34 (2014): 336–48.

Saucier, Catherine. *A Paradise of Priests: Singing the Civic and Episcopal Hagiography of Medieval Liège.* Rochester, NY: University of Rochester Press, 2014.

———. "Sacred Music and Musicians at the Cathedral and Collegiate Churches of Liège, 1330–1500." PhD diss., University of Chicago, 2005.

Sauval, Henri. *Histoire et recherches des antiquités de la ville de Paris.* 3 vols. Paris: Charles Moette et Jacques Chardon, 1724.

Schildbach, Martin. *Das einstimmige Agnus Dei und seine handschriftliche Überlieferung vom 10. bis zum 16. Jahrhundert.* Erlangen: J. Hogl, 1967.

Schlager, Karlheinz. *Alleluia-Melodien II ab 1100.* Monumenta monodica medii aevi. Vol. 8. Kassel: Bärenreiter, 1987.

Schrade, Leo. *Polyphonic Music of the Fourteenth Century.* Monaco: Editions de L'Oiseau-Lyre, 1956.

Schribner, Robert. *Popular Culture and Popular Movements in Reformation Germany.* London: Hambledon Press, 1987.

Severin, Corsten. "Universities and Early Printing." In *Bibliography and the Study of 15th Century Civilization,* edited by Lotte Hellinga and John Goldfinch, 83–123. London: British Library, 1987.

Seybolt, Robert Francis. "Fifteenth-Century Editions of the Legenda Aurea." *Speculum* 21, no. 3 (1946): 327–38.

Sherr, Richard. "The Performance of Chant in the Renaissance and its Interactions with Polyphony." In *Plainsong in the Age of Polyphony,* edited by Thomas Forrest Kelly, 178–208. Cambridge: Cambridge University Press, 1992.

Simiz, Stefano. *Confréries urbaines et devotion en Champagne (1450–1830).* Lille: Presses Universitaires du Septentrion, 2002.

Slavin, Arthur J. "The Rochepot Affair." *The Sixteenth Century Journal* 10, no. 1 (1979): 3–19.

Slocum, Kay Brainerd. "Confrerie, Bruderschaft, and Guild: The Formation of Musicians' Fraternal Organizations in Thirteenth- and Fourteenth-Century Europe." *Early Music History* 14 (1995): 257–74.

———. *Liturgies in Honour of Thomas Becket.* Toronto: University of Toronto Press, 2004.

Sluhovsky, Moshe. *Patroness of Paris: Rituals of Devotion in Early Modern France.* Leiden: Brill, 1998.

Small, Graeme. "Centre and Periphery in Late Medieval France: Tournai, 1384–1477." In *War, Government and Power in Late Medieval France,* edited by Christopher Allmand, 145–74. Liverpool: Liverpool University Press, 2000.

Smith, Anthony D. *Chosen Peoples: Sacred Sources of National Identity*. Oxford: Oxford University Press, 2003.

Snow, Emily. "The Lady of Sorrows: Music, Devotion, and Politics in the Burgundian-Habsburg Netherlands." PhD diss., Princeton University, 2010.

Soil, Eugène. "Les tapisseries tournaisiennes. Les tapissiers et les hautelissuers de cette ville. Recherches et documents sur l'histoire, la fabrication et les produits des ateliers de Tournai." *Memoires de la Société historique et littéraire de Tournai* 22 (1891): 1–455.

Stäblein-Harder, Hanna. *Fourteenth-Century Mass Music in France*. Critical Text. Tubingen: American Institute of Musicology, 1962.

———. *Fourteenth-Century Mass Music in France*. Music Score. Tubingen: American Institute of Musicology, 1962.

Stein, Henri. *L'atelier typographique de Wolfgang Hopyl*. Fontainebleu: Impr. de E. Bourges, 1891.

———. *Nouveaux documents sur Wolfgang Hopyl, imprimeur à Paris*. Extrait du Bibliographe modern. Paris: A. Picard et fils, 1905.

Stoessel, Jason, and Denis Collins. "New Light on the Mid-Fourteenth-Century *Chace*: Canons Hidden in the Tournai Manuscript." *Music Analysis* 38 (2019): 1–49.

Stones, Alison. "Missel de la cathedrale de Tournai." In *Trésors sacrés des églises et couvents de Tournai. Cathédrale Notre-Dame de Tournai, 9 mai-1er août 1971*, Exhibition Catalogue, 51–53. Tournai: Publication du Trésor de la Cathédrale et des Archives de la Cathédrale, 1971.

Strohm, Reinhard. "The Ars Nova Fragments of Gent." *Tijdschrift van de Vereniging voor Nederlandse Muziekgeschiedenis* 34, no. 2 (1984): 109–31.

———. *Music in Late Medieval Bruges*. Oxford: Clarendon Press, 1990.

Suau, Jean-Pierre. "Les Vertus des Heures imprimées à Paris par Philippe Pigouchet pour Simon Vostre (22 août 1498) et les Vertus de type français de dossiers de stalles (XVI siècle) de la cathédrale d'Auch." *Bulletin de la Société archéologique, historique, littéraire et scientifique du Gers* 90, no. 1 (1989): 40–62.

Surius, Laurentius. *De probatis Sanctorum historiis*. Cologne: Calenius & Quentel, 1581.

Sutch, Susie Speakman, and Anne-Laure van Bruaene. "The Seven Sorrows of the Virgin Mary: Devotional Communication and Politics in the Burgundian Habsburg Low Countries, c.1490–1520." *Journal of Ecclesiastical History* 61 (2010): 252–78.

Symes, Carol. "The Appearance of Early Vernacular Plays: Forms, Functions, and the Future of Medieval Theater." *Speculum* 77 no. 3 (2002): 778–831.

———. *A Common Stage: Theater and Public Life in Medieval Arras*. Ithaca, NY: Cornell University Press, 2007.

————. "The Lordship of Jongleurs." In *The Experience of Power in Medieval Europe, 950–1350*, edited by Robert Berkhofer, Alan Cooper, and Adam Kosto, 237–52. Aldershot, UK: Ashgate, 2005.

Tagage, J. M. B. *De Ordinarius van de Collegiale Onze Lieve Vrouwekerk te Maastricht*. Assen: Van Gorcum, 1984.

Tangari, Nicola. "Mensural and Polyphonic Music of the Fourteenth Century and a New Source for the Credo of Tournai in a Gradual of the Basilica di Santa Maria Maggiore in Rome." *Plainsong and Medieval Music* 24 (2015): 25–70.

Taylor, Larissa J. ed., *Encyclopedia of Medieval Pilgrimage*. Leiden: Brill, 2009.

Terry-Fritsch, Allie. "Proof in Pierced Flesh: Caravaggio's Doubting Thomas and the Beholder of Wounds in Early Modern Italy." In *Beholding Violence in Medieval and Early Modern Europe*, edited by Allie Terry-Fritsch and Erin Felicia Labbie, 15–37. New York: Routledge, 2012.

Thannabaur, Peter Josef. *Das einstimmige Sanctus der römischen Messe in der handschriftlichen Uberlieferung des 11. Bis 16 Jahrhunderts*. Munich: W. Ricke, 1962.

Thelen, Emily S. "The Feast of the Seven Sorrows of the Virgin: Piety, Politics and Plainchant at the Burgundian-Habsburg Court." *Early Music History* 35 (2016): 261–307.

————. *The Seven Sorrows Confraternity of Brussels*. Turnhout: Brepols, 2016.

Thijssen, Hans J. M. M. H. *Censure and Heresy at the University of Paris, 1200–1400*. Philadelphia: University of Pennsylvania Press, 1998.

Thiriet, Marcel. "Essai sur la géographie du culte de Saint Nicolas en France." In *Saint Nicolas: Actes du Symposium des 8–9 Juin, 1985*, 9–26. Saint-Nicolas-de-Port: La ville de Saint-Nicolas-de-Port, 1988.

Tomasello, Andrew. "Scribal Design in the Compilation of Ivrea MS 115." *Musica Disciplina* 42 (1988): 73–100.

————. "The Transmission of the Las Huelgas Credo." *Revisita de Musicologia* 13, no. 2 (1990): 501–9.

Trio, Paul. "Les confréries des Pays-Bas face au problème de la pauvreté (XVème–XVIème siècle)." In *Confraternite, Chiesa e Società*, edited by L. B. Lenoci, 277–88. Fasano: Schena, 1994.

————. "Lay Persons in Power: The Crumbling of the Clerical Monopoly on Urban Devotion in Flanders as a Result of the Rise of Lay Confraternities in the Late Middle Ages." In *Early Modern Confraternities in Europe and the Americas: International and Interdisciplinary Perspectives*, edited by Christopher Black and Pamela Gravestock, 53–63. Aldershot, UK: Ashgate, 2006.

————. "A Medieval Students' Confraternity at Ypres: The Notre Dame Confraternity of Paris Students." *History of Universities* 5 (1985): 14–53.

Turner, Bruno. "Spanish Liturgical Hymns: A Matter of Time." *Early Music* 23, no. 3 (1995): 473–82.

Updike, Daniel. *Printing Types: Their History, Forms, and Use*. Cambridge, MA: Harvard University Press, 1962.

Van Bruaene, Anne-Laure. "In Principio Erat Verbum. Drama, Devotion, Reformation and Urban Association in the Low Countries." In *Early Modern Confraternities in Europe and the Americas: International and Interdisciplinary Perspectives*, edited by Christopher Black and Pamela Gravestock, 64–80. Aldershot, UK: Ashgate, 2006.

———. "Repertorium van rederijkerskamers in de Zuidelijke Nederlanden en Luik 1400–1650." *De Digitale Bibliotheek voor de Nederlandse Letteren* (2004). Accessed February 12, 2020. https://www.dbnl.org/tekst/brua002repe01_01/ brua002repe01_01_0156.php.

Van Cranenbroeck, Fabienne. "Analyse codicologique de l'antiphonaire A 12." Unpublished description of the manuscript. 2008. Archives de la Cathédrale de Tournai, Tournai.

Van den Borren, Charles. "Inventaire des manuscrits de musique polyphonique qui se trouvent en Belgique." *Acta musicologica*, VI (1934): 116–21.

———. *Missa Tornacensis*. Corpus Mensurabilis Musicae 13. Rome: American Institute of Musicology, 1957.

Vanderputten, Steven. "Itinerant Lordship: Relic Translations and Social Change in Eleventh- and Twelfth-Century Flanders." *French History* 6 (2011): 143–63.

Van Deusen, Nancy. "Songs of Exile, Songs of Pilgrimage." In *Western Plainchant in the First Millennium: Studies in the Medieval Liturgy and its Music*, edited by Sean Gallagher, James Haar, John Nádas, and Timothy Striplin, 105–18. Aldershot, UK: Ashgate, 2003.

Van Orden, Kate. *Music, Discipline, and Arms in Early Modern France*. Chicago: University of Chicago Press, 2005.

Verroken, Eric. "Gaspar van Weerbeke (c.1445–after 1517), a Composer from Oudenaarde." *Journal of the Alamire Foundation* 11 (2019): 167–94.

Vincent, Catherine. *Des charités bien ordonnées: Les confréries normandes de la fin du XIIIe siècle au début du XVIe siècle*. Paris: École Normale Supérieure, 1988.

———. *Les confréries médiévales dans le royaume de France XIIIe–XVe siècle*. Paris: Albin Michel, 1994.

Vleeschouwers-Van Melkebeek, Monique. *De Officialiteit van Doornik: Oorsprong en Vroege Ontwikkeling (1192–1300)*. Brussels: Paleis der Academièn, 1985.

Voisin, Charles Joseph. "Drames liturgiques de Tournai." *Bulletins de la Société historique et littéraire de Tournai* 6 (1860): 261–91.

———. "Note sur l'église de Saint-Nicolas à Tournai." *Bulletins de la Societe historique et litteraire de Tournai* 13 (1869): 173–88.

———. "Notice sur la confrérie de la Transfiguration." *Bulletins de la Société historique et littéraire de Tournai* 3 (1853): 139–44.

Voragine, Jacobus de. *La légende dorée en François*. Paris: Antoine Vérard, 1496. *Gallica*. Accessed February 12, 2020. http://gallica.bnf.fr/ark:/12148/ btv1b8604292q.

————. *The Golden Legend of Jacobus de Voragine: Translated and Adapted from the Latin by Granger Ryan and Helmut Ripperger*. London: Longmans, Green and Co., 1941.

————. *The Golden Legend, or, Lives of the Saints / as Englished by William Caxton*. 6 vols. London: J. M. Dent and Co., 1939.

Walsh, Christine. *The Cult of St. Katherine of Alexandria in Early Medieval Europe*. Aldershot, UK: Ashgate, 2007.

Ward, Tom R. "Polyphonic Settings of Mensurally Notated Hymn Melodies." In *Der lateinische Hymnus im Mittelalter*, edited by Andreas Haug, 331–43. Kassel: Bärenreiter, 2004.

————. *The Polyphonic Office Hymn 1400–1520: A Descriptive Catalogue*. Neuhausen-Stuttgart: American Institute of Musicology-Hänssler, 1980.

Warichez, Joseph. *La cathédrale de Tournai et son chapitre*. Wetteren: Imprimerie de Meester, 1934.

Warolin, Christian. "L'hôpital et la chapelle Sainte-Catherine, rue Saint-Denis, et la confrérie des apothicaires de Paris." *Revue d'histoire de la pharmacie* 87 (1999): 417–24.

Weber, Max. *General Economic History*. New Brunswick, NJ: Rutgers University Press, 1981.

Wegman, Rob. "For Whom the Bell Tolls: Reading and Hearing Busnoys's *Anthoni usque limina*." In *Hearing the Motet: Essays on the Motet of the Middle Ages and Renaissance*, edited by Dolores Pesce, 122–41. Oxford: Oxford University Press, 1997.

————. "From Maker to Composer: Improvisation and Musical Authorship in the Low Countries, 1450–1500." *Journal of the American Musicological Society* 49, no. 3 (1996): 409–79.

————. "Mensural Intertextuality in Busnoys." In *Antoine Busnoys: Method, Meaning, and Context in Late Medieval Music*, edited by Paula Higgins, 175–214. Oxford: Oxford University Press, 2000.

————. "Music and Musicians at the Guild of Our Lady in Bergen op Zoom, c. 1470–1510." *Early Music History* 9 (1990): 175–249.

Wieck, Roger. *Time Sanctified: The Book of Hours in Medieval Art and Life*. Baltimore: The Walters Art Museum, 1988.

Williamson, Beth. "Sensory Experience in Medieval Devotion: Sound and Vision, Invisibility and Silence." *Speculum* 88 (2013): 1–43.

Williamson, Magnus. "Affordable Splendour: Editing, Printing and Marketing the Sarum Antiphoner (1519–1520)." *Renaissance Studies* 26 (2012): 60–87.

Wilson, Blake. *Music and Merchants: The Laudesi Companies of Republican Florence*. New York: Oxford University Press, 1992.

Wolf, Kirsten. *The Old Norse-Icelandic Legend of Saint Barbara*. Toronto: Pontifical Institute of Medieval Studies, 2000.

Wolinski, Mary E. "Music for the Confraternity of St. James in Paris." In *Chant, Liturgy and the Inheritance of Rome: Essays in Honour of Joseph Dyer*, edited by Daniel J. DiCenso and Rebecca Maloy, 525–41. London: Boydell & Brewer, 2017.

Wright, Craig. "A Fragmentary Manuscript of Early 15th-Century Music at Dijon." *Journal of the American Musicological Society* 27, no. 2 (1974): 306–15.

———. *The Maze and the Warrior: Symbols in Architecture, Theology, and Music.* Cambridge, MA: Harvard University Press, 2004.

———. *Music and Ceremony at Notre Dame of Paris 500–1500.* Cambridge: Cambridge University Press, 1989.

Young, Karl. *The Drama of the Medieval Church.* 2 vols. Oxford: Clarendon Press, 1933.

Zieman, Katherine. *Singing the New Song: Literacy and Liturgy in Late Medieval England.* Philadelphia: University of Pennsylvania Press, 2008.

Index of Chant and Polyphonic Compositions

Index of Early Printed
Liturgical Books

Index of Manuscripts

General Index

William of St. Pathus, 99
women as business owners in Paris,
   245n6

Wright, Craig, 4, 59